IoT Development for ESP32 and ESP8266 with JavaScript

A Practical Guide to XS and the Moddable SDK

Peter Hoddie
Lizzie Prader

Apress®

IoT Development for ESP32 and ESP8266 with JavaScript: A Practical Guide to XS and the Moddable SDK

Peter Hoddie
Menlo Park, CA, USA

Lizzie Prader
Menlo Park, CA, USA

ISBN-13 (pbk): 978-1-4842-5069-3
https://doi.org/10.1007/978-1-4842-5070-9

ISBN-13 (electronic): 978-1-4842-5070-9

Copyright © 2020 by Peter Hoddie and Lizzie Prader

Managing Director, Apress Media LLC: Welmoed Spahr
Acquisitions Editor: Natalie Pao
Development Editor: James Markham
Coordinating Editor: Jessica Vakili

Distributed to the book trade worldwide by Springer Science+Business Media New York, 233 Spring Street, 6th Floor, New York, NY 10013. Phone 1-800-SPRINGER, fax (201) 348-4505, e-mail orders-ny@springer-sbm.com, or visit www.springeronline.com. Apress Media, LLC is a California LLC and the sole member (owner) is Springer Science + Business Media Finance Inc (SSBM Finance Inc). SSBM Finance Inc is a **Delaware** corporation.

For information on translations, please e-mail rights@apress.com, or visit http://www.apress.com/rights-permissions.

Apress titles may be purchased in bulk for academic, corporate, or promotional use. eBook versions and licenses are also available for most titles. For more information, reference our Print and eBook Bulk Sales web page at http://www.apress.com/bulk-sales.

Any source code or other supplementary material referenced by the author in this book is available to readers on GitHub via the book's product page, located at www.apress.com/978-1-4842-5069-3. For more detailed information, please visit http://www.apress.com/source-code.

Printed on acid-free paper

Table of Contents

About the Authors

Peter Hoddie is an engineer and entrepreneur focused on client software. He is recognized for crafting compact and efficient code that pushes the boundaries of user experience on consumer hardware. The software he and his teams have built has powered mass-market consumer products from companies including Apple, Palm, Sling, HP, Sony, and Whirlpool. Peter recognizes that the first users of any product are the developers creating it, and that those developers cannot build compelling consumer products on a foundation that's unstable, complex, or confusing. He therefore champions investments in great tools and a simple runtime architecture.

Peter has founded several companies, including Kinoma, which merged into Marvell Semiconductor. He led QuickTime development at Apple during the 1990s as a Distinguished Engineer. He contributed to the development of the QuickTime file format and its adoption by ISO into the MPEG-4 standard. He is currently a member of the JavaScript language standards committee (ECMA TC39) and chair of ECMA TC53 for "Smart wearable systems and sensor-based devices." Peter is particularly proud of his work putting both the KinomaJS framework and Darwin Streaming Server into open source. He continues to come to terms with the ten patents that bear his name.

Lizzie Prader is a software engineer at Moddable in the San Francisco Bay Area. She is an IoT skeptic working in the IoT space, hoping to make consumer IoT products and other embedded systems more open and customizable for the end user. She specializes in developing touch screen user interfaces for embedded systems and creating developer resources.

ABOUT THE AUTHORS

Before Moddable, Lizzie worked as a developer relations engineer for the Kinoma team at Marvell Semiconductor, helping customers get the most out of Kinoma's JavaScript-powered prototyping products. She earned her bachelor's degree in Computer Science from UC Berkeley. When not sitting behind a computer, she enjoys being outdoors (in particular running, hiking, and swimming), reading, and playing the piano.

About the Technical Reviewers

Mark Wharton was born in England, was raised in Papua New Guinea and Australia, and worked as a software engineer for startups and large corporations in Australia, Japan, and the United States. He currently works at Amazon on the Alexa Automotive initiative. Since his early days programming the 6502 assembly language on Apple IIe and Commodore 64 computers, Mark excels at making the most of limited resources in constrained environments. Now in his spare time, Mark enjoys applying those skills to a new generation of low-cost, low-power devices using the Moddable SDK.

Masahiro Shioji is a product creator who likes to bring technologies into easy-to-use products and release them to the world. He started in product development in the digital camera industry, at Sanyo Electric in Japan, and produced a QuickTime/MPEG-4 direct encoding video camera in collaboration with Peter Hoddie when Peter worked at Apple. Masahiro went on to spread the joy of creating something to university students, including operating a lab toward that end while continuing his own work in product development and new business development.

About the Editor

Caroline Rose is a freelance technical writer and editor based in Palo Alto, California. With a career that has included 7 years working as a programmer, her focus has been on producing highly technical documentation, most notably as lead writer and editor of the original *Inside Macintosh*. Caroline was also Manager of Publications at NeXT and the editor of Apple's quarterly technical journal, *develop*. Her subsequent freelance work began with coauthoring updated versions of Adobe's PostScript and PDF reference manuals and went on to include clients such as AMD, Apple, Apress, Kinoma, Logitech, Nokia, and Sony. In her free time, Caroline enjoys playing guitar, singing, swimming, hiking, traveling, and working on her memoir.

Acknowledgments

This book is better because of the generous assistance of many talented individuals we're fortunate to call friends.

- **Caroline Rose, editor** – Caroline brought her legendary precision and clarity to this book. Everything about this book is better thanks to her patient work.

- **Mark Wharton, technical reviewer** – Mark carefully reviewed the entire text, and then ran and reviewed every single example.

- **Masahiro Shioji, technical reviewer, Chapter 2** – Shioji-san brought the perspective of an embedded C developer to his thoughtful review.

- **Brian Friedkin, BLE advisor** – Creator of the BLE implementation in the Moddable SDK, Brian made sure the explanations and examples in Chapter 4 are just right.

- **Patrick Soquet, advisor** – As the inventor of the XS JavaScript engine, Patrick is the starting point for everything we know about embedded JavaScript.

- **Chris Krueger, illustrator** – Chris turned our rough ideas and rougher sketches into the simple, clear images you see throughout the book.

- **Team Moddable** – Our colleagues at Moddable have been incredibly supportive and patient over the many months it took to create this book.

Foreword

Those of you who have read Wikipedia cover to cover will remember the definition of hybrid vigor. For the rest of you:

> **Heterosis, hybrid vigor,** or **outbreeding enhancement** is the improved or increased function of any biological quality in a hybrid offspring. An offspring is heterotic if its traits are enhanced as a result of mixing the genetic contributions of its parents.
>
> — Wikipedia, page 69105

The practical upshot of this is that if you take separate, inbred strains of, say, corn and breed them together, you get a great big vigorous plant, hence the name hybrid vigor.

The Moddable SDK, as described in this book, represents the hybrid vigor between embedded and JavaScript development. Using Moddable is a short path to very large amounts of corn.

If you're an embedded developer, you delight in the ability to get close to the metal, to program on tiny, inexpensive devices without the affordances offered by development on large systems. Writing in C/C++ and/or assembly language gives you a great deal of control, but you often struggle with shoehorning functionality into these small devices, wrestle brittle development and debugging environments, and build ad hoc device-specific ways of updating code and managing resources. If the embedded device has a display or is capable of wireless communications, you need to track down the right tools to build, simulate, and test a wide variety of functionality in the absence of a rich underlying OS. A great deal of your energy goes into managing the constraints of these small systems rather than into the applications themselves.

If you're a JavaScript developer, you delight in its productivity, versatility, and ubiquity. The language is forgiving to a novice yet extremely powerful in the hands of a master. It's versatile enough to be used in front-end development as well as back-end infrastructure. Its huge community continually enriches the language and libraries and makes it arguably the most popular language ever. All this versatility and power comes with a price; until now a robust version of JavaScript has not scaled down to the point where it will fit on a small embedded device.

Moddable takes the best of these two strains and blends them together on an emerging class of powerful new microcontrollers. Embedded developers no longer have to regard JavaScript with envious eyes. They now have access to a versatile high-level language that still allows them to stay close to the metal and maintain tight control. JavaScript developers can reach ridiculously inexpensive devices with none of the friction of traditional embedded development, yet still work with affordances present on much larger systems.

It's embarrassingly easy to be productive in the Moddable environment, with its rich SDK for managing secure web connectivity, Wi-Fi, Bluetooth, sound, graphics, user interfaces, and more; its elegant, full-featured debugging; and a wide variety of target hardware that ranges from inexpensive to nearly free.

My day job is investing in technology startups, and as such it pains me to see companies attempting embedded development with blunt tools. Moddable can save developers time and money and produce beautifully polished embedded applications. As an investor, I love tools that reduce risk and make companies more capital-efficient. As an avid maker, I love tools that make making even more fun.

If you develop embedded products, or if you're a hobbyist or even just someone who loves writing code, Moddable's hybrid vigor changes the game. Go grow some corn.

— Peter Barrett

Introduction

This book is a hands-on guide to writing the software for IoT products. Each chapter is filled with compact, focused examples for you to learn from, study, run, and modify. When you finish this book, you'll know the fundamentals of building sophisticated IoT products on low-cost hardware using modern JavaScript.

IoT products differ from traditional products in two ways: they have the ability to run software and they have the ability to communicate. Their communication is often over the internet, but it may be more local—for example, between products on your home Wi-Fi network or with your phone over a Bluetooth connection.

IoT products are often created by adding a microcontroller with Wi-Fi or Bluetooth capabilities to a traditional product. The cost of adding a microcontroller with communication capabilities is about one dollar today and continues to fall. At that price, nearly every product is going to be an IoT product—not just televisions and thermostats but also light bulbs, light switches, electric wall plugs, door locks, window shades, garage door openers, ceiling fans, rice cookers, refrigerators, and more.

The code in this book runs on the ESP32 and ESP8266 microcontrollers from Espressif, which offer remarkable power at an unprecedented cost. Unsurprisingly, they're widely deployed in IoT products and extremely popular with makers and hobbyists. What you'll learn in this book isn't limited to these microcontrollers, however; it can be applied to a growing number of microcontrollers from manufacturers including Nordic, Qualcomm, and Silicon Labs.

Adding IoT hardware to a traditional product is the easy part; the hard part is the software. Software defines the product's features and behavior.

It determines whether the product is reliable and easy to use and whether it's secure from external attacks and respects the privacy of users. Software decides what other products the product can communicate with, its energy use, the ease of adding new features over time, and much more.

Software is fundamental to IoT products, yet most of the industry continues to write the software for them using the same tools and techniques embedded software developers have used for decades. While the hardware has advanced by orders of magnitude, the software has not. That's a problem, because much more is expected of the software in an IoT product today than the software in a digital thermostat from 1999.

JavaScript: A New Tool

This book introduces a new way of building the software for IoT products—a way that doesn't try to reinvent the wheel by starting over. It adds one new tool to the many that embedded software developers have used for years: the JavaScript programming language. It may sound like a stretch to suggest that a programming language can transform the software of an IoT product, but it can. A modern high-level language is the perfect antidote to decades-old, low-level development methods.

JavaScript may seem an unlikely starting point for future generations of IoT products. After all, JavaScript began as a simple programming language to add a little interactivity to web pages at the dawn of the web. But as the web has evolved, JavaScript has evolved with it; it's now a formally defined programming language standardized by an international committee with representatives from major companies, including Apple, Facebook, Google, Microsoft, Mozilla, and PayPal. The language has been made secure by two decades of attacks in the web browser. It's been made powerful by the demands of increasingly sophisticated web pages. And it's been made reliable and easy to use to meet the needs of millions of web developers around the world.

Developers working in JavaScript are incredibly productive and nimble. Within hours of a natural disaster, new websites appear with impressive features implemented in JavaScript. Major websites like Facebook and LinkedIn aren't just built in JavaScript but deploy new features daily using JavaScript. Server-side JavaScript with Node.js now powers entire businesses, and many mobile apps are built in JavaScript.

JavaScript is ready for IoT developers to use. This book gets IoT developers ready to use JavaScript.

Recent Technical Advances

JavaScript wasn't always a good fit for IoT. While the JavaScript engines built into web browsers are breathtakingly fast, that speed comes at a cost. Those engines are far too big to store in a low-cost microcontroller, and they require orders of magnitude more memory than is built into the hardware. The XS JavaScript engine is different: created by Kinoma and maintained by Moddable, it's optimized for the constraints of the microcontrollers that power low-cost IoT products. XS is very small and still plenty fast.

To keep the engine small, you might expect XS to support only a subset of the JavaScript programming language, but that's not the case. XS implements over 99% of the 2020 version of the JavaScript language specification; that's more than any web browser. As an optimization, XS allows you to omit many features of the language to make the engine even smaller—but that's your choice. All the features are there if you want to use them.

Having a small, efficient, and compatible JavaScript engine isn't enough. The JavaScript language only performs computations; it needs a runtime to interact with the outside world. For a web page, the runtime is the web browser; for a web server, the runtime is Node.js. For IoT products, this book uses the Moddable SDK as the runtime.

The Moddable SDK includes a large collection of efficient modules for common tasks like communicating over the internet, controlling IoT hardware, managing security, and storing data. The Moddable SDK also has something unusual for an IoT runtime: deep support for high-quality, rich user interfaces on low-cost touch screens. While you may not yet be considering a screen for your IoT product, your future customers probably wish you would, because a screen makes your product easier to set up and use and enables it to provide more features.

For Embedded Programmers and Web Developers

There are no veteran IoT software developers, because the field is too new. We're all still learning. Most IoT developers come from one of two backgrounds: there are developers building software for embedded systems, who are now being called on to create IoT products with connectivity, complex behaviors, and countless features; and there are developers working on the web, who are being called on to build IoT products on hardware that comes with resource and performance limits that are unimaginable on the web.

JavaScript is at the intersection of developers coming from the embedded and web software worlds. The JavaScript language itself embodies this intersection, arriving from the web with a syntax that looks a lot like the C and C++ languages long favored by embedded developers. JavaScript and C/C++ code can call each other, making it natural to combine both in a product. JavaScript has long been used for communication on the web, even giving rise to the JSON data interchange format commonly by IoT products to communicate.

This book is for developers with a background in either embedded software or web development. For experienced embedded developers unfamiliar with JavaScript, an early chapter introduces C and C++

programmers to JavaScript. For experienced web developers getting started in embedded systems, the book provides tips on memory and performance optimization unique to IoT product development.

Organization of This Book

Here's how this book is organized:

- Chapter 1 takes you through gathering all the hardware and software required for this book and running your first JavaScript application on a microcontroller. Along the way, it shows how to use the helpful features of xsbug, the JavaScript source-level debugger.

- Chapter 2 is a fast-paced, practical introduction to JavaScript for developers who are already familiar with C or C++. The JavaScript language introduced here is the same language that's used on the web, but since this book focuses on embedded systems, the chapter addresses some aspects of JavaScript that are seldom used by web developers.

- Chapter 3 is all about your IoT device's connection to the network, including different ways to connect, how to communicate using various network protocols, how to make secure connections, and the advanced topics of how to turn your device into a private Wi-Fi base station and how to use JavaScript promises with networking APIs.

- Chapter 4 focuses on Bluetooth Low Energy (BLE), a wireless communication widely used between two devices in close proximity to each other. Products choose to use BLE instead of Wi-Fi if minimizing energy use is particularly important and when direct communication with another device, such as a mobile phone, is an acceptable alternative to internet access.

- Chapter 5 explains how to work with stored data on embedded systems, given their code size limitations, constrained RAM, and performance constraints. It explains the three primary ways to store data—files, preferences, and resources—and introduces direct access to flash memory, an advanced technique that offers the greatest flexibility.

- Chapter 6 gets you started on writing your own JavaScript code to interact with hardware. It includes examples that require just a few widely available, inexpensive sensors and actuators and shows you how to communicate with them directly using different hardware protocols.

- Chapter 7 explains how to play sounds using an inexpensive speaker that's easy to attach directly to an ESP32 or ESP8266. You'll also learn how you can achieve higher-quality audio playback using an external I^2S audio driver and how to choose the optimal audio format for your project.

- Chapter 8 covers first the benefits and cost-effectiveness of adding a display to your IoT product and then the fundamentals of graphics on microcontrollers, including background on optimizations and constraints, information about how to add graphics assets to projects, and an introduction to various drawing methods. The next two chapters provide more details.

- Chapter 9 discusses the Poco renderer through examples showing how to deliver high-quality, high-performance graphics on inexpensive microcontrollers. Poco is part of the Commodetto graphics library, which adds features including offscreen graphics buffers, bitmaps, and instantiation of graphics assets from resources, as demonstrated in some of the examples.

- Chapter 10 elaborates on Piu, the object-oriented user interface framework that uses the Poco renderer to draw and simplifies the process of creating sophisticated user interfaces. The chapter provides an overview of how Piu works and introduces its key capabilities through a series of examples.

- Chapter 11 presents the advanced topic of XS in C, the low-level C API provided by the XS JavaScript engine so that you can integrate C code into your JavaScript projects (or JavaScript code into your C projects). Using XS in C enables you to optimize memory use, improve performance, reuse existing C and C++ code libraries, and access unique hardware capabilities.

Finally, there's a Glossary to remind you of the meanings of terms defined in this book.

What's Next

As you work your way through the chapters of this book, you'll acquire new knowledge and skills. There are many paths ahead:

- If you're a professional product developer, you can apply what you've learned to your IoT products.

- If you operate a cloud service, you can build modules to help IoT product developers connect more easily with your service.

- If you're a sensor manufacturer, you can create modules to gather data from your sensors, streamlining the process of using those sensors in IoT products.

- If you're a maker or hobbyist, you can use your new knowledge and skills in your next project.

As you become proficient in using JavaScript to create IoT products, you may find that you spend less time and energy trying to make the product work at all and more time making it work better, do more, and be easier to use. That's the real power of building IoT products in JavaScript.

One reason the JavaScript language has evolved so quickly for so long is that JavaScript developers have always shared their knowledge and experience in online communities. This sharing has resulted in a huge body of JavaScript source code being published under free and open source software licenses. This code is available to you to learn from, improve, and build on. As you create your own IoT projects using JavaScript, consider sharing them with others, so that other developers can learn from you and build on your work.

When you're ready to explore more, there are many resources on the web to help:

- The GitHub repository for this book contains all the examples in the book, updates, and errata to correct any errors. You can open an issue to report a problem or ask a question.

  ```
  https://github.com/Moddable-OpenSource/iot-
  product-dev-book
  ```

- The Moddable SDK includes reference documentation and examples for all the capabilities introduced in this book. It also includes the source code for the modules, so you can learn from how they work and enhance them to meet your needs. If you have questions or find a problem, you can open an issue.

  ```
  https://github.com/Moddable-OpenSource/
  moddable
  ```

- The Moddable blog has in-depth articles about building IoT products using JavaScript. You can learn about the latest language capabilities supported by the XS JavaScript engine, security capabilities, and new features of the Moddable SDK.

  ```
  https://blog.moddable.com/blog/
  ```

- Twitter is a great way to keep up with the latest developments. You can follow the authors of this book on Twitter at **@lizzieprader** and **@phoddie** and follow **@moddabletech** for the latest on the Moddable SDK, events, meetups, and new projects that developers have created.

CHAPTER 1

Getting Started

This chapter takes you through gathering all the hardware and software required for this book and running your first JavaScript application on a microcontroller. Along the way, the chapter also shows how to use the helpful features of xsbug, the JavaScript source-level debugger.

Installing all the software tools and setting up your development environment takes a little time, but once you can run one example you'll be ready to run any example in this book. You'll also have everything you need to begin writing your own applications using the Moddable SDK.

Hardware Requirements

The majority of the examples in this book require very little hardware, but you at least need the following:

- A computer with a USB port (macOS Sierra version 10.12 or later, Windows 7 Pro SP1 or later, or Linux)

- A Micro USB cable (high-speed, data sync–capable)

- An ESP32 NodeMCU module or ESP8266 NodeMCU module

© Peter Hoddie and Lizzie Prader 2020
P. Hoddie and L. Prader, *IoT Development for ESP32 and ESP8266 with JavaScript*,
https://doi.org/10.1007/978-1-4842-5070-9_1

Note   All the examples run on the ESP32 or the ESP8266, with the exception that the examples using Bluetooth Low Energy (BLE), as discussed in Chapter 4, run only on the ESP32, because the ESP8266 doesn't support BLE. If you're interested in experimenting with the BLE examples in this book, you'll need to use an ESP32.

The examples were tested with the ESP32 and ESP8266 modules, shown in Figure 1-1.

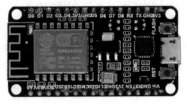

Figure 1-1. *ESP32 (left) and ESP8266 (right)*

The examples using sensors and actuators (Chapters 6 and 7) require a few additional components:

- Tactile button

- Tri-color LED (common anode)

- Three 330 Ohm resistors

- Micro servo

- TMP36 temperature sensor

- TMP102 temperature sensor

- Mini metal speaker (8 Ohm, 0.5W)

- Jumper wires

These hardware components are shown in Figure 1-2. More information on where you can purchase them is provided in the chapters where they're discussed.

Figure 1-2. *Hardware components for Chapters 6 and 7*

The examples that use the Poco renderer (Chapter 9) or the Piu user interface framework (Chapter 10) can be run on the hardware simulator on your computer, but it's highly recommended that you use an actual display and run them on your ESP32 or ESP8266. If you're comfortable wiring together components on a breadboard, here's what you need:

- An ILI9341 QVGA touch display (Figure 1-3), which is available on eBay and elsewhere online; search for "spi display 2.4 touch" and you should find several inexpensive options. Note that although this display works well, there are many other choices. The Moddable SDK includes built-in support for several other displays of varying cost and quality; see the documentation/displays directory of the Moddable SDK for more information.

- A breadboard.

- Male-to-female jumper wires.

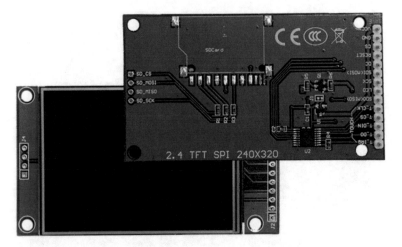

Figure 1-3. *ILI9341 QVGA touch display*

If you'd rather not do the wiring yourself, you can purchase a Moddable One or Moddable Two from the Moddable website. Moddable One is an ESP8266 wired to a capacitive touch screen; Moddable Two is an ESP32 wired to the same touch screen. Both come as ready-to-use development kits in a compact form factor. Figure 1-4 shows a Moddable One.

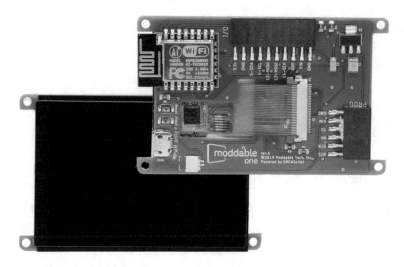

Figure 1-4. *Moddable One*

The Moddable SDK also supports ESP32-based development kits with built-in screens. A popular choice is the M5Stack FIRE, shown in Figure 1-5. See the Moddable SDK repository on GitHub for more information about supported development kits.

Figure 1-5. *M5Stack FIRE*

Software Requirements

You need the following software:

- Code editor

- Example code files

- Moddable SDK

- Build tools for the ESP32 and/or ESP8266

You can choose whichever code editor you prefer. There are many JavaScript-friendly editors, including Visual Studio Code, Sublime Text 3, and Atom.

The next sections explain how to download the example code files and set up the Moddable SDK and build tools for your device.

Downloading the Example Code

All the examples are available at https://github.com/Moddable-OpenSource/iot-product-dev-book. You can download the example code using the git command line tool.

Note In this book, commands that you enter on the command line are preceded by a > symbol. This symbol is not part of the command; it's included only to clarify where each separate command begins.

- On macOS/Linux, use the terminal:

  ```
  > cd ~/Projects
  > git clone https://github.com/Moddable-OpenSource/
      iot-product-dev-book
  ```

- On Windows, use the Command Prompt (changing `<username>` to your username):

```
> cd C:\Users\<username>\Projects
> git clone https://github.com/Moddable-OpenSource/
    iot-product-dev-book
```

You also need to set the `EXAMPLES` environment variable to point at your local copy of the examples repository, as follows:

- On macOS/Linux:

```
> export EXAMPLES=~/Projects/iot-product-dev-book
```

- On Windows:

```
> set EXAMPLES=C:\Users\<username>\Projects\
    iot-product-dev-book
```

Setting Up Your Build Environment

Before building and running the examples, follow the instructions in the "Moddable SDK – Getting Started" document in the `documentation` directory of the Moddable SDK. This document provides step-by-step instructions for installing, configuring, and building the Moddable SDK for macOS, Linux, and Windows, as well as instructions for installing tools you need in order to work with the ESP32 and ESP8266.

Using `xsbug`

The `xsbug` debugger provides source-level debugging of JavaScript code running on the XS JavaScript engine. It connects to devices via USB and has a graphical user interface (shown in Figure 1-6) to make it easy to use.

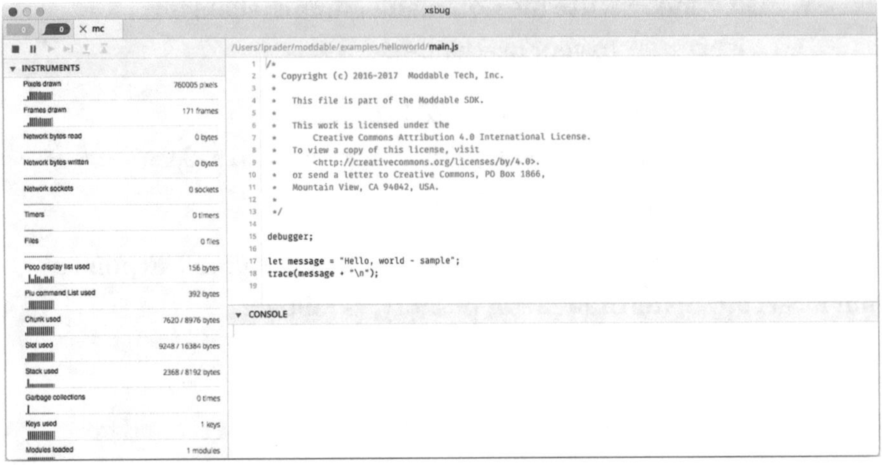

Figure 1-6. xsbug debugger

Similar to other debuggers, xsbug supports setting breakpoints and browsing source code, the call stack, and variables. It also provides real-time instrumentation to track memory usage and to profile application and resource consumption.

When you're developing for a microcontroller, the build system automatically opens xsbug before launching your application on the target device.

When developing for the desktop simulator, you need to open xsbug yourself, by either double-clicking its application icon or opening it from the command line as follows:

- On macOS:

```
> open $MODDABLE/build/bin/mac/release/xsbug.app
```

- On Windows/Linux:

```
> xsbug
```

Important Features for Examples in This Book

This book doesn't refer to xsbug often because the examples have already been debugged. However, xsbug is an invaluable tool as you create your own applications. The most important xsbug features used in this book are as follows:

- **Machine tabs** – Each XS virtual machine connected to xsbug gets its own tab in the upper left of the window (as highlighted by the dashed border in Figure 1-7). Clicking a tab changes the left pane to the machine tab view, where you can view instrumentation, use control buttons, and more.

- **Control buttons** – These graphically labeled buttons (highlighted by the dotted border in the figure) at the top of the machine tab view control the virtual machine. From left to right, they are **Kill**, **Break**, **Run**, **Step**, **Step In**, and **Step Out**.

- **Console** – It's often useful to be able to view diagnostic messages during execution of an application. The trace function writes messages to the debug console in the bottom right of xsbug.

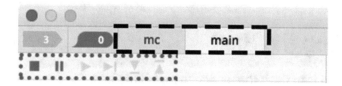

Figure 1-7. *xsbug machine tabs and control buttons*

See the xsbug document in the documentation/xs directory of the Moddable SDK for full documentation of all the features of xsbug.

Running Examples

The examples in the repository for this book are organized by chapter, each one having several examples. To make it faster to build and launch the examples, each chapter has its own *host*, which contains the software environment needed to run the examples for that chapter; the host is the collection of JavaScript modules, configuration variables, and other software available for your application to use. Because space is very limited in microcontrollers, it isn't possible to have a single host that contains all the modules used in the examples in this book.

You can think of the host as essentially the base application. The web browser is the host when you run JavaScript in a web browser; Node.js is the host when you run JavaScript on a web server.

Installing the host separately, rather than installing the host and example together, significantly speeds up development, by minimizing the amount of software that needs to be downloaded. Installing a host on your device typically takes between 30 and 90 seconds. Once that's done, you can install most examples in just a few seconds, because the host already contains the device firmware and JavaScript modules required by the examples.

The next sections walk you through the entire process of installing a host and then an example, starting with helloworld. Note that in the context of this book, installing an application causes the application to then run on the device.

Installing the Host

The first step is to flash the device to install the host. The source code for each chapter's host is available to read in the host directory, if you're curious. To use the host, all you really need to know is that it includes all the modules necessary for the corresponding examples.

You use the mcconfig command line tool to flash the device.

mcconfig

The mcconfig command line tool builds and installs applications on microcontrollers or in the simulator. The commands to use to install this chapter's host on each supported platform are provided here.

On the ESP32, use these commands:

- On macOS/Linux:

```
> cd $EXAMPLES/ch1-gettingstarted/host
> mcconfig -d -m -p esp32
```

- On Windows:

```
> cd %EXAMPLES%\ch1-gettingstarted\host
> mcconfig -d -m -p esp32
```

On the ESP8266, use these commands:

- On macOS/Linux:

```
> cd $EXAMPLES/ch1-gettingstarted/host
> mcconfig -d -m -p esp
```

- On Windows:

```
> cd %EXAMPLES%\ch1-gettingstarted\host
> mcconfig -d -m -p esp
```

Confirming the Host Was Installed

Once the host is installed, it writes the message shown in Figure 1-8 to the debug console.

Figure 1-8. *Message from host in* xsbug

Installing `helloworld`

The `helloworld` example consists of just three lines of JavaScript:

```
debugger;
let message = "Hello, World";
trace(message + "\n");
```

This example uses two important features:

- The debugger statement, which halts execution and breaks into xsbug.

- The trace function, which writes messages to the debug console. Note that trace doesn't automatically add a newline character (\n) at the end of the message. This enables you to use several trace statements to

generate the output of a single line. Be sure to include
the newline character at the end of the line so that the
text displays properly in xsbug.

You use mcrun to install examples.

mcrun

The mcrun command line tool builds and installs additional JavaScript
modules and resources that change the behavior or appearance of
Moddable applications on microcontrollers or in the simulator. Both
mcconfig and mcrun build scripts and resources. Unlike mcrun, mcconfig
also builds native code. In JavaScript terms, mcconfig builds the host.

After you install an example using mcrun, the device reboots. This
relaunches the host, which in turn runs the example you installed.

Use the following commands to install the helloworld example. Make
sure you change <platform> to the correct platform for your device, either
esp32 or esp.

- On macOS/Linux:

```
> cd $EXAMPLES/ch1-gettingstarted/helloworld
> mcrun -d -m -p <platform>
```

- On Windows:

```
> cd %EXAMPLES%\ch1-gettingstarted\helloworld
> mcrun -d -m -p <platform>
```

Finishing Up

You should immediately break into xsbug once the application is installed.
Click the **Run** button to see the message Hello, World written to the
debug console, as shown in Figure 1-9.

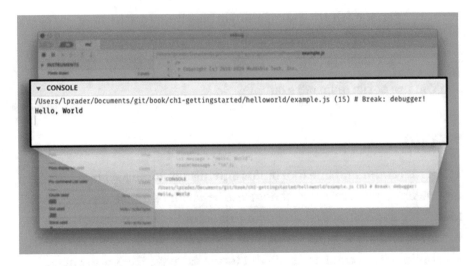

Figure 1-9. *Hello, World written to console in* xsbug

If everything goes well, you can move on to the "Conclusion" section of this chapter if you're working with a bare NodeMCU board. If you want to add a display—which is highly recommended—continue with the "Adding a Display" section instead.

If you ran into issues, see the next section.

Troubleshooting

When you're trying to install an application, you may experience roadblocks in the form of errors or warnings; this section explains some common issues and how to solve them.

Device Not Connected/Recognized

The error message

```
error: cannot access /dev/cu.SLAB_USBtoUART
```

means that the device is not connected to your computer or the computer doesn't recognize the device. There are a few reasons this can happen:

- Your device is not plugged into your computer. Make sure it's plugged in when you run the build commands.

- You have a USB cable that is power only. Make sure you're using a data sync–capable USB cable.

- The computer does not recognize your device. To fix this problem, see the instructions that follow for your operating system.

macOS/Linux

To test whether your computer recognizes your device, unplug the device and enter the following command:

```
> ls /dev/cu*
```

Then plug in the device and repeat the same command. If nothing new appears, the device isn't being seen. Make sure you have the correct VCP driver installed.

If it is seen, you now have the device name and you need to edit the UPLOAD_PORT environment variable. Enter the following command, replacing /dev/cu.SLAB_USBtoUART with the name of the device on your system:

```
> export UPLOAD_PORT=/dev/cu.SLAB_USBtoUART
```

Windows

Check the list of USB devices in Device Manager. If your device shows up as an unknown device, make sure you have the correct VCP driver installed.

If your device shows up on a COM port other than COM3, you need to edit the UPLOAD_PORT environment variable. Enter the following command, replacing COM3 with the appropriate device COM port for your system:

```
> set UPLOAD_PORT=COM3
```

Incompatible Baud Rate

The following warning message is normal and is no cause for concern:

```
warning: serialport_set_baudrate: baud rate 921600 may not work
```

However, sometimes the upload starts but does not complete. You can tell an upload is complete after the progress bar traced to the console goes to 100%. For example:

```
.................................................. [  16% ]
.................................................. [  33% ]
.................................................. [  49% ]
.................................................. [  66% ]
.................................................. [  82% ]
.................................................. [  99% ]
..                                                 [ 100% ]
```

There are a few reasons the upload may fail partway through:

- You have a faulty USB cable.

- You have a USB cable that does not support higher baud rates.

- You're using a board that requires a lower baud rate than the default baud rate that the Moddable SDK uses.

To solve the last two problems, you can change to a slower baud rate as follows:

1. If you're working with an ESP32, open `moddable/tools/mcconfig/make.esp32.mk`; if an ESP8266, open `moddable/tools/mcconfig/make.esp.mk`.

2. Find this line, which sets the upload speed to 921,600:

   ```
   UPLOAD_SPEED ?= 921600
   ```

3. Set the speed to a smaller number. For example:

   ```
   UPLOAD_SPEED ?= 115200
   ```

Device Not in Bootloader Mode

This issue is not uncommon if you're using certain ESP32-based boards. Status messages stop being traced briefly when you attempt to flash the device, and after several seconds you receive this error message:

```
A fatal error occurred: Failed to connect to ESP32: Timed out waiting for packet header
```

If the device is not in bootloader mode, you cannot flash the device. If you're using a NodeMCU module, follow these steps every time you flash:

1. Unplug the device.

2. Hold down the BOOT button (circled in Figure 1-10).

3. Plug the device into your computer.

4. Enter the `mcconfig` command.

5. Wait a few seconds and release the BOOT button.

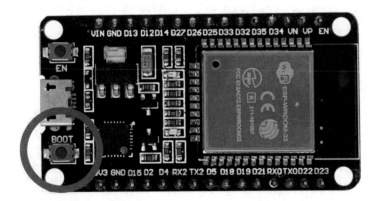

Figure 1-10. BOOT button on ESP32

Adding a Display

Although most of the examples in this book don't require a display, adding a display to the ESP32 or ESP8266 greatly improves the user experience. It enables you to do the following:

- Show more information than a few blinking lights

- Create modern user interfaces

- Add functionality

The examples in this book are designed for a display with 240 x 320 or 320 x 240 resolution (for example, QVGA). These displays are typically between 2.2" and 3.5" in size and were common in early smart phones. Displays of other sizes may be connected to these microcontrollers, but this size is a good match for the capabilities of these microcontrollers.

The following sections show how to connect the ILI9341 QVGA touch display to the ESP32 or ESP8266. If you're using a development board like the Moddable One or Moddable Two, you can skip to the "Installing helloworld-gui" section.

Connecting a Display to the ESP32

Table 1-1 and Figure 1-11 show how to connect a display to the ESP32.

Table 1-1. *Wiring to connect display to ESP32*

ILI9341 Display	ESP32
SDO/MISO	GPIO12
LED	3.3V
SCK	GPIO14
SDI/MOSI	GPIO13
CS	GPIO15
DC	GPIO2
RESET	3.3V
GND	GND
VCC	3.3V
T_DO	GPIO12
T_DIn	GPIO13
T_CLK	GPIO14
T_IRQ	GPIO23
T_CS	GPIO18

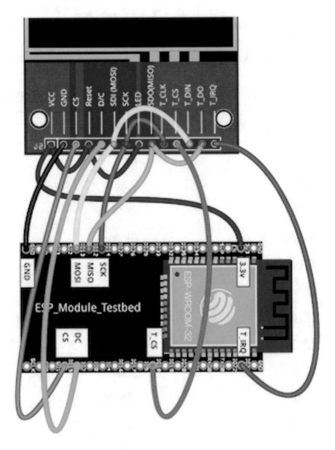

Figure 1-11. *Wiring diagram for connecting display to ESP32*

Connecting a Display to the ESP8266

Table 1-2 and Figure 1-12 show how to connect a display to the ESP8266.

Table 1-2. Wiring to connect display to ESP8266

ILI9341 Display	ESP8266
SDO/MISO	GPIO12
LED	3.3V
SCK	GPIO14
SDI/MOSI	GPIO13
CS	GPIO15
DC	GPIO2
RESET	3.3V
GND	GND
VCC	3.3V
T_DO	GPIO12
T_DIn	GPIO13
T_CLK	GPIO14
T_IRQ	GPIO16
T_CS	GPIO0

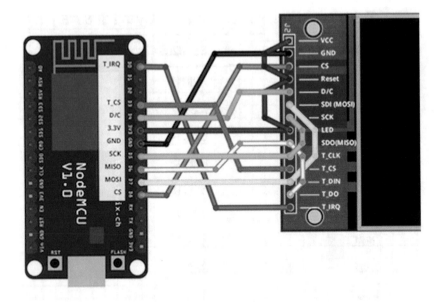

Figure 1-12. *Wiring diagram for connecting display to ESP8266*

Installing `helloworld-gui`

The `helloworld-gui` example is a version of `helloworld` that displays text on the screen. If you wired a display to a device yourself, reflashing the device with the `helloworld-gui` application is a good way to test whether the wiring is correct.

The commands to use are very similar to the ones used to install `helloworld`. The only difference is the platform identifier. The platform identifier tells the build system to include the proper display and touch drivers. If you're using a Moddable One, the platform identifier is `esp/moddable_one`; for a Moddable Two, it's `esp32/moddable_two`. If you added a display according to the instructions in the preceding sections, the platform identifier is either `esp32/moddable_zero` or `esp/moddable_zero`.

Use the following commands to install the `helloworld-gui` example. Make sure you change `<platform>` to the correct platform for your device.

- On macOS/Linux:

```
> cd $EXAMPLES/ch1-gettingstarted/helloworld-gui
> mcconfig -d -m -p <platform>
```

- On Windows:

```
> cd %EXAMPLES%\ch1-gettingstarted\helloworld-gui
> mcconfig -d -m -p <platform>
```

If you specify the correct platform and your wiring is correct, you will see the screen shown in Figure 1-13.

Figure 1-13. *Graphical helloworld application*

Conclusion

Now that your development environment is set up and you're familiar with the process of installing this chapter's examples on your device, you're ready to try some more examples!

At this point, you have all the materials and skills you need to follow along with Chapters 2 through 10. These chapters are independent of each other, so you can read them in any order. As you start working with the examples in a chapter, be sure to install that chapter's host or you'll encounter errors when launching the examples. Once you feel comfortable with the APIs of the Moddable SDK, you can move on to Chapter 11, which covers more advanced topics.

CHAPTER 2

JavaScript for Embedded C and C++ Programmers

This chapter is a fast-paced, practical introduction to JavaScript for developers who are already familiar with C or C++. It assumes that you already know how to program and, perhaps, have some development experience with embedded systems. The JavaScript language introduced here is exactly the same language that's used on the web. But since the focus here is on embedded systems rather than web browsers, this chapter addresses some aspects of JavaScript that are seldom used by developers working on the web. For example, consider that it's almost impossible to write embedded software without manipulating binary data (such as an array of bytes); JavaScript supports binary data with built-in typed array classes, yet most web developers never use that feature because it's unnecessary when building a web page. So even if you're familiar with JavaScript on the web, you may want to read this chapter to familiarize yourself with language features more common on embedded systems than on the web.

C and C++ programmers have a big advantage when getting started with JavaScript, because the language looks quite similar to C. That's no accident: the JavaScript programming language was designed to be similar

© Peter Hoddie and Lizzie Prader 2020
P. Hoddie and L. Prader, *IoT Development for ESP32 and ESP8266 with JavaScript*,
https://doi.org/10.1007/978-1-4842-5070-9_2

to the Java programming language; Java was created as an evolution of C++; and C++ was created to bring object-oriented programming to C. The many similarities will help you quickly read and write JavaScript code. Still, the languages are also different in many respects. This chapter uses the similarities as a foundation to introduce you to some of the differences.

JavaScript is now more than 20 years old, and it's constantly evolving. This chapter introduces modern JavaScript, including the features in the 2019 edition of JavaScript as well as some (like private fields) that are on track for inclusion in a future edition. Only features of JavaScript that are part of the standard language are described here. Because of JavaScript's long history, certain features are no longer recommended for use; this chapter identifies some of them. In particular, JavaScript 5th Edition, standardized in 2012, introduced *strict mode,* which eliminates a handful of confusing and inefficient features. Those original behaviors remain available in *sloppy mode,* which is primarily used for backward compatibility for websites, but this book uses strict mode exclusively.

Fundamental Syntax

This section introduces fundamentals such as how to use JavaScript to make function calls, declare variables, and control the flow of execution with `if`, `switch`, `for`, and `while` statements. All of these are very similar in C and JavaScript, but you'll learn about some important differences along the way.

"Hello, world"

The traditional starting point for learning C is the `hello, world` program from Kernighan and Ritchie's book *The C Programming Language.* In JavaScript, it's just one line:

```
trace("hello, world\n");
```

Here, the C printf function is replaced by the trace function from the Moddable SDK. (Developers working with JavaScript on the web use console.log instead of trace.) As in C, the argument to the function is passed inside parentheses and the statement is terminated with a semicolon. The string literal passed to the function is identical, too—a string surrounded by double quotes—and uses the familiar backslash (\) notation as in C to escape special characters, such as the newline character here.

Semicolons

One significant difference between C and C++ is that the semicolon at the end of a statement is optional in JavaScript, thanks to the automatic semicolon insertion (ASI) feature. The following code is allowed in JavaScript but fails in C:

```
trace("hello, ")
trace("world")
trace("\n")
```

While this is convenient, since it saves a keystroke and silently fixes the common mistake of leaving out the semicolon, it creates ambiguities in certain obscure cases, which can result in bugs. Therefore, you should always end statements with a semicolon rather than relying on ASI. JavaScript linters, such as ESLint, include a check for missing semicolons.

Declaring Variables and Constants

Variables in JavaScript are declared with the let statement:

```
let a = 12;
let b = "hello";
let c = false;
```

Unlike in C, the variable declaration doesn't include any type information (such as int, bool, or char *). That's because any variable may hold any type. This dynamic typing, which is further explained later in this chapter, is one feature of JavaScript that takes C programmers a little time to get used to.

Variable names in JavaScript generally follow C conventions: they're case-sensitive, so i and I are distinct names, and there's no limit on the length of variable names. JavaScript variable names may also include Unicode characters, as in these examples:

```
let garçon = "boy";
let 東京都 = "Tokyo";
let $ = "dollar";
let under_score = "_";
```

You declare constant values with const:

```
const PRODUCT_NAME = "Light Sensor";
const LUMEN_REGISTER = 2;
const USE_OPTIMIZATIONS = true;
```

Any attempt to assign a value to a constant generates an error; however, unlike in C, this error is generated at runtime rather than at build time.

As shown in Listing 2-1, declarations made with let and const obey the same scoping rules as declarations in C.

Listing 2-1.

```
let x = 1;
const y = 2;
let z = 3;
if (true) {
    const x = 2;
```

```
    let y = 1;
    trace(x);    // output: 2
    trace(y);    // output: 1
    trace(z);    // output: 3
    y = 4;
    z += y;
}
trace(x);        // output: 1
trace(y);        // output: 2
trace(z);        // output: 7
```

JavaScript also lets you use var to declare variables and this is still common, since let is a relatively new addition. However, this book recommends using let exclusively, because var doesn't obey the same scoping rules as declarations in C.

The if Statement

The if statement in JavaScript has the same structure as in C, as illustrated in Listing 2-2.

Listing 2-2.

```
if (x) {
    trace("x is true\n");
}
else {
    trace("x is false\n");
}
```

As in C, when the if or else block is a single statement you can omit the braces that delimit the block:

```
if (!x)
    trace("x is false\n");
else
    trace("x is true\n");
```

The condition in the if statement in Listing 2-2 is simply x. In C, this means that if x is 0, the condition is false; otherwise, it's true. In JavaScript, this is more complex, because the variable x may be of any type, not just a number (or a pointer, but pointers don't exist in JavaScript). JavaScript has defined the following rules to evaluate whether a given value is true or false:

- For a boolean value, this determination is simple: the value is either true or false.

- For a number, JavaScript follows the rule of C, treating a value of 0 as false and all other values as true.

- An empty string (a string with length 0) evaluates to false, and all non-empty strings evaluate to true.

In JavaScript, a value that evaluates to true in a condition is called "truthy," and one that evaluates to false is called "falsy."

A compact form of an if statement, the conditional (ternary) operator, is available in JavaScript and has the same structure as in C:

```
let x = y ? 2 : 3;
```

The switch Statement

As shown in Listing 2-3, the switch statement in JavaScript looks very much as it does in C.

Listing 2-3.

```
switch (x) {
    case 0:
        trace("zero\n");
        break;
    case 1:
        trace("one\n");
        break;
    default:
        trace("unexpected!\n");
        break;
}
```

There's one important difference, however: the value following the case keyword is not limited to integer values. For example, you can use a floating-point number (see Listing 2-4).

Listing 2-4.

```
switch (x) {
    case 0.25:
        trace("one quarter\n");
        break;
    case 0.5:
        trace("one half\n");
        break;
}
```

You can also use strings (Listing 2-5).

Listing 2-5.

```
switch (x) {
    case "zero":
    case "Zero":
        trace("0\n");
        break;
    case "one":
    case "One":
        trace("1\n");
        break;
    default:
        trace("unexpected!\n");
        break;
}
```

In addition, JavaScript lets you mix the types of values in the case statements, though that's seldom necessary.

Loops

JavaScript has both for and while loops that look similar to their C language counterparts (see Listing 2-6).

Listing 2-6.

```
for (i = 0; i < 10; i++)
    trace(i);

let j = 12;
while (j--)
    trace(j);
```

JavaScript loops support both continue and break (Listing 2-7).

Listing 2-7.

```
for (i = 0; i < 10; i++) {
    if (i & 1)
        continue;     // Skip odd numbers
    trace(i);
}
let j = 0;
do {
    let jSquared = j * j;
    if (jSquared > 100)
        break;
    trace(jSquared);
    j++;
} while (true);
```

Types

JavaScript has just a handful of built-in types, from which all other types are created. Many of these types are familiar to C and C++ programmers, such as Boolean, Number, and String, though there are differences in the JavaScript versions of these that you need to understand. Other types, such as undefined, do not have an equivalent in C or C++.

Note that this section doesn't introduce all the types. It omits RegExp, BigInt, and Symbol, for example, because they're not commonly used when developing in JavaScript for embedded systems; they are available, however, should your project require them.

undefined

In C and C++, an operation can have a result that's not defined by the language. For example, if you forget to initialize x in the following code, the value of y is unknown:

```
int x;
int y = x + 1;        // ??
```

Also, the result of a function is unknown if you forget to include a return statement:

```
int add(int a, int b) {
    int result = a + b;
}
int z = add(1, 2);  // ??
```

Your C or C++ compiler usually detects these kinds of mistakes and issues warnings so you can fix the problem. Still, there are many ways to make mistakes in C and C++ that result in code with results that are unpredictable.

In JavaScript, there's never a situation in which the result is unpredictable. One part of how this is achieved is with the special value undefined, which indicates that no value has been assigned. In C, 0 is sometimes used as an invalid value for a similar purpose, but it's ambiguous in situations where 0 is a valid value.

When you define a new local variable, it has the value of undefined until you assign another value to it. If your function exits without a return statement, its return value is undefined. You'll see other uses of undefined throughout this chapter.

Strictly speaking, JavaScript has an undefined type, which always has the value undefined.

Boolean Values

The boolean values in JavaScript are true and false. These are not the same as 1 and 0 in C; they're distinct values defined by the language.

```
let x = 42;
let y = x == 42;    // true
let z = x == "dog"; // false
```

Numbers

Every number value in JavaScript is defined to be a double-precision (64-bit) IEEE 754 floating-point value. Before you gasp in horror at the performance implications of this on a microcontroller, know that the XS JavaScript engine used in the Moddable SDK internally stores numbers as integers and performs integer math operations on them when possible. This ensures that the implementation is efficient on microcontrollers without an FPU while maintaining full compatibility with standard JavaScript.

```
let x = 1;
let y = -2.3;
let z = 5E2;      // 500
```

There are some benefits to having every number defined to be 64-bit floating-point. For one thing, integer overflow is much less likely. If the result of an integer operation overflows a 32-bit integer, it's automatically promoted to a floating-point value. A 64-bit floating-point value can store integers up to 53 bits before losing precision. If you do happen to perform a math operation that generates a fractional result—for example, dividing an odd integer by 2—JavaScript returns the accurate fractional result as a floating-point value.

Infinity and NaN

JavaScript has some special values for numbers:

- Dividing by 0 doesn't generate an error but instead returns Infinity.

- Attempting to perform a nonsense operation returns NaN, meaning "not a number." For example, 5 / "a string" and 5 + undefined return NaN because it doesn't make sense to divide an integer by a string value or add undefined to an integer.

Bases

JavaScript has special notation for hexadecimal and binary constants:

- A 0x prefix on a number means it's in hexadecimal notation, just as it does in C.

- A 0b prefix on a number means it's in binary notation, as supported in C++14.

These prefixes are useful when working with binary data, as in the following examples:

```
let hexMask = 0x0F;
let bitMask = 0b00001111;
```

Unlike C, JavaScript doesn't support octal numbers with a leading 0, as in 0557; if you try to use one, it generates an error when building. Octal numeric literals are supported in the form 0o557.

Numeric Separators

JavaScript lets you use the underscore character (_) as a numeric separator, to separate digits in a number. The separator doesn't change the value of the number but can make it easier to read. C++14 also has a numeric separator, but it uses the single quote character (') instead.

```
let mask = 0b0101101011110000;
let maskWithSeparators = 0b0101_1010_1111_0000;
```

Bitwise Operators

JavaScript provides bitwise operators for numbers, including the following:

- ~ – bitwise NOT
- & – bitwise AND
- | – bitwise OR
- ^ – bitwise XOR

It also provides these bitwise operators, for shifting bits:

- >> – signed shift right
- >>> – unsigned shift right
- << – shift left

There's no unsigned shift left because shifting left by a nonzero value always discards the sign bit. When performing any bitwise operation, JavaScript always first converts the value to a 32-bit integer; any fractional component or additional bits are discarded.

The Math Object

The Math object provides many of the functions C programmers use from the math.h header file. In addition to common constants such as Math.PI, Math.SQRT2, and Math.E, it includes common functions such as those shown in Listing 2-8.

Listing 2-8.

```
let x = Math.min(1, 2, 3);  // minimum = 1
let y = Math.max(2, 3);     // maximum = 3
let r = Math.random();      // random number between 0 and 1
```

```
let z = Math.abs(-3.2);       // absolute value = 3.2
let a = Math.sqrt(100);       // square root = 10
let b = Math.round(3.9);      // rounded value = 4
let c = Math.trunc(3.9);      // truncated value = 3
let z = Math.cos(Math.PI);    // cosine of pi = -1
```

Consult a JavaScript reference for a complete listing of the constant values and functions provided by the Math object.

Converting Numbers to Strings

In C, a common way to convert a number to a string is to use sprintf to print the number to a string buffer. In JavaScript, you convert a number to a string by calling the number's toString method (yes, in JavaScript even a number is an object!):

```
let a = 1;
let b = a.toString();    // "1"
```

The default base for toString is 10; to convert to a non-decimal value, such as hexadecimal or binary, pass the base as the argument to toString:

```
let a = 240;
let b = a.toString(16);    // "f0"
let c = a.toString(2);     // "11110000"
```

To convert to floating-point notation, use toFixed instead of toString and specify the number of digits after the decimal point:

```
let a = 24.328;
let b = a.toFixed(1);    // "24.3"
let c = a.toFixed(2);    // "24.33"
let d = a.toFixed(4);    // "24.3280"
```

The functions toExponential and toPrecision provide additional formatting options for converting numbers to strings.

Converting Strings to Numbers

In C, a common way to convert a string to a number is to use `sscanf`. In JavaScript, use either `parseInt` or `parseFloat` depending on whether you want the result as an integer or a floating-point value:

```
let a = parseInt("12.3");       // 12
let b = parseFloat("12.30");    // 12.3
```

The default base for `parseInt` is 10, except when the string begins with 0x, in which case the default is 16. The `parseInt` function takes an optional second argument indicating the base. The following example parses a hexadecimal value:

```
let a = parseInt("F0", 16);     // 240
```

You can also access the functionality of `parseInt` and `parseFloat` as `Number.parseInt` and `Number.parseFloat`; however, this is less common.

Strings

In C, strings are not a distinct type but just an array of 8-bit characters. Because strings are so common, the C standard library provides many functions for working with them. Still, working with strings isn't easy in C and can easily lead to security errors, like buffer overflows. C++ addresses some of the issues, though working with strings is still not easy or safe. JavaScript, by contrast, has a built-in `String` type that was designed to be easy for programmers to use and to use safely; this reflects JavaScript's origin as the language of the web, where string manipulations are common in building web pages.

In JavaScript, strings differ from common C strings in many ways. A string is a sequence of 16-bit Unicode characters (UTF-16), not an array of 8-bit characters. Using Unicode to represent strings ensures that all applications can work reliably with string values in any language. Although the characters are conceptually 16-bit Unicode, the JavaScript engine may store them internally in any representation. The XS engine stores strings in UTF-8, so there's no additional memory overhead for characters from the common 7-bit ASCII character set.

Accessing Individual Characters

JavaScript strings are not arrays; however, they do support C's array syntax for accessing individual characters. Unlike in C, though, the result is not the Unicode (numeric) value of the character but a one-character string containing the character at that index.

```
let a = "garçon";
let b = a[3];    // "ç"
let c = a[4];    // "o"
```

In C, accessing an invalid index—for example, past the end of the string—returns an undefined value. For a declared as shown in the preceding code, a[100] will access whatever happens to be in memory 100 bytes after the start of the string. The access might even cause a memory fault by accessing unmapped memory. In JavaScript, attempting to read a character outside the valid range of a string returns the value undefined.

To get the Unicode value of a character at a given index, use the charCodeAt function:

```
let a = "garçon";
let b = a.charCodeAt(3);     // 231
let c = a.charCodeAt(4);     // 111
let d = a.charCodeAt(100);   // NaN
```

Modifying Strings

C lets you both read from and write to the characters in a string. JavaScript strings are read-only, also called *immutable*; you cannot modify a string "in place." For example, the assignment to a[0] in the following code does nothing in JavaScript:

```
let a = "a string";
a[0] = "A";
```

This restriction can be a little difficult to get used to coming from C, but it becomes familiar with some experience using the many methods provided to operate on a string.

Determining the Length of Strings

To determine the length of a string in C, you use the strlen function, which returns the number of bytes in the string. It determines the length by scanning for a byte with the value 0, because strings in C are defined to end on a 0 byte. In JavaScript, strings are a sequence of Unicode characters, with no terminating null character; the number of characters in the sequence is known to the JavaScript engine and is available through the length property.

```
let a = "hello";
let b = a.length;    // 5
```

One problem with strlen is that number of bytes in a string is only equal to the string's length when the characters are 8-bit ASCII characters. For Unicode characters, strlen doesn't provide the character count. Of course, there are other functions that do, but it's a common mistake for C programmers to use strlen incorrectly with strings to get the character count, leading to bugs. The JavaScript length property avoids this problem because it always returns a character count.

41

The example in Listing 2-9 uses the length property to count the spaces in a string.

Listing 2-9.

```
let a = "zéro un deux";
let spaces = 0;
for (let i = 0; i < a.length; i++) {
    if (a[i] == " ")
        spaces += 1;
}
trace(spaces);
```

Embedding Quotes and Control Characters

The string literal values in this chapter up to this point have all used double quote marks (") to define the beginning and end of the string. Strings delimited by double quotes may contain single quotes (').

```
let a = "Let's eat!";
```

As in C, such strings cannot contain a double quote. Unlike in C, you can delimit a string with single quotes instead of double quotes, which is convenient for strings that contain double quotes.

```
let a = '"This is a test," she said.';
```

Strings delimited by single or double quotes must be entirely contained on a single line. You can include line breaks in the string by using \n to specify the newline character; the backslash (\) lets you escape characters just as in C.

```
let a = 'line 1\nline 2\nline 3\n';
```

Another way to delineate a string in JavaScript is to use the backtick character (`` ` ``). Strings defined in this way are called *template literals* and have several useful properties, including that they can span multiple lines (potentially making your strings more readable; compare Listing 2-10 to the preceding example).

Listing 2-10.

```
let a =
`line 1
line 2
line 3
`;
```

String Substitution

Template literals provide a substitution mechanism that's useful for composing a string from several parts. The functionality this provides is very similar to using `printf` in C with a formatting string. However, whereas C separates the formatting string from the values to be formatted, JavaScript merges them. This may feel unfamiliar at first, but putting the values to be formatted directly into the string is less error-prone.

```
let a = "one";
let b = "two";
let c = `${a}, ${b}, three`;     // "one, two, three"
```

Inside a template literal, the characters between ${ and } are evaluated as a JavaScript expression, which enables you to perform calculations and apply formatting to the result:

```
let a = `2 + 2 = ${2 + 2}`;      // "2 + 2 = 4"
let b = `Pi to three decimals is ${Math.PI.toFixed(3)}`;
        // "Pi to three decimals is 3.142"
```

A special feature, called *tags*, enables a function to modify the default behavior of template literals. For example (as Chapter 4 will demonstrate), you can use this feature to convert the string representation of a UUID to binary data. The details of how tagged template literals work are beyond the scope of this chapter, but using them is easy: just put the tag before the template literal.

```
let a = uuid`1805`;
let b = uuid`9CF53570-DDD9-47F3-BA63-09ACEFC60415`;
```

Adding Strings

You can combine strings in JavaScript by using the addition operator (+):

```
let a = "one";
let b = "two";
let c = a + ", " + b + ", three";    // "one, two, three"
```

JavaScript lets you add strings to non-string values, such as numbers. Its rules for how this works usually give you the expected result, but not always:

```
let a = "2 + 2 = " + 4;        // "2 + 2 = 4"
let b = 2 + 2 + " = 2 + 2";    // "4 = 2 + 2"
let c = "2 + 2 = " + 2 + 2;    // "2 + 2 = 22"
```

Because remembering all the rules about type conversion during string addition can be difficult, it's recommended that you instead use template literals, which are more predictable and often more readable.

Converting String Case

Converting strings to uppercase or lowercase in C is challenging, especially when you're working with the complete set of Unicode characters. JavaScript has built-in functions for doing these conversions.

```
let a = "Garçon";
let b = a.toUpperCase();    // "GARÇON"
let c = a.toLowerCase();    // "garçon"
```

Notice that the toUpperCase and toLowerCase functions do not modify the original string, stored in the variable a in the preceding example, but rather return a new string with the modified value. All JavaScript functions that operate on strings behave this way, because all strings are immutable.

Extracting Parts of Strings

To extract part of a string into another string, use the slice function. Its arguments are the starting and ending indices, where the ending index is the index *before which* to end extraction. If the ending index is omitted, the string's length is used.

```
let a = "hello, world!";
let b = a.slice(0, 5);      // "hello"
let c = a.slice(7, 12);     // "world"
let d = a.slice(7);         // "world!"
```

JavaScript also has a substr function, which provides similar functionality to slice but with slightly different arguments. However, slice is preferred over substr, which is maintained primarily for legacy code on the web.

Repeating Strings

To create a string that repeats a particular value several times, use the repeat function:

```
let a = "-";
let b = a.repeat(3);     // "---"
let c = ".-";
let d = c.repeat(2);     // ".-.-"
```

Trimming Strings

When parsing strings, you often want to remove white space (space character, tab, carriage return, line feed, and so on) at the start or end. The trim functions remove white space in a single step:

```
let a = " JS ";
let b = a.trim();         // "JS"
let c = a.trimStart();    // "JS "
let d = a.trimEnd();      // " JS"
```

The trim functions could be implemented entirely in JavaScript (as could most of the string functions), but building them into the language means their implementation is considerably faster and their behavior is consistent across all applications.

Searching Strings

The strstr function in C finds one string inside another. The indexOf function in JavaScript is similar to strstr. As shown in Listing 2-11, the first argument to indexOf is the substring to search for, the optional second argument is the character index at which to begin searching, and the result of the function is the index where the substring is found, or –1 if not found.

Listing 2-11.

```
let string = "the cat and the dog";
let a = string.indexOf("cat");      // 4
let b = string.indexOf("frog");     // -1
let c = string.indexOf("the");      // 0
let d = string.indexOf("the", 2);   // 12
```

Sometimes you want to find the last occurrence of a substring. In C, this requires calling strstr several times until no further matches are found. JavaScript provides the lastIndexOf function for this situation.

```
let string = "the cat and the dog";
let a = string.lastIndexOf("the");          // 12
let b = string.lastIndexOf("the", a - 1); // 0
```

When evaluating strings, it's useful to check whether the string begins or ends with a particular string. You use strcmp and strncmp to do this in C. This situation is common enough that JavaScript provides dedicated startsWith and endsWith functions.

```
if (string.startsWith("And "))
    trace(`Don't start sentence with "and"`);
if (string.endsWith("..."))
    trace(`Don't end sentence with ellipsis`);
```

Functions

JavaScript has functions, of course, as does C. Some functions are very similar in both languages.

```
function add(a, b) {
    return a + b;
}
```

Function Arguments

Because JavaScript variables may hold any type of value, the type of arguments is not given, just their name. Also unlike in C and C++, there are no function declarations; you just write the source code to the function and then any code that can access the function can call it. This ad hoc approach allows for faster coding.

In C and C++, you can pass an argument value by reference, using a pointer, but in JavaScript you must always pass arguments by value. Consequently, a JavaScript function never changes the value of a variable passed to it. For example, the add function in Listing 2-12 doesn't change the value of x.

Listing 2-12.

```
function add(a, b) {
    a += b;
    return a;
}
let x = 1;
let y = 2;
let z = add(x, y);
```

When you pass an object to a function, the function can modify the properties of the object but not the call's local variable holding the object. This is similar to passing a pointer to a data structure in C. In Listing 2-13, the setName function adds the name property to the object passed to it. The assignment it makes, of a new empty object to its parameter a, doesn't change the value of b.

Listing 2-13.

```
function setName(a, name) {
    a.name = name;
    a = {};
}

let b = {};
setName(b, "thermostat");
// b.name is "thermostat"
```

In C and C++, the implementation of a function can determine the number of arguments passed to it and can access each one using va_start, va_end, and va_arg. These are powerful tools but can be complicated to use. JavaScript also provides tools for working with the arguments to a function. Any arguments not passed by the caller are set to undefined, so (as done for b in Listing 2-14), you can check whether an argument has not been passed.

Listing 2-14.

```javascript
function add(a, b) {
    if (b == undefined)
        return NaN;
    return a + b;
}

add(1);
```

Another way to access the parameters passed to the function is by using the special `arguments` variable, which behaves like an array containing the arguments. This approach is similar to using `va_arg` with the added benefit of knowing the number of arguments. In Listing 2-15, the add function accepts any number of arguments and returns their sum.

Listing 2-15.

```javascript
function add() {
    let result = 0;
    for (let i = 0; i < arguments.length; i++)
        result += arguments[i];
    return result;
}

let c = add(1, 2);
let d = add(1, 2, 3);
```

The use of `arguments` is common in JavaScript, but it's not available in all situations. It's introduced here because you're likely to see it in code. Modern JavaScript has an additional feature, called *rest parameters*, which provides similar functionality, is always available, and is more flexible (see Listing 2-16).

Listing 2-16.

```
function add(...values) {
    let result = 0;
    for (let i = 0; i < values.length; i++)
        result += values[i];
    return result;
}
```

Here ...values indicates that all remaining arguments (all arguments, in this example) are to be placed in an array named values. The code in Listing 2-17 adds a round parameter to control whether the values should be rounded before being summed.

Listing 2-17.

```
function addR(round, ...values) {
    let result = 0;
    for (let i = 0; i < values.length; i++)
        result += round ? Math.round(values[i]) : values[i];
    return result;
}

let c = addR(false, 1.1, 2.9, 3.5); // c = 7.5
let d = addR(true, 1.1, 2.9, 3.5);  // d = 8
```

Just as rest parameters combine several arguments into an array, *spread syntax* separates the content of an array into individual arguments. Spread syntax uses the same three-dot syntax as rest parameters. The function in Listing 2-18 sums the absolute value of its arguments; it first takes the absolute value of the arguments and then calls the add function using spread syntax to compute the sum.

Listing 2-18.

```
function addAbs(...values) {
    for (let i = 0; i < values.length; i++)
        values[i] = Math.abs(values[i]);
    return add(...values);
}

let c = addAbs(-1, -2, 3);  // c = 6
```

There are many other uses of spread syntax—for example, to clone an array:

```
let a = [1, 2, 3, 4];
let b = [...a];           // b = [1, 2, 3, 4]
```

You can also use spread syntax to concatenate two arrays:

```
let a = [1, 2];
let b = [3, 4];
let c = [...a, ...b];    // c = [1, 2, 3, 4]
```

In some situations, it's useful to provide a default value for an argument. This isn't possible in C but it is done in C++, using the same syntax as in JavaScript. In JavaScript, since arguments not passed by the caller are set to undefined, you can provide a default value for any parameter that has that value. The function in Listing 2-19 accepts a temperature value; if the units aren't specified, a default of Celsius is used.

Listing 2-19.

```
function setCelsiusTemperature(temperature) {
    trace(`setCelsiusTemperature ${temperature}\n`);
}
```

```
function setTemperature(temperature, units = "Celsius") {
    switch (units) {
        case "Fahrenheit":
            temperature -= 32;
            temperature /= 1.8;
            break;
        case "Kelvin":
            temperature -= 273.15;
            break;
        case "Celsius":
            // no conversion needed
            break;
    }
    setCelsiusTemperature(temperature);
}

setTemperature(14); // units argument defaults to Celsius
setTemperature(14, "Celsius");
setTemperature(57, "Fahrenheit");
```

Unlike in C, every function in JavaScript has a return value; there's no way for a function to exit without a well-defined return value. Consider the three functions shown in Listing 2-20.

Listing 2-20.

```
function a() {
    return undefined;
}
function b() {
    return;
}
function c() {
}
```

Function a explicitly returns the value undefined. Function b provides no value to the return statement and so returns undefined. Function c has no return statement but returns undefined just like function b because undefined is the default value that all functions return. You'll find all three of these forms in JavaScript code, depending on the preference of the code's author. They're indistinguishable by the caller of the function.

By contrast, the following code is allowed in C. The result of function c is whatever value happens to be in the memory or register reserved for the return value.

```
int c(void) {
}
int b = c();    // b is unknown
```

Passing Functions As Arguments

In C, it's common to pass a function a pointer to another function, enabling you to customize the behavior of the function being passed—for example, to provide a comparison function to use when sorting. Similarly, JavaScript functions may be passed as arguments to another function, as shown in Listing 2-21.

Listing 2-21.

```
function square(a) {
    return a * a;
}
function circleArea(r) {
    return Math.PI * r * r;
}
function sum(filter, ...values) {
    let result = 0;
```

```
    for (let i = 0; i < values.length; i++)
        result += filter(values[i]);
    return result;
}

let a = sum(square, 1, 2, 3);    // 14
let b = sum(circleArea, 1);      // 3.14...
```

You can also pass built-in functions as arguments. For example, the following code calculates the sum of the square roots of the remaining arguments:

```
let c = sum(Math.sqrt, 1, 4, 9);    // 6
```

Often when a function is passed, that function is used in only that one place. In C, the function implementation is often not located near where it's called, which hurts readability. Unlike C, JavaScript allows anonymous (unnamed) inline functions. The following example calls the sum function defined in Listing 2-21 to calculate the sum of areas of equilateral triangles using an anonymous inline function as the filter:

```
let a = sum(function(a) {
    return a * (a / 2);
}, 1, 2, 3);    // 7
```

Anonymous functions are widely used in JavaScript code for various kinds of callbacks. Seeing the source code to a function as the argument to a function call is a little unusual, but you do get used to it. If you prefer to keep function implementations separate from function calls, you can use nested functions instead. In Listing 2-22, the function triangleArea is visible only inside the function main. Using a nested function keeps the implementation of the filter function near the place where it's used, often improving the maintainability of the code.

Listing 2-22.

```
function main() {
    function triangleArea(a) {
        return a * (a / 2);
    }

    let a = sum(triangleArea, 1, 2, 3);  // 7
}
```

Declaring Functions

As noted earlier, there are no function declarations in JavaScript, unlike in C and C++: when you declare a function in JavaScript, you're actually declaring a variable. The following line of code, using the common syntax for declaring a function, creates a local variable named example:

```
function example() {}
```

The following line also creates a local variable named example, assigning an anonymous function to it:

```
let example = function() {};
```

These two lines of code are equivalent, and both functions can be called in the same way. But because both forms create a local variable, you can't have a function and a local variable with the same name. You can, however, change the function that a local variable references, as shown in Listing 2-23.

Listing 2-23.

```
function log(a) {
    trace(a);
}

log("one");
```

```
// Disable logging
let originalLog = log;
log = function(a) {}

log("two");

// Reenable logging
log = originalLog;

log("three");
```

Closures

One of the most powerful features of JavaScript functions is closures. They're commonly used for callback functions. A *closure* binds together a function with a group of variables outside the function. The references to outside variables persist for the lifetime of the closure. Closures don't exist in C and were only added to in C++ in 2011, as lambda expressions; consequently, many developers working in C and C++ are unfamiliar with them. Despite the obscure name, closures are so easy to use that it's easy to forget you're using them.

Listing 2-24 uses a closure to implement a counter. The makeCounter function returns a function. You can have one function return a pointer to another function in C, but there's a difference here: the anonymous function that's returned references a variable named value, and that variable is not local to the anonymous function; instead it's a local variable in the makeCounter function that the anonymous function is contained in.

Listing 2-24.

```
function makeCounter() {
    let value = 0;

    return function() {
        value += 1;
```

```
    return value;
  }
}
```

Each time the function returned by makeCounter is called, it increments value and returns that value. Here's how it works: When a function references variables outside its own local scope, it's said to "close" over those variables, automatically creating a closure. In this example, using the variable value in the anonymous function creates a closure that lets it access the local variable value from makeCounter. JavaScript makes it safe to use that local variable even after makeCounter returns and the stack frame of makeCounter has been deallocated (see Listing 2-25).

Listing 2-25.

```
let counter = makeCounter();

let a = counter();   // 1
let b = counter();   // 2
let c = counter();   // 3
```

The example in Listing 2-25 does what you expect: the makeCounter function returns a counter function; each time the counter function is called, it increments the counter and returns the new value. But what happens if you call makeCounter twice? Does the second call return a separate counter or a reference to the first counter? For the answer, see Listing 2-26.

Listing 2-26.

```
let counterOne = makeCounter();
let counterTwo = makeCounter();

let a = counterOne();   // 1
let b = counterOne();   // 2
```

```
let c = counterTwo();    // 1
let d = counterTwo();    // 2
let e = counterOne();    // 3
let f = counterTwo();    // 3
```

As you can see, each time `makeCounter` is called, the function it returns has a new closure with a separate copy of `value`.

If it's difficult right now to imagine how you might use closures in your own code, don't worry; many programmers use them without even realizing it. Closures are common in APIs that use callback functions; when the callback function is installed, it often closes over variables that it uses when the callback is invoked.

If you have experience with object-oriented programming, you may recognize closures used this way as being similar to object instances, and in fact they can be used for that. However, JavaScript has better alternatives, using classes (introduced later in this chapter).

Objects

JavaScript is an object-oriented programming language; C is not. There are few practical ways to use JavaScript without using objects. In the earlier sections of this chapter, even common operations on numbers and strings required calling methods of the number and string objects. C++ is an object-oriented language, but C++ and JavaScript take very different approaches to objects. For example, C++ has class templates, operator overloading, and multiple inheritance—none of which are part of JavaScript. If you're coming from C, you'll need to learn a bit about objects. If you're coming from C++, you'll need to learn about JavaScript's more compact approach to objects. The good news is that millions of developers have successfully used objects in JavaScript to build web pages, web services, mobile apps, and embedded firmware.

To create objects in JavaScript, you use the new keyword, as in C++. All objects in JavaScript descend from Object, a built-in object. The following lines create an instance of Object:

```
let a = new Object();
let b = new Object;
```

Object is a special kind of function called a *constructor*. When the Object constructor is invoked with new, an instance of Object is created and the constructor function is executed to initialize the instance. If the constructor function is passed no arguments, the parentheses for the argument list are optional. Therefore, the preceding two lines are identical; which form you use is a matter of personal coding style.

There are many other objects that are built into JavaScript. Listing 2-27 shows examples of how the constructor is called for some of them. Details about these and other built-in objects are provided in later sections of this chapter.

Listing 2-27.

```
let a = new Array(10);              // array of length 10
let b = new Date("September 6, 2019");
let c = new Date;                   // current date and time
let d = new ArrayBuffer(128);       // 128-byte buffer
let e = new Error("bad value");
```

The base object, Object, doesn't do much by itself. Still, it's common in JavaScript code because it can be used as an ad hoc record. In C, you use a structure (struct) to hold a set of values; in C++, you use either a structure or a class (struct or class). A JavaScript object, unlike a structure in C or C++, is not a fixed set of fields. What C calls fields are called *properties* in JavaScript. As illustrated in Listing 2-28, you can add properties to an object whenever you want; they don't have to be declared in advance.

Listing 2-28.

```
let a = new Object;
a.one = 1;
a.two = "two";
a.object = new Object;
a.add = function(a, b) {
    return a + b;
};
```

Because creating these ad hoc objects is so common, JavaScript provides a shortcut: you can use {} in place of new Object. The result is identical, but the code is more compact. You can initialize properties of an object by enumerating the properties within the braces. The following is equivalent to the preceding example:

```
let a = {one: 1, two: "two", object: {},
          add: function(a, b) {return a + b;}};
```

JavaScript developers tend to prefer the braces style (and this book uses it almost exclusively) because it's more compact and more readable.

Object Shorthand

It's common to store the result of several calculations in local variables and then put those into an object. When the local variables have the same name as the properties of the object, the code looks redundant, as in the example in Listing 2-29.

Listing 2-29.

```
let one = 1;
let two = "two";
let object = {};
```

```
let add = function(a, b) {return a + b;};
let result = {one: one, two: two, object: object, add: add};
```

Because this situation happens frequently, JavaScript provides a shortcut for it. The code in Listing 2-30 is equivalent to the preceding example.

Listing 2-30.

```
let one = 1;
let two = "two";
let object = {};
let add = function(a, b) {return a + b;};
let result = {one, two, object, add};
```

Another shortcut is available for defining properties that have a function as their value. Listing 2-31 shows the straightforward approach.

Listing 2-31.

```
let object = {
    add: function(a, b) {
        return a + b;
    },
    subtract: function(a, b) {
        return a - b;
    }
};
```

Listing 2-32 shows the shortcut version, which eliminates the colon (:) and the function keyword.

Listing 2-32.

```
let object = {
    add(a, b) {
        return a + b;
    },
    subtract(a, b) {
        return a - b;
    }
};
```

In addition to being more compact and readable, this same syntax is used for defining classes in JavaScript, as you'll soon see.

Deleting Properties

Not only can you add properties to a JavaScript object at any time, but you can also remove them. Properties are removed using the delete keyword:

```
delete a.one;
delete a.missing;
```

Once a property is deleted, getting it from the object gives the value undefined. You may recall that this is the same value that's returned when you try to access a character of a string beyond the string's length. It's not an error to use delete on a property that the object doesn't have. For example, no error is generated when (given object a with properties one, two, and object) a.missing is deleted as shown previously.

C++ programmers are familiar with delete as the way to destroy an object and so might expect that deleting a property would destroy the object referenced by the property; however, the delete keyword in JavaScript is different, as discussed later in the "Memory Management" section.

Checking for Properties

Because properties can come and go at any time, sometimes you need to check whether a particular property is present on an object. There are two ways to do this. Since any missing property has the value undefined, you could check whether getting a property gives the value undefined.

```
if (a.missing == undefined)
    trace("a does not have property 'missing'");
```

But don't do that! There are several subtle problems that can arise. For example, consider this code:

```
let a = {missing: undefined};
if (a.missing == undefined)
    trace("a does not have property 'missing'");
```

Here, the object has a missing property that happens to have a value of undefined. There are other ways this check can fail, but for now this example is enough to demonstrate the need for a better solution. Using the keyword in is a better way to check for the existence of a property. The following example works in all situations:

```
if (!("missing" in a))
    trace("a does not have property 'missing'");
```

Adding Properties to Functions

Functions in JavaScript are objects, which means you can add and remove properties of a function just as you would with any other object. Listing 2-33 defines a function named calculate that supports three operations, each corresponding to a property of the function that's assigned a constant: add is 1, subtract is 2, and multiply is 3. The operations defined here are similar to an enumeration in C or C++. However, instead of being defined separately from the calculate function as an enum in C or C++, the operation values are attached directly to the function that uses them. This way of providing names for constants is used in some parts of the Moddable SDK.

Listing 2-33.

```
function calculate(operation, a, b) {
    if (calculate.add == operation)
        return a + b;
    if (calculate.subtract == operation)
        return a - b;
    if (calculate.multiply == operation)
        return a * b;
}
calculate.add = 1;
calculate.subtract = 2;
calculate.multiply = 3;

let a = calculate(calculate.add, 1, 2);          // 3
let b = calculate(calculate.subtract, 1, 2);     // -1
```

Freezing Objects

There are situations in which you want to ensure that the properties of an object cannot be changed. You might be tempted to use const to achieve that:

```
const a = {
    b: 1
};
```

However, that doesn't work. Using const doesn't make the object on the right side of the = in the constant declaration read-only; in this example, it makes only a read-only. Consider these subsequent assignments:

```
a = 3;       // generates an error
a.b = 2;     // OK - can change existing property
a.c = 3;     // OK - can add new property
```

To prevent modifications to the object that is the value of the constant, you can use Object.freeze, a built-in function that makes all existing properties of the object read-only and prevents new properties from being added. As you can see in Listing 2-34, attempts to change the value of a property in the frozen object or add a new property to the object generate errors.

Listing 2-34.

```
const a = Object.freeze({
    b: 1
});

a = 3;       // generates an error
a.b = 2;     // error - can't change existing property
a.c = 3;     // error - can't add new property
```

Note that Object.freeze returns the object passed to it, which is convenient in this example because it avoids adding a line of code. Object.freeze is rarely used in JavaScript for the web today, but the Moddable SDK uses it extensively because it enables objects to be stored efficiently in ROM or flash memory on embedded devices, saving limited RAM.

Object.freeze is a shallow operation, which means it doesn't freeze nested objects. In Listing 2-35, for example, the nested object assigned to the property c is not frozen.

Listing 2-35.

```
const a = Object.freeze({
    b: 1,
    c: {
        d: 2
    }
});
a.c.d = 3;  // OK
a.c.e = 4;  // OK
a.b = 2;    // error - can't change existing property
a.e = 3;    // error - can't add new property
```

You could explicitly freeze c, but that begins to get verbose and error-prone, as shown in Listing 2-36.

Listing 2-36.

```
const a = Object.freeze({
    b: 1,
    c: Object.freeze({
        d: 2
    })
});
```

Because freezing objects helps optimize memory use on embedded devices, the XS JavaScript engine used in the Moddable SDK extends Object.freeze with an optional second argument which enables a deep freeze—that is, recursively freezing all nested objects (see Listing 2-37).

Listing 2-37.

```
const a = Object.freeze({
    b: 1,
    c: {
        d: 2
    }
}, true);
a.c.d = 3;  // error - can't change existing property
a.c.e = 4;  // error - can't add new property
```

Note that this extension to Object.freeze isn't part of the JavaScript language standard, so it doesn't work in most environments. It does, however, address a common need in embedded development. Perhaps a future edition of the JavaScript language will support this capability.

If your code needs to know whether an object is frozen, you can use Object.isFrozen. Like Object.freeze, this is a shallow operation, so it doesn't tell you whether any nested objects are frozen.

```
if (!Object.isFrozen(a)) {
    a.b = 2;
    a.c = 3;
}
```

Freezing an object is a one-way operation: there is no Object.unfreeze. This is because Object.freeze is sometimes used as a security measure to prevent untrusted client code from tampering with the object. If the untrusted code could unfreeze the object, it would enable the security measure to be breached.

null

Like C and C++, JavaScript code uses the value null. In C and C++, this is written as NULL to indicate that it's defined using a macro; in JavaScript, null is a built-in value.

C uses NULL as the value for pointers that don't currently reference anything. JavaScript has no pointers, so this meaning doesn't make sense. In JavaScript, null is a value indicating that there's no reference to an object. The value null is considered as a special null object and consequently has a type of Object.

It's easy to get null and undefined confused. They're similar, but not identical: undefined means no value has been given; null explicitly states that there's no object reference, which implies that the variable or property will hold an object at some point during its execution. As a rule, when a local variable or object property is intended to reference an object, assign the value null when there's no object.

Comparisons

Comparing two values in C is straightforward, for the most part, because you're usually comparing two values of the same type. In a few cases, the C language applies type conversion before comparing. This enables you to, for example, compare a uint8_t value to a uint32_t value without having to explicitly convert the type of either value. C++ makes comparisons considerably more powerful by providing operator overloading, enabling programmers to provide their own implementations of the comparison operators for types they define. JavaScript is much more like C than C++ in this regard; it doesn't support operator overloading, so the behavior of comparisons is fully defined by the JavaScript language.

Like C, JavaScript implicitly converts certain types when performing a comparison with the equality operator (==). Listing 2-38 shows a few examples.

Listing 2-38.

```
let a = 1 == "1";          // true
let b = 0 == "";           // true
let c = 0 == false;        // true
let d = "0" == false;      // true
let e = 1 == true;         // true
let f = 2 == true;         // false
let g = Infinity == "Infinity";  // true
```

As you can see, the rules for how types are converted in a comparison aren't always what you might expect. For this reason, JavaScript programmers often avoid implicit conversions by using the *strict equality operator* (===) instead, as shown in Listing 2-39. The strict equality operator never performs type conversion; if the two values are of different types, they're always unequal.

Listing 2-39.

```
let a = 1 === "1";         // false
let b = 0 === "";          // false
let c = 0 === false;       // false
let d = "0" === false;     // false
let e = 1 === true;        // false
let f = 2 === true;        // false
let g = Infinity === "Infinity";  // false
```

JavaScript also provides a *strict inequality operator* (`!==`), which can be used in place of the inequality operator (`!=`) to avoid type conversion:

```
let a = 1 !== "1";      // true
let b = 0 !== "";       // true
let c = 0 !== false;    // true
```

In many cases, there's no harm in using `==` and `!=` instead of the strict versions. However, the edge cases in which the behaviors are different can introduce bugs that are difficult to track down. Therefore, the current best practice in JavaScript programming is to always use the strict versions of the operators.

Some of the examples in this chapter that precede the introduction of the strict comparison operators use `==` and `!=`. Now that you know about the strict versions of these operators and why they're preferred, the examples in the remainder of this book will use only the strict operators.

Comparing Objects

When two objects are compared in JavaScript, they're equal only if they reference the same instance. This is usually what you expect, though sometimes developers incorrectly expect that if all the properties of two different instances are equal, the result of the equality comparison is `true`. This kind of deep comparison is not provided directly by JavaScript, though it may be implemented in your application if needed.

```
let a = {b: 1};
let b = a === {b: 1};    // false
let c = a;
let d = a === c;         // true
```

In C++, the default behavior for comparing objects is the same as in JavaScript. Using operator overloading, C++ programmers can perform deep comparisons if the class implements support.

Errors and Exceptions

JavaScript includes a built-in `Error` type which is used to report problems that occur during execution. Errors are almost exclusively used together with JavaScript's exception mechanism, which is similar in many ways to C++ exceptions. The C language doesn't include exceptions, though similar functionality is often built using `setjmp` and `longjmp` in the C standard library.

To create an error, invoke the `Error` constructor. To help with debugging, you can provide an optional error message.

```
let a = new Error;
let b = new Error("invalid value");
```

There are other kinds of errors, which are used to indicate a specific problem. These include `RangeError`, `TypeError`, and `ReferenceError`. You use them in the same way as `Error`. It's most common to simply use `Error`, but you can use the others if they fit your situation.

Once you have an error, you report it using a `throw` statement (Listing 2-40).

Listing 2-40.

```
function setTemperature(value) {
    if (value < 0)
        throw new RangeError("too cold");
    ...
}
```

You can specify any value following the `throw` statement, though by convention the value is usually an instance of an error.

When an exception is thrown, the current execution path ends. Execution resumes at the first `catch` block on the stack. If there are no catch blocks on the stack, the exception is considered an unhandled exception. Unhandled exceptions are ignored, meaning the host doesn't attempt to handle the exception. To catch an exception, you write `try` and `catch` blocks just as in C++; Listing 2-41 follows from the preceding example to illustrate this.

Listing 2-41.

```
try {
    setTemperature(-1); // throws an exception
    // Execution never reaches here
    displayMessage("Temperature set to -1\n");
}
catch (e) {
    trace(`setTemperature failed: ${e}\n`);
}
```

When `setTemperature` generates an exception in this example, execution jumps to the `catch` block, skipping over the call to `displayMessage`. The argument to the `throw` statement as shown in Listing 2-40—the `RangeError` instance created by the `setTemperature` function—is provided here in the local variable named e that's specified in parentheses following the `catch` keyword. If your `catch` block doesn't use that value, you can omit the parentheses following `catch`, as shown in Listing 2-42.

Listing 2-42.

```
try {
    setTemperature(-1); // throws an exception
    // Execution never reaches here
    displayMessage("Temperature set to -1\n");
}
catch {
    trace("setTemperature failed\n");
}
```

After catching the error, you have the option to propagate it, as if it hadn't been caught. This is useful if you want to perform cleanup when the error occurs and the error also needs to be handled by code farther up the call stack. To propagate the exception, use the throw statement inside the catch block (Listing 2-43).

Listing 2-43.

```
try {
    setTemperature(-1); // throws an exception
    // Execution never reaches here
    displayMessage("Temperature set to -1");
}
catch (e) {
    trace(`setTemperature failed: ${e}\n`);
    throw e;
}
```

Your exception handling may also include a finally block, as shown in Listing 2-44. (Standard C++ doesn't provide finally, but it's part of Microsoft's dialect of C++.) The finally block is always called, no matter how the exception is handled, or even if it isn't caught by a catch block.

Listing 2-44.

```
try {
    setTemperature(-1);
}
catch (e) {
    trace(`setTemperature failed: ${e}\n`);
    throw e;
}
```

```
finally {
    displayMessage(`Temperature set to ${getTemperature()}\n`);
    // always executes
}
```

In Listing 2-44, the call to displayMessage happens regardless of whether setTemperature throws an exception. When using finally, you can omit the catch block (Listing 2-45), in which case the exception will continue to propagate up the stack after the finally block executes.

Listing 2-45.

```
try {
    setTemperature(-1);
}
finally {
    displayMessage(`Temperature set to ${getTemperature()}`);
}
```

When an exception is not handled—for example, when setTemperature throws an exception in Listings 2-44 and 2-45—a warning is traced to the debug console. It isn't necessarily a mistake to leave an exception caught, but it can be an indication of a problem. The warning may include the name of the function that detected the uncaught exception; this is a native function, often part of the Moddable SDK runtime, so the name may be unfamiliar.

While these examples have just a few lines of code in the try blocks, real-world code often has large blocks of code within a single try block. This enables you to keep the code for handling errors small and isolated, rather than having it be part of each function call as can be the case in C.

The combination of try, catch, and finally blocks gives you a great deal of flexibility in how your code responds or doesn't respond to exceptions. Don't worry too much about using them as you get started. It's common to write code without exception handling and then add it later when you address the failure cases.

Classes

Like C++, JavaScript lets you create your own kinds of objects by defining classes. In JavaScript, you use the class keyword to define and implement your classes. Classes in JavaScript are quite a bit simpler than in C++. Even if you don't expect to create your own classes, you should become familiar with JavaScript classes so that you'll be able to understand code written by others.

Earlier versions of JavaScript didn't have the class keyword, making it more difficult to create classes. The keyword was introduced in the 6th Edition of the language standard (often referred to as "ES6") in 2015. Before that, JavaScript developers created classes using lower-level approaches, including Object.create, or directly manipulated the object's prototype property. While these techniques still work and are common in legacy code in the web, this section focuses on modern JavaScript, where class enables code to be more readable and has no impact on runtime performance.

Class Constructor and Methods

Listing 2-46 shows a simple class, Bulb, representing a light bulb that can be either on or off.

Listing 2-46.

```
class Bulb {
    constructor(name) {
        this.name = name;
        this.on = false;
    }
    turnOn() {
        this.on = true;
    }
    turnOff() {
        this.on = false;
    }
    toString() {
        return `"${this.name}" is ${this.on ? "on" : "off"}`;
    }
}
```

Unlike in C++, there's no declaration of the class; there's only an implementation. The syntax used to define the functions in the class is the same as you've already seen for functions outside a class (in the "Object Shorthand" section). However, unlike when functions are defined as properties in an ordinary object, in a class there are no commas between the functions.

As you can see in Listing 2-46, the Bulb class is a collection of functions. The function named constructor in a class is special; it's called automatically when the object is created. The constructor performs any necessary initialization before the new instance is returned to the creator. The following code creates an instance of Bulb:

```
let wallLight = new Bulb("wall light");
wallLight.turnOn();
```

Another special function in JavaScript classes is toString. This function is called automatically in situations where JavaScript wants the string representation of the object. The toString method of Bulb provides a summary of the current state, which is useful for debugging.

```
let wallLight = new Bulb("wall light");
wallLight.turnOn();
trace(wallLight);
// output: "wall light" is on
```

Because the trace function outputs strings, it converts its argument to a string, which invokes the toString method. You can also call toString directly, as in wallLight.toString().

The toString method is a special case in JavaScript; there are no other conversion functions, such as toNumber.

Note   The invocation of a class constructor must occur after the class is defined. This means that you can only call new Bulb after the definition of the class in Listing 2-46, not before. Invoking it before that throws a runtime exception with the message get Bulb: not initialized yet!.

Static Methods

As in C++, a JavaScript class may include static methods, meaning functions that are accessed through the class rather than the instance. A simple example of a static method is one that returns the version of the implementation (Listing 2-47).

Listing 2-47.

```
class Bulb {
    ...       // as earlier
    static getVersion() {
        return 1.2;
    }
}
```

Static methods are attached to the class and therefore can be called even before an instance is created.

```
if (Bulb.getVersion() < 1.5)
    throw new Error("incompatible version");
```

Subclasses

Much of the power of classes comes from the ability to create subclasses. In JavaScript, you use the extends keyword to create a subclass. The code in Listing 2-48 implements DimmableBulb as a subclass of the Bulb class defined in Listing 2-46.

Listing 2-48.

```
class DimmableBulb extends Bulb {
    constructor(name) {
        super(name);
        this.dimming = 100;
    }
    setDimming(value) {
        if ((value < 0) || (value > 100))
            throw new RangeError("bad dimming value");
        this.dimming = value;
    }
}
```

As you'd expect from a subclass, the DimmableBulb class inherits the turnOff and turnOn methods from Bulb. The constructor function requires some explanation. It immediately calls super with the same argument as was passed to it. In a JavaScript class, super is a reference to the constructor of the superclass—here, the constructor of Bulb. Therefore, the first task performed by the DimmableBulb constructor is to construct its superclass, Bulb.

While the constructor of a subclass may perform calculations before calling the constructor of its superclass, it must eventually call it. Until it does, this is undefined, so any attempt to get or set properties on the instance will fail. For example, modifying the DimmableBulb constructor as shown in Listing 2-49 generates an exception when it attempts to set the dimming property, because this is not yet available.

Listing 2-49.

```
class DimmableBulb extends Bulb {
    constructor(name) {
        this.dimming = 100; // throws an exception
        super(name);
    }
    ...
}
```

The DimmableBulb implementation also inherits the toString method from Bulb. The implementation of toString for Bulb doesn't print the dimming level; the implementation of toString for DimmableBulb (Listing 2-50) adds the dimming level, by first calling the toString method in Bulb (as specified by super) and then appending the dimming level to that result.

Listing 2-50.

```
class DimmableBulb extends Bulb {
    ...
    toString() {
        return super.toString() +
                ` with dimming ${this.dimming}`;
    }
}
```

The built-in Object class is the ultimate superclass of all JavaScript classes. The Bulb class inherits directly from Object. This is implied by the absence of an extends clause in its implementation, but it can also be stated explicitly, as shown in Listing 2-51.

Listing 2-51.

```
class Bulb extends Object {
    constructor(name) {
        super();
        this.name = name;
        this.on = false;
    }
    ...
}
```

Note that because Bulb now explicitly extends Object, the Bulb constructor must invoke the constructor of the class it extends by calling super. If the call to super is omitted, accessing this throws an exception with the message Bulb: this is not initialized yet!.

Classes that descend directly from Object aren't usually written this way, to keep the source code concise. But this example does hint at another feature of JavaScript classes: the ability to subclass built-in objects. The example in Listing 2-52 subclasses the built-in Array class (which you'll learn more about soon) to add methods for finding the total and average of the values in the array.

Listing 2-52.

```javascript
class MyArray extends Array {
    sum() {
        let total = 0;
        for (let i = 0; i < this.length; i++)
            total += this[i];
        return total;
    }
    average() {
        return this.sum() / this.length;
    }
}

let a = new MyArray;
a[0] = 1;
a[1] = 2;
let b = a.sum();        // 3
let c = a.average();    // 1.5
```

When building a product, you may have more than a single instance of Bulb. For example, you might be making a light switch that controls several light bulbs, and you might keep that list of lights in an array. You could create a subclass of Array for this purpose, with the subclass (Bulbs in the example in Listing 2-53) providing batch operations on the bulbs.

Listing 2-53.

```
class Bulbs extends Array {
    allOn() {
        for (let i = 0; i < this.length; i++)
            this[i].turnOn();
    }
    allOff() {
        for (let i = 0; i < this.length; i++)
            this[i].turnOff();
    }
}

let bulbs = new Bulbs;
bulbs[0] = new Bulb("hall light");
bulbs[1] = new DimmableBulb("wall light");
bulbs[2] = new DimmableBulb("floor light");
bulbs.allOn();
```

It would be nice to have a dimAll method in Bulbs, but that would only work for instances of DimmableBulb; calling setDimming on an instance of Bulb throws an exception because the method doesn't exist. The JavaScript instanceof operator helps here, by enabling you to determine whether an instance corresponds to a particular class (Listing 2-54).

Listing 2-54.

```
let a = new Bulb("hall light");
let b = new DimmableBulb("wall light");
let c = a instanceof Bulb;         // true
let d = b instanceof Bulb;         // true
let e = a instanceof DimmableBulb; // false
let f = b instanceof DimmableBulb; // true
```

As you can see, `instanceof` checks the specified class, including its superclasses. In the example in Listing 2-54, this means that b is an instance of both `DimmableBulb` and `Bulb`, since `Bulb` is the superclass of `DimmableBulb`. With this knowledge, the implementation of `dimAll` is now possible (Listing 2-55).

Listing 2-55.

```
class Bulbs extends Array {
    ...
    dimAll(value) {
        for (let i = 0; i < this.length; i++) {
            if (this[i] instanceof DimmableBulb)
                this[i].setDimming(value);
        }
    }
}
```

The properties of the `Bulb` instance are ordinary JavaScript properties, making them available both to the class implementation and to code using the class:

```
let wallLight = new Bulb("wall light");
wallLight.turnOn();
trace(`Light on: ${wallLight.on}\n`);
```

That's useful, but sometimes you want to use a different representation for the value inside the implementation than what you use in the API. For example, the `setDimming` method accepts values from 0 to 100, because percentages are a natural way to describe a dimming level; however, the implementation may prefer to store a value from 0 to 1.0 because that's more efficient for its internal calculations. JavaScript classes support getters and setters that are useful for these kinds of transformations. The implementation in Listing 2-56 replaces the `setDimming` method with a getter and setter for the `dimming` property.

Listing 2-56.

```
class DimmableBulb extends Bulb {
    constructor(name) {
        super(name);
        this._dimming = 1.0;
    }
    set dimming(value) {
        if ((value < 0) || (value > 100))
            throw new RangeError("bad dimming value");
        this._dimming = value / 100;
    }
    get dimming() {
        return this._dimming * 100;
    }
}

let a = new DimmableBulb("hall light");
a.dimming = 50;
a.dimming = a.dimming / 2;
```

Users of the class access the dimming property as an ordinary JavaScript property. However, when the property is set, the set dimming setter method of the class is invoked, and when the property is read, the get dimming getter method is invoked.

Private Fields

The getter and setter in Listing 2-56 store the value in a property named _dimming. JavaScript code has long used an underscore (_) at the start of property names to indicate that they're only for internal use. Unlike C++, JavaScript has not provided private fields in classes. Work on adding private fields to the JavaScript standard is nearly complete; this section introduces private fields as they're expected to be in the JavaScript standard. Private fields are supported by the XS JavaScript engine for use in your embedded development.

Private fields in JavaScript are indicated by prefixing the field name with a hash character (#). The private field must be declared in the class body. Listing 2-57 shows the version of DimmableBulb in Listing 2-56 rewritten to use a private field named #dimming in place of _dimming.

Listing 2-57.

```
class DimmableBulb extends Bulb {
    #dimming = 1.0;

    set dimming(value) {
        if ((value < 0) || (value > 100))
            throw new RangeError("bad dimming value");
        this.#dimming = value / 100;
    }
    get dimming() {
        return this.#dimming * 100;
    }
}

let a = new DimmableBulb("hall light");
a.dimming = 50;
a.dimming = a.dimming / 2;
a.#dimming = 100;    // error
```

Notice that the private field #dimming is initialized to 1.0 in its declaration in the class body. This is optional; it can instead be initialized in the constructor. Until it's initialized, it has a value of undefined.

Notice also that the example in Listing 2-57 eliminates the constructor entirely. That's possible here because #dimming is already initialized. Since DimmableBulb inherits from Bulb, when there's no constructor on

DimmableBulb the constructor of Bulb is automatically called when an instance is created. As you'd expect from C++, the code outside the class has no access to private fields; consequently, the final line of the example, which attempts to assign a value to #dimming, generates an error.

JavaScript doesn't support the C++ friends or protected class features. The private properties of a class are only directly accessible to code inside the class body. Private fields are truly private, remaining invisible even to subclasses and superclasses.

Private Methods

Together with private fields, the JavaScript language standard is adding *private methods*—functions that can only be called from within a class's implementation. For example, the DimmableBulb class in Listing 2-58 has a private #log method.

Listing 2-58.

```
class DimmableBulb extends Bulb {
    #dimming = 1.0;

    set dimming(value) {
        if ((value < 0) || (value > 100))
            throw new RangeError("bad dimming value");
        this.#dimming = value / 100;

        this.#log(`set dimming ${this.#dimming}`);
    }
    get dimming() {
        this.#log("get dimming");
        return this.#dimming * 100;
    }
```

```
    #log(msg) {
        trace(msg);
    }
}
let a = new DimmableBulb("hall light");
a.#log("test");      // error
```

Using Callback Functions in Classes

There are times when a class implementation passes a function to an
API as a callback. A common example is when an API uses a timer to
delay an action into the future. JavaScript web developers commonly use
setTimeout for this purpose; in embedded JavaScript, the equivalent is
Timer.set. The example in Listing 2-59 adds a method to the Bulb class to
turn the light on or off after a specified time interval elapses.

Listing 2-59.

```
class Bulb {
    ...
    setOnAfter(value, delayInMS) {
        let bulb = this;
        Timer.set(function() {
            if (value)
                bulb.turnOn();
            else
                bulb.turnOff();
        }, delayInMS);
    }
}
```

The setOnAfter method calls Timer.set with two arguments: an anonymous function to execute after the timer expires and the time to wait in milliseconds. The callback function uses a closure to access bulb; this is necessary because the value of this in the callback is not the instance of bulb that setOnAfter was called with, but rather is the global object (that is, globalThis). This code works, but JavaScript has better tools to implement this functionality.

Like modern C++, modern JavaScript has *lambda functions*— commonly called *arrow functions* because of the => syntax used to declare them. Like closures, arrow functions are a little difficult to understand but easy to use. When an arrow function is called, its this value is the same as the this value of the function in which the arrow function is defined. This feature of arrow functions is referred to as *lexical this* because the value of this inside the arrow function is taken from the enclosing function.

Arrow functions are popular because they maintain the value of this and they're more concise in source code. The examples in Listing 2-60 show the same functions using the function keyword and arrow function syntax.

Listing 2-60.

```
function randomTo100() {
    return Math.random() * 100;
}
let randomTo100 = () => Math.random() * 100;

function cube(a) {
    return a * a * a;
}
let cube = a => a * a * a;

function add(a, b) {
    return a + b;
}
let add = (a, b) => a + b;
```

```
function upperFirst(str) {
    let first = str[0].toUpperCase();
    return first + str.slice(1);
}
let upperFirst = str => {
    let first = str[0].toUpperCase();
    return first + str.slice(1);
};
```

All of the pairs of examples in Listing 2-60 are functionally equivalent, apart from the value of this in the functions; however, the examples don't use this. The code in Listing 2-61 uses an arrow function to improve the implementation of setOnAfter (in Listing 2-59) by taking advantage of the lexical this to eliminate the bulb local variable. Using this approach, the code of the callback is able to use this in the same way that class methods can.

Listing 2-61.

```
class Bulb {
    ...
    setOnAfter(value, delayInMS) {
        Timer.set(
            () => value ? this.turnOn() : this.turnOff(),
            delayInMS
        );
    }
}
```

It's important to be familiar with arrow functions because they're very common in JavaScript. You'll encounter them in some of the examples in this book. Keep in mind that arrow functions aren't just an alternative way of writing the source code of functions; they also change the value of this inside the function.

Modules

Modules are the mechanism in JavaScript for packaging a library of code. There are some similarities between JavaScript modules and shared or dynamic libraries in C and C++: both specify exports to share a limited number of classes, functions, and values; and both can import classes, functions, and values from other libraries. Like dynamic libraries in C, JavaScript modules are loaded at runtime. There are also many differences, including that there's no JavaScript equivalent to a statically linked C library.

Importing from Modules

To use the capabilities provided by a module, you must first import the corresponding classes, functions, or values. There are many different ways to import from a module, with a flexibility that gives you control over what you import and how you name those imports.

Examples in the preceding section used the Timer class without showing where it came from. The Timer class is contained in the timer module. To import from a module, you use the import statement.

```
import Timer from "timer";

Timer.set(() => trace("done"), 1000);
```

The import statement is special in JavaScript in that it's executed before all other code. It's customary to put the import statement at the top of the source code, like include statements in C, but even if they're not first, they still execute first.

The preceding form of the import statement consists of two parts:

- The name of the variable in which to store the import.
  Here it's Timer, but you can use any name you like.
  The ability to select the name can help avoid name
  conflicts, especially when you're working with many
  modules.

- After the from keyword, the module specifier. Here it's
  "timer".

A module specifier that, like "timer", is not a path is called a *bare module specifier*. For embedded JavaScript, these are more common; in fact, this book uses only bare module specifiers. One reason for this is that there's often no file system in an embedded device to resolve the path. By contrast, JavaScript on the web currently only uses paths for module specifiers, so there you'll see import statements with a from clause, like from "./modules/timer.js".

The form of the import statement illustrated previously imports the default export of the timer module. Every module has a default export. Some modules have additional exports; for example, the http module used in Chapter 3 exports both a Request class and a Server class. Listing 2-62 shows different ways to import these non-default exports from http.

Listing 2-62.

```
import {Server} from "http";    // server only
new Server;

import {Request} from "http";    // client only
new Request;

import {Server, Request} from "http";
new Server;
new Request;
```

You can use the as keyword to rename non-default exports that you import. Listing 2-63 renames Server to HTTPServer and Request to HTTPClient.

Listing 2-63.

```
import {Server as HTTPServer, Request as HTTPClient} from "http";
new HTTPServer;
new HTTPClient;
new Request;     // fails, Request is undefined
new Server;      // fails, Server is undefined
```

If you prefer for readability, you may use the same module specifier in multiple import statements:

```
import {Server as HTTPServer} from "http";
import {Request as HTTPClient} from "http";
```

You can also import all the exports from a module. When you do this, you assign the imports to an object. By avoiding name conflicts, this feature of JavaScript serves a similar purpose to namespaces in C++.

```
import * as HTTP from "http";
new HTTP.Server;
new HTTP.Request;
```

Once you import a class from a module, you can use it like a class declared in the same source file or a JavaScript built-in class. As you've seen, you can instantiate the class with the new operator. You can also create subclasses of an imported class:

```
import {Request} from "http";
class MyRequest extends Request {
    ...
}
```

Exporting from Modules

When you start writing your own classes, you'll want to package them into your own modules; those modules need to export their classes so that they can be used by other code (and functions and values may likewise be exported). The following line uses the export statement to provide the Bulb class as the module's default export:

```
export default Bulb;
```

You can optionally put the export statement before the declaration of a class, which here means you could combine export default with the definition of the Bulb class, as follows:

```
export default class Bulb {
    ...
}
```

This approach is valid but less common. Current JavaScript best practices recommend putting all your import statements together at the start of the source file and all export statements together at the end, making your code easier to read and maintain.

The following example shows two ways to provide non-default exports of Bulb and DimmableBulb:

```
export {Bulb};
export {DimmableBulb};

export {Bulb, DimmableBulb};
```

Like the import statement, an export statement can perform renaming using as. This is useful when you want to export a different name from that used in your implementation.

```
export {Bulb as BULB, DimmableBulb as DIMMABLEBULB};
```

The only way a module can access the contents of another module is through its exports. Classes, functions, and values that are not exported cannot be accessed directly; they're equivalent to classes, functions, and values defined using the static keyword in C and C++, but with this important difference: by default in C and C++, everything is exported unless declared static, whereas in JavaScript nothing is exported except as indicated by an export statement. The JavaScript approach—a whitelist instead of a blacklist of exports as in C—helps with security and maintainability by avoiding unintended exports.

ECMAScript Modules vs. CommonJS Modules

The modules used in this book are part of the JavaScript language specification. They're sometimes referred to as ECMAScript modules, or ESMs. Before modules were added to the official specification, a module system named CommonJS was used in some environments, particularly in Node.js. Because of that history, you may still see CommonJS documentation and modules. However, they don't work in the hosts used in this book, and most environments (including Node.js) are migrating to standard JavaScript modules.

Globals

Like C and C++, JavaScript has global variables. You've used some of them already, such as Object, Array, and ArrayBuffer. These built-in classes are assigned to global variables that have the same name as the class. You access these globals simply by using their name. If that name isn't in the current scope, the global variable is used. If no global variable is available with that name, an error is generated. This is similar to the link error generated when you access a nonexistent global in C.

```
function example() {
    let a = Date;        // OK, Date is built in
    let b = DateTime;    // error, DateTime is not defined
}
```

In C and C++, you create a global variable by declaring a variable at the top-level scope of a source code file. Unless it's marked as static, the variable is visible to all code statically linked to that file. In JavaScript, you must be explicit about creating a global variable. To define a new global variable in JavaScript, you add it to an object named globalThis. The following line creates a global variable named AppName and sets its initial value:

```
globalThis.AppName = "light bulb";
```

Once the global variable is defined, you can access it either implicitly by stating only its name or explicitly by reading the property from globalThis:

```
AppName = "Light Bulb";
globalThis.AppName += " App";
```

If you want to know whether a particular global variable is already defined, use the in keyword introduced in the "Objects" section of this chapter.

```
if ("AppName" in globalThis)
    trace(`AppName is ${AppName}\n`);
else
    trace("AppName not available");
```

In the same way that you remove properties from an object with the delete operator, you can remove global variables:

```
delete globalThis.AppName;
```

Note that the original name of the globalThis object was global, which is easier to remember and type; it was changed for compatibility reasons. Some environments support global as an alias for globalThis.

When you work with modules, they can seem to have global variables. Consider the module example in Listing 2-64.

Listing 2-64.

```
let counter = 0;

function count() {
    return ++counter;
}

export default count;
```

The way the counter variable is declared at the top-level scope, it appears to be like a global variable declaration in C or C++, but it's not. The counter variable is private to the module, since it isn't explicitly exported. Such variables are local to the module. In C or C++, the equivalent result is achieved by preceding the variable declaration with static to limit its visibility to the current source code file.

Arrays

In C and C++, any pointer to a type (such as char *) or to a structure (such as struct DataRecord *) may access a single element (as in *ptr) or an array (as in ptr[0], ptr[1]). These uses of a pointer can lead to errors—for example, writing to an index beyond the end of the memory reserved for an array. To help avoid some of the dangers of working with arrays, C++ provides an std:array class template, which also provides iterators and other common helper functions. JavaScript's built-in Array object is more like std:array in C++ in that it's designed to be safe and it provides many helper functions to perform common operations.

Unlike C and C++, JavaScript doesn't permanently set the number of elements when an array is instantiated; arrays may contain a variable number of elements. You can optionally indicate the number of elements when calling the constructor.

```
let a = new Array;       // empty array
let b = new Array(10);   // 10-element array
```

As you might have guessed, all array entries are initialized to undefined. Notice that when an array is created, there's no indication of the type of data it will hold. That's because each array element may contain any value; the values don't need to be of the same type.

Array Shorthand

Because creating arrays is so common, JavaScript provides a shortcut:

```
let a = []; // empty array
```

Using this shortcut syntax, you can provide the initial values of the array:

```
let a = [0, 1, 2];
let b = [undefined, 1, "two", {three: 3}, [4]];
```

Accessing Elements of an Array

Accessing elements of an array uses the same syntax as in C and C++. Elements are numbered starting at 0.

```
let a = [0, 1, 2];
a[0] += 1;
trace(a[0]);
a[1] = a[2];
```

Reading the value of an array beyond the end of the array returns undefined. Writing a value beyond the end of an array creates the value, extending the length of the array.

```
let sparse = [0, 1, 2];
sparse[3] = 3;
sparse[1_000_000] = "big array";
```

You might expect that this assignment to the millionth element of the array will fail on a microcontroller with limited memory: the ESP8266 has only about 64 KB of RAM, so how can it hold an array with a million elements? Yet the assignment succeeds, and accessing sparse[1_000_000] returns "big array". How does that work?

An array in JavaScript may be *sparse,* meaning that not all elements must be present. Any elements that aren't present have a value of undefined. In the case here of the array sparse, there are only five elements, which just happen to be at indices 0, 1, 2, 3, and 1,000,000.

Arrays have a length property, which indicates the number of elements in the array. The length is used, for example, to iterate over the elements in the array. For a sparse array, length is not the number of elements with an assigned value, but 1 more than the highest index that has an assigned value. In the case here of the array sparse, length is 1,000,001 even though there are only five elements with assigned values.

Setting the length property changes the array. Setting it to a smaller value truncates the array. The following truncates the preceding sparse array to four elements:

```
sparse.length = 4;   // [0, 1, 2, 3]
```

Setting an array's length property to a larger value doesn't change the array's contents.

Iterating over Arrays

As shown in Listing 2-65, you can use the length property to iterate over the elements in an array using a for loop, as in C and C++.

Listing 2-65.

```
let a = [0, 1, 2, 3, 4, 5];
let total = 0;
for (let i = 0; i < a.length; i++)
    total += a[i];
```

Instead of using the C-style for loop, you can use the JavaScript for-of loop.

```
for (let value of a)
    total += value;
```

The for-of loop approach is more compact, eliminating the code to manage the value i and the lookup of the value in the array a[i]. Both the C-style for loop and the for-in loop iterate through all the values from index 0 to the length of the array, even for sparse arrays where there are unassigned values. Because the unassigned values have a value of undefined, total has a value of NaN at the end of the code in Listing 2-66.

Listing 2-66.

```
let a = [0, 1, 2, 3, 4, 5];
a[1_000_000] = 6;
let total = 0;
for (let i in a)
    total += a[i];
```

You can modify this code to ignore array elements with the value undefined, as follows:

```
for (let i in a)
    total += (undefined === a[i]) ? 0 : a[i];
```

An alternative solution is to iterate over the values in the array using a for-of loop that includes only array elements that have an assigned value, as shown in Listing 2-67; the value of total at the end of this code is 21 rather than NaN as in Listing 2-66.

Listing 2-67.

```
let a = [0, 1, 2, 3, 4, 5];
a[1_000_000] = 6;
let total = 0;
for (let value of a)
    total += value;
```

The Array object also has methods for iterating over an array in many different ways, each of which uses a callback function. The forEach method is similar to the for-in loop (see Listing 2-68). Like the for-of loop, this method skips array elements that don't have a value assigned.

Listing 2-68.

```
let a = [0, 1, 2, 3, 4, 5];
let total = 0;
a.forEach(function(value) {
    total += value;
});
```

Using arrow functions reduces the iteration code to a single line:

```
let a = [0, 1, 2, 3, 4, 5];
let total = 0;
a.forEach(value => total += value);
```

As you might guess, not all of the many ways to iterate over an array in JavaScript are equally efficient. The forEach approach, for example, is the most compact code but requires a function call on every element, which can add overhead. For small arrays, use whichever approach is most convenient; for large arrays, it can be worth measuring the performance of different approaches to find the fastest one.

The map method is helpful when you need to perform an operation on each element of an array. It invokes a callback on each element and returns a new array containing the results. The following example creates an array containing the square of the values in the original array. The arrow function invoked for each element uses the exponentiation operator (**) to calculate the square.

```
let a = [-2, -1, 0, 1, 2];
let b = a.map(value => value ** 2); // [4, 1, 0, 1, 4]
```

Adding and Removing Elements of an Array

Because JavaScript arrays aren't a fixed length, they have uses beyond a simple ordered list. The push and pop functions enable you to use an array as a stack (last in, first out), as shown in Listing 2-69.

Listing 2-69.

```
let stack = [];
stack.push("a");
stack.push("b");
stack.push("c");
```

```
let c = stack.pop();      // "c"
stack.push("d");
let d = stack.pop();      // "d"
let b = stack.pop();      // "b"
```

With the unshift and pop functions, you can use an array as a queue (first in, first out). The unshift function adds values to the start of an array; see Listing 2-70. (There's also shift, which removes the first item from an array.)

Listing 2-70.

```
let queue = [];
queue.unshift("first");
queue.unshift("second");
let a = queue.pop();      // "first"
queue.unshift("third");
let b = queue.pop();      // "second"
```

Using unshift and pop to add and remove elements of a queue is useful but not entirely intuitive. These functions would be easier to use if they had names that make more sense for a queue; you can do this by creating a subclass of Array, as shown in Listing 2-71.

Listing 2-71.

```
class Queue extends Array {
    add(element) {
        this.unshift(element);
    }
    remove(element) {
        return this.pop();
    }
}
```

```
let queue = new Queue;
queue.add("first");
queue.add("second");
let a = queue.remove(); // "first"
queue.add("third");
let b = queue.remove(); // "second"
```

To extract part of an array into another array, use the slice function. As when you use slice to extract parts of strings, it takes two arguments: the starting and ending indices (where the ending index is the index before which to end extraction). If the ending index is omitted, the string's length is used. The slice function never changes the content of the array it's operating on.

```
let a = [0, 1, 2, 3, 4, 5];
let b = a.slice(0, 2);  // [0, 1]
let c = a.slice(2, 4);  // [2, 3]
```

To remove part of an array, use splice. The name splice is very similar to slice, and the two operate similarly: they take the same arguments, and both functions return an array containing the section of the array identified by the arguments. However, splice also deletes the elements from the original array.

```
let a = [0, 1, 2, 3, 4, 5];
let b = a.splice(0, 2); // [0, 1]
let c = a.splice(0, 2); // [2, 3]
// a = [4, 5] here
```

Searching Arrays

Searching for a particular value within an array is common, and there are several functions to help with that. As shown in Listing 2-72, you can use indexOf to search from the start of an array or lastIndexOf to search from the end. The first parameter is the value to search for; an optional second parameter indicates the index at which to begin searching in the array. If the value isn't found, both functions return –1.

Listing 2-72.

```
let a = [0, 1, 2, 3, 2, 1, 0];
let b = a.indexOf(1);           // 1
let c = a.lastIndexOf(1);       // 5
let d = a.indexOf(1, 3);        // 5
let e = a.lastIndexOf(1, 3);    // 1
let f = a.indexOf("one");       // -1
```

The indexOf and lastIndexOf functions use the strict equality operator to test whether a match is found. If you want to apply a different test, use the findIndex function, which invokes a callback function to test for a match. The following example performs a case-insensitive match:

```
let a = ["Zero", "One", "Two"];
let search = "one";
let b = a.findIndex(value =>
                    value.toLowerCase() === search); // 1
```

Sorting Arrays

Sorting is another common operation on arrays. The sort function on arrays is similar to the qsort function in C and C++, though it may be implemented using a different sorting algorithm. Like qsort, JavaScript's sort operates in place, so no new array is created. The built-in sort function's default behavior is to compare the array values as strings.

```
let a = ["Zero", "One", "Two"];
a.sort();
// ["One", "Two", "Zero"]
```

To implement other behaviors, you provide a callback function to perform the comparison. The comparison is similar to that of the callback function in the C and C++ qsort function, receiving two values to compare and returning a negative number, 0, or a positive number depending on the result of the comparison. For example, the following code sorts an array of numbers:

```
let a = [0, 1, 2, 3, 2, 1, 0];
a.sort((x, y) => x - y);
// [0, 0, 1, 1, 2, 2, 3]
```

The example in Listing 2-73 uses a more complex comparison function to perform a case-insensitive sort of strings.

Listing 2-73.

```
let a = ["Zero", "zero", "two", "Two"];
a.sort();
// ["Two", "Zero", "two", "zero"]
a.sort((x, y) => {
    x = x.toLowerCase();
    y = y.toLowerCase();
    if (x > y)
        return +1;
    if (x < y)
        return -1;
    return 0;
});
// ["Two", "two", "Zero", "zero"]
```

Binary Data

JavaScript didn't always support binary data, unlike C, which has supported memory buffers containing native integer types from the start. In C, one of the first things you learn is how to allocate memory with malloc and how to fill that memory with arrays and other data structures. The ability to operate on memory buffers directly is essential for many kinds of embedded development—for example, when working with binary messages in various network and hardware protocols. JavaScript supports the same kinds of operations as you're accustomed to when coding in C and C++, though the way you perform those operations is quite different.

Another benefit to using binary data in JavaScript is that it can reduce your project's memory use. One of the fundamental characteristics of JavaScript is that any value may hold any type, but this powerful feature comes with a cost: additional memory is required on each value to store the value's type. While a boolean value in C is just one byte (or a bit, using bit fields), a boolean value in JavaScript can be much more—for example, 8 or 16 bytes. Using binary data in JavaScript, you can store a boolean value in a byte (or even a bit) with just a little work. If your project maintains a large amount of data in memory, consider using JavaScript's binary data features, as the memory savings can be significant. Creating a 1,000-element array of JavaScript booleans using a standard Array object may require 16 KB of RAM, more than may be free on an ESP8266, but creating it using a Uint8Array object requires just 1 KB of RAM—exactly the same as in C.

ArrayBuffer

The JavaScript equivalent of calloc is the ArrayBuffer class. An ArrayBuffer is a block of memory of a fixed number of bytes. The memory is initially set to 0, to avoid any surprises with uninitialized memory.

```
let a = new ArrayBuffer(10);    // 10 bytes
```

If the buffer can't be allocated because not enough free memory is available, the ArrayBuffer constructor throws an exception.

To retrieve the number of bytes in an ArrayBuffer, get the byteLength property. The number of bytes contained in an ArrayBuffer instance is fixed at the time it's created. There's no equivalent to realloc; you cannot set the byteLength property of an ArrayBuffer.

```
let a = new ArrayBuffer(16);
let b = a.byteLength;    // 16
a.byteLength = 20;       // exception thrown
```

As with an array, you use the slice method to extract a section of the buffer into a new ArrayBuffer instance:

```
let a = new ArrayBuffer(16);
let b = a.slice(0, 8);        // copy first half
let c = a.slice(8, 16);       // copy second half
let d = a.slice(0);           // clone entire buffer
```

You might expect to be able to access the content of an ArrayBuffer using array syntax (for example, a[0]), but this is not the case. An ArrayBuffer is only a buffer of bytes. Because there's no type associated with the data, JavaScript doesn't know how to interpret the bytes—for example, whether the byte values are signed or unsigned. To access the data in an ArrayBuffer, you wrap it in a view. The following sections introduce two kinds of view: typed array and data view.

Typed Arrays

JavaScript *typed arrays* are a collection of classes that let you work with arrays of integers and floating-point values stored in an ArrayBuffer. You don't work with the TypedArray class directly but with its subclasses for specific types, such as Int8Array, Uint16Array, and Float32Array. Using a typed array is similar to creating a memory buffer in C with calloc and assigning the result to a pointer to an integer or floating-point type.

You can create a typed array that wraps an existing `ArrayBuffer`. The following example wraps an `ArrayBuffer` into a `Uint8Array`:

```
let a = new ArrayBuffer(16);
let b = new Uint8Array(a);
```

Now that you have a view on the buffer, you can access the content using array bracket syntax as you'd expect:

```
b[0] = 12;
b[1] += b[0];
```

Typed arrays, such as the `Uint8Array` in the earlier example, have a `byteLength` property, as does `ArrayBuffer`, but they also have a `length` property indicating the number of elements in the array. When the elements are bytes, these two values are equal, but for larger types, they differ (see Listing 2-74).

Listing 2-74.

```
let a = new ArrayBuffer(24);
let b = new Uint8Array(a);
let c = new Uint16Array(a);
let d = new Uint32Array(a);
let e = b.length;    // 24
let f = c.length;    // 12
let g = d.length;    // 6
```

Here a single `ArrayBuffer` is wrapped by several views; this is allowed. In C, it's called "aliasing," and it's dangerous because it interferes with certain compiler optimizations. In JavaScript, it's safe, though you should use it with care to avoid unexpected surprises when reading and writing to overlapping views.

You can create a typed array view that references a subset of a buffer, by including an offset in bytes to the start of the view and the number of elements in the view. This is like assigning an integer pointer a value in the middle of a memory buffer. In JavaScript, however, there's no unpredictable result when you read past the end of the buffer; that always returns undefined (see Listing 2-75).

Listing 2-75.

```
let a = new ArrayBuffer(18)
let b = new Int16Array(a);
b[0] = 0;
b[1] = 1;
b[2] = 2;
b[3] = 3;
let c = new Int16Array(a, 6, 1);
        // c begins 6 bytes into a and has one element
let d = c[0];    // 3
let e = c[1];    // undefined (read past end of view)
```

The Int16Array view created in Listing 2-75 for variable c begins at offset 6, but it could begin at any offset, including an odd-numbered one. Accessing the 16-bit values in that array requires misaligned reads. Not all microcontrollers support misaligned reads and writes; the ESP8266 is one microcontroller that doesn't support misaligned memory access. When C code performs a misaligned read or write, a hardware exception is generated, causing the microcontroller to reset. JavaScript code doesn't have this problem because the language guarantees that misaligned operations give the same result as aligned operations—another way JavaScript makes coding on embedded products a little easier.

Typed Array Shorthand

It's common to create small integer arrays. In C and C++, you can easily declare static arrays on the stack.

```
static uint16_t values[] = {0, 1, 2, 3};
```

In JavaScript, you can achieve the same result using the static of method on typed arrays:

```
let a = Uint16Array.of(0, 1, 2, 3);
let b = a.byteLength;    // 8
let c = a.length;        // 4
```

The of function automatically creates an ArrayBuffer of the size needed to store the values. You can access the ArrayBuffer created by of by getting the buffer property of the typed array. This buffer may be used with other views, such as data views.

```
let a = Uint16Array.of(0, 1, 2, 3);
let b = a.buffer;
let c = b.byteLength;    // 8
```

Copying Typed Arrays

In C and C++, you use memcpy and memmove to copy data values within a single buffer or between two buffers. You've already seen how to use slice on an ArrayBuffer in JavaScript to copy part or all of the buffer to a new buffer; you can use copyWithin to copy values within a single buffer and set to copy values from one buffer to another. In C, you need to take special care when copying within a single buffer when the source and destination overlap, whereas JavaScript's copyWithin method guarantees the results are predictable and correct. The first argument to copyWithin is the destination index, and the second and third arguments are the starting and ending source indices to copy (where the ending index is the index before which to end).

110

```
let a = Uint16Array.of(0, 1, 2, 3, 4, 5, 6);
a.copyWithin(4, 1, 3);
// [0, 1, 2, 3, 1, 2, 6]
```

The set method writes one typed array into another. The first argument is the source data to write, and the second argument is the index at which to begin writing the data.

```
let a = Int16Array.of(0, 1, 2, 3, 4, 5, 6);
let b = Int16Array.of(-2, -3);
a.set(b, 2);
// [0, 1, -2, -3, 4, 5, 6]
```

To write only a subset of the source data, you need to create another view. The subarray method is convenient for that, as shown in Listing 2-76. Given the starting and ending indices of a typed array, subarray returns a new typed array that references only those indices. Note that subarray doesn't allocate a new ArrayBuffer; it just references the same ArrayBuffer.

Listing 2-76.

```
let a = Int16Array.of(0, 1, 2, 3, 4, 5, 6);
let b = Int16Array.of(0, -1, -2, -3, -4, -5, -6);
let c = b.subarray(2, 4);
a.set(c, 2);
// [0, 1, -2, -3, 4, 5, 6]
```

You could use slice in place of subarray to copy the subset in a new Int16Array, but that temporarily uses additional memory, so subarray is preferred in this case.

The TypedArray classes are not subclasses of Array; they're entirely independent classes, but they're designed to share common APIs. For example, the copyWithin method you learned about for typed arrays is available with Array. Similarly, many of the Array methods, including map, forEach, indexOf, lastIndexOf, findIndex, and sort, are also available for typed arrays.

Filling Typed Arrays

Another useful method available for both Array and TypedArray is fill, which is similar to memset in C and C++. But while memset operates only on byte values, fill operates on values of the type of the typed array. As shown in Listing 2-77, the first argument to fill is the value to assign, and the optional second and third arguments are the beginning and ending indices to fill (where the ending index is the index before which to end the fill). If the optional arguments are not provided, the entire array is filled.

Listing 2-77.

```
let a = new Uint16Array(4);
a.fill(0x1234);
// [0x1234, 0x1234, 0x1234, 0x1234]

a.fill(0, 1, 3);
// [0x1234, 0, 0, 0x1234]

let b = new Uint32Array(2);
b.fill(0x12345678);
// [0x12345678, 0x12345678]
```

Writing Typed Array Values

Writing values into a typed array usually behaves as in C. For example, if you write a 16-bit value into an 8-bit typed array, the least significant 8 bits are used (see Listing 2-78).

Listing 2-78.

```
let a = new Uint32Array(1);
a[0] = 0x12345678;   // 0x12345678

let b = new Uint16Array(1);
b[0] = 0x12345678;   // 0x5678
```

```
let c = new Uint8Array(1);
c[0] = 0x12345678;  // 0x78
```

JavaScript also has a Uint8ClampedArray, which implements a different behavior: rather than taking the least significant bits, it pins the input value to a value between 0 and the maximum value that the typed array instance can store.

```
let a = new Uint8ClampedArray(1);
a[0] = 5;    // 5
a[0] = 256; // 255
a[0] = -1;  // 0
```

Floating-Point Typed Arrays

There are two floating-point typed arrays: Float32Array and Float64Array. Since number values in JavaScript are 64-bit IEEE 754 floating-point, Float64Array is able to store these values without any loss of precision. Float32Array reduces the precision and range of the values that may be stored but is sufficient for some situations.

Note   The typed array classes make no guarantee about the order of bytes when storing values (that is, whether big-endian or little-endian). The JavaScript engine implementation is free to store values in any way it chooses, as long as the accuracy of the value is preserved. It usually stores them in the same order as the host microcontroller, for maximum efficiency. To control the byte order of values, use a data view (discussed next).

Data Views

The DataView class provides another kind of view onto an ArrayBuffer. Unlike typed arrays, in which all the values are of the same type, *data views* are used to read and write different-sized integers and floating-point values into a buffer. You can use DataView to access binary data that corresponds to a C or C++ struct containing values of different types.

You instantiate a data view by passing the DataView constructor an ArrayBuffer for the view to wrap, just as you can pass an ArrayBuffer to a typed array constructor:

```
let a = new ArrayBuffer(16);
let b = new DataView(a);
```

Also as with typed arrays, you can pass an offset and size to the DataView constructor to restrict the view to a subset of the total buffer. This capability is useful for accessing data structures embedded in a larger memory buffer.

```
let a = new ArrayBuffer(16);
let b = new DataView(a, 4, 12);
// b may only access bytes 4 through 12 of a
```

Accessing Values of a Data View

A DataView instance is able to get and set all the same types as a typed array, as shown in Listing 2-79. The getter and setter methods all have the offset into the view as their first argument. The second argument of the setter methods specifies the value to set.

Listing 2-79.

```
let a = new DataView(new ArrayBuffer(8));
a.setUint8(0, 0);
a.setUint8(1, 1);
```

```
a.setUint16(2, 0x1234);
a.setUint32(4, 0x01020304);
```

Because the DataView methods write multi-byte values in big-endian byte order by default, the buffer a contains the following hexadecimal bytes after the example in Listing 2-79 executes:

```
00 01 12 34 01 02 03 04
```

You read the values back using the corresponding getter methods. The following example assumes the DataView instance a shown previously:

```
let b = a.getUint8(0);      // 0
let c = a.getUint8(1);      // 1
let d = a.getUint16(2);     // 0x1234
let e = a.getUint32(4);     // 0x01020304
```

The DataView methods have an optional final parameter to control the byte order. If the parameter is omitted or false, the byte order is big-endian; if true, it's little-endian (see Listing 2-80).

Listing 2-80.

```
let a = new DataView(new ArrayBuffer(8));
a.setUint8(0, 0);
a.setUint8(1, 1);
a.setUint16(2, 0x1234, true);
a.setUint32(4, 0x01020304, true);
```

Because setUint8 writes a single-byte value, there's no byte order, so the third parameter is unnecessary. The calls to setUint16 and setUint32 in Listing 2-80 set the byte order parameter to true, so the output is little-endian.

```
00 01 34 12 04 03 02 01
```

To read values stored in little-endian order, pass true as the final parameter to the getter methods:

```
let b = a.getUint16(2, true);   // 0x1234 (little-endian get)
let c = a.getUint16(2);         // 0x3412 (big-endian get)
```

The DataView class includes getter and setter methods that correspond to all the types available in TypedArray: Int8, Int16, Int32, Uint8, Uint16, Uint32, Float32, and Float64.

The DataView class is a very flexible way to manipulate binary data structures, but the code isn't particularly readable. Instead of writing a.value to access a field as you would in C, you have to write something like a.getUint16(6, true). One way to improve the readability and reduce the possibility of errors is to create a subclass of DataView for the data structure. Imagine that you have the C data structure shown in Listing 2-81 for a network packet header that you want to use from JavaScript. For simplicity, assume there's no padding between the fields.

Listing 2-81.

```
typedef struct Header {
    uint8_t     kind;
    uint8_t     priority;
    uint16_t    sequenceNumber;
    uint32_t    value;
}
```

The JavaScript Header class in Listing 2-82 subclasses DataView to implement easy access to the C Header structure. Because network packets typically use big-endian byte ordering, the multi-byte values are written in big-endian order.

Listing 2-82.

```
class Header extends DataView {
    constructor(buffer = new ArrayBuffer(8)) {
        super(buffer);
    }
    get kind() {return this.getUint8(0);}
    set kind(value) {this.setUint8(0, value);}
    get priority() {return this.getUint8(1);}
    set priority(value) {this.setUint8(1, value);}
    get sequenceNumber() {return this.getUint16(2);}
    set sequenceNumber(value) {this.setUint16(2, value);}
    get value() {return this.getUint32(4);}
    set value(value) {this.setUint32(4, value);}
}
```

Because the class uses getters and setters, the resulting code for users of the class is similar to C. The example in Listing 2-83 uses the Header class to read values from a packet received in the variable p.

Listing 2-83.

```
let a = new Header(p);
let b = a.kind;
let c = a.priority;
let d = a.sequenceNumber;
let e = a.value;
```

Listing 2-84 creates a new packet, initializes the values, and calls a send function to transmit the ArrayBuffer a.buffer used by the Header instance for storage.

Listing 2-84.

```
let a = new Header;
a.kind = 1;
a.priority = 2;
a.sequenceNumber = 3;
a.value = 4;
send(a.buffer);
```

As you can see, defining a class representing the binary data structure makes the code that works with that data structure much clearer. Working with binary data is one area where C has an advantage in the compactness of the code; still, it's possible to achieve the same result with readable code in JavaScript. JavaScript has benefits here, too: Consider that code that reads from data received over the network is often fragile. In this example, if the packet received has only four bytes instead of the needed eight bytes, the read of the value field has an undefined result, which could leak private data or even cause a crash. If that situation occurs in JavaScript, the attempt to read value using getUint32 fails with an exception because the read is out of range.

Memory Management

Memory management is one place where JavaScript differs significantly from C and C++. In C and C++, you explicitly allocate memory with malloc, calloc, and realloc and deallocate it with free. These memory allocation and deallocation functions are not in the language itself but in the standard library. In C++, you also allocate memory when you instantiate a class using new, and you deallocate that memory when you use delete to invoke the class's destructor.

JavaScript builds memory management into the language. When you create an object, string, ArrayBuffer, or any other built-in object that requires memory, that memory is transparently allocated by the JavaScript engine. As you'd expect, the language also deallocates the memory; however, rather than requiring your code to make a call like free or use the C++ delete operator, JavaScript automatically frees the memory when it determines it's safe to do so. This approach to memory management is implemented using a garbage collector. At certain points in time, the JavaScript engine runs the garbage collector, which scans all memory allocated by the engine, identifies any allocations that are no longer referenced, and deallocates any unreferenced memory blocks.

Consider this code:

```
let a = "this is a test";
a = {};
a = new ArrayBuffer(16);
```

This example does the following:

1. The first line allocates a string and assigns it to a. Because the string is referenced by a, it cannot be garbage-collected.

2. The second line assigns an empty object to a, deleting the reference to the string. Since no other variable or properties refer to the string, it's eligible to be garbage collected.

3. After the ArrayBuffer assignment on the third line, the empty object becomes eligible for garbage collection.

The JavaScript language doesn't define when the garbage collector runs. The garbage collector in the XS engine used in the Moddable SDK runs whenever it's out of memory; that may be never, once an hour, or many times a second, depending on the code running.

The garbage collector works well for managing memory. It reduces the amount of code you need to write, because both allocations and deallocations happen automatically. It eliminates the bug of forgetting to deallocate memory, which causes memory leaks; this is a major concern in embedded systems, many of which must run for months or years at a time, because a small memory leak that occurs periodically eventually leads to a system failure. The garbage collector also eliminates the bug of reading memory that has been deallocated, since memory isn't deallocated if code is still able to reference.

For all its benefits, the garbage collector is not a general-purpose solution for resource management. Consider Listing 2-85, which opens a file twice, first in write mode and then in read-only mode.

Listing 2-85.

```
let f = new File("/foo.txt", 1);     // 1 for write
f.write("this is a test");
f = undefined;

...

let g = new File("/foo.txt");        // read-only
```

At the time undefined is assigned to f in this example, the instance of the File class corresponding to the file opened for write access is eligible for garbage collection. In most file systems, when a file is opened for write access the access is exclusive, meaning the file cannot be opened a second time. Because the garbage collector may run at any time, the call to open the file in read-only mode may or may not succeed, depending on whether the write-access file object has been collected yet. For this reason, objects used to represent non-memory resources, such as an open file, usually provide a way to explicitly release the resource. In the Moddable SDK, the close method is used to release the resources, similar to using the delete operator in C++.

```
let f = new File("/foo.txt", 1);      // 1 for write
f.write("this is a test");
f.close();
```

The call to close closes the file immediately. Any further attempt to write to the instance in f will fail. The file may now be opened again, in read or write mode.

The Date Class

The C standard library provides the gettimeofday and localtime functions to determine the current date, time, time zone, and daylight saving time offset. The strftime function in the same library converts the date and time to text format using format strings. JavaScript provides equivalent functionality in the built-in Date class.

The following code creates an instance of the Date class. The instance contains a time value, which is initialized to the current time when the Date constructor is called with no arguments.

```
let now = new Date;
trace(now.toString());
// Tue Sep 24 2019 11:18:26 GMT-0700 (PDT)
```

The Date constructor accepts arguments to initialize the value to something other than the current time. You can initialize it from a string, though this is not recommended because of the ease of making mistakes in the string format.

```
let d = new Date("Tue Sep 24 2019 11:18:26 GMT-0700 (PDT)");
```

Instead, you can pass the components of the time (hours, minutes, year, and so on) as arguments to the constructor:

```
let d = new Date(2019, 8, 24);
        // September 24 2019 midnight
let e = new Date(2019, 8, 24, 11, 18, 26);
        // September 24 2019 11:18:26
```

Note here that the value for the month of September is 8, rather than 9 as you might expect. That's because month numbers in the JavaScript Date API start from 0 instead of 1; this was decided early in the development of JavaScript to match the Java language's java.util.Date object. Also note that the time specified in the second declaration is local time, not UTC (Coordinated Universal Time). To specify UTC time, use the Date.UTC function together with the Date constructor.

```
let d = new Date(Date.UTC(2019, 8, 24));
        // September 24 2019 midnight UTC
```

A Date instance stores a time value in milliseconds and always in UTC time. To retrieve that value, call the getTime method.

```
let now = new Date;
let utcTimeInMS = now.getTime();
```

If your code needs to retrieve the time frequently, the preceding example is inefficient, as it creates a new instance of Date every time the current time is needed. For such situations, the static method now returns the current UTC time in milliseconds as a number.

```
let utcTimeInMS = Date.now();
```

The Date class provides access to all the parts that make up a date and time (see Listing 2-86).

Listing 2-86.

```
let now = new Date;
let ms = now.getMilliseconds();      // 0 to 999
let seconds = now.getSeconds();      // 0 to 59
let minutes = now.getMinutes();      // 0 to 59
let hours = now.getHours();       // 0 to 23
let day = now.getDay();           // 0 (Sunday) to 6 (Saturday)
let date = now.getDate();         // 1 to 31
let month = now.getMonth();       // 0 (January) to 11 (December)
let year = now.getFullYear();
```

The values returned in Listing 2-86 are local time, with the time zone and daylight saving time offsets applied. Versions of the same functions for the UTC values are also available; they begin with getUTC, as in getUTCMilliseconds, getUTCSeconds, and so on.

There are also setter methods corresponding to all the getter methods. Listing 2-87 creates a date object and modifies it to be midnight of the following New Year's Day.

Listing 2-87.

```
let d = new Date;
d.setMilliseconds(0);
d.setSeconds(0);
d.setMinutes(0);
d.setHours(0);
d.setDate(1);
d.setMonth(0);
d.setFullYear(d.getFullYear() + 1);
```

The setHours and setFullYear methods support additional parameters, enabling the example in Listing 2-87 to be written more compactly:

```
let d = new Date;
d.setHours(0, 0, 0, 0);
d.setFullYear(d.getFullYear() + 1, 0, 1);
```

To retrieve the current time zone offset from UTC time, call the getTimezoneOffset method. The value returned is in minutes and has the current daylight saving time offset applied.

```
let timeZoneOffset = d.getTimezoneOffset();
// timeZoneOffset = 420 (offset in minutes from UTC)
```

As shown earlier in this section, the toString method of the Date object provides a string representing the local time with the time zone and daylight saving time offsets applied. For some situations—for example, networking—it's helpful to have a text representation of the string in UTC time. Use the toUTCString method to create a string representing the UTC time.

```
let d = new Date;
trace(d.toUTCString());
// "Tue, 24 Sep 2019 18:18:26 GMT"
```

Another time and date format used by many standards is ISO 8601. The toISOString method provides an ISO 8601–compatible version of the date as a string.

```
let d = new Date;
trace(d.toISOString());
// "2019-09-24T18:18:26.000Z"
```

While toUTCString and toISOString are convenient, you can use your knowledge of JavaScript dates and strings to generate strings in any format your project needs.

Event-Driven Programming

Embedded programs, particularly those running on less powerful devices, are often organized around a single loop that executes continuously. Listing 2-88 shows a trivial example.

Listing 2-88.

```
while (true) {
    if (readButton())
        lightOn();
    else
        lightOff();
}
```

This style of programming works for very simple embedded devices. However, it doesn't work well for larger systems with many different inputs and outputs; for such systems, event-driven programming is preferred. Event-driven programs wait for events to occur, such as a button press. When the event occurs, a callback is invoked to respond to it. JavaScript is designed for use with event-driven programs because that's how web browsers work.

Listing 2-89 is an event-driven version of the infinite loop in the preceding example. Here, the onRead callback is invoked when the button changes so that the code doesn't need to continuously poll the button state.

Listing 2-89.

```
let button = new Button;
button.onRead = function(value) {
    if (value)
        lightOn();
```

```
    else
        lightOff();
}
```

As a rule, callbacks that deliver events are invoked only when the microcontroller is idle. When JavaScript code is executing, callbacks are deferred until the code completes. In Listing 2-88, since the loop is infinite, no callbacks can be invoked. Therefore, it's generally impossible to use a single loop as the basis for your JavaScript application; you must adopt the event-driven programming style.

If you haven't done much event-driven programming before, don't worry. The examples in this book are all written to show you how to use embedded JavaScript APIs in an event-driven programming style. With a little practice, it should become second nature.

Conclusion

With this introduction to JavaScript under your belt, you're ready to move on in this book. The remaining chapters are about how to use JavaScript on embedded systems to create IoT products using features provided by the Moddable SDK.

The JavaScript language specification is huge—over 750 pages. This book can't possibly explain every feature and nuance of the language, but many excellent resources are available to help you learn more. Mozilla's MDN Web Docs (`developer.mozilla.org`) is the de facto reference for the JavaScript language. It's up to date with the latest standard, provides plenty of examples, and is extremely detailed. It's a great resource for embedded developers because many of the examples it presents can be understood even if you're not a web developer.

CHAPTER 3

Networking

There are so many different kinds of IoT devices—from thermostats to door locks, from smart watches to smart light bulbs, from washing machines to security cameras—that it's easy to forget they all have something in common: the network. What separates an IoT device from an ordinary everyday device is its connection to the network. This chapter is all about that connection, starting with different ways to connect to the network.

Once your device is connected to the network, it can communicate in many different ways. This chapter shows you how to communicate using the same HTTP networking protocol used by the web browser on your computer and phone. It also shows how to use the WebSocket protocol for interactive two-way communication and the MQTT protocol used for publish-and-subscribe.

Securing communication is essential for many products, so you'll also learn how to make secure connections using TLS (Transport Layer Security) in combination with protocols like HTTP, WebSocket, and MQTT.

The chapter closes with two advanced topics. The first is how to turn your device into a Wi-Fi base station, a technique used by many commercial IoT products for easy configuration. You can connect your computer, phone, and other devices to this private Wi-Fi base station without installing any special software. The second advanced topic is how to use JavaScript promises with networking APIs.

P. Hoddie and L. Prader, *IoT Development for ESP32 and ESP8266 with JavaScript*, https://doi.org/10.1007/978-1-4842-5070-9_3

About Networking

This book focuses on hardware that connects to the network using Wi-Fi. Your Wi-Fi *access point,* also called a *base station* or *router,* connects your Wi-Fi network to the internet. The access point also creates a local network which allows devices connected to it to communicate with each other. The HTTP, MQTT, and WebSocket protocols are used to communicate with servers on the internet, but they can also be used to communicate between devices on your local Wi-Fi network. Communicating directly between devices is faster and can be more private because your data never leaves your Wi-Fi network. It eliminates the cost of a cloud service. Using the mDNS network protocol makes it easy for devices on your local network to communicate directly with each other.

All the networking examples in this chapter are *non-blocking* (or *asynchronous*). This means, for example, that when you request data from the network using the HTTP protocol, your application continues running while the request is made. This is the same way networking works when you use JavaScript on the web but different from much of the networking implementations in embedded environments. For various reasons, many embedded development environments use *blocking* networking instead; this leaves the device unresponsive to user input during the network operation unless a more complex and memory-intensive technique, such as threads, is also used.

The classes in the Moddable SDK that implement networking capabilities use callback functions to provide status and deliver network data. Callbacks are simple to implement, and they operate efficiently even on hardware with relatively little processing power and memory. On the web, developers have long used callbacks for network operations. More recently, a feature of JavaScript called *promises* has become a popular alternative to callbacks for some situations. Because promises require more resources, they're used sparingly here. Promises are supported in the XS engine that powers the Moddable SDK. The networking capabilities introduced in this chapter may be adapted to use promises; an example is included in the section on promises at the end of this chapter.

Connecting to Wi-Fi

You already know how to connect your computer and phone (and probably even your television!) to the internet, and that experience will help you when writing the code to connect your device. You'll need to learn a few new things too, because IoT devices don't always have a screen, and without a screen the user can't simply tap the name of the Wi-Fi network to connect to.

This section describes three different ways to connect to Wi-Fi:

- From the command line

- With simple code to connect to a known Wi-Fi access point

- By scanning for an open Wi-Fi access point

Each of these is useful for different situations; you'll choose the best one for your projects. Using the command line is great for development, but the other two approaches are needed when you move beyond experimenting to building sophisticated prototypes and real products.

Note   This section uses a different installation pattern from the one you learned in Chapter 1: rather than installing the host with `mcconfig` and then installing examples using `mcrun`, you install the examples using `mcconfig`.

Connecting from the Command Line

In Chapter 1, you learned to use the `mcconfig` command line tool to build and install the host. The `mcconfig` command can define variables. As shown in the following command, you can connect to a Wi-Fi access point by defining the variable `ssid` with the value of the name of the Wi-Fi access point. *SSID* stands for *service set identifier* and is the technical term for the human-readable name of a Wi-Fi network provided by a Wi-Fi base station.

```
> mcconfig -d -m -p esp ssid="my wi-fi"
```

Defining `ssid` in this way causes a configuration variable to be added to your application which is used by the device's base networking firmware to connect automatically to Wi-Fi when the device powers up. After the Wi-Fi connection is established, your application is run. This is convenient because it means your application can assume that the network is always available.

If your Wi-Fi access point requires a password, include that on the command line as the value of the `password` variable:

```
> mcconfig -d -m -p esp ssid="my wi-fi" password="secret"
```

During the Wi-Fi connection process, diagnostic trace messages are displayed in the debug console. Watch the messages to help diagnose connection troubles. Here's an example of a successful connection:

```
Wi-Fi connected to "Moddable"
IP address 10.0.1.79
```

If the Wi-Fi password is rejected by the Wi-Fi access point, the following message is displayed:

```
Wi-Fi password rejected
```

All other unsuccessful connection attempts display the following message:

```
Wi-Fi disconnected
```

Install the $EXAMPLES/ch3-network/wifi-command-line example on your device to test this connection method.

Connecting with Code

Using command line options to define your Wi-Fi credentials is convenient for development, but for projects you share with others you'll often want to store the Wi-Fi credentials in a preference instead. This section looks at the code to connect to a Wi-Fi access point defined in your application. (Managing preferences is described in Chapter 5.)

The wifi module contains the JavaScript class used to manage Wi-Fi network connections. To use the wifi module in your code, first import the WiFi class from it:

```
import WiFi from "wifi";
```

Use the static connect method of the WiFi class to connect to a Wi-Fi network. In the $EXAMPLES/ch3-network/wifi-code example, the SSID and password are passed to the constructor as properties in a dictionary (Listing 3-1).

Listing 3-1.

```
WiFi.connect({
        ssid: "my wi-fi",
        password: "secret"
    }
);
```

This call begins the process of establishing a connection. The call is asynchronous, which means that the actual work of connecting takes place in the background; the application keeps running while the connection is being established. This is just like on your phone, where you can continue using apps while a Wi-Fi connection is being established. In an IoT device, you often want to know when the network connection is available so that you'll know when your application can make connections to other devices and the internet.

To monitor the connection status, create an instance of the WiFi class and provide a monitoring callback function (Listing 3-2) to be called whenever the connection status changes.

Listing 3-2.

```
let wifiMonitor = new WiFi({
        ssid: "my wi-fi",
        password: "secret"
    },
    function(msg) {
        switch (msg) {
            case WiFi.gotIP:
                trace("network ready\n");
                break;

            case WiFi.connected:
                trace("connected\n");
                break;

            case WiFi.disconnected:
                trace("connection lost\n");
                break;
        }
    }
);
```

The callback function is called with one of these three messages, depending on the connection status:

- connected – Your device has connected to the Wi-Fi access point. It's not yet ready to use, however, because it hasn't yet received its IP address. When you see this message, you know that the SSID and password are valid.

- gotIP – Your device has received its IP address and is now ready to communicate with other devices on the local network and the internet.

- disconnected – Your device has lost its network connection. On some devices, you receive this message before receiving a connect message.

Some projects keep the WiFi object active all the time to monitor for network disconnections. If you don't need to monitor for a dropped network connection, you should close the WiFi object to free the memory it's using.

```
wifiMonitor.close();
```

Closing the WiFi object does not disconnect from the Wi-Fi network. It simply means your callback function will no longer be called with notifications about the callback status.

To disconnect from the Wi-Fi network, call the WiFi class's static disconnect method:

```
WiFi.disconnect();
```

To test this connection method, take these steps:

1. Open $EXAMPLES/ch3-network/wifi-code/main.js in your text editor.

2. Change lines 4 and 5 so that ssid and password match your network credentials.

3. Install the $EXAMPLES/ch3-network/wifi-code example
    on your device from the command line using mcconfig.

If the connection is successful, you'll see the following messages traced
to the debug console:

```
connected
network ready
```

If the connection is unsuccessful, you'll instead see connection lost
displayed repeatedly.

Connecting to Any Open Access Point

Sometimes you'll want your IoT device to connect to any available open
Wi-Fi access point (for example, one that doesn't require a password).
Connecting to an unknown network isn't a good idea from a security
perspective, but in some situations the convenience is more important.

To connect to an open access point, the first step is to find one. The
WiFi class provides the static scan method to look for access points. The
code in Listing 3-3 performs a single scan for access points, logging the
results to the debug console. It gets the signal strength from the rssi
property of accessPoint. *RSSI* stands for *received signal strength indication*
and is a measure of the strength of the signal received from the Wi-Fi
access point. Its values are negative numbers, and stronger signals have an
RSSI value closer to 0.

Listing 3-3.

```
WiFi.scan({}, accessPoint => {
    if (!accessPoint) {
        trace("scan complete\n");
        return;
    }
```

```
    let name = accessPoint.ssid;
    let open = "none" === accessPoint.authentication;
    let signal = accessPoint.rssi;
    trace(`${name}: open=${open}, signal=${signal}\n`);
});
```

Here's an example of this code's output:

```
ESP_E5C7AF: open=true, signal=-62
Large Conf.: open=false, signal=-85
Expo 2.4: open=false, signal=-74
PAB: open=true, signal=-77
Kanpai: open=false, signal=-66
Moddable: open=false, signal=-70
scan complete
```

The duration of a scan is typically less than 5 seconds, varying somewhat by device. During the scan, the example traces the name of the access point, whether it's open, and its signal strength. When the scan is complete, the scan callback function is called with the accessPoint argument set to undefined and the message scan complete is traced.

If you're in a location with many access points, a single scan may not discover every available access point. To build a complete list, your application can merge the results of several scans. See wifiscancontinuous in the Moddable SDK for an example.

A user choosing a Wi-Fi access point to connect to usually selects the one with the strongest strength. The $EXAMPLES/ch3-network/wifi-open-ap example performs the same selection process using the code in Listing 3-4.

Listing 3-4.

```
let best;

WiFi.scan({}, accessPoint => {
    if (!accessPoint) {
        if (!best) {
            trace("no open access points found\n");
            return;
        }
        trace(`connecting to ${best.ssid}\n`);
        WiFi.connect({ssid: best.ssid});
        return;
    }

    if ("none" !== accessPoint.authentication)
        return; // not open

    if (!best) {
        best = accessPoint; // first open access point found
        return;
    }

    if (best.rssi < accessPoint.rssi)
        best = accessPoint; // new best
});
```

This code uses the variable best to keep track of the open access point with the strongest signal strength during scanning. After the scan completes, the code connects to that access point.

To test this method, install the wifi-open-ap example on your device.

Installing the Network Host

The host is in the $EXAMPLES/ch3-network/host directory. Navigate to this directory from the command line and install it with mcconfig.

Installing Examples

The examples in this chapter only work properly if the device is connected to a Wi-Fi access point. Earlier in this chapter, you learned how to specify the SSID and password of an access point by defining variables in the mcconfig command. You can use these same variables in the mcrun command to connect your device to Wi-Fi before the example runs.

```
> mcrun -d -m -p esp ssid="my wi-fi"
```

```
> mcrun -d -m -p esp ssid="my wi-fi" password="secret"
```

Getting Network Information

When working with the network, you may need information about the network interface or network connection, for debugging purposes or to implement features. This information is available from the net module.

```
import Net from "net";
```

Information is retrieved from the Net object using its static get method. This example retrieves the name of the Wi-Fi access point that the device is connected to:

```
let ssid = Net.get("SSID");
```

Here are some other pieces of information you can retrieve:

- IP – the IP address of the network connection; for example, `10.0.1.4`

- MAC – the MAC address of the network interface; for example, `A4:D1:8C:DB:C0:20`

- SSID – the name of the Wi-Fi access point

- BSSID – the MAC address of the Wi-Fi access point; for example, `18:64:72:47:d4:32`

- RSSI – the Wi-Fi signal strength

Making HTTP Requests

The most commonly used protocol on the internet is HTTP, and there are many good reasons for its popularity: it's relatively simple, it's widely supported, it works well for small and large amounts of data, it has proven to be extremely flexible, and it can be supported on a wide range of devices, including the relatively inexpensive ones found in many IoT products. This section shows how to make different kinds of HTTP requests to an HTTP server. (The next section will show how to secure those connections.)

Fundamentals

The `http` module contains support for making HTTP requests and creating an HTTP server. To make an HTTP request, first import the `Request` class from the module:

```
import {Request} from "http";
```

The Request class uses a dictionary to configure the request. There are just two required properties in the dictionary:

- Either a host property or an address property to define the server to connect with, where host specifies the server by name (for example, www.example.com) and address defines the server by IP address (for example, 10.0.1.23)

- A path property to specify the path to the HTTP resource to access (for example, /index.html or /data/lights.json)

All other properties are optional; the kind of HTTP request you're making determines whether they're present and what their values are. Many of the optional properties are introduced in the following sections.

In addition to the configuration dictionary, each HTTP request has a callback function that's invoked throughout the various stages of the request. The callback receives a message corresponding to the current stage. Here's the complete list of the stages of an HTTP request:

- requestFragment – The callback is being asked to provide the next part of the request body.

- status – The status line of the HTTP response has been received. The HTTP status code (for example, 200, 404, or 301) is available. The status code indicates the success or failure of the request.

- header – An HTTP response header has been received. This message is repeated for each HTTP header received.

- headersComplete – This message is received between receipt of the final HTTP response header and receipt of the response body.

- responseFragment – This message provides a fragment of the HTTP response and may be received multiple times.

- responseComplete – This message is received after all HTTP response fragments.

- error – A failure occurred while processing the HTTP request.

If this looks overwhelming, don't worry; many HTTP requests use only one or two of these messages. Two of the messages, requestFragment and responseFragment, are only used to work with HTTP data that's too big to fit in the memory of the device. The sections that follow show how to use many of the available messages.

GET

The most common HTTP request is GET, which retrieves a piece of data. The code in Listing 3-5 from the $EXAMPLES/ch3-network/http-get example performs an HTTP GET to get the home page from the web server www.example.com.

Listing 3-5.

```
let request = new Request({
    host: "www.example.com",
    path: "/",
    response: String
});

request.callback = function(msg, value) {
    if (Request.responseComplete === msg)
        trace(value, "\n");
}
```

The `response` property in the call to the `Request` constructor specifies how you would like the body of the response to be returned. In this case, you're specifying that it should be returned as a JavaScript string. The callback receives the `responseComplete` message when the response—the entire web page—is received. The web page is stored in the `value` parameter. The call to `trace` displays the source HTML in the debug console.

You can use this approach in your projects to retrieve text data. If you want to retrieve binary data, you can do that by passing a value of `ArrayBuffer` instead of `String` for the `response` property, as in Listing 3-6.

Listing 3-6.

```
let request = new Request({
    host: "httpbin.org",
    path: "/bytes/1024",
    response: ArrayBuffer
});
```

Getting the entire HTTP response at once works perfectly well as long as there's enough memory on the device to hold it. If there's not enough memory, the request fails with an `error` message. The next section explains how to retrieve sources that are bigger than available memory.

Streaming GET

In situations where the response to an HTTP request may not fit into available memory, you can make a streaming HTTP GET request instead. This is just a little more complicated, as shown in Listing 3-7 from the `$EXAMPLES/ch3-network/http-streaming-get` example.

Listing 3-7.

```
let request = new Request({
    host: "www.bing.com",
    path: "/"
});

request.callback = function(msg, value, etc) {
    if (Request.responseFragment === msg)
        trace(this.read(String), "\n");
    else if (Request.responseComplete === msg)
        trace(`\n\nTransfer complete.\n\n`);
}
```

Notice that in the call to the constructor, the response property is not present. The absence of that property tells the HTTP Request class to deliver each fragment of the response body to the callback as it's received, with the responseFragment message. In this example, the callback then reads the data as a string to trace to the debug console, but it could also read the data as an ArrayBuffer. Instead of tracing to the debug console, the callback might write the data to a file; you'll learn how to do this in Chapter 5.

When you stream an HTTP request, the body of the response is not provided in the value argument with the responseComplete message.

The Request class supports the *chunked transfer encoding* feature of the HTTP protocol. This feature is often used to deliver large responses. The HTTP Request class decodes the chunks before invoking the callback function. Therefore, your callback function doesn't need to parse the chunk headers, simplifying your code.

GET JSON

IoT products don't usually request web pages unless they're scraping a
page to extract data; instead, they use REST APIs, which very often respond
with JSON. Since JSON is a very small data-only subset of JavaScript, it's
extremely convenient to use in JavaScript code. Listing 3-8 is an example
of a request to a REST weather service. The application ID used in
$EXAMPLES/ch3-network/http-get-json is only an example; you should
sign up for your own application ID (APPID) at openweathermap.org and
use it instead.

Listing 3-8.

```
const APPID = "94de4cda19a2ba07d3fa6450eb80f091";
const zip = "94303";
const country = "us";

let request = new Request({
    host: "api.openweathermap.org",
    path: `/data/2.5/weather?appid=${APPID}&` +
          `zip=${zip},${country}&units=imperial`
    response: String
});

request.callback = function(msg, value) {
    if (Request.responseComplete === msg) {
        value = JSON.parse(value);
        trace(`Location: ${value.name}\n`);
        trace(`Temperature: ${value.main.temp} F\n`);
        trace(`Weather: ${value.weather[0].main}.\n`);
    }
}
```

Notice that in the dictionary passed to the `Request` constructor, `response` is set to `String`, just as in the `GET` example earlier. The response is requested as `String` because JSON is a text format. Once the response is available, the callback receives the `responseComplete` message, and then it uses `JSON.parse` to convert the string it received to a JavaScript object. Finally, it traces three values from the response to the debug console.

If you want to know all the available values returned by the weather service, you can either read their documentation or look at the response directly in the debug console. To look in the debugger, set a breakpoint on the first `trace` call; when stopped at the breakpoint, expand the `value` property to see the values, as shown in Figure 3-1.

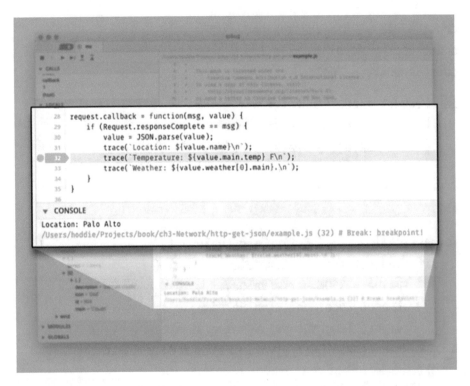

Figure 3-1. *Expanded JSON weather response shown in xsbug*

As you can see in this figure, the JSON returned by the server contains many properties that the JavaScript code doesn't use, such as `clouds` and `visibility`. In some situations there's enough memory on the device to hold the entire JSON text but not enough memory to hold the JavaScript object created by calling `JSON.parse`. The object may use more memory than the text because of the way JavaScript objects are stored in memory. To help solve this problem, the XS JavaScript engine supports an optional second parameter to the `JSON.parse` call. If the second parameter is an array, only the property names in the array are parsed from the JSON. This can significantly reduce the memory used, and the parsing runs faster too. Here's how to change the call to `JSON.parse` in the preceding example to decode only the properties the example uses:

```
value = JSON.parse(value, ["main", "name", "temp", "weather"]);
```

Subclassing an HTTP Request

The HTTP Request class is a low-level class that provides a great deal of functionality with a high degree of efficiency, giving it the power and flexibility necessary for a broad range of IoT scenarios. Still, for any given situation, the functional purpose of the code can be obscured by details related to the HTTP protocol. Consider the code in Listing 3-8 from the preceding section: the inputs are the ZIP code and country, and the outputs are the current weather conditions, but everything else is an implementation detail.

A good way to simplify the code is to create a subclass. A well-designed subclass provides a focused, easy-to-use API that takes only the relevant inputs (for example, the ZIP code) and provides only the desired outputs (for example, the weather conditions). The `$EXAMPLES/ch3-network/http-get-subclass` example (Listing 3-9) shows a subclass design for the weather request in the preceding section.

Listing 3-9.

```
const APPID = "94de4cda19a2ba07d3fa6450eb80f091";

class WeatherRequest extends Request {
    constructor(zip, country) {
        super({
            host: "api.openweathermap.org",
            path: `/data/2.5/weather?appid=${APPID}&` +
                  `zip=${zip},${country}&units=imperial`,
            response: String
        });
    }
    callback(msg, value) {
        if (Request.responseComplete === msg) {
            value = JSON.parse(value,
                            ["main", "name", "temp", "weather"]);
            this.onReceived({
                temperature: value.main.temp,
                condition: value.weather[0].main}
            );
        }
    }
}
```

Using this WeatherRequest subclass is easy (Listing 3-10), as all the details of the HTTP protocol, the openweathermap.org API, and JSON parsing are hidden in the implementation of the subclass.

Listing 3-10.

```
let weather = new WeatherRequest(94025, "us");

weather.onReceived = function(result) {
    trace(`Temperature is ${result.temperature}\n`);
    trace(`Condition is ${result.condition}\n`);
}
```

Setting Request Headers

The HTTP protocol uses headers to communicate additional information about the request to the server. For example, it's common to include the name and version of the product making the HTTP request in the User-Agent header, one of the standard HTTP headers. You may also include nonstandard HTTP headers with the request to communicate information to a particular cloud service.

Listing 3-11 shows how to add headers to an HTTP request. It adds the standard User-Agent header and a custom X-Custom header. The headers are provided in an array, with the name of each header followed by its value.

Listing 3-11.

```
let request = new Request({
    host: "api.example.com",
    path: "/api/status",
    response: String,
    headers: [
        "User-Agent", "my_iot_device/0.1 example/1.0",
        "X-Custom", "my value"
    ]
});
```

Specifying the headers in an array rather than in a dictionary or a Map object is somewhat unusual. It's done here because it's more efficient and reduces the resources needed on the IoT device.

Getting Response Headers

The HTTP protocol uses headers to communicate additional information about the response to the client. A common header is Content-Type, which indicates the data type of the response (such as text/plain, application/json, or image/png). The response headers are delivered to the callback function with the header message. One header is delivered at a time, to reduce memory use by avoiding the need to store all received headers in memory at once. When all response headers have been received, the callback is invoked with the headersComplete message.

Listing 3-12 checks all headers received for a Content-Type header. If one is found, its value is stored in the variable contentType. After all headers are received, the code checks to see that a Content-Type header was received (that is, contentType is not undefined) and that the content type is text/plain.

Listing 3-12.

```
let contentType;

request.callback = function(msg, value, etc) {
    if (Request.header === msg) {
        if ("content-type" === value)
            contentType = etc;
    }
    else if (Request.headersComplete === msg) {
        trace("all headers received\n");
```

```
        if ((undefined === contentType) ||
            !contentType.toLowerCase().startsWith("text/plain"))
            this.close();
    }
}
```

The names of HTTP headers are case-insensitive by definition, so Content-Type, content-type, and CONTENT-TYPE all refer to the same header. The HTTP Request class converts the name of the header to lowercase, so the callback can always use lowercase letters in header name comparisons.

POST

All the examples of HTTP requests so far have used the default HTTP request method of GET and have had an empty request body. The HTTP Request class supports setting the request method to any value, such as POST, and providing a request body.

The $EXAMPLES/ch3-network/http-post example (Listing 3-13) makes a POST call to a web server with a JSON request body. The method property of the dictionary defines the HTTP request method, and the body property defines the contents of the request body. The request body may be either a string or an ArrayBuffer. The request is posted to a server that echoes back the JSON response. The callback function traces the echoed JSON values to the debug console.

Listing 3-13.

```
let request = new Request({
    host: "httpbin.org",
    path: "/post",
    method: "POST",
    body: JSON.stringify({string: "test", number: 123}),
    response: String
});
```

```
request.callback = function(msg, value) {
    if (Request.responseComplete === msg) {
        value = JSON.parse(value);
        trace(`string: ${value.json.string}\n`);
        trace(`number: ${value.json.number}\n`);
    }
}
```

This example stores the entire request body in memory. In some situations, there's not enough free memory available to store the request body, such as when uploading a large file. The HTTP Request class supports streaming of the request body; for an example of this, see the examples/network/http/httppoststreaming example in the Moddable SDK.

Handling Errors

Sometimes an HTTP request fails, possibly due to a network failure or a problem with the request. In all cases, the failure is nonrecoverable. Therefore, you need to decide how to handle the error in a way that's appropriate for your IoT product, such as reporting it to the user, retrying immediately, retrying later, or just ignoring the error. If you're not yet ready to add error handling to your project, adding a diagnostic trace on error is a good start, as it helps you see failures during development.

When the failure is due to a network error—network failure, DNS failure, or server fault—your callback is invoked with the error message. The following example shows a callback that traces the failure to the debug console:

```
request.callback = function(msg, value) {
    if (Request.error === msg)
        trace(`http request failed: ${value}\n`);
}
```

If the failure is due to a problem with the request—it was badly formed, the path is invalid, or you're not properly authorized—the server responds with an error in the HTTP status code. The HTTP Request class provides the status code to the callback in the status message. For many web services, a status code from 200 to 299 means the request succeeded, while others indicate a failure. Listing 3-14 demonstrates handling HTTP status codes.

Listing 3-14.

```
request.callback = function(msg, value) {
    if (Request.status === msg) {
        if ((value < 200) || (value > 299))
            trace(`http status error: ${value}\n`);
    }
}
```

Securing Connections with TLS

Secure communication is an important part of most IoT products. It helps maintain the privacy of the data generated by the product and prevents tampering with the data while it's moving from the device to the server. On the web, most communication is secured using *Transport Layer Security,* or *TLS*, which replaces Secure Sockets Layer (SSL). TLS is a low-level tool for securing communication that works with many different protocols. This section explains how to use TLS with the HTTP protocol. The same approach applies to the WebSocket and MQTT protocols, described later.

Working with TLS on an embedded device is a bit more challenging than on a computer, server, or mobile device because of the reduced memory, processing power, and storage. In fact, establishing a secure TLS connection is the most computationally demanding task many IoT products perform.

151

Using TLS with the SecureSocket Class

The SecureSocket class implements TLS in a way that can be used with various network protocols. To use SecureSocket, you must first import it:

```
import SecureSocket from "securesocket";
```

To make a secure HTTP request (HTTPS), add a Socket property with the value of SecureSocket, which tells the HTTP Request class to use the secure socket instead of the default standard socket. Listing 3-15 is an excerpt from the $EXAMPLES/ch3-network/https-get example that shows the dictionary from the earlier HTTP GET example (Listing 3-5) modified to make an HTTPS request.

Listing 3-15.

```
let request = new Request({
    host: "www.example.com",
    path: "/",
    response: String,
    Socket: SecureSocket
});
```

The callback does not change from the original example.

Public Certificates

Certificates are an important part of how TLS provides security: they enable the client to verify the identity of the server. Certificates are built into the software of the IoT product just as they're built into a web browser, with one difference: whereas a web browser can store hundreds of certificates—enough to verify the identity of all publicly available servers on the internet—an IoT product doesn't have enough storage to hold so many certificates. Fortunately, an IoT product typically communicates with only a few servers, so you can include only the certificates you need.

Certificates are data, so they're stored in resources that applications can access rather than in code. The manifest for the HTTPS GET example includes the certificate needed to verify the identity of www.example.com (Listing 3-16).

Listing 3-16.

```
"resources": {
    "*": [
        "$(MODULES)/crypt/data/ca107"
    ]
}
```

If you try to access a website and the certificate's resource is not available, the TLS implementation throws an error like the one shown in Figure 3-2.

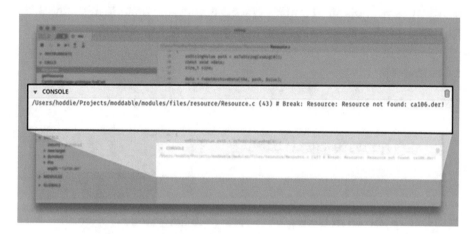

Figure 3-2. *TLS certificate error message in* xsbug

The error shows the number of the missing resource, so you can modify the manifest to include that resource (Listing 3-17).

Listing 3-17.

```
"resources": {
    "*": [
        "$(MODULES)/crypt/data/ca106"
    ]
}
```

This works because the Moddable SDK includes the certificates for most public websites. The next section describes how to connect to a server that uses a private certificate.

Private Certificates

Private certificates provide additional security by ensuring that only IoT products that have the private certificate are able to connect to the server. The private certificate is usually provided in a file with a .der extension. To use a private certificate in your project, first put the certificate in the same directory as your manifest and modify the manifest to include it (Listing 3-18). Note that the manifest does not include the .der file name extension.

Listing 3-18.

```
"resources": {
    "*": [
        "./private_certificate"
    ]
}
```

Next, as shown in Listing 3-19, your application loads the certificate from the resource and passes it to the HTTP request in the secure property of the constructor's dictionary.

Listing 3-19.

```
import Resource from "resource";

let cert = new Resource("private_certificate.der");
let request = new Request({
    host: "iot.privateserver.net",
    path: "/",
    response: String,
    Socket: SecureSocket,
    secure: {
        certificate: cert
    }
});
```

Creating an HTTP Server

Including an HTTP server in your IoT product opens up many possibilities, such as enabling your product to do the following:

- Provide web pages to users on the same network, which is a great way to provide a user interface for products without a display

- Provide a REST API for applications and other devices to communicate with

Fundamentals

To create an HTTP server, first import the Server class from the http module:

```
import {Server} from "http";
```

Like the HTTP Request class, the HTTP Server class is configured with a dictionary object. There are no required properties in the dictionary. Also like HTTP Request, HTTP Server uses a callback function to deliver messages at the various stages of responding to an HTTP request. Here's the complete list of the stages of an HTTP request:

- connection – The server has accepted a new connection.

- status – The status line of the HTTP request has been received. The request path and request method are available.

- header – An HTTP request header has been received. This message is repeated for each HTTP header received.

- headersComplete – This message is received between receipt of the final HTTP request header and receipt of the request body.

- requestFragment – (For streaming request bodies only) A fragment of the request body is available.

- requestComplete – The entire request body has been received.

- prepareResponse – The server is ready to begin delivering the response. The callback returns a dictionary describing the response.

- responseFragment – (For streaming responses only) The callback responds to this message by providing the next fragment of the response.

- responseComplete – The entire response has been delivered successfully.

- error – A failure occurred before the HTTP response was completely delivered.

The examples that follow show how to use many of these messages. Most applications working with the HTTP Server class use only a few of them.

Responding to a Request

An HTTP server responds to all kinds of different requests. Listing 3-20 is an excerpt from the $EXAMPLES/ch3-network/http-server-get example that responds to each request with plain text that indicates the HTTP method used for the response (usually GET) and the path of the HTTP resource requested. Both the method and the path are provided to the callback with the status message. The callback stores these values to return them in the text when it receives the prepareResponse message.

Listing 3-20.

```
let server = new Server({port: 80});
server.callback = function(msg, value, etc) {
    if (Server.status === msg) {
        this.path = value;
        this.method = etc;
    }
    else if (Server.prepareResponse === msg) {
        return {
            headers: ["Content-Type", "text/plain"],
            body: `hello. path "${this.path}".
                method "${this.method}".`
        };
    }
}
```

When you run this example, the IP address of the device is displayed in the debug console as follows:

```
Wi-Fi connected to "Moddable"
IP address 10.0.1.5
```

After the IP address is displayed, you can use a web browser on the same network to connect to the web server. When you enter `http://10.0.1.5/test.html` in the address bar of the browser, you receive the following response:

```
hello. path "/test.html". method "GET".
```

Notice that the callback does not set the `Content-Length` field. When you use the body property, the server implementation adds the `Content-Length` header automatically.

The body property in this example is a string, but it may also be an `ArrayBuffer` to respond with binary data.

Responding to JSON PUT

Often a REST API receives its input as JSON in the request body and provides its output as JSON in the response body. The `$EXAMPLES/ch3-network/http-server-put` example is a JSON echo server which replies to every message it receives by sending back that message. The example expects the client to use the PUT method to send a JSON object. The response embeds that JSON object into a larger JSON object that also includes an `error` property.

When the `status` message is received, the server verifies that it's a PUT method; otherwise, the server closes the connection to reject the request. The callback returns `String` when it receives the `status` message, to indicate that it wants the entire request body at one time as a string. To receive the request body as binary data instead, it may return `ArrayBuffer`.

In response to the requestComplete message, the server parses the JSON input and embeds it into the object used to generate the response. When the prepareResponse message is received, the server in Listing 3-21 returns the response body JSON as a string and sets the Content-Type header to application/json.

Listing 3-21.

```
let server = new Server;

server.callback = function(msg, value, etc) {
    switch (msg) {
        case Server.status:
            if ("PUT" !== etc)
                this.close();
            return String;

        case Server.requestComplete:
            this.json = {
                error: "none",
                request: JSON.parse(value)
            };
            break;

        case Server.prepareResponse:
            return {
                headers: ["Content-Type", "application/json"],
                body: JSON.stringify(this.json)
            };
    }
}
```

Since this example doesn't pass a dictionary to the Server constructor, the default of port 80 is used.

You can use the following command to try the http-server-put example using the curl command line tool. You'll need to change <IP_address> to match the IP address of your development board (for example, 192.168.1.45). The command posts the simple JSON message in the --data argument to the server and displays the result to the debug console.

```
> curl http://<IP_address>/json
    --request PUT
    --header "Content-Type: application/json"
    --data '{"example": "data", "value": 101}'
```

Receiving a Streaming Request

When a large request body is sent to the HTTP server, it may be too large to fit in memory. This can happen, for example, when you upload data to store in a file. The solution is to receive the request body in fragments rather than all at once. Listing 3-22 from the $EXAMPLES/ch3-network/http-server-streaming-put example logs an arbitrarily large text request to the debug console. To ask the HTTP Server class to deliver the request body in fragments, the callback returns true to the prepareRequest message. The fragments are delivered with the requestFragment message and traced to the debug console. The requestComplete message indicates that all request body fragments have been delivered.

Listing 3-22.

```
let server = new Server;

server.callback = function(msg, value) {
    switch (msg) {
        case Server.status:
            trace("\n ** begin upload to ${value} **\n");
            break;
```

```
case Server.prepareRequest:
    return true;

case Server.requestFragment:
    trace(this.read(String));
    break;

case Server.requestComplete:
    trace("\n ** end of file **\n");
    break;
    }
}
```

You can adapt this example to write the received data where your application needs it rather than to the debug console. For example, in Chapter 5 you'll learn the APIs to write the data to a file.

To try this example, use the `curl` command line tool as shown in the following. You'll need to change `<directory_path>` and `<IP_address>` for your configuration.

```
> curl --data-binary "@/users/<directory_path>/test.txt"
    http://<IP_address>/test.txt -v
```

Sending a Streaming Response

If the response to an HTTP request is too large to fit into memory, the response can be streamed instead. This approach is appropriate for file downloads. As shown in Listing 3-23, the `$EXAMPLES/ch3-network/http-server-streaming-get` example generates a response of random length containing random integers from 1 to 100. To indicate that the response body is to be streamed, the callback sets the body property to `true` in the dictionary returned from the `prepareResponse` message. The server invokes the callback repeatedly with the `responseFragment` message to get the next part of the response. The callback returns `undefined` to indicate the end of the response.

Listing 3-23.

```
let server = new Server;

server.callback = function(msg, value) {
    if (Server.prepareResponse === msg) {
        return {
            headers: ["Content-Type", "text/plain"],
            body: true
        };
    }
    else if (Server.responseFragment === msg) {
        let i = Math.round(Math.random() * 100);
        if (0 === i)
            return;
        return i + "\n";
    }
}
```

This example returns string values for the response body, but it may also return ArrayBuffer values to provide binary data. When the responseFragment message is received, the value argument to the callback indicates the maximum number of bytes that the server is prepared to accept for this fragment. When you stream a file, this can be used as the number of bytes to read from the file for the fragment.

The HTTP Server class sends streaming response bodies using chunked transfer encoding. For response bodies where the length is known, the server uses the default identity encoding to send the body without a transfer encoding header and includes a Content-Length header.

mDNS

Multicast DNS, or *mDNS*, is a collection of capabilities that make it easier for devices to work together on a local network. You probably know the DNS (Domain Name System) protocol because it's how your web browser finds the network address for the website you enter in the address bar (for example, it's how the browser converts www.example.com to 93.184.216.34). DNS is designed to be used by the entire internet. In contrast, mDNS is designed to work only on your local network—for example, for all the devices connected to your Wi-Fi access point. DNS is a centralized design that depends on authoritative servers to map names to IP addresses, whereas mDNS is entirely decentralized, with each individual device answering requests to map its name to an IP address.

In this section, you'll learn how to use mDNS to give your IoT device a name, like porch-light.local, so that other devices can find it by name rather than have to know its IP address. You'll also learn to use another part of mDNS, DNS-SD (DNS Service Discovery), to find services provided by devices (such as finding all printers or all web servers) and to advertise your device's services on the local network.

The mdns module contains the JavaScript classes you use to work with mDNS and DNS-SD from your application. To use the mdns module in your code, first import it as follows:

```
import MDNS from "mdns";
```

Note   mDNS is well supported on macOS, Android, iOS, and Linux. Windows 10 does not fully support mDNS yet, so you may need to install additional software to use it there.

Claiming a Name

mDNS is commonly used to assign a name to a device for use on the local network. mDNS names are always in the .local domain, as in thermostat.local. You can pick any name you like for a device. The device must check to see whether the name is already in use, because it won't work to have multiple devices responding to the same name. The process of checking is called *claiming*. The claiming process lasts a few seconds. If a conflict is found, mDNS defines a negotiation process. At the end of the negotiation, only one device has the requested name and the other selects an unused name. For example, if you try to claim iotdevice unsuccessfully, you may end up with iotdevice-2.

The $EXAMPLES/ch3-network/mdns-claim-name example shows the process of claiming a name (see Listing 3-24). The MDNS constructor is invoked with a dictionary that contains the hostName property with the value of the desired name. There's a callback function that receives progress messages during the claiming process. When the name message is received with a non-null value, the claimed name is traced to the debug console.

Listing 3-24.

```
let mdns = new MDNS({
        hostName: "iotdevice"
    },
    function(msg, value) {
        if ((MDNS.hostName === msg) && value)
            trace(`Claimed name ${value}.\n`);
    }
);
```

Once a device has claimed a name, you can use the name to access the device. For example, you can use the ping command line tool to confirm that the device is online.

```
> ping iotdevice.local
```

Finding a Service

By claiming a name, your device becomes easier to communicate with, but at best the name gives only a small hint about what the device does. It would be helpful to know that the device is a light, thermostat, speaker, or web server so that you could write code that works with it without any configuration. That's the problem that DNS-SD solves: it's a way to advertise the capabilities of your IoT product on the local network.

Each kind of DNS-SD service has a unique name. For example, a web server service has the name http and a network file system has the name nfs. The $EXAMPLES/ch3-network/mdns-discover example shows how to search for all the web servers advertising on your local network. There may be web servers on your network that you aren't aware of, because many printers have a built-in web server for configuration and management.

As shown in Listing 3-25, the mdns-discover example creates an MDNS instance without claiming a name. It installs a monitoring callback function to be notified when an http service is found. For each service found, it makes an HTTP request for the home page of the device and traces its HTTP headers to the debug console.

Listing 3-25.

```
let mdns = new MDNS;
mdns.monitor("_http._tcp", function(service, instance) {
    trace(`Found ${service}: "${instance.name}" @ ` +
          `${instance.target} ` +
          `(${instance.address}:${instance.port})\n`);
```

```
let request = new Request({
    host: instance.address,
    port: instance.port,
    path: "/"
});
request.callback = function(msg, value, etc) {
    if (Request.header === msg)
        trace(`   ${value}: ${etc}\n`);
    else if (Request.responseComplete === msg)
        trace("\n\n");
    else if (Request.error === msg)
        trace("error \n\n");
};
});
```

The instance argument to the callback function has several properties for working with the device:

- name – the human-readable name of the device

- target – the mDNS name of the device
  (for example, lightbulb.local)

- address – the IP address of the device

- port – the port used to connect to the service

Here's the output from the example when it finds an HP printer with an http service:

```
Found _http._tcp: "HP ENVY 7640 series"
              @hpprinter.local (192.168.1.223:80)
    server: HP HTTP Server; HP ENVY 7640 series - E4W44A;
    content-type: text/html
```

```
last-modified: Mon, 23 Jul 2018 10:53:51 GMT
content-language: en
content-length: 658
```

Advertising a Service

Your device can use DNS-SD to advertise the services it provides, which enables other devices on the same network to find and use those services.

The $EXAMPLES/ch3-network/mdns-advertise example defines the service it provides in a JavaScript object stored in the variable httpService. The service description says that the example supports the http service and makes it available on port 80. Listing 3-26 defines the HTTP service for DNS-SD.

Listing 3-26.

```
let httpService = {
    name: "http",
    protocol: "tcp",
    port: 80
};
```

The example then creates an MDNS instance to claim the name server. Once the name has been claimed, the script in Listing 3-27 adds the http service. The service cannot be added before the name is claimed because DNS-SD requires each service to be associated with an mDNS name.

Listing 3-27.

```
let mdns = new MDNS({
        hostName: "server"
    },
```

```
    function(msg, value) {
        if ((MDNS.hostName === msg) && value)
            mdns.add(httpService);
    }
);
```

After the service is added, other devices may find it, as shown earlier in the section "Finding a Service."

The full mdns-advertise example also contains a simple web server that listens on port 80. When you run the example, you can type server.local into your web browser to view the response from the web server.

WebSocket

The *WebSocket* protocol is a good alternative to HTTP when you need frequent two-way communication between devices. When two devices communicate using WebSocket, a network connection is kept open between them, enabling efficient communication of brief messages such as sending a sensor reading or a command to turn on a light. In HTTP, one device is the client and the other is the server; only the client can make a request, and the server always responds. WebSocket, on the other hand, is a peer-to-peer protocol, enabling both devices to send and receive messages. It's often a good choice for IoT products that need to send many small messages. However, because it keeps a connection open at all times between two devices, it usually requires more memory than HTTP.

The WebSocket protocol is implemented by the websocket module, which contains both WebSocket client and WebSocket server support. Your project can import one or both, as needed.

```
import {Client} from "websocket";
import {Server} from "websocket";
import {Client, Server} from "websocket";
```

Because WebSocket is a peer-to-peer protocol, the code for a client and a server is very similar. The primary difference is in the initial setup.

Connecting to a WebSocket Server

The $EXAMPLES/ch3-network/websocket-client example uses a WebSocket echo server, which replies to every message it receives by sending back that message. The WebSocket Client class constructor takes a configuration dictionary. The only required property is host, the name of the server. If no port property is specified, the WebSocket default of 80 is assumed.

```
let ws = new Client({
    host: "echo.websocket.org"
});
```

You can establish a secure connection using TLS by passing SecureSocket for the Socket property, as explained earlier in the section "Using TLS with the SecureSocket Class."

You provide a callback function to receive messages from the WebSocket Client class. The WebSocket protocol is simpler than HTTP, so the callback is also simpler. In the websocket-client example, the connect and close messages just trace a message. The WebSocket protocol's connection process consists of two steps: the connect message is received when the network connection is established between the client and server, and the handshake message is received when the client and server agree to communicate using WebSocket, indicating that the connection is ready for use.

When the example receives the handshake message, it sends the first message, a JSON string with count and toggle properties. When the echo server sends that JSON back, the callback in Listing 3-28 is invoked with the receive message. It parses the string back to JSON, modifies the count and toggle values, and sends the modified JSON back to the echo server. This process repeats indefinitely, with count increasing each time.

Listing 3-28.

```
ws.callback = function(msg, value) {
    switch (msg) {
        case Client.connect:
            trace("connected\n");
            break;

        case Client.handshake:
            trace("handshake success\n");
            this.write(JSON.stringify({
                count: 1,
                toggle: true
            }));
            break;

        case Client.receive:
            trace(`received: ${value}\n`);
            value = JSON.parse(value);
            value.count += 1;
            value.toggle = !value.toggle;
            this.write(JSON.stringify(value));
            break;

        case Client.disconnect:
            trace("disconnected\n");
            break;
    }
}
```

Here's the output of this code:

```
connected
handshake success
received: {"count":1,"toggle":true}
```

```
received: {"count":2,"toggle":false}
received: {"count":3,"toggle":true}
received: {"count":4,"toggle":false}
...
```

Each call to write sends one WebSocket message. You can send a message at any time after receiving the handshake message, not just from inside the callback:

```
ws.write("hello");
ws.write(Uint8Array.of(1, 2, 3).buffer);
```

Messages are either a string or an ArrayBuffer. When you receive a WebSocket message, it's either a string or an ArrayBuffer depending on what was sent. Listing 3-29 shows how to check the type of value, the received message.

Listing 3-29.

```
if (typeof value === "string")
    ...;    // a string

if (value instanceof ArrayBuffer)
    ...;    // an ArrayBuffer, binary data
```

Creating a WebSocket Server

The $EXAMPLES/ch3-network/websocket-server example implements a WebSocket echo server (again, meaning that whenever the server receives a message, it sends back the same message). The WebSocket Server class is configured with a dictionary that has no required properties. The optional port property indicates the port to listen on for new connections; it defaults to 80.

```
let server = new Server;
```

The server callback function in Listing 3-30 receives the same messages as the client. In this example, all messages just trace status to the debug console, except for receive, which echoes back the received message.

Listing 3-30.

```
server.callback = function(msg, value) {
    switch (msg) {
        case Server.connect:
            trace("connected\n");
            break;

        case Server.handshake:
            trace("handshake success\n");
            break;

        case Server.receive:
            trace(`received: ${value}\n`);
            this.write(value);
            break;

        case Server.disconnect:
            trace("closed\n");
            break;
    }
}
```

This server supports multiple simultaneous connections, each of which has a unique this value when the callback is invoked. If your application needs to maintain state across a connection, it can add properties to this. When a new connection is established, the connect message is received; when the connection ends, the disconnect message is received.

MQTT

The *Message Queuing Telemetry Transport* protocol, or *MQTT*, is a publish-and-subscribe protocol designed for use by lightweight IoT client devices. The server (sometimes called the "broker" in MQTT) is more complex, and consequently isn't typically implemented on resource-constrained devices. Messages to and from an MQTT server are organized into *topics*. A particular server may support many topics, but a client receives only the messages for the topics it subscribes to.

The client for the MQTT protocol is implemented by the mqtt module:

```
import MQTT from "mqtt";
```

Connecting to an MQTT Server

The MQTT constructor is configured by a dictionary with three required parameters: the host property indicates the MQTT server to connect to, port is the port number to connect to, and id is a unique ID for this device. It's an error for two devices with the same ID to connect to an MQTT server, so take care to ensure that these are truly unique. The $EXAMPLES/ch3-network/mqtt example excerpt in Listing 3-31 uses the device's MAC address for the unique ID.

Listing 3-31.

```
let mqtt = new MQTT({
    host: "test.mosquitto.org",
    port: 1883,
    id: "iot_" + Net.get("MAC")
});
```

If the MQTT server requires authentication, the user and password properties are added to the configuration dictionary. The password is always binary data, so Listing 3-32 uses the ArrayBuffer.fromString static method to convert a string to an ArrayBuffer.

Listing 3-32.

```
let mqtt = new MQTT({
    host: "test.mosquitto.org",
    port: 1883,
    id: "iot_" + Net.get("MAC"),
    user: "user name",
    password: ArrayBuffer.fromString("secret")
});
```

To use an encrypted MQTT connection, use TLS as described earlier in the section "Securing Connections with TLS," by adding a Socket property and optional secure property to the dictionary.

Some servers use the WebSocket protocol to transport MQTT data. If you're using a server that does this, you need to specify the path property to tell the MQTT class the endpoint to connect to, as shown in Listing 3-33. Transporting MQTT over a WebSocket connection has no benefit and uses more memory and network bandwidth, so it should be used only if the remote server requires it.

Listing 3-33.

```
let mqtt = new MQTT({
    host: "test.mosquitto.org",
    port: 8080,
    id: "iot_" + Net.get("MAC"),
    path: "/"
});
```

The MQTT client has three callback functions (Listing 3-34). The onReady callback is invoked when a connection is successfully established to the server, onMessage when a message is received, and onClose when the connection is lost.

Listing 3-34.

```
mqtt.onReady = function() {
    trace("connection established\n");
}

mqtt.onMessage = function(topic, data) {
    trace("message received\n");
}

mqtt.onClose = function() {
    trace("connection lost\n");
}
```

Once the onReady callback has been invoked, your MQTT client is ready to subscribe to message topics and publish messages.

Subscribing to a Topic

To subscribe to a topic, send the server the name of the topic to subscribe to. Your client can subscribe to multiple clients by calling subscribe more than once.

```
mqtt.subscribe("test/string");
mqtt.subscribe("test/binary");
mqtt.subscribe("test/json");
```

Messages are delivered to the onMessage callback function for all topics that your client has subscribed to. The topic argument is the name of the topic and the data argument is the complete message.

```
mqtt.onMessage = function(topic, data) {
    trace(`received message on topic "${topic}"\n`);
}
```

The data argument is always provided in binary form, as an ArrayBuffer. If you know the message is a string, you can convert it to a string; if you know the string is JSON, you can convert it to a JavaScript object.

```
data = String.fromArrayBuffer(data);
data = JSON.parse(data);
```

String.fromArrayBuffer is a feature of XS to make it easier for applications to work with binary data. There is a parallel ArrayBuffer.fromString function. These are not part of the JavaScript language standard.

Publishing to a Topic

To send a message to a topic, call publish with either a string or an ArrayBuffer:

```
mqtt.publish("test/string", "hello");
mqtt.publish("test/binary", Uint8Array.of(1, 2, 3).buffer);
```

To publish JSON, first convert it to a string:

```
mqtt.publish("test/json", JSON.stringify({
    message: "hello",
    version: 1
}));
```

SNTP

Simple Network Time Protocol, or *SNTP,* is a lightweight way to retrieve the current time. Your computer probably uses SNTP (or its parent, NTP) to set its time behind the scenes. Unlike your IoT device, your computer also has a real-time clock backed up by a battery, so it always knows the current time. If you need the current time on an IoT device, you need to retrieve it. If you're using the command line method of connecting to Wi-Fi, the current time is retrieved once the Wi-Fi connection is established if you specify a time server on the command line.

```
> mcconfig -d -m -p esp ssid="my wi-fi" sntp="pool.ntp.org"
```

When connecting to Wi-Fi with code, you also need to write some code to set your IoT device's clock. You get the current time with the SNTP protocol, which is implemented in the sntp module, and you set the device's time using the time module.

```
import SNTP from "sntp";
import Time from "time";
```

Listing 3-35 shows the $EXAMPLES/ch3-network/sntp example requesting the current time from the time server at pool.ntp.org. When the time is received, the device's time is set and displayed in UTC (Coordinated Universal Time) in the debug console. The SNTP instance closes itself to free the resources it's using, since it's no longer needed.

Listing 3-35.

```
new SNTP({
        host: "pool.ntp.org"
    },
    function(msg, value) {
        if (SNTP.time !== msg)
            return;
```

```
        Time.set(value);
        trace("UTC time now: ",
                (new Date).toUTCString(), "\n");
    }
);
```

Most IoT products keep a list of several SNTP servers for situations where one is unavailable. The SNTP class supports this scenario without needing to create additional instances of the SNTP class. See the `examples/network/sntp` example in the Moddable SDK to learn how to use this fail-over feature.

Advanced Topics

This section introduces two advanced topics: how to turn your device into a private Wi-Fi base station and how to use JavaScript promises with networking APIs.

Creating a Wi-Fi Access Point

Sometimes you don't want to connect your IoT product to the entire internet but you do want to let people connect to your device to configure it or check its status. At other times, you do want to connect your device to the internet but you don't have the name and password for the Wi-Fi access point yet. In both these situations, creating a private Wi-Fi access point may be a solution. In addition to being a Wi-Fi client that connects to other access points, many IoT microcontrollers (including the ESP32 and ESP8266) can be an access point.

You can turn your IoT device into an access point with a call to the static `accessPoint` method of the `WiFi` class:

```
WiFi.accessPoint({
    ssid: "South Village"
});
```

The `ssid` property defines the name of the access point and is the only required property. As shown in Listing 3-36, optional properties enable you to set a password, select the Wi-Fi channel to use, and hide the access point from appearing in Wi-Fi scans.

Listing 3-36.

```
WiFi.accessPoint({
    ssid: "South Village",
    password: "12345678",
    channel: 8,
    hidden: false
});
```

A device is either an access point or the client of an access point. It cannot be both at the same time, so once you've entered access point mode, you cannot access the internet.

You can provide a web server on your access point, as shown earlier in the section "Responding to a Request." In Listing 3-37, from the `$EXAMPLES/ch3-network/accesspoint` example, the import of the HTTP Server class is a little different because it renames, or aliases, the class to `HTTPServer` to avoid a name collision with the DNS server (introduced following this example).

Listing 3-37.

```
import {Server as HTTPServer} from "http";

(new HTTPServer).callback = function(msg, value) {
    if (HTTPServer.prepareResponse === msg) {
        return {
            headers: ["Content-Type", "text/plain"],
            body: "hello"
        };
    }
}
```

How will other devices know the address of your web server so that they can connect to it? You could claim a local name with mDNS. But since your IoT product is the access point, it's also now the router for the network, so it can resolve DNS requests. This means that whenever a device on the network looks up a name, such as www.example.com, your application can direct the request to your HTTP server. Listing 3-38 is a simple DNS server that does exactly that.

Listing 3-38.

```
import {Server as DNSServer} from "dns/server";

new DNSServer(function(msg, value) {
    if (DNSServer.resolve === msg)
        return Net.get("IP");
});
```

The DNS Server class constructor takes a callback function as its sole parameter. The callback function is invoked with the resolve message whenever any device connected to the access point tries to resolve a DNS name. In response, the callback provides its own IP address. When most computers or phones connect to a new Wi-Fi point, they perform a check to see if they're connected to the internet or if a login is required. When this check is performed on your access point, it will cause your web server's access point to be called to get the web page to show. In this example, it will simply show hello, but you can change this to show device status, configure Wi-Fi, or anything else you like.

Promises and Asynchronous Functions

Promises are a feature of JavaScript to simplify programming with callback functions. Callback functions are simple and efficient, which is why they're used in so many places. Promises can improve the readability of code that performs a sequence of steps using callback functions.

This section is not intended as a complete introduction to promises and asynchronous functions. If you aren't familiar with these JavaScript features, read through this section to see if they look useful to your projects; if they do, many excellent resources are available on the Web to help you learn more.

The $EXAMPLES/ch3-network/http-get-with-promise example excerpt in Listing 3-39 builds on the HTTP Request class to implement a fetch function that returns a complete HTTP request as a string.

Listing 3-39.

```
function fetch(host, path = "/") {
    return new Promise((resolve, reject) => {
        let request = new Request({host, path, response: String});
        request.callback = function(msg, value) {
            if (Request.responseComplete === msg)
                resolve(value);
            else if (Request.error === msg)
                reject(-1);
        }
    });
}
```

The implementation of the fetch function is tricky, requiring an in-depth understanding of how promises work in JavaScript. But using the fetch function is easy (Listing 3-40).

Listing 3-40.

```
function httpTrace(host, path) {
    fetch(host, path)
        .then(body => trace(body, "\n"))
        .catch(error => trace("http get failed\n"));
}
```

Reading the code for httpTrace, you might imagine that the HTTP request happens synchronously, but that's not the case, as all network operations are non-blocking. The arrow functions passed to the .then and .catch calls are executed when the request completes—.then if the call succeeds or .catch if it fails.

The recent versions of JavaScript provide another way to write this code: as an asynchronous function. Listing 3-41 shows the call to fetch rewritten in an asynchronous function. The code looks like ordinary JavaScript apart from the keywords async and await.

Listing 3-41.

```
async function httpTrace(host, path) {
    try {
        let body = await fetch(host, path);
        trace(body, "\n");
    }
    catch {
        trace("http get failed\n");
    }
}
```

The `httpTrace` function is asynchronous, so it returns immediately when called. The keyword `await` before the call to `fetch` tells the JavaScript language that when `fetch` returns a promise, execution of `httpTrace` should be suspended until the promise is ready (resolved or rejected).

Promises and asynchronous functions are powerful tools, and they're used in JavaScript code for much more powerful systems, including web servers and computers. They're available for your IoT projects, even on resource-constrained devices, because you're using the XS JavaScript engine. Still, callback functions are preferred in most situations, because they require less code, execute faster, and use less memory. When building your project, you'll need to decide whether the convenience of using them outweighs the additional resources used.

Conclusion

In this chapter you've learned various ways for your IoT device to communicate over a network. The different protocols described in this chapter all follow the same basic API pattern:

- The protocol's class provides a constructor that accepts a dictionary to configure the connection.

- Callback functions deliver information from the network to your application.

- Communication is always asynchronous to avoid blocking, an important consideration on IoT products that don't always have the luxury of multiple threads of execution.

- Callbacks can be turned into promises using small helper functions so that applications can use asynchronous functions in modern JavaScript.

You, as the developer of an IoT product, need to decide the communication methods it supports. There are many factors to consider. If you want your device to communicate with the cloud, HTTP, WebSocket, and MQTT are all possible choices, and they all support secure communication using TLS. For direct device-to-device communication, mDNS is a good starting point to enable devices to advertise their services, and HTTP is a lightweight way to exchange messages between devices.

Of course, your product doesn't have to choose just one network protocol for communication. Starting from the examples in this chapter, you're ready to try different protools to find what works best for the needs of your device.

CHAPTER 4

Bluetooth Low Energy (BLE)

There are many ways to enable wireless communication between devices. Chapter 3 introduced many protocols that operate over a Wi-Fi connection to communicate with devices anywhere in the world. This chapter focuses on *Bluetooth Low Energy*, or *BLE*, a wireless communication widely used between two devices in close proximity to each other. Products choose to use BLE instead of Wi-Fi if minimizing energy use is particularly important, such as in battery-powered products, and when direct communication with another device, such as a mobile phone, is an acceptable alternative to internet access. Many IoT products use BLE, from heart rate monitors to electric toothbrushes to ovens. Product manufacturers often offer a mobile app or desktop companion application to monitor or control these products.

BLE is version 4 of the Bluetooth standard and was first introduced in 2010. The original Bluetooth was standardized in 2000 to send streams of data over short distances. BLE significantly reduces the energy use of the original Bluetooth, enabling it to operate much longer on a single battery charge. BLE achieves this, in part, by reducing the amount of data transmitted. Transmitting over shorter distances also uses less energy; BLE devices typically have a range of no more than 100 meters, whereas Wi-Fi has a much larger range. BLE's lower power consumption and cost make it well suited for many IoT products.

© Peter Hoddie and Lizzie Prader 2020
P. Hoddie and L. Prader, *IoT Development for ESP32 and ESP8266 with JavaScript*,
https://doi.org/10.1007/978-1-4842-5070-9_4

Using the information in this chapter, you can build your own BLE devices that run on a microcontroller.

Note   The examples in this chapter are for the ESP32. If you attempt to build them for the ESP8266, the build will fail because the ESP8266 doesn't have BLE hardware. The examples do, however, run on other devices with integrated BLE supported by the Moddable SDK, including Qualcomm's QCA4020 and the Blue Gecko by Silicon Labs.

BLE Basics

If you're new to working with BLE, the information in this section is essential, as it explains concepts used throughout the rest of this chapter. If you're familiar with BLE, still consider giving this section a quick scan to familiarize yourself with the terminology used in this book and how it relates to the BLE API of the Moddable SDK.

GAP Centrals and Peripherals

The *Generic Access Profile*, or *GAP*, defines how devices advertise themselves, how they establish connections with each other, and security. The two main roles defined by GAP are *Central* and *Peripheral*.

A Central scans for devices acting as Peripherals and initiates requests to establish a new connection with a Peripheral. A device acting as a Central usually has relatively high processing power and plenty of memory—for example, a smart phone, tablet, or computer—whereas Peripherals are often small and battery-powered. Peripherals advertise themselves and accept requests to establish a connection.

The BLE specification enables a Central to be connected to multiple Peripherals, and a Peripheral to be connected to multiple Centrals. It's common for a Central to connect to several Peripherals at the same time. For example, you may use your smart phone to connect to your heart rate monitor, smart watch, and lights. It's uncommon for a Peripheral to connect to more than one Central at a time; most Peripherals do not allow for multiple concurrent connections. The BLE API of the Moddable SDK enables a Peripheral to connect with a single Central at a time.

GATT Clients and Servers

The *Generic Attribute Profile*, or *GATT*, defines the way BLE devices transfer data back and forth after a connection is established between them—a client-server relationship.

A *GATT Client* is a device that accesses data from a remote GATT Server by sending read/write requests. A *GATT Server* is a device that stores data locally, receives read/write requests, and notifies the remote GATT Client of changes to the values of its characteristics. In this chapter, the term *Server* is used to mean a GATT Server, and *Client* means a GATT Client.

GAP vs. GATT

Many BLE tutorials incorrectly use the terms *Central* and *Client* interchangeably and the terms *Peripheral* and *Server* interchangeably. This is because Centrals usually take on the Client role and Peripherals usually take on the Server role. However, the BLE specification says that either Centrals or Peripherals may take on the role of Client, Server, or both.

Central and *Peripheral* are terms defined by GAP, telling you how the BLE connection is managed. *Client* and *Server* are terms defined by GATT, telling you about the storage and flow of data after a connection has been established. GATT comes into the picture only after the advertising and connection process defined by GAP is complete.

Profiles, Services, and Characteristics

GATT also defines the format of data, with a hierarchy of *profiles, services,* and *characteristics.* As illustrated in Figure 4-1, the top level of the hierarchy is a profile.

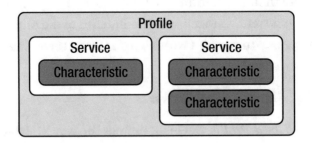

Figure 4-1. *GATT profile hierarchy*

Profiles

A *profile* defines a specific use of BLE for communication between multiple devices, including the roles of the devices involved and their general behaviors. For example, the standard Health Thermometer profile defines the roles of a Thermometer device (a sensor) and a Collector device; the Thermometer device measures the temperature, and the Collector device receives the temperature measurement and other data from the Thermometer. The profile specifies the services that the Thermometer must instantiate (the Health Thermometer service and the Device Information service) and states that the intended use of the profile is in healthcare applications.

Profiles don't exist on a BLE device; rather, they are specifications implemented by a BLE device. The list of officially adopted BLE profiles is available at bluetooth.com/specifications/gatt. When you're implementing your own BLE device, it's a good idea to check whether a standard profile is available that meets the needs of your product. If there is, you'll benefit from interoperability with other products that support the standard, saving you the time of designing a new profile.

Services

A *service* is a collection of characteristics that describe the behavior of part of a BLE device. For example, the Health Thermometer service provides temperature data from a Thermometer device. A service may have one or more characteristics and is distinguished by a UUID. Officially adopted BLE services have 16-bit UUIDs. The Health Thermometer service is assigned the number 0x1809. You can create your own custom services by giving them a 128-bit UUID.

Services are advertised by a BLE device. The list of officially adopted BLE services is available at bluetooth.com/specifications/gatt/services.

Characteristics

A *characteristic* is a single value or data point that provides information about a GATT service. The format of the data depends on the characteristic; for example, the Heart Rate Measurement characteristic used by the Heart Rate service provides a heart rate measurement as an integer, and the Device Name characteristic provides the name of a device as a string.

The list of officially adopted BLE characteristics is available at bluetooth.com/specifications/gatt/characteristics. As with services, officially adopted BLE characteristics have 16-bit UUIDs and you can create your own with a 128-bit UUID.

The BLE API of the Moddable SDK

The Moddable SDK does not have distinct classes in its BLE API for the roles defined by GAP and for GATT. Instead, it provides functions for Centrals and GATT Clients in a single BLEClient class, and functions for Peripherals and GATT Servers in a single BLEServer class. This class organization reflects the two most common configurations of BLE devices: devices that act as Centrals and take on the Client role and devices that act as Peripherals and take on the Server role.

The BLEClient Class

The BLEClient class provides functions you use to create Centrals and GATT Clients. The functions for Centrals perform the following operations:

1. Scan for Peripherals.

2. Initiate requests to establish a connection with Peripherals.

The functions for GATT Clients perform these operations:

1. Find the GATT services of interest.

2. Find characteristics of interest in each service.

3. Read, write, and enable notifications for characteristics within each service.

You subclass the BLEClient class to implement a specific BLE device that supports the operations your device requires. Subclasses call methods of the BLEClient class to initiate the preceding operations. All BLE operations performed by BLEClient are asynchronous to avoid blocking execution for an indeterminate period of time. Consequently, instances of the BLEClient class receive results through callbacks. For example, the BLEClient class has a startScanning method that you call to start scanning for Peripherals, and an onDiscovered callback that's automatically invoked when a Peripheral is discovered.

You only need to implement the callbacks required to work with the Peripherals, services, and characteristics your device requires.

The BLEServer Class

The BLEServer class provides functions you use to create Peripherals and GATT Servers. The functions for Peripherals perform the following operations:

1. Advertise so that Centrals can discover the Peripheral.

2. Accept connection requests from a Central.

The functions for GATT Servers perform these operations:

1. Deploy services.

2. Respond to characteristic read and write requests from a Client.

3. Accept characteristic value change notification requests from a Client.

4. Notify a Client of characteristic value changes.

You can implement standard BLE profiles like Heart Rate or your own custom-defined profile to support your product's unique capabilities. In both cases, you first define GATT services in JSON files and then subclass the BLEServer class to implement specific BLE devices. Subclasses call methods of the BLEServer class to initiate the preceding operations. All BLE operations performed by BLEServer are asynchronous to avoid blocking execution for an indeterminate period of time. Consequently, instances of the BLEServer class receive results through callbacks.

Installing the BLE Host

The examples in this chapter are installed using the pattern described in Chapter 1: you install the host on your device using mcconfig, then install example applications using mcrun.

The host is in the $EXAMPLES/ch4-ble/host directory. Navigate to this directory from the command line and install it with mcconfig.

Creating a BLE Scanner

The $EXAMPLES/ch4-ble/scanner example implements a Central that scans for nearby Peripherals and traces their names to the console. It's implemented using the BLEClient class. Listing 4-1 shows most of the source code for this example.

Listing 4-1.

```
class Scanner extends BLEClient {
    onReady() {
        this.startScanning();
    }
    onDiscovered(device) {
        let scanResponse = device.scanResponse;
        let completeName = scanResponse.completeName;
        if (completeName)
            trace(`${completeName}\n`);
    }
}
```

The Scanner class implements two BLEClient callbacks:

- The onReady callback is invoked when the BLE stack is ready to use. In this example, the onReady callback calls startScanning to enable scanning for nearby Peripherals.

- The onDiscovered callback is invoked one or more times for each Peripheral discovered. In this example, the onDiscovered callback traces the discovered Peripheral's name to the console.

With this simple example, your Central discovers Peripherals around you and tells you their names. Now you're ready to go a step further: the next example demonstrates how to use other features of the `BLEClient` class to create a BLE device that communicates with a virtual Peripheral.

Creating Two-Way Communication

The `$EXAMPLES/ch4-ble/text-client` example implements a Central that connects to a Peripheral and receives text data via characteristic value change notifications.

To see the example working, you'll need a Peripheral that provides the text data characteristic. You can create one using Bluefruit, a mobile app available for free on iOS and Android devices. To create the Peripheral, take the following steps, illustrated in Figures 4-2 and 4-3:

1. Download and open Bluefruit and enter Peripheral mode. In the ADVERTISING INFO section, change the **Local Name** field to esp.

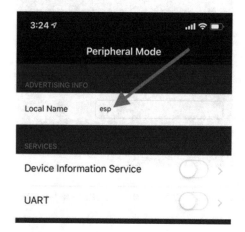

Figure 4-2. *Peripheral mode in Bluefruit*

2.   Make sure the UART service is turned on.

Figure 4-3. *UART service enabled*

The next sections explain the code that runs on the ESP32 to implement the Central device.

Connecting to the Peripheral

The constants at the top of the application correspond to the device name you set in Bluefruit and the service and characteristic UUID used by the UART service:

```
const PERIPHERAL_NAME = 'esp';
const SERVICE_UUID = uuid`6E400001B5A3F393E0A9E50E24DCCA9E`;
const CHARACTERISTIC_UUID = uuid`6E400003B5A3F393E0A9E50E24DCCA9E`;
```

Like the scanner example, this example implements the onReady and onDiscovered callbacks, as shown in Listing 4-2. But instead of just tracing the names of devices to the console, this example checks the name of each discovered Peripheral to see if it matches the PERIPHERAL_NAME constant. If it does, it stops scanning for Peripherals and calls the connect method, which initiates a connection request between the BLEClient and a target Peripheral device.

Listing 4-2.

```
class TextClient extends BLEClient {
    onReady() {
        this.startScanning();
    }
    onDiscovered(device) {
        if (PERIPHERAL_NAME ===
                device.scanResponse.completeName) {
            this.stopScanning();
            this.connect(device);
        }
    }
}
    ...
```

The argument to connect is an instance of the Device class, representing a single Peripheral. BLEClient automatically creates instances of the Device class when a Peripheral is discovered; applications do not instantiate them directly. Applications do, however, interact with instances of the Device class directly—for example, by calling methods to perform GATT service and characteristic discovery.

The onConnected Callback

The onConnected method is a callback that's invoked when the Central connects to a Peripheral. This example calls the device object's discoverPrimaryService method to obtain the primary GATT service from the Peripheral. The argument to discoverPrimaryService is the UUID of the service to discover.

```
onConnected(device) {
    device.discoverPrimaryService(SERVICE_UUID);
}
```

You can discover all of the primary services of a Peripheral using the discoverAllPrimaryServices method. For example, the onConnected callback could instead be written as follows:

```
onConnected(device) {
    device.discoverAllPrimaryServices();
}
```

The onServices Callback

The onServices method is a callback that's invoked when service discovery is complete. The services argument is an array of service objects—instances of the Service class—each of which provides access to a single service. If discoverPrimaryService was called to find a single service, the services array contains only the one service found.

As shown in Listing 4-3, this example checks to see if the Peripheral provides a service with the UUID that matches the one defined by the SERVICE_UUID constant. If it does, it calls the service object's discoverCharacteristic method to look for the service characteristic with the UUID that matches the one defined by the CHARACTERISTIC_UUID constant.

Listing 4-3.

```
onServices(services) {
    let service = services.find(service =>
            service.uuid.equals(SERVICE_UUID));
    if (service) {
        trace(`Found service\n`);
        service.discoverCharacteristic(CHARACTERISTIC_UUID);
    }
    else
        trace(`Service not found\n`);
}
```

You can discover all of the service characteristics using the discoverAllCharacteristics method. For example, the onServices callback could replace the line that calls discoverCharacteristic with the following line:

```
service.discoverAllCharacteristics();
```

The onCharacteristics Callback

The onCharacteristics method is a callback that's invoked when characteristic discovery is complete. The characteristics argument is an array of characteristic objects—instances of the Characteristic class—each of which provides access to a single service characteristic.

If discoverCharacteristic was called to find a single characteristic, the characteristics array contains the single characteristic found.

When the desired characteristic is found, the example calls the characteristic object's enableNotifications method to enable notifications when the characteristic's value changes, as shown in Listing 4-4.

Listing 4-4.

```
onCharacteristics(characteristics) {
    let characteristic = characteristics.find(characteristic =>
            characteristic.uuid.equals(CHARACTERISTIC_UUID));
    if (characteristic) {
        trace(`Enabling notifications\n`);
        characteristic.enableNotifications();
    }
    else
        trace(`Characteristic not found\n`);
}
```

If you set up your Peripheral correctly, you'll see the following messages in the debug console when you run the text-client application:

```
Found service
Enabling notifications
```

Receiving Notifications

After notifications are enabled, you can send notifications to the Client by changing the value of the Peripheral's characteristic from your smart phone. To change the value, tap the **UART** button. This will take you to the screen shown in Figure 4-4. Enter text in the input field at the bottom of the screen and tap **Send** to update the characteristic value.

Figure 4-4. *UART screen in Bluefruit*

The characteristic value is delivered to the Client through the onCharacteristicNotification callback in an ArrayBuffer. This example assumes the value is a string, so it converts the ArrayBuffer to a string using String.fromArrayBuffer (a feature of XS to make it easier for applications to work with binary data). There is a parallel ArrayBuffer.fromString. These are not part of the JavaScript language standard.

```
onCharacteristicNotification(characteristic, buffer) {
    trace(String.fromArrayBuffer(buffer)+"\n");
}
```

Creating a Heart Rate Monitor

Now that you know the basics of implementing a Client that receives notifications from a Server, this example will show you how to use features of the BLEServer class to implement a Peripheral that takes on the Server role after connecting to a Central.

The $EXAMPLES/ch4-ble/hrm example advertises the standard Heart Rate and Battery services, accepts connection requests from Centrals, sends notifications for simulated heart rate values, and responds to read requests from a Client for a simulated battery level. The next few sections explain how it's implemented using the BLEServer class.

Defining and Deploying Services

GATT services are defined in JSON files located in the host's bleservices directory. The JSON is automatically converted to platform-specific native code at build time, and the compiled object code is linked to the application.

Each GATT service is defined in its own JSON file. Listing 4-5 shows the standard Heart Rate service.

Listing 4-5.

```
{
    "service": {
        "uuid": "180D",
        "characteristics": {
            "bpm": {
```

```
        "uuid": "2A37",
        "maxBytes": 2,
        "type": "Array",
        "permissions": "read",
        "properties": "notify"
      }
    }
  }
}
```

Here are explanations of some of the important properties:

- The uuid property of the service object is the number assigned to the service by the GATT specification. The Heart Rate service has the UUID 180F.

- The characteristics object describes each characteristic supported by the service. Each immediate property is the name of a characteristic. In this example there is just one characteristic: bpm, which stands for beats per minute.

- The uuid property of a characteristic object is the unique number assigned to the characteristic by the GATT specification. The bpm characteristic of the Heart Rate service has the UUID 2A37.

- The type property specifies the type of the characteristic value used in your JavaScript code. The BLEServer class uses the value of the type property to convert the binary data transferred by the Client to JavaScript types. This saves your Server code the work of converting back and forth between different types of data (ArrayBuffer, String, Number, and so on).

- The permissions property defines whether the
  characteristic is read-only, write-only, or read/write
  and whether accessing the characteristic requires an
  encrypted connection. The bpm property is read-only
  because in a heart rate monitor, the beats per minute
  is determined by sensor readings and consequently
  cannot be written by a Client. The read permission
  indicates that a Client can read the characteristic
  over a nonencrypted or encrypted connection; use
  readEncrypted when the value is only accessible
  over an encrypted connection. Similarly, use write
  or writeEncrypted for write permissions. To indicate
  that a characteristic supports both reading and
  writing, include both a read and a write value in
  the permissions string, separated by a comma—for
  example, "readEncrypted,writeEncrypted".

- The properties property defines the characteristic's
  properties. It may be read, write, notify, indicate,
  or a combination of those (comma-separated). The
  read and write values permit reads and writes of the
  characteristic value, notify permits the Server to notify
  the Client of changes to the characteristic value without
  its being requested and without acknowledgment that
  the notification was received, and indicate is the same
  as notify except that it requires acknowledgment that
  the notification was received before another indication
  can be sent.

Once the BLE stack completes its initialization, it invokes the
onReady callback. The hrm example implementation of onReady initiates
advertising, enabling its services to be discovered by Clients. The following
section explains how the subclass manages when advertising is active.

Advertising

Peripherals broadcast advertisement data to announce themselves. The BLEServer class has a startAdvertising method to begin broadcasting advertisement packets and a stopAdvertising method to stop.

The hrm example calls startAdvertising when the BLE stack is ready to use and also when the connection to a Central is lost. When startAdvertising is called, the Peripheral broadcasts its advertising data type flags value, its name, and its services (Heart Rate and Battery), as shown in Listing 4-6. The UUIDs for the Heart Rate and Battery services come from the GATT specification.

Listing 4-6.

```
this.startAdvertising({
    advertisingData: {
        flags: 6,
        completeName: this.deviceName,
        completeUUID16List: [uuid`180D`, uuid`180F`]
    }
});
```

When a connection is successfully established to a Central, the Peripheral stops sending advertising packets, as it supports only a single connection at a time:

```
onConnected() {
    this.stopAdvertising();
}
```

When the connection is lost, the Peripheral again starts advertising.

A BLE advertisement may contain additional data—for example, to implement a BLE beacon. BLE beacons advertise data for many Centrals to see without connecting to them. The code in Listing 4-7 is from the examples/network/ble/uri-beacon example in the Moddable SDK, which implements a UriBeacon that advertises the Moddable website. The UUID here comes from the Assigned Numbers specification (see bluetooth.com/specifications/assigned-numbers/16-bit-uuids-for-members). The encodeData method encodes the URI in the format specified by the UriBeacon spec. See the uri-beacon example for the source code.

Listing 4-7.

```
this.startAdvertising({
    advertisingData: {
        completeUUID16List: [uuid`FED8`],
        serviceDataUUID16: {
            uuid: uuid`FED8`,
            data: this.encodeData("http://www.moddable.com")
        }
    }
});
```

Advertising data only transmits data; there is no way to reply. Bidirectional communication requires one device to take on the GATT Client role and one device to take on the GATT Server role. Before this can happen, the connection process defined by GAP must be complete.

Establishing a Connection

Once the heart rate Peripheral starts advertising, it waits for a Central to request to connect to it. You can use any of a variety of mobile apps to create a Central that does this. In this section, you'll use LightBlue, which is available for free on iOS and Android devices. LightBlue has a Central mode that enables you to scan for, connect to, and send read/write requests to Peripherals. You can use it as the Client for your Peripheral by taking the following steps:

1. Run the example on your ESP32.

2. Download and open LightBlue and wait for the
   Heart Rate Monitor Peripheral to appear, as shown
   in Figure 4-5.

Figure 4-5. Heart Rate Monitor *Peripheral in LightBlue*
Peripherals list

3. Tap the **Heart Rate Monitor** Peripheral to establish a connection to it.

The onConnected callback is invoked when a Central connects to the heart rate Peripheral. In this example, it stops broadcasting advertisement and responding to scan response packets, as shown in Listing 4-8.

Listing 4-8.

```
class HeartRateService extends BLEServer {
    ...
    onConnected() {
        this.stopAdvertising();
    }
    ...
}
```

Sending Notifications

BLE Clients may request notifications for characteristics that have the notify property, such as the bpm characteristic in this example. When notifications are enabled, Servers notify the Client of changes to the characteristic's value without the Server's having to request the value. Notifications save energy, a key feature of the design of BLE, by eliminating the need for the Client to poll the Server for changes in characteristics.

To receive notifications for the simulated heart rate in LightBlue, take the following steps (as illustrated in Figures 4-6, 4-7, and 4-8):

1. Tap the **Heart Rate Measurement** characteristic.

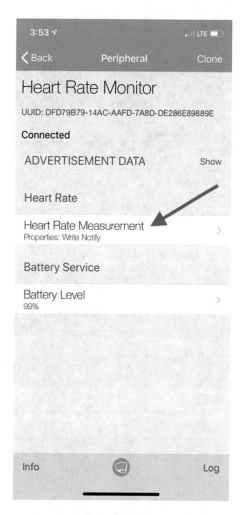

Figure 4-6. *Heart Rate Monitor characteristics screen with **Heart Rate Measurement** button*

2. Tap **Listen for notifications** to enable notifications.

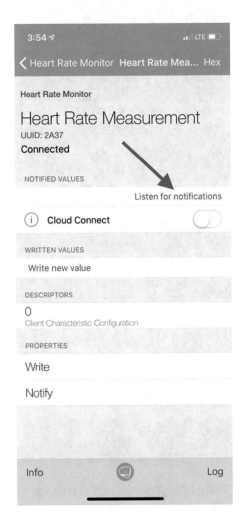

Figure 4-7. *Heart Rate Measurement screen with* ***Listen for notifications*** *button*

3. Watch the simulated heart rate values appear.

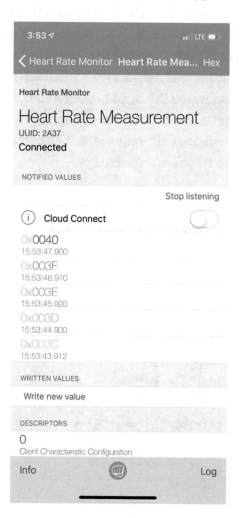

Figure 4-8. *Heart rate values appearing in NOTIFIED VALUES section*

Now let's take a look at the code that implements notifications for the Heart Rate service on the Server side. The onCharacteristicNotifyEnabled method is a callback that's invoked when a Client enables notifications on a characteristic. The onCharacteristicNotifyDisabled method is a callback that's invoked when a Client disables notifications on a characteristic. The characteristic argument for both is an instance of the Characteristic class, which provides access to a single service characteristic.

The onCharacteristicNotifyEnabled method (shown in Listing 4-9) calls the notifyValue method, which sends a characteristic value change notification to the connected Client, at 1,000-millisecond (1-second) intervals. This simulates a heart rate sensor, although a real heart rate monitor would not send periodic updates; rather, it would send a notification when the value actually changes.

Listing 4-9.

```
onCharacteristicNotifyEnabled(characteristic) {
    this.bump = +1;
    this.timer = Timer.repeat(id => {
        this.notifyValue(characteristic, this.bpm);
        this.bpm[1] += this.bump;
        if (this.bpm[1] === 65) {
            this.bump = -1;
            this.bpm[1] = 64;
        }
        else if (this.bpm[1] === 55) {
            this.bump = +1;
            this.bpm[1] = 56;
        }
    }, 1000);
}
```

The onCharacteristicNotifyDisabled method (Listing 4-10) ends the sending of notifications by calling the stopMeasurements method.

Listing 4-10.

```
onCharacteristicNotifyDisabled(characteristic) {
    this.stopMeasurements();
}
...
stopMeasurements() {
    if (this.timer) {
        Timer.clear(this.timer);
        delete this.timer;
    }
    this.bpm = [0, 60]; // flags, beats per minute
}
```

Responding to Read Requests

Clients may request the value of characteristics that support the read property, like the Battery service in this example. To send requests to read the value of the simulated battery level in LightBlue, take the following steps (as illustrated in Figures 4-9, 4-10, and 4-11):

1. Tap the **Battery Level** characteristic.

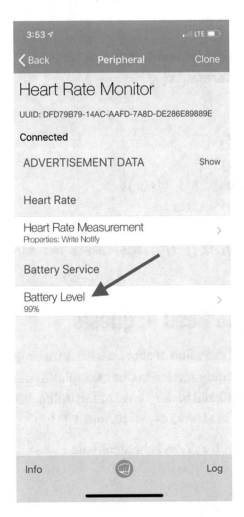

Figure 4-9. *Heart Rate Monitor characteristics screen with **Battery Level** button*

2. Tap **Read again**.

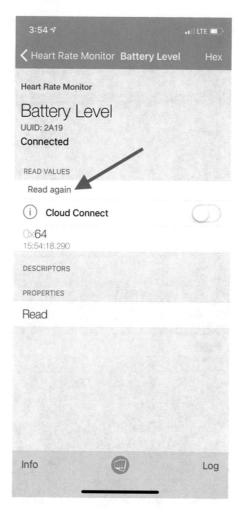

Figure 4-10. *Battery Level screen with **Read again** button*

3. Watch the simulated battery level appear.

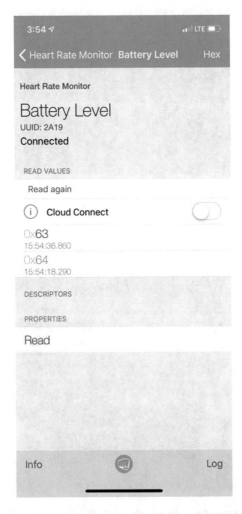

Figure 4-11. *Battery level value appearing in READ VALUES section*

Now let's take a look at the code that handles the battery level service notifications. The onCharacteristicRead method (Listing 4-11) is a callback that's invoked when a Client reads a service characteristic value on demand. The BLEServer instance is responsible for handling the read request. In this example, the battery level starts at 100; each time it's read, the callback returns the value and decrements it by 1.

Listing 4-11.

```
onCharacteristicRead(params) {
    if (params.name === "battery") {
        if (this.battery === 0)
            this.battery = 100;
            return this.battery--;
    }
}
```

Establishing Secure Communication

The Moddable SDK supports enhanced security features introduced in version 4.2 of the Bluetooth Core Specification: LE Secure Connections with Numeric Comparison, Passkey Entry, and Just Works pairing methods. Both the BLEClient and BLEServer classes have an optional securityParameters property that requests that devices establish an LE Secure Connection. The pairing method used depends on the devices' capabilities and options set in the securityParameters property. Security callback functions are hosted by the BLEClient and BLEServer classes. The next section walks through a simple example.

Secure Heart Rate Monitor

The $EXAMPLES/ch4-ble/hrm-secure example is a secure version of the $EXAMPLES/ch4-ble/hrm example that requires passkey entry for pairing.

Again, you can use LightBlue as the Client. Follow the same steps as before, and when you're prompted to enter the code from the heart rate monitor (as shown in Figure 4-12), enter the passkey traced to the console in xsbug (Figure 4-13).

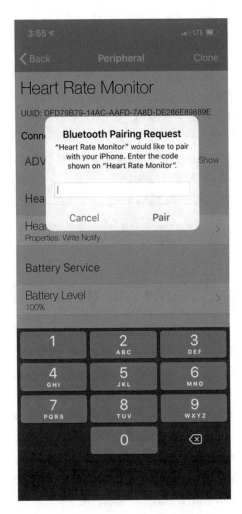

Figure 4-12. *Prompt to enter code in LightBlue*

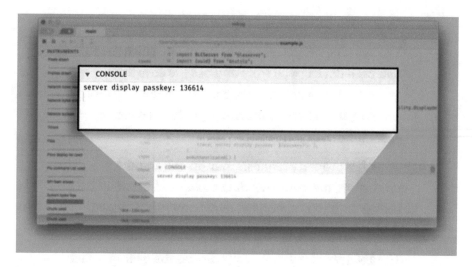

Figure 4-13. *Passkey in debug console*

Now you can enable notifications for the heart rate value and read the battery value on demand as before, but the connection between the Server and Client is secure.

The code has just a few differences from the $EXAMPLES/ch4-ble/hrm example. As shown in Listing 4-12, the onReady callback includes additional code to configure the device security requirements and I/O capabilities of the Peripheral.

Listing 4-12.

```
this.securityParameters = {
    bonding: true,
    mitm: true,
    ioCapability: IOCapability.DisplayOnly
};
```

The properties in this code specify the following:

- The bonding property enables bonding, which means that both devices will store and use the keys they exchange the next time they connect. Without bonding enabled, the devices will have to go through pairing every time they connect.

- The mitm property requests man-in-the-middle protection, meaning that data exchanged between two paired devices is encrypted to prevent an untrusted device from eavesdropping.

- The ioCapability property indicates the user interface capabilities for the device related to confirming the passkey. This device doesn't have a display, but it has display capability because it can trace to the debug console. Other Peripherals may have more input/output capabilities (for example, a device with a keyboard) or fewer input/output capabilities (such as a device with no way to display text). The ioCapability properties of both devices are used to determine the pairing method. For example, if neither device has a keyboard or display, the Just Works pairing method is used.

Two additional callbacks of the BLEServer class are implemented (see Listing 4-13):

- The onPasskeyDisplay callback is invoked when you try to establish a connection to the Peripheral. In this case, it's called when you tap the name of the Peripheral in LightBlue. As you saw before, this example traces the passkey to the debug console.

- The onAuthenticated callback is invoked after successful device pairing. This example simply changes the authenticated property to indicate that a secure connection was established.

Listing 4-13.

```
onPasskeyDisplay(params) {
    let passkey = this.passkeyToString(params.passkey);
    trace(`server display passkey: ${passkey}\n`);
}
onAuthenticated() {
    this.authenticated = true;
}
```

The Server checks that the authenticated property is set when the Client enables notifications. The code inside the if block looks the same as the onCharacteristicNotifyEnabled method of the hrm example.

```
onCharacteristicNotifyEnabled(characteristic) {
    if (this.authenticated) {
        ...
}
```

The Server also defines an additional helper method, named passkeyToString. Passkey values are integers and must always include six digits when displayed to the user. This method pads the passkey with leading zeros, when necessary, for display.

```
passkeyToString(passkey) {
    return passkey.toString().padStart(6, "0");
}
```

Conclusion

Now that you understand the essentials of these examples, there's a lot you can do with BLE on your ESP32. Instead of connecting to virtual Peripherals that you create in LightBlue, you can connect to BLE products in your home. Instead of sending simulated data like the heart rate monitor example, you can send actual sensor data from your favorite off-the-shelf sensors.

If you want to try more BLE examples, see the `examples/network/ble` directory in the Moddable SDK on GitHub. Examples that enable your device to become a URI-transmitting beacon, pair your device with the iPhone Music app, and more are available. If you want to learn more about the BLE API of the Moddable SDK, see the `documentation/network/ble` directory.

CHAPTER 5

Files and Data

Nearly every product has some data that it needs to ensure is available across restarts of the device, even if power is lost. On microcontrollers, flash memory is typically used for this non-volatile storage (NVS) memory. The same flash memory that holds the code of your application also stores the data your application uses and the data it creates. Here are some kinds of data your application might store:

- Read-only data, such as the images that make up the user interface of your product or files containing static web pages served from an embedded web server

- Small pieces of data that are both read and written—for example, user preferences and other long-term state

- Large collections of data that are created as your product monitors operations—for example, while gathering data from its sensors

On computers and mobile devices, it's common to use the file system for most, if not all, data storage needs. However, because of the constraints of embedded systems—code size limitations, highly constrained RAM, and severe performance constraints—the firmware often doesn't even include a file system.

© Peter Hoddie and Lizzie Prader 2020
P. Hoddie and L. Prader, *IoT Development for ESP32 and ESP8266 with JavaScript*,
https://doi.org/10.1007/978-1-4842-5070-9_5

This chapter explains three different ways to work with stored data on embedded systems: files, preferences, and resources. The final section introduces direct access to flash memory, an advanced technique that provides the greatest flexibility.

When building your product, choose the data storage methods that best match your needs. Before assuming that files are the right choice, consider preferences and resources, which are lighter-weight ways to work with stored data.

Installing the Files and Data Host

You can run all of the examples referred to in this chapter by following the pattern described in Chapter 1: install the host on your device using mcconfig, then install example applications using mcrun.

The host is in the $EXAMPLES/ch5-files/host directory. Navigate to this directory from the command line and install it with mcconfig.

Files

The ESP32 and ESP8266 use SPIFFS (Serial Peripheral Interface Flash File System) for their file system in flash memory. SPIFFS is designed specifically for working with the NOR (NOT OR) flash memory used with many microcontrollers. While SPIFFS is nowhere near as fully featured as the file systems on a computer, it provides all the fundamental features you'll need.

When using files on an embedded device, it's important to keep in mind these limitations of the file system implementation:

- SPIFFS is a flat file system, meaning that there are no real directories. All files are together in the SPIFFS root directory.

- File names are limited to 32 bytes.

- There are no file permissions or locks. All files may be read, written, and deleted.

- The length of time for a write is unpredictable. It's often fast, but when the file system needs to consolidate blocks it may block for some time.

This section focuses on accessing files using SPIFFS, which is available without adding any hardware and has a relatively small code size. On the ESP32, these same APIs may also be used to access an SD memory card formatted using the FAT32 file system.

File Classes

All access to the file system is done using classes in the file module:

```
import {File, Iterator, System} from "file";
```

The file module exports these three classes, as explained in detail in the following sections:

- The File class performs operations on individual files, including read, write, delete, and rename.

- The Iterator class returns the contents of a directory. On a flat file system like SPIFFS, Iterator is only available for the root directory.

- The System class provides information about the file system storage, including total amount of storage and free space available.

File Paths

File paths are the strings you use to identify files and directories. The file module uses the slash character (/) to separate the parts of a path, as in /spiffs/data.txt.

Although SPIFFS is a flat file system with no subdirectories, it's accessed with a root of /spiffs/ instead of / to support embedded devices that have more than one file system—for example, a built-in flash file system and an external SD card.

On the desktop simulator, the root varies based on the host platform. For example, on macOS, the default file system root is /Users/Shared/. When you write code intended to work in more than one environment, you can use the predefined value in the mc/config module to find the root for your host platform.

```
import config from "mc/config";

const root = config.file.root;
```

Because there may be multiple file systems, this root is just a convenient default place for files, not necessarily the sole file system available.

Each file system may have a different limit for the length of a file or directory name. Use the System.config static method to retrieve the maximum length for names in a specified root.

```
const spiffsConfig = System.config("/spiffs/");
let name = "this is a very long file name.txt";
if (name.length > spiffsConfig.maxPathLength)
    throw new Error("file name too long");
```

File Operations

This section describes methods that perform operations on a file, including deleting, creating, and opening. There are no methods to read or write the full content of a file, as that would often fail due to memory limitations; later sections introduce techniques for reading and writing.

Determining Whether a File Exists

Use the static `exists` method of the `File` class to determine whether a file exists:

```
if (File.exists(root + "test.txt"))
    trace("file exists\n");
else
    trace("files does not exist\n");
```

Deleting a File

To delete a file, use the static `delete` method of the `File` class:

```
File.delete(root + "goaway.txt");
```

The `delete` method returns `true` if successful and `false` otherwise. If the file doesn't exist, `delete` returns `true` rather than throw an error, so there's no need to surround its invocation with a `try/catch` block. The method does throw an error if the delete operation fails, but this happens only in rare circumstances, such as when the flash memory is worn out or the file system data structures are corrupt.

Renaming a File

To rename a file, use the static `rename` method of the `File` class. The first argument is the full path of the file to rename, whereas the second argument is only the new name.

```
File.rename(root + "oldname.txt", "newname.txt");
```

Note   The `rename` method is only for renaming a file. On file systems that support subdirectories, `rename` cannot be used to move a file from one directory to another.

Opening a File

To open a file, create an instance of the File class. The File constructor's first parameter is the full path of the file to open. The optional second parameter is true to open in write mode (creating the file if it doesn't exist) and either absent or false to open in read mode. Here's an example of opening a file in read mode:

```
let file = new File(root + "test.txt");
```

The following example opens a file in write mode, creating the file if it doesn't exist:

```
let file = new File(root + "test.txt", true);
```

The File constructor throws an error if there's an error in opening a file, such as trying to open a nonexistent file in read mode.

When you're done accessing a file, close the file instance to free the system resources it's using:

```
file.close();
```

Writing to a File

This section introduces techniques for writing data to a file. You can use the File class to write both text and binary data. A file must be opened in write mode, or write operations will throw an error. To open in write mode, pass true as the second argument to the File constructor.

The file system automatically grows the file when you write data beyond the current size. There's no support for truncating a file. To reduce a file's size, create another file and copy the needed data into it from the original file.

Writing Text

The write method of the File class determines the kind of data you want to write from the type of the JavaScript object you pass to the call. To write text, pass a string. The following code from the $EXAMPLES/ch5-files/files example writes a single string to a file:

```
let file = new File(root + "test.txt", true);
file.write("this is a test");
file.close();
```

Strings are always written as UTF-8 data.

Writing Binary Data

To write binary data to a file, pass an ArrayBuffer to write. The following code from the $EXAMPLES/ch5-files/files example writes five 32-bit unsigned integers to a file. The values are in a Uint32Array, which uses an ArrayBuffer for its storage. The call to write gets the ArrayBuffer from the buffer property of the bytes array.

```
let bytes = Uint32Array.of(0, 1, 2, 3, 4);
let file = new File(root + "test.bin", true);
file.write(bytes.buffer);
file.close();
```

To write bytes (8-bit unsigned values), pass an integer value as the argument (see Listing 5-1).

Listing 5-1.

```
let file = new File(root + "test.bin", true);
file.write(1);
file.write(2);
file.write(3);
file.close();
```

227

Getting File Size

To determine the size of a file in bytes, you first open the file and then check its length property:

```
let file = new File(root + "test.txt");
let length = file.length;
trace(`test.txt is ${length} bytes\n`);
file.close();
```

The length property is read-only. It cannot be set to change the size of the file.

Writing Mixed Types

The write method lets you pass multiple arguments to write several pieces of data in a single call. This executes a little faster and keeps your code a little smaller. The following example writes an ArrayBuffer, four bytes, and one string in a single call to write:

```
let bytes = Uint32Array.of(0x01020304, 0x05060708);
let file = new File(root + "test.bin", true);
file.write(bytes.buffer, 9, 10, 11 12, "ONE TWO!");
file.close();
```

A hex dump of the file after the write looks like this:

```
04 03 02 01 08 07 06 05    .... ....
09 0A 0B 0C 79 78 69 32    .... ONE
84 87 79 33                TWO!
```

You might expect the first four bytes to be 01 02 03 04, but remember that instances of TypedArray, which includes Uint32Array, are stored in the host platform's byte order, and the ESP32 and ESP8266 microcontrollers are both little-endian devices.

Reading from a File

This section introduces techniques for retrieving data from a file. You can use the File class to read both text and binary data. Most files are one or the other—all binary or all text data—though this is not required.

The File class supports reading a file in pieces, which enables you to control the maximum memory used when reading from the file.

Reading Text

Sometimes it's useful to retrieve the entire contents of a file as a single text string. You do this by calling the read method with a single argument of String, which tells the file instance to read from the current position to the end of the file and put the result in a string. The following code from the $EXAMPLES/ch5-files/files example reads the contents from the test.txt file created earlier:

```
let file = new File(root + "test.txt");
let string = file.read(String);
trace(string + "\n");
file.close();
```

The read method always starts reading from the current position. In this case, since the file has just been opened, the current position is 0, the start of the file.

Reading Text in Pieces

You may also use the read method to retrieve parts of a file, to minimize peak memory use. The optional second argument to read indicates the maximum number of bytes to read. This is the number of bytes that are read, with one exception: if reading the requested number of bytes would pass the end of the file, the text from the current position to the end of the file is read.

The example in Listing 5-2 reads a file in ten-byte pieces and traces them to the console. It compares the position property to the length property to determine when it has read all data from the file.

Listing 5-2.

```
let file = new File(root + "test.txt");
while (file.position < file.length) {
    let string = file.read(String, 10);
    trace(string + "\n");
}
file.close();
```

On a computer, you might memory-map the file to simplify access to the data; however, that approach is not generally available on microcontrollers, as they typically lack an MMU (memory management unit) to perform the mapping. If you want to memory-map read-only data, resources are a good alternative, as explained later in this chapter.

Reading Binary Data

To read the entire file as binary data, call read with the single argument ArrayBuffer. The following code from the $EXAMPLES/ch5-files/files example reads the contents from the test.bin file created earlier:

```
let file = new File(root + "test.bin");
let buffer = file.read(ArrayBuffer);
file.close();
```

As when reading text, the binary read starts from the current position, which is 0 when the file opened, and continues to the end of the file. The data is returned in an ArrayBuffer. The following example wraps the returned buffer in a Uint8Array and displays the hexadecimal byte values on the console:

```
let bytes = new Uint8Array(buffer);
for (let i = 0; i < bytes.length; i++)
    trace(bytes[i].toString(16).padStart(2, "0"), "\n");
```

Reading Binary Data in Pieces

The read method may also be used to retrieve binary data from arbitrary locations in a file. The example in Listing 5-3 reads the last four bytes of the file and displays the result as a 32-bit unsigned integer. The read location is specified by setting the position property to four bytes from the end of the file.

Listing 5-3.

```
let file = new File(root + "test.bin");
file.position = file.length - 4;
let buffer = file.read(ArrayBuffer, 4);
file.close();
let value = (new Uint32(buffer))[0];
```

Directories

The SPIFFS file system implements only a single directory, the root directory. Other file systems, such as FAT32, support an arbitrary number of subdirectories. In all cases, you use the Iterator class of the file module to list the files and subdirectories contained in a directory.

Iterating over Directories

Retrieving a list of the items in a directory is a two-step process. First you create an instance of the Iterator class for the directory over which to iterate; then you call the next method of the iterator to retrieve each item. When all items have been returned, the iterator returns undefined. Listing 5-4 from the $EXAMPLES/ch5-files/files example traces the files and directories contained in the root directory to the console.

Listing 5-4.

```
let iterator = new Iterator(root);
let item;
while (item = iterator.next()) {
    if (undefined === item.length)
        trace(`${item.name.padEnd(32)} directory\n`);
    else
        trace(`${item.name.padEnd(32)} file ${item.length}` +
            "bytes\n");
}
```

The next method returns an object with properties that describe the item. The name property is always present. The length property is present only for files and indicates the number of bytes in the file. There's no separate property to indicate whether the item is a file or directory, as the presence of the length property is sufficient for this purpose.

The iterator instance has a close method, which may be called to free the system resources used by the iterator. This is not usually necessary, however, because the iterator implementation automatically frees any system resources when it reaches the end of the items.

The Iterator class returns one item at a time, rather than a list of all items, to keep memory use to a minimum. The order in which items are returned depends on the underlying file system implementation. In the general case, you cannot assume, for example, that the items are returned in alphabetical order or that directories are returned before files.

Iterating with JavaScript Iterators

The JavaScript language provides an iterator feature that makes it easier to write code that uses iterators. For example, you can use the for-of loop syntax to iterate through the items. This language feature works with any instance that implements the *iterator protocol*, which the file module's Iterator class does. This approach is a little more concise for you to code, at the expense of using a little more memory and CPU time. Listing 5-5 adapts Listing 5-4 to use the JavaScript iterator.

Listing 5-5.

```
for (let item of new Iterator(root)) {
    if (undefined === item.length)
        trace(`${item.name.padEnd(32)} directory\n`);
    else
        trace(`${item.name.padEnd(32)} file ${item.length}` +
            "bytes\n");
}
```

Where iterators really shine is as inputs to functions that operate on iterators. For example, if you need an array containing all the items contained in a directory, you can simply pass the iterator instance to Array.from.

```
let items = Array.from(new Iterator(root));
```

Getting File System Information

The file module's System object contains an info method to provide information about each file system root. You use this method to determine the total number of bytes of storage available and the number of bytes currently in use.

```
let info = System.info(root);
trace(`Used ${info.used} of ${info.total}\n`);
```

Preferences

Preferences are another tool for storing data on a microcontroller in your IoT product. They're much more efficient than files but also much more limited. A file is well suited to storing a lot of information, whereas a preference stores only small pieces of information. Often in your product, you only need to keep track of a handful of user settings, and preferences are all you need for those situations; you may even exclude the file system entirely from your product.

Another advantage of using preferences is their reliability. The implementations of preferences for ESP32 and ESP8266 take steps to ensure that the preference data is not corrupted even if power is lost while the preferences are being updated. That level of reliability is more difficult to achieve in a file system, because the data structures are more complex.

The Preference Class

The preference module provides access to preferences. To use preferences in your code, import the Preference class from the preference module.

```
import Preference from "preference";
```

The JavaScript Preferences API introduced in this chapter is the same between microcontrollers; however, the underlying implementation is different. For example, on the ESP32, preferences are implemented using the NVS library in the ESP32 IDF SDK, whereas on the ESP8266, preferences are implemented by the Moddable SDK because there's no system-provided equivalent. Since the implementations are different, there also are differences in behavior. The following sections note the differences you need to keep in mind.

Preference Names

Each preference is identified by two values, a domain and a name. These are similar to a simple file system path: the domain is like the directory name, and the name is like the file name. For example, consider a Wi-Fi light, where you want to save the user settings to restore when the power is turned on. You could use a `light` domain for all the light state preferences, with `on`, `brightness`, and `color` for names. The light might keep statistics data (such as the number of times the light has been turned on) in another domain, such as `stats`.

The domain and name values of a preference are always strings. Names are limited to 15 bytes on the ESP32 and 31 bytes on the ESP8266.

Preference Data

Preferences are not intended to replace a file system; it's a common mistake to try to use them that way. Because the size of each individual preference is limited, as is the total storage available for all preferences, they're far less general than a file system.

Each preference has a data type: a boolean, a 32-bit signed integer, a string, or an `ArrayBuffer`. Floating-point numeric values are not supported. The string type is often the most convenient to use but is also often the least efficient use of storage space. It you need to combine several values in a single preference, consider using an `ArrayBuffer`.

When you write a value, the type of the value is established based on the data provided. To change the type, write the value again. When you read a value, the value returned has the same type as the value that was written.

Note these differences between preference data on the ESP32 and on the ESP8266:

- On the ESP32, the preference data space is configurable and is set to 16 KB in the hosts used in this book. On the ESP8266, the space for preference data is 4 KB.

- On the ESP32, each preference may be up to 4,000 bytes of data; on the ESP8266, this value is limited to 64 bytes. If you're writing code that you expect to run on several different microcontroller platforms, you need to design your preference values for the 64-byte data size.

Reading and Writing Preferences

Because preferences are just small pieces of data with a type, they're much easier to read and write than a file. Listing 5-6 from the $EXAMPLES/ch5-files/preferences example writes four preferences to the example domain. The type of each value is used as the preference name. The set implementation determines the type of the preference based on the value passed in the third argument.

Listing 5-6.

```
Preference.set("example", "boolean", true);
Preference.set("example", "integer", 1);
Preference.set("example", "string", "my value");
Preference.set("example", "arraybuffer",
               Uint8Array.of(1, 2, 3).buffer);
```

Use the static get call to retrieve preference values, as shown in Listing 5-7. The type of the value returned matches the type of the value used in the set call.

Listing 5-7.

```
let a = Preference.get("example", "boolean");     // true
let b = Preference.get("example", "integer");     // 1
let c = Preference.get("example", "string");      // "my value"
let d = Preference.get("example", "arraybuffer");
        // ArrayBuffer of [1, 2, 3]
```

If no preference is found with the specified domain and name, the get call returns undefined:

```
let on = Preference.get("light", "on");
if (undefined === on)
    on = false;
```

Deleting Preferences

Use the delete method to remove a preference:

```
Preference.delete("example", "integer");
```

No error is thrown if a preference cannot be found with the specified domain and name. If there's an error while updating flash memory to remove the preference, delete throws an error.

Don't Use JSON

When building products in JavaScript for the web or computers, it's common to store preferences using JSON—an approach that's extremely easy to code and is flexible. It's tempting to do the same when creating an embedded product using JavaScript; however, although it works in some products, it isn't recommended, because it's more likely to lead to failures later in the development process. Consider the following:

- Storing preferences in a JSON file requires that your project include a file system—a large body of code that takes up some of the limited space in your flash memory.

- A JSON object must be loaded into memory all at once, which means that accessing one preference value requires enough memory to hold all preference values.

- Loading the JSON string data from a file and then parsing it to JavaScript objects takes considerably more time than just loading one value from a preference.

- File systems are generally less error-resilient to power failures than preferences. Consequently, there's a higher chance that user settings will be lost.

Using JSON may also seem like a good way to store several values in a single preference. This does work, but it has two limitations that make it an inadvisable choice in many cases. First, because preference data is limited to just 64 bytes on some devices, you cannot combine many values this way. Second, the overhead of the JSON format almost certainly means the preference data uses more storage than other methods. For example, the following code uses 24 bytes of storage to store three small integer values as JSON:

```
Preference.set("example", "json",
                JSON.stringify({a: 1, b: 2, c: 3}));
```

In contrast, this example requires just three bytes by using Uint8Array:

```
Preference.set("example", "bytes",
                Uint8Array.of(1, 2, 3).buffer);
```

Reading the values from the JSON version is easier:

```
let pref = JSON.parse(Preference.get("example", "json"));
```

Reading the values from the more storage-efficient version requires an additional line of code:

```
let pref = new Uint8Array(Preference.get("example", "bytes"));
pref = {a: pref[0], b: pref[1], c: pref[2]};
```

Security

The preference module provides no guarantees about the security of preference data. The domain, name, and value may be stored "in the clear" without any encryption or obfuscation. As with user data in files, you should take appropriate steps in your product to ensure that user data is adequately protected. Examples of sensitive user data that are commonly stored in IoT products are Wi-Fi passwords and cloud service account identifiers. At a minimum, you should consider applying some form of encryption to these values so that they cannot be read by an attacker scanning the flash memory of the device.

Some hosts do provide encrypted storage for preference data. With additional configuration, this is available on the ESP32, for example.

Resources

Resources are a tool for working with read-only data. They're the most efficient way to embed large pieces of data in your project. Resources are usually accessed in place in flash memory, where they're stored, and therefore use no RAM no matter how large the resource data is. The Moddable SDK uses resources for many different purposes, including TLS certificates, images, and audio, but there's no restriction on the kind of data you can store in a resource.

The `$EXAMPLES/ch5-files/resources` example hosts a simple web page defined by `mydata.dat`, which is included as a resource. After you run the example, open a web browser and enter the IP address of your device, and you'll see a web page that says "Hello, world".

Adding Resources to a Project

Including a resource in your project requires two steps:

1. You add a file containing the resource data to your project. Often the resource files are placed in a subdirectory such as `assets`, `data`, or `resources`, but you can store them anywhere you like.

2. You add the file to the `resources` section of your manifest to tell the build tools to copy the file's data to a resource.

Listing 5-8 is from the `resources` example's manifest. It includes just one resource, `mydata.dat`, from the directory containing the manifest.

Listing 5-8.

```
"resources": {
    "*": [
        "./mydata"
    ],
},
```

The data file must have a `.dat` extension. However, the file name in the manifest must not include the extension; the build tools automatically locate your file with the `.dat` extension. It's important that you do not include several files with the same name but different extensions (for example, `mydata.dat` and `mydata.bin`), as the tools may not find the one you expect first.

This chapter describes resource data that's copied directly from your input file to the output binary without any changes. The build tools also have the ability to apply transformations to the data, such as converting images to a format optimized for your target microcontroller; Chapter 8 explains how to use resource transformations.

Accessing Resources

To access a resource, import the Resource class from the resource module:

```
import Resource from "resource";
```

You call the Resource class constructor with the path of the resource from the manifest. Note that the path always includes the file extension—.dat in this case.

```
let data = new Resource("mydata.dat");
```

The Resource constructor throws an error if it cannot find the requested resource. If you want to check whether a resource exists before calling the constructor, use the static exists method:

```
if (Resource.exists("mydata.dat")) {
    let data = new Resource("mydata.dat");
    ...
}
```

Using Resources

The Resource constructor returns the binary data as a HostBuffer. A HostBuffer is similar to an ArrayBuffer but, unlike an ArrayBuffer, the data of a HostBuffer may be read-only and consequently may be located in flash memory.

To get the number of bytes in a resource, use the byteLength property, just as with an ArrayBuffer:

```
let r1 = new Resource("mydata.dat");
let length = r1.byteLength;
```

Also as with an ArrayBuffer, you cannot access the data of a HostBuffer directly but must wrap it in a typed array or data view. The following example wraps a resource in a Uint8Array and traces the values to the console:

```
let r1 = new Resource("mydata.dat");
let bytes = new Uint8Array(r1);
for (let i = 0; i < bytes.length; i++)
    trace(bytes[i], "\n");
```

This example wraps the resource in a DataView object to access its content as big-endian 32-bit unsigned integers:

```
let r1 = new Resource("mydata.dat");
let view = new DataView(r1);
for (let i = 0; i < view.byteLength; i += 4)
    trace(view.getUint32(i, false), "\n");
```

Sometimes you want to modify the data in a resource. Because the data is read-only, you need to make a copy. The HostBuffer returned by the Resource constructor has a slice method that may be used to copy the resource data, in the same way as the slice method on an ArrayBuffer instance. For example, you could copy the entire resource to an ArrayBuffer in RAM as follows:

```
let r1 = new Resource("mydata.dat");
let clone = r1.slice(0);
```

The first argument to slice is the starting offset of the data to copy. The optional second argument is the ending offset to copy; if omitted, data is copied to the end of the resource. The following example extracts ten bytes of resource data starting at byte 20:

```
let r1 = new Resource("mydata.dat");
let fragment = r1.slice(20, 30);
```

The slice method supports an optional third argument, which is not provided by ArrayBuffer. This argument controls whether the data is copied into RAM. If it's set to false, slice returns a HostBuffer referring to a fragment of the resource data, which is useful when you want to associate just part of a resource with an object without copying its data into RAM. For example, if there's an array of five unsigned 16-bit data at offset 32 of the resource, you can create a Uint16Array that references it, as follows:

```
let r1 = new Resource("mydata.dat");
let values = new Uint16Array(r1.slice(32, 10, false));
```

You could achieve a similar result by using the optional byteOffset and length parameters of the Uint16Array constructor:

```
let r1 = new Resource("mydata.dat");
let values = new Uint16Array(r1, 32, 10);
```

The advantage of using slice is that it ensures that the full resource is unavailable to untrusted code with access to the values array. In the first of the preceding two examples, values.buffer has access to the entire resource, whereas in the second example it may be used only to access the five values in the Uint16Array.

Accessing Flash Memory Directly

All of the modules described in this chapter for storing and retrieving data—files, preferences, and resources—use the flash memory attached to the controller for data storage. Each approach for working with data in flash memory has its own benefits and limitations. In most cases, one of these approaches is a good fit for your product's needs; in some situations, a more specialized approach may be more efficient. The flash module gives you direct access to flash storage. Using it well requires more work, but it's worth the effort in some cases.

Warning   This is an advanced topic. Accessing flash memory directly is dangerous. You may crash your device or corrupt your data. You may even damage the flash memory, leaving your device unusable. Proceed with caution!

Flash Hardware Fundamentals

To be able to use the API provided by the flash module, it's important to understand the fundamentals of the flash hardware.

The flash memory used with the ESP32 and ESP8266 microcontrollers is connected using an SPI (Serial Peripheral Interface) bus. Although reasonably fast to access, it's still many times slower than accessing data in RAM.

Flash memory is organized into *blocks* (also called "sectors"). The size of a block varies depending on the flash memory component used. A common value is 4,096 bytes. When you're reading and writing flash memory, you don't usually need to be aware of the block size. However, the block size is important when you're initializing flash memory.

The flash memory uses NOR technology to store data. This has the curious implication that an erased byte of flash memory has all bits set to 1, whereas it's common to think of erased storage as being set to 0. You might think that you could simply set the freshly erased bytes to all zeros but, as you'll see, that's not a good idea with NOR flash memory.

When you write to NOR flash memory, you're only writing 0 bits. Because the flash memory is erased to all 1 bits, this doesn't matter on the first write. Consider two bytes (16 bits) of flash memory. They start out erased to all 1 bits.

```
11111111 11111111
```

Write two bytes to that, 1 and 2, and the result is straightforward:

```
00000001 00000010
```

The next step is where the result is unexpected. Here's what happens when you then write the two bytes 2 and 1 to the same location:

```
00000000 00000000
```

The result is that both bytes are set to 0. Why? Remember that with NOR flash memory, a write sets only the 0 bits. Any bits in flash memory that are already set to 0 cannot be changed back to 1 with a write.

- Flash 0. Write 0 => Flash 0.

- Flash 0. Write 1 => Flash 0.

- Flash 1. Write 0 => Flash 0.

- Flash 1. Write 1 => Flash 1.

If a write can only change bits from 1 to 0, how are bits changed from 0 to 1? You use the flash erase method to do that. Unlike read and write, which may access any byte in the flash memory directly, erase is a bulk operation that sets all the bits in a block of flash memory to 1. You erase blocks aligned to the block size boundary, which means bytes 0 to 4,095 or bytes 4,096 to 8,191—not 1 to 4,096 because that's not aligned to the start of a block, and not bytes 1 to 2 because that's not a full block.

If you want to change one bit, you can read the entire block into RAM, erase the block, change the bit in RAM, and then write the block back. That works, but it's slow, because erase is a relatively slow operation—many times slower than read and write. This approach also requires enough RAM to hold a full block, and there's not always that much memory on a resource-constrained microcontroller. The biggest problem, however, is that flash memory wears out. Each block may be erased only a certain number of times, after which that block no longer stores data reliably; to preserve the device, you need to minimize the number of times you erase each block.

The good news is that the flash memory in your ESP32 or ESP8266 supports thousands, if not tens of thousands, of erase operations. The preference and file module implementations are aware of the limits and characteristics of NOR flash memory and take steps to minimize erases. If you're accessing flash memory directly in a product that's intended to be used for years, you need to do the same.

One commonly used strategy is incremental writes. In this approach, the current values are zeroed out and the new values written after the zeros in the block. This enables a single value to be updated many times without an erase. This approach is used by the preference module. The Frequently Updated Integer example later in this section explores the details of incremental writes.

Another common strategy is wear leveling. This approach attempts to erase each flash storage block the same number of times over the lifetime of the product, to ensure that no block (for example, the first block) wears out much sooner than the others due to more frequent access. The SPIFFS file system underlying the file module uses this technique.

Accessing Flash Partitions

The flash memory available to your microcontroller is accessed using the Flash class from the flash module:

```
import Flash from "flash";
```

Flash memory is divided into segments called *partitions.* For example, one partition contains your project's code, another the preference data, and another the storage for the SPIFFS file system. Each partition is identified by a name.

To access the bytes in a partition, instantiate the Flash class with the name of the partition. When you install example applications using mcrun as introduced in Chapter 1, the byte code for the application is stored in the xs partition. The following line instantiates the Flash class to access it:

```
let xsPartition = new Flash("xs");
```

The partitions available to your code vary depending on the microcontroller and the host implementation. The xs partition that contains applications installed with mcrun is always available. The area used for the SPIFFS file system, named storage, is also generally always available; if you're not using the SPIFFS file system in your project, you can use it for other purposes. Although these partitions are both present, their sizes vary by device.

On the ESP32, the ESP32 IDF from Espressif defines the partitions. The IDF provides a flexible partition mechanism that makes it possible for you to define your own partitions. On the ESP8266, the Moddable SDK defines the partitions, and they cannot easily be reconfigured.

On the ESP32, the Flash constructor searches the IDF partition map to match the partition name requested. Consequently, you can access the partition that contains the ESP32 preferences—which are implemented in the NVS library—with the name nvs, as declared in the partition map (the partitions.csv file in an IDF project).

```
let nvsPartition = new Flash("nvs");
```

Getting Partition Information

An instance of the Flash class has two read-only properties that provide important information about the partition: blockSize and byteLength.

The blockSize property indicates the number of bytes in a single block of the flash hardware. This value is often 4,096, but for robustness you should use the blockSize property rather than hardcode a constant value in your code. That way, your code can work unchanged on hardware that incorporates a different flash hardware component.

```
let storagePartition = new Flash("storage");
let blockSize = storagePartition.blockSize;
```

The blockSize property is important because it tells you both the alignment and the size of erase operations on the partition.

The byteLength property provides the total number of bytes available in the partition. The following example calculates the number of blocks in the partition:

```
let blocks = storagePartition.byteLength / blockSize;
```

The value of the byteLength property is always an integer multiple of the value of blockSize property, so the number of blocks is always an integer.

Reading from a Flash Partition

Use the read method to retrieve bytes from the flash storage partition. The read method takes two arguments: the offset into the partition and the number of bytes to read. The result of the read call is an ArrayBuffer. The following is an excerpt from the $EXAMPLES/ch5-files/flash-readwrite example:

```
let buffer = partition.read(0, 10);
let bytes = new Uint8Array(buffer);
```

```
for (let i = 0; i < bytes.byteLength; i++)
    trace(bytes[i] + "\n");
```

This code retrieves the first ten bytes from the partition. It wraps the returned ArrayBuffer in a Uint8Array to trace the byte values to the console.

There are no restrictions on the offset and number of bytes to read, beyond the requirement that they're within the partition. Specifically, a single call to read may cross a block boundary.

The read call copies the requested data from the partition into a new ArrayBuffer. Consequently, you should read flash memory in small fragments to use as little RAM as practical.

Erasing a Flash Partition

Use the erase method to reset all the bits in a flash partition to 1. The method takes a single argument, the number of the blocks to reset. This line erases the first block of the partition:

```
partition.erase(0);
```

The following code resets the entire partition. The erase operation is relatively slow; for a large partition—for example, the storage partition on the ESP8266—this operation takes several seconds.

```
let blocks = partition.byteLength / partition.blockSize;
for (let block = 0; block < blocks; block++)
    partition.erase(block);
```

Writing to a Flash Partition

Use the write method to change the values stored in the flash partition. This method takes three arguments: the offset at which to write the data into the partition, the number of bytes to write, and an ArrayBuffer containing the data. When the number of bytes to write is less than the size of the ArrayBuffer, only that number of bytes are written. The following example sets the first ten bytes of the partition to integers from 1 to 10:

```
let buffer = Uint8Array.of(1, 2, 3, 4, 5, 6, 7, 8, 9, 10).buffer;
partition.write(0, 10, buffer);
```

Keep in mind that writing sets only the 0 bits, as explained earlier in the "Flash Hardware Fundamentals" section. Therefore, it may be necessary to perform an erase before calling write.

Mapping a Flash Partition

On the ESP32, you have the option of memory-mapping the partition, which gives you read-only access to the contents of the partition using a typed array or data view constructor. To memory-map a partition, call the map method. The following code is taken from the $EXAMPLES/ch5-files/flash-map example:

```
let partition = new Flash("storage");
let buffer = partition.map();
let bytes = new Uint8Array(buffer);
```

The map property returns a HostBuffer that may be passed to a typed array or data view constructor to access the data. Memory-mapped partitions are a more convenient way to access data than the read call in some situations. Furthermore, because the data in the partition is not copied to RAM by the map method, RAM use is minimized.

The map method is unavailable on ES8266 due to hardware limitations that allow only memory mapping of the first megabyte of flash memory, the area reserved to store the firmware.

Example: Frequently Updated Integer

This section presents an example of directly accessing flash memory to maintain a 32-bit value more efficiently than is possible using a file or a preference. The example is for the situation where your product needs to update a value frequently in flash storage to ensure that it's maintained reliably across reboots of the product.

The example uses a single block of flash memory. That's typically 4,096 bytes, which is 1,024 times bigger than the 32-bit (four-byte) value being stored. The example takes advantage of the additional storage to reduce the number of erase operations, thereby prolonging the lifetime of the flash memory. For convenience, the block used is the first block of the `storage` partition, which prevents this example from being used with the SPIFFS file system.

The complete Frequently Updated Integer example is available at `$EXAMPLES/ch5-files/flash-frequentupdate`.

Initializing the Block

The first step is to open the storage partition:

```
let partition = new Flash("storage");
```

As shown in Listing 5-9, the next step is to check whether the block has been initialized. This is done by looking for a unique signature at the start of the block. If the signature is not found, the block is erased and the signature is written.

Listing 5-9.

```
const SIGNATURE = 0xa82aa82a;

let signature = partition.read(0, 4);
signature = (new Uint32Array(signature))[0];
```

```
if (signature !== SIGNATURE)
    initialize(partition);

function initialize(partition) {
    let signature = Uint32Array.of(SIGNATURE);

    partition.erase(0);
    partition.write(0, 4, signature.buffer);
}
```

Updating the Value

After the signature, the block has space to store 1023 copies of the counter. Listing 5-10 shows a write function that updates the value of the counter. It searches for the first unused 32-bit integer in the block and writes the value there. Recall that when a block is erased, all the bits are set to 1. That means any unused entries contain the value 0xFFFFFFFF (a 32-bit integer with all bits set to 1). If the block is full, it reinitializes the block and writes the value in the first free position.

Listing 5-10.

```
function write(partition, newValue) {
    for (let i = 1; i < 1024; i++) {
        let currentValue = partition.read(i * 4, 4);
        currentValue = (new Uint32Array(currentValue))[0];
        if (0xFFFFFFFF === currentValue) {
            partition.write(i * 4, 4,
                            Uint32Array.of(newValue).buffer);
            return;
        }
    }
    initialize(partition);
    partition.write(4, 4, Uint32Array.of(newValue).buffer);
}
```

Reading the Value

The final part is the read function, shown in Listing 5-11. Like the write function, it searches for the first free entry. Once that's found, read returns the value of the previous entry. If the search reaches the end of the block, the last value in the block is returned.

Listing 5-11.

```
function read(partition) {
    let i;

    for (i = 1; i < 1024; i++) {
        let currentValue = partition.read(i * 4, 4);
        currentValue = (new Uint32Array(currentValue))[0];
        if (0xFFFFFFFF === currentValue)
            break;
    }

    let result = partition.read((i - 1) * 4, 4);
    return (new Uint32Array(result))[0];
}
```

Benefits and Future Work

This example efficiently stores an integer value in flash memory. The value may be updated 1,023 times before the block needs to be erased. To understand the impact of this, consider a product that updates that value once a minute. That works out to 514 erase operations per year (60 * 24 * 365, which is 525,600 minutes per year, divided by 1,023 updates per erase rounds up to 514). Using a flash chip with support for 10,000 erase operations (a conservative estimate), the product has about a 19.5-year lifetime. If each write operation required an erase, the same product would wear out in only 7 days (60 * 24 * 7 is 10,080 writes per week).

The careful reader has noticed two limitations of this example: if power is lost in the `write` function after the erase and before the write, the current value will be lost; and the value cannot be set to `0xffffffff` because that value is used to identify unused entries in the block. Solutions to these shortcomings are possible and are left as exercises for the reader.

Conclusion

In this chapter, you learned several different ways to store information in an embedded product. Files, preferences, and resources are the three primary ways to store data, and each is optimized for a different use of storage. You can use any combination of these approaches in your product. When designing your product, consider your storage needs to determine which approaches to use to make optimal use of available storage. Some situations are so specialized that none of these standard storage techniques are optimal; to address those cases, this chapter showed how flash memory works so that you can create your own storage methods.

CHAPTER 6

Hardware

Sensors and actuators are integral parts of nearly every IoT product. Sensors gather data from the environment, such as the temperature, humidity, and light levels, and translate it into electrical signals that a microcontroller or other system can react to. Actuators do the opposite: they take electrical signals and translate them into physical actions, such as turning a motor or a light on or playing a sound.

Just as there are different networking protocols that define how data is shared over the network, there are different hardware protocols that define how sensors and actuators communicate with the microcontroller they're connected to. The Moddable SDK includes JavaScript APIs for a variety of hardware protocols, including digital, analog, PWM, servo, and I²C. These APIs enable you to interact with off-the-shelf hardware or your own circuits from your ESP32 or ESP8266.

In this chapter, you'll learn how to get started writing your own JavaScript code to interact with hardware. The chapter includes many examples that require just a few simple, widely available, inexpensive sensors and actuators.

The code in this chapter communicates with hardware directly using different hardware protocols. Once you learn how to work with a few common hardware protocols, you'll have the knowledge you need to incorporate the many hardware components that use those protocols into your own projects. When attaching new hardware to a computer, it's often necessary to install a software driver—that is, software that knows how

© Peter Hoddie and Lizzie Prader 2020
P. Hoddie and L. Prader, *IoT Development for ESP32 and ESP8266 with JavaScript*,
https://doi.org/10.1007/978-1-4842-5070-9_6

to interact with the hardware through the low-level hardware protocols; in effect, this chapter teaches you how to write the software drivers for various hardware components. IoT products that control the hardware directly in this way have many benefits, including more precise control, smaller code, and lower latency. Of course, software drivers are also available for many components; in the Moddable SDK, you'll find them in `modules/drivers`.

Installing the Hardware Host

The examples in this chapter are installed using the pattern described in Chapter 1: you install the host on your device using `mcconfig`, then install example applications using `mcrun`.

The host is in the `$EXAMPLES/ch6-hardware/host` directory. Navigate to this directory from the command line and install it with `mcconfig`.

Notes on Wiring

This chapter, unlike most other chapters in this book, requires you to do additional setup of your device before running most examples: you need to wire various sensors and actuators to your device. If you're new to this, it may be confusing as you get started. If you've done this before, you know that it's easy to make mistakes and that troubleshooting can sometimes take time. This section provides important information on wiring that you should know before running the examples.

Following the Wiring Instructions

This chapter provides wiring tables and diagrams for most sensors and actuators used in the examples. The wiring diagrams show the wiring for NodeMCU boards and therefore NodeMCU pin numbers, such as D6 or

D7. These labels don't necessarily match the GPIO number used in code. If you're using a different development board, make sure you look at the wiring tables, which provide the GPIO number—for example, GPIO12 or GPIO13—along with the NodeMCU pin numbers in parentheses. All development boards label pins differently, so you have to map the pins accordingly. The Moddable development boards are labeled with "GP" followed by the GPIO number used in code—for example, GP12 or GP13— so if the wiring table says a pin should be wired to GPIO12, plug it into the pin labeled GP12 on the Moddable boards.

Troubleshooting Wiring Issues

It's important to follow the wiring instructions carefully. If you make a mistake in your wiring, a few things might happen:

- An error is thrown. This is common and is generally the easiest issue to fix. For example, if you swap the SDA and SCL pins of an I^2C sensor, you'll get errors when reading and writing. Take advantage of xsbug and use the error messages to diagnose your issue. Sometimes you just have to fix your wiring; other times you may have a faulty sensor or actuator.

- The application works but gives unexpected results. This is also common, but it can be hard to catch. For example, if you plug the digital pin of a sensor into the wrong pin on your development board, the application reads from a pin that's not connected to anything; it doesn't throw an error but it does give unexpected results. If you're pressing a button and the application isn't responding as expected, or you're writing to a pin of a tri-color LED and the color isn't updated, double-check your wiring.

- You destroy your sensor or actuator. This is less common than the first two issues, but it can happen. For example, powering a sensor with 5V when it's designed to accept 3.3V can damage the electronics on the sensor.

Blinking an LED

The simplest physical output you can create with your ESP32 or ESP8266 is to turn the on-board LED (Figure 6-1) on and off. Both the ESP32 and ESP8266 NodeMCU boards have an on-board LED connected to pin 2.

Figure 6-1. *On-board LED on ESP8266 (top) and ESP32 (bottom)*

The Digital class provides access to the GPIO pins on your device:

```
import Digital from "pins/digital";
```

You can configure a digital pin for input or output. Once configured, the pin can take on a value of 1, meaning the voltage is high, or 0, meaning the voltage is low. The $EXAMPLES/ch6-hardware/blink example uses the Digital class and a timer to blink the on-board LED. As shown in Listing 6-1, the example uses the static write method of the Digital class, which sets the pin (specified by the first argument) to Digital.Output mode and sets its value to 0 or 1 (the second argument).

Listing 6-1.

```
let blink = 1;
Timer.repeat(() => {
    blink = blink ^ 1;
    Digital.write(2, blink);
}, 200);
```

Alternatively, you can construct an instance of the Digital class and call the instance's write method. Using the constructor allows for full configuration of the pin. When you call the constructor, you pass in a dictionary with pin and mode properties. The following mode values are available for digital output pins:

```
Digital.Output
Digital.OutputOpenDrain
```

Listing 6-2 shows another way to write the blink example, using the Digital constructor.

Listing 6-2.

```
let led = new Digital({
    pin: 2,
    mode: Digital.Output
});

let blink = 1;
Timer.repeat(() => {
    blink = blink ^ 1;
    led.write(blink);
}, 200);
```

Using an instance of Digital is more efficient for writing than using the static Digital.write method; the constructor initializes the pin once, whereas Digital.write must initialize it on each write. Digital.write is convenient for infrequent writes, but if your project writes to a digital output frequently, create an instance once and write to it instead.

Reading a Button

Buttons are a simple way to add physical input to projects. The ESP32 and ESP8266 NodeMCU modules have two buttons built in. One of the buttons is wired to digital pin 0 and may be used as a digital input in your projects; this button is labeled FLASH, BOOT, or IO0, depending on which module you have.

The $EXAMPLES/ch6-hardware/button example uses the Digital class and a timer to read the on-board button. As shown in Listing 6-3, the example uses the static read method of the Digital class, which sets the pin (specified by the first argument) to Digital.Input mode and reads its value, returning 0 or 1. The example traces to the debug console each time the button is pressed. It also maintains a count of the number of button presses and includes it in the output.

Listing 6-3.

```
let previous = 1;
let count = 0;
Timer.repeat(id => {
    let value = Digital.read(0);
    if (value !== previous) {
        if (value)
            trace(`button pressed: ${++count}\n`);
        previous = value;
    }
}, 100);
```

Alternatively, you can construct an instance of the Digital class and call the instance's read method. Using the constructor allows for full configuration of the pin. When you call the constructor, you pass in a dictionary with pin and mode properties. The following mode values are available for digital input pins:

```
Digital.Input
Digital.InputPullUp
Digital.InputPullDown
Digital.InputPullUpDown
```

Listing 6-4 shows how the button example could be rewritten to use the Digital constructor.

Listing 6-4.

```
let button = new Digital({
    pin: 0,
    mode: Digital.Input
});
let previous = 1;
```

```
let count = 0;
Timer.repeat(id => {
    let value = button.read();
    if (value !== previous) {
        if (value)
            trace(`button pressed: ${++count}\n`);
        previous = value;
    }
}, 100);
```

Other Digital Input Modes

The modes Digital.InputPullUp, Digital.InputPullDown, and
Digital.InputPullUpDown are used to enable pull-up and pull-down
resistors that are built into some of the GPIO pins on the ESP32 and ESP8266.
This isn't always necessary, but it's useful for buttons like the one shown in
Figure 6-2, which requires a pull-down resistor to prevent it from receiving
random noise when it's in an unpressed sate. You can get buttons like this
from SparkFun (product ID COM-10302) and Adafruit (product ID 1009).

Figure 6-2. *Tactile button*

The $EXAMPLES/ch6-hardware/external-button example has the
same functionality as the button example, but it works with a button like
the one in Figure 6-2 rather than the built-in button. If you want to run this
example, first follow the wiring instructions given here to connect it to your
ESP32 or ESP8266.

ESP32 Wiring Instructions

Table 6-1 and Figure 6-3 show how to connect the button to the ESP32.

Table 6-1. *Wiring to connect the button to ESP32*

Button	ESP32
PWR	3V3
DIN	GPIO16 (RX2)

Figure 6-3. *Wiring diagram for connecting the button to ESP32*

ESP8266 Wiring Instructions

Table 6-2 and Figure 6-4 show how to connect the button to the ESP8266.

Table 6-2. *Wiring to connect the button to ESP8266*

Button	ESP8266
PWR	3V3
DIN	GPIO16 (D0)

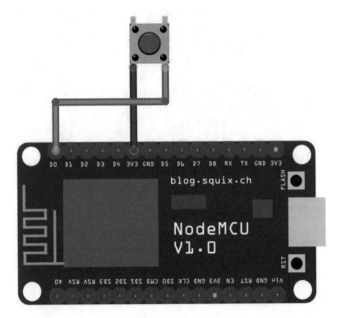

Figure 6-4. *Wiring diagram for connecting the button to ESP8266*

Understanding the `external-button` Code

The `external-button` example uses the `Digital` constructor as shown in the following code. It configures pin 16 with the mode `Digital.InputPullDown`, which enables the built-in pull-down resistor on pin 16.

```
let button = new Digital({
    pin: 16,
    mode: Digital.InputPullDown
});
```

The rest of the code is very similar to the rewritten `button` example (Listing 6-4), except for a few small changes to account for the use of the pull-down resistor.

More About Pull-Up and Pull-Down Resistors

Both the ESP32 and the ESP8266 have a built-in pull-down resistor on pin 16, which is why the `external-button` example runs on either one without any changes to the code. That said, you can modify it to use any pin with a built-in pull-down resistor, and other applications you build can use the other pins as well. The ESP32 has built-in pull-down resistors on all GPIO pins except pins 34–39, whereas the ESP8266 only has a built-in pull-down resistor on pin 16.

Other sensors may require a pull-up resistor. The ESP32 has built-in pull-up resistors on all GPIO pins except pins 34–39; the ESP8266 has built-in pull-up resistors on GPIO pins 1–15.

Instead of using the built-in resistors, you can also add pull-up or pull-down resistors directly to sensors. If you do this, you can use any GPIO pin, not just pins with a built-in resistor. Also note that if you do this, you should always use the mode `Digital.Input`. In other words, do not enable a built-in pull-down resistor if you add a pull-down resistor to the sensor itself, and likewise do not enable a built-in pull-up resistor if you add a pull-up resistor to the sensor itself.

Monitoring for Changes

You can more efficiently detect changes on the value of a digital input by using the digital Monitor class. Instead of periodic polling, it uses a feature of the microcontroller to monitor for changes. An instance of Monitor is configured to trigger on changes from 0 to 1 (that is, rising edge) and/or changes from 1 to 0 (falling edge). When the hardware detects a trigger event, the Monitor class invokes a callback function.

Listing 6-5 shows how the button example could use the Monitor class. Notice that this version is quite a bit smaller.

Listing 6-5.

```
let monitor = new Monitor({
    pin: 0,
    mode: Digital.Input,
    edge: Monitor.Rising
});
let count = 0;
monitor.onChanged = function() {
    trace(`button pressed: ${++count}\n`);
}
```

The original button example uses the value and previous variables to keep track of the button's state; using the Monitor class simplifies the code considerably because the class keeps track of the button's state itself, notifying the application only when the state has changed.

Like the Digital constructor, the Monitor constructor takes a dictionary with pin and mode properties. It also includes an edge property specifying the events that trigger the onChanged callback; edge may be Monitor.Rising, Monitor.Falling, or Monitor.Rising | Monitor.Falling. An application must install an onChanged callback on the instance, to be invoked when the specified edge events occur.

Using the Monitor class instead of polling has advantages beyond simplifying your code. Because the class uses the microcontroller's built-in hardware to detect changes, there's no need to run any code to watch for changes, freeing up CPU cycles for other work. Additionally, the monitor detects changes immediately, whereas the polling approach checks for a change only every 100 milliseconds. Of course, you can poll more frequently, but that requires even more CPU cycles. Further, the polling approach misses very quick button presses that happen between reads, whereas the monitor is always active and so doesn't miss any button presses.

Controlling a Tri-color LED

Unlike the basic on/off single-color LED in the earlier blink example, a tri-color LED (also called an RGB LED) combines three LEDs—red, green, and blue—into a single package, enabling you to precisely control both the color and the brightness. Controlling the three colors of a tri-color LED requires four pins: one to control each of the three LEDs, plus a power pin shared by all the colors.

The examples in this section assume you're using a common anode LED, like the one shown in Figure 6-5, which is available from SparkFun (product ID COM-10821) and Adafruit (product ID 159).

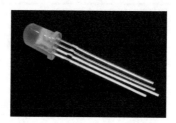

Figure 6-5. *Tri-color LED*

Before you run the examples, follow the instructions to set up your tri-color LED and the wiring instructions to connect it to your ESP32 or ESP8266.

LED Setup

As shown in Figure 6-6, the LED requires that current limiting resistors be added to all the pins except for the power pin, to prevent them from drawing too much current. Use 330 Ohm resistors.

Figure 6-6. *Tri-color LED with current limiting resistors*

ESP32 Wiring Instructions

Table 6-3 and Figure 6-7 show how to connect the LED to the ESP32.

Table 6-3. *Wiring to connect the LED to ESP32*

LED	ESP32
PWR	3V3
R	GPIO12 (D12)
G	GPIO13 (D13)
B	GPIO14 (D14)

Figure 6-7. *Wiring diagram for connecting the LED to ESP32*

ESP8266 Wiring Instructions

Table 6-4 and Figure 6-8 show how to connect the tri-color LED to the ESP8266.

Table 6-4. *Wiring to connect the LED to ESP8266*

LED	ESP8266
PWR	3V3
R	GPIO12 (D6)
G	GPIO13 (D7)
B	GPIO14 (D5)

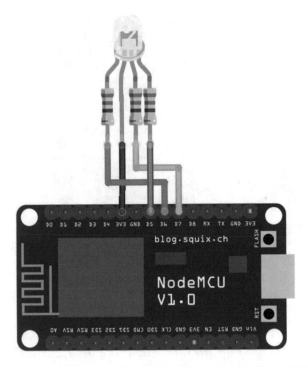

Figure 6-8. *Wiring diagram for connecting the LED to ESP8266*

Using `Digital` with a Tri-color LED

The red, green, and blue pins of the tri-color LED are connected to digital outputs. In the `$EXAMPLES/ch6-hardware/tricolor-led-digital` example, they can be controlled individually using the same `Digital` class you used in the `blink` example to control a simple single-color LED. As shown in Listing 6-6, the difference is that you can display eight different colors by mixing the three primary colors.

Listing 6-6.

```
let r = new Digital(12, Digital.Output);
let g = new Digital(13, Digital.Output);
let b = new Digital(14, Digital.Output);
```

```
Timer.repeat(() => {
    // black (all off)
    r.write(1);
    g.write(1);
    b.write(1);
    Timer.delay(100);

    // red (red on)
    r.write(0);
    Timer.delay(100);

    // magenta (red and blue on)
    b.write(0);
    Timer.delay(100);

    // white (all on)
    g.write(0);
    Timer.delay(100);
}, 1);
```

The tri-color LED can display more than just the primary and secondary colors of black, white, red, green, blue, magenta, cyan, and yellow. To achieve that, you need more control than simply turning the red, green, and blue LEDs on and off; you need to be able to set them to values between on and off—that is, between 0 and 1. A digital output can't do that, since its output is always either 0 or 1. In the next section, you'll learn how to overcome this limitation.

Using PWM with a Tri-color LED

To display a greater range of color and brightness, a tri-color LED may instead be controlled using *pulse-width modulation*, or *PWM*, a special type of digital signal commonly used in motors and LEDs, including tri-color LEDs. PWM is roughly equivalent to an analog output but is generated using a digital signal. More specifically, the digital pin outputs a square wave with varied widths of high and low values. Taking the average of these high and low pulses over time creates a power level between the high and low values, proportional to the pulse widths. The result is that instead of being limited to 0 and 1 as output values, you can output any value in between.

The PWM class provides access to the PWM output pins. The $EXAMPLES/ch6-hardware/tricolor-led-pwm example uses PWM and a timer to cycle through different colors.

```
import PWM from "pins/pwm";
```

The example needs three instances of the PWM class, one for each wire on the tri-color LED that controls the brightness of an individual color. The PWM constructor takes a dictionary specifying the pin number.

```
let r = new PWM({pin: 12});
let g = new PWM({pin: 13});
let b = new PWM({pin: 14});
```

The write method sets the current value of the pin. The value you pass is a number from 0 to 1023, the analog value to synthesize. Lower values correspond to higher brightness. When the application runs, it makes the LED turn green. A PWM value of 0 is equivalent to a digital output set to 0, and a PWM value of 1023 is equivalent to a digital output set to 1. The following code sets the tri-color LED to green by setting the green LED to full brightness and the red and blue LEDs to off:

```
r.write(1023);
g.write(0);
b.write(1023);
```

As shown in Listing 6-7, the code then cycles through colors by adjusting the value of individual pins. First it changes the color from green to cyan by decreasing the value of the blue pin. Between calls to write, the delay method of the Timer class is used to delay execution for 50 milliseconds.

Listing 6-7.

```
while (bVal >= 21) {
    bVal -= 20;
    b.write(bVal);
    Timer.delay(50);
}
b.write(1);
```

After fading from green to cyan, the LED fades from cyan to blue, blue to magenta, and finally magenta to red (Listing 6-8).

Listing 6-8.

```
while (gVal <= 1003) {
    gVal += 20;
    g.write(gVal);
    Timer.delay(50);
}
g.write(1023);

while (rVal >= 21) {
    rVal -= 20;
    r.write(rVal);
    Timer.delay(50);
}
r.write(0);

while (bVal <= 1003) {
    bVal += 20;
    b.write(bVal);
    Timer.delay(50);
}
b.write(1023);
```

Rotating a Servo

Servos are motors that control a rotating output. The output may be precisely turned to a specified position within an arc, typically 180 degrees. Servos are commonly used in robotics to control movements of robots and for rotating objects such as the lens of a camera to control focus and zoom. Figure 6-9 shows a micro servo available from Adafruit (product ID 169). Micro servos like this one can be powered using an ESP32 or ESP8266. There are also larger, more powerful servos for moving larger objects; these servos require more power to operate than the microcontroller can provide and therefore require an external power supply.

Figure 6-9. *Micro servo from Adafruit*

Servos are configured with the Servo class, which uses digital pins to control servo motors.

The $EXAMPLES/ch6-hardware/servo example rotates a servo from 0 degrees up to 180 degrees, 2.5 degrees at a time. Before you run the example, follow the wiring instructions given here to connect it to your ESP32 or ESP8266.

ESP32 Wiring Instructions

Table 6-5 and Figure 6-10 show how to connect the servo to the ESP32.

Table 6-5. *Wiring to connect the servo to ESP32*

Servo	ESP32
PWR	3V3
GND	GND
Servo (DOUT)	GPIO14 (D14)

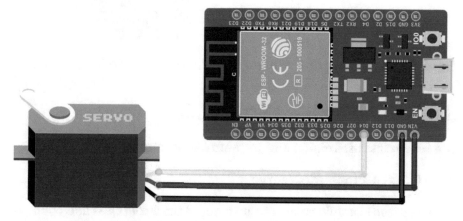

Figure 6-10. *Wiring diagram for connecting the servo to ESP32*

ESP8266 Wiring Instructions

Table 6-6 and Figure 6-11 show how to connect the servo to the ESP8266.

Table 6-6. *Wiring to connect the servo to ESP8266*

Servo	ESP8266
PWR	3V3
GND	GND
Servo (DOUT)	GPIO14 (D5)

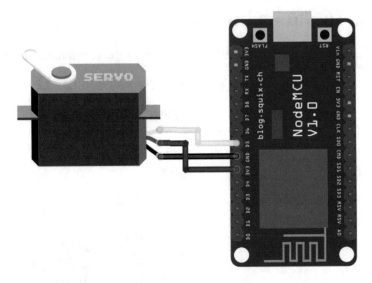

Figure 6-11. *Wiring diagram for connecting the servo to ESP8266*

Understanding the `servo` Code

The Servo class uses digital pins to control servo motors:

```
import Servo from "pins/servo";
```

The `servo` example creates an instance of the Servo class and changes the position at a regular interval by calling the instance's `write` method. As shown in Listing 6-9, the argument to the `write` method is the angle to rotate to; note that this may be a fractional number.

Listing 6-9.

```
let servo = new Servo({pin: 14});
let angle = 0;
Timer.repeat(() => {
    angle += 2.5;
```

```
    if (angle > 180)
        angle -= 180;
    servo.write(angle);
}, 250);
```

It takes time for the servo to rotate to a new position; the amount of time depends on the servo you're using. Depending on the servo, using a shorter interval may not make the servo rotate faster but instead may result in a confused behavior as the servo does its best to keep up with the changes, which are coming in faster than it can operate.

The Servo class also has a writeMicroseconds method, which allows for greater precision by letting you provide the number of microseconds (instead of degrees) for the signal pulse. The range of acceptable values varies from servo to servo; setting the pulse length to a value that's too low or too high can break the servo, so be sure to check your servo's datasheet.

Getting the Temperature

Measuring temperature is such a common task for IoT products that sensor manufacturers have created many different temperature sensors. These sensors use a variety of hardware protocols to communicate with the microcontroller. This section explains two that are easy to use and widely available:

- The TMP36 (Figure 6-12) uses an analog value to communicate the temperature. The simpler of the two sensors, it has only a single output—an analog output that connects to the analog input of a microcontroller— and has no configuration options. It's available from SparkFun (product ID SEN-10988) and Adafruit (product ID 165).

Figure 6-12. *TMP36 sensor*

- The TMP102 (Figure 6-13) uses the I²C bus to communicate the temperature. It connects using the I²C hardware protocol, which is considerably more complex to work with than an analog input but enables the sensor to offer additional functionality and configuration options. It's available from SparkFun (product ID SEN-13314).

Figure 6-13. *TMP102 sensor*

This section also explains how to use a sensor's datasheet to understand the data provided by the sensor and convert it to a human-readable format.

TMP36

The $EXAMPLES/ch6-hardware/tmp36 example reads the temperature from a TMP36 sensor and traces the value in degrees Celsius to the debug console. Before you run the example, follow the wiring instructions given here to connect the TMP36 to your ESP32 or ESP8266.

ESP32 Wiring Instructions

Table 6-7 and Figure 6-14 show how to connect the TMP36 to the ESP32.

Table 6-7. *Wiring to connect the TMP36 to ESP32*

TMP36	ESP32
PWR	3V3
Analog	ADC0 (VP) on NodeMCU board ADC7 (GP35) on Moddable Two
GND	GND

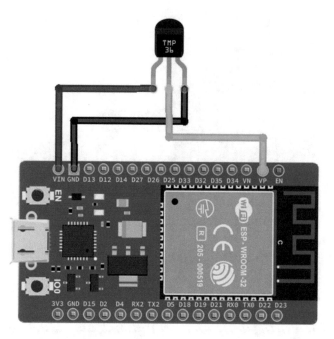

Figure 6-14. *Wiring diagram for connecting the TMP36 to ESP32*

ESP8266 Wiring Instructions

Table 6-8 and Figure 6-15 show how to connect the TMP36 to the ESP8266.

Table 6-8. *Wiring to connect the TMP36 to ESP8266*

TMP36	ESP8266
PWR	3V3
Analog	ADC0 (A0)
GND	GND

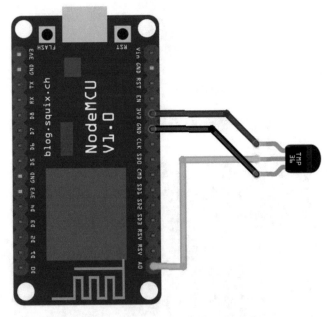

Figure 6-15. *Wiring diagram for connecting the TMP36 to ESP8266*

Understanding the `tmp36` Code

The analog pin on the TMP36 outputs a voltage proportional to the temperature. The `Analog` class provides access to the analog inputs on your device:

```
import Analog from "pins/analog";
```

Unlike other hardware protocol classes, the `Analog` class is never instantiated. It provides only one static method: a `read` method that samples the value of the specified pin, returning a value from 0 to 1023. The `tmp36` example calls the `read` method and converts the returned voltage to the temperature.

The excellent Adafruit tutorial for the TMP36 (`learn.adafruit.com/tmp36-temperature-sensor/overview`) provides the following formula to convert the voltage to the temperature:

Temp in °C = [(Vout in mV) – 500] / 10

The `tmp36` example is based on this formula, as you can see here:

```
let value = (Analog.read(0) / 1023) * 330 - 50;
trace(`Celsius temperature: ${value}\n`);
```

Note   If you're running on Moddable Two, you'll need to change the pin number from 0 to 7 due to the difference in wiring.

The TMP36 is designed to accurately measure temperatures between –40°C and +125°C. For temperatures outside this range, it returns readings but with less accuracy. The analog input has 10 bits of resolution, allowing for readings with an accuracy of about 0.25°C. This accuracy is sufficient for many purposes, but not all; as described next, the TMP102 temperature sensor provides greater resolution for temperature measurements.

TMP102

The $EXAMPLES/ch6-hardware/tmp102 example reads the temperature from a TMP102 sensor and traces the value in degrees Celsius to the debug console. Before you run the example, follow the wiring instructions given here to connect the TMP102 to your ESP32 or ESP8266.

This section refers to the TMP102 schematic and the TMP102 datasheet, both of which can be found on the TMP102 product page on SparkFun's website: sparkfun.com/products/13314.

ESP32 Wiring Instructions

Table 6-9 and Figure 6-16 show how to connect the TMP102 to the ESP32.

Table 6-9. *Wiring to connect the TMP102 to ESP32*

TMP102	ESP32
GND	GND
VCC	3V3
SDA	GPIO21 (D21)
SCL	GPIO22 (D22)

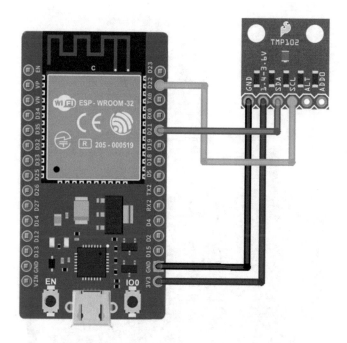

Figure 6-16. *Wiring diagram for connecting the TMP102 to ESP32*

ESP8266 Wiring Instructions

Table 6-10 and Figure 6-17 show how to connect the TMP102 to the ESP8266.

Table 6-10. *Wiring to connect the TMP102 to ESP8266*

TMP102	ESP8266
GND	GND
VCC	3V3
SDA	GPIO5 (D1)
SCL	GPIO4 (D2)

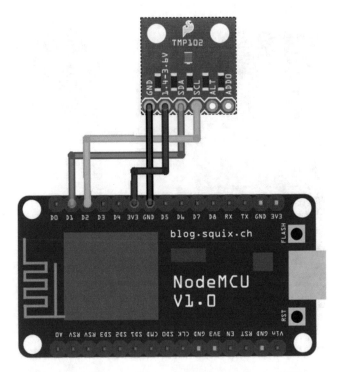

Figure 6-17. *Wiring diagram for connecting the TMP102 to ESP8266*

Understanding the `tmp102` Code

The `tmp102` example retrieves temperature data from the TMP102 and converts it to degrees Celsius for output to the debug console. This particular example is worth a careful look because it introduces the I^2C hardware protocol, which is used in a vast number of sensors. I^2C is a serial protocol for connecting multiple devices to a single two-wire bus.

Once you learn the fundamentals of working with I^2C in JavaScript, you can often quickly write the code to communicate with a new sensor based on a review of the hardware datasheet or a sample implementation, such as an Arduino sketch. An alternative method, using the SMBus subset of I^2C, is discussed in the next section. Understanding how to use I^2C and SMBus will enable you to explore the many options of a huge array of available sensors.

Note that this chapter introduces many, but not all, of the capabilities of the TMP102. The datasheet is the best way to learn about the capabilities of any sensor. Further reading on the TMP102 shows that it includes features designed for use in thermostats, for example.

One of the features that make I²C popular is that, because it's a bus, it allows several different sensors to be connected to the same two microcontroller pins. Each sensor has a unique address, enabling them to be accessed independently. Using a bus for this hardware protocol reduces the total number of pins needed to connect multiple sensors, which is valuable because often the number of available pins is limited.

The I2C class provides access to the I²C bus connected to a pair of pins:

```
import I2C from "pins/i2c";
```

The tmp102 example creates an instance of the I2C class. The dictionary passed to the constructor contains the I²C address of the target device. You can include pin numbers in the dictionary by specifying sda and scl properties; this example uses the default pins for the target device and therefore does not specify pin numbers in the dictionary. The default pin numbers for the ESP32 or ESP8266 match the wiring in the preceding diagrams. The address of the board, 0x48, is specified in the TMP102 schematic.

```
let sensor = new I2C({address: 0x48});
```

This instance of the I2C class can now access the sensor on the I²C bus at address 0x48. The TMP102 maintains four 16-bit registers, which are accessed over I²C using reads and writes. The registers are shown in Table 6-11. (See also Tables 1 and 2 of the TMP102 datasheet.)

Table 6-11. *TMP102 registers*

Register #	Register Name	Purpose
0	Temperature	Read the most recent temperature
1	Configuration	Read or set options for temperature conversion rate, power management, and so on
2	T_{LOW}	Read or set the low temperature when using the built-in comparator
3	T_{HIGH}	Read or set the high temperature when using the built-in comparator

To read or write to a register, you first write the target register number to the device. Once that's complete, you read or write the register value. The example reads the temperature (register 0), so it first writes the value 0 to the sensor and then reads two bytes.

```
const TEMPERATURE_REG = 0;
sensor.write(TEMPERATURE_REG);
let value = sensor.read(2);
```

The read method returns the bytes in a Uint8Array instance named value. It can read up to 40 bytes from the target device, although most I²C reads are just a few bytes.

Of the two bytes read, the first is the most significant byte. The second byte, the least significant, has the low 4 bits set to 0, giving a resolution of 12 bits. The following line of the code combines the two bytes in the value array into a 12-bit integer value:

```
value = (value[0] << 4) | (value[1] >> 4);
```

This value is in the format described in Table 5 of the TMP102 datasheet. Negative values are represented in two's complement format. If the first bit of value is 1, the temperature is below 0°C, requiring additional calculations (Listing 6-10) to generate the correct negative value.

Listing 6-10.

```
if (value & 0x800) {
    value -= 1;
    value = ~value & 0xFFF;
    value = -value;
}
```

The final step is to convert the value to degrees Celsius and trace it to the debug console. Because there are 12 bits of total resolution and 4 of those bits are used for the fractional part of the value, the TMP102 provides temperature values accurate to within 0.0625°C. The accurate range of temperature readings is from –55°C to +128°C.

```
value /= 16;
trace(`Celsius temperature: ${value}\n`);
```

Using SMBus

The *System Management Bus*, or *SMBus*, protocol is built on top of I²C. It uses a subset of the methods defined by I²C to formalize a convention used by many register-based I²C devices, including the TMP102. As mentioned previously, the TMP102 uses four registers to read and write values between the sensor and the microcontroller. To read from or write to a register, you first send the register number, then send the read or write command.

You can use I²C to communicate with SMBus devices as you did earlier, but since SMBus devices are quite common the Moddable SDK includes an SMBus class for convenience:

```
import SMBus from "pins/smbus";
```

The SMBus class is a subclass of the I2C class, and its constructor accepts the same dictionary arguments. SMBus adds additional calls to I2C to read and write registers directly. In the tmp102 example, using I2C directly to read a register requires two calls: a write to set the register to read and then the actual read. SMBus combines these two calls into a single readWord call.

```
let sensor = new SMBus({address: 0x48});
let value = sensor.readWord(TEMPERATURE_REG, true) >> 4;
```

The readWord method takes two arguments: first the register to read and then true if the two bytes are in big-endian order or false if little-endian (the default). Because the first byte returned here is the most significant byte, the value is big-endian, so the second argument is true. Since the two bytes have already been combined into an integer, all that remains is to shift right by 4 bits to generate the 12-bit value.

The SMBus class provides readByte to read a single byte and readBlock to read a specified number of bytes. It also provides the corresponding write methods writeByte, writeWord, and writeBlock.

Configuring the TMP102

The TMP102 is able to support a variety of configuration options because it communicates over I²C, a flexible and extensible hardware protocol. This section discusses four such options.

Note that to simplify the code, the examples in this section use the SMBus subclass of I2C instead of I2C directly.

Reading Higher Temperatures with Extended Mode

The TMP102 can measure temperatures up to 150°C, but to do so requires increasing the resolution from the default of 12 bits to 13 bits, which is done by enabling *extended mode*. This mode, like most of the options of the TMP102, is controlled by the 16-bit configuration register, which is register 1. To enable extended mode, you set the EM bit in the configuration register to 1.

Because the configuration register controls many options, to avoid unintentionally changing an option the code (Listing 6-11) first reads the current value of the configuration register, then sets the EM bit, and finally writes the value back.

Listing 6-11.

```
const CONFIGURATION_REG = 1;
const EM_MASK = 0b0000_0000_0001_0000;

let configuration = sensor.readWord(CONFIGURATION_REG, true);
sensor.writeWord(CONFIGURATION_REG, configuration | EM_MASK,
                true);
```

In your own IoT product, you may already know the value of the configuration register, without needing to read it. In that case, you can set it directly, without the initial read.

With extended mode enabled, the temperature register returns 13-bit values instead of 12-bit values, which requires a small adjustment in the calculations of the Celsius degrees. In the SMBus version, the right shift value changes from 4 to 3 and the calculations for negative numbers change. Listing 6-12 shows the modified code.

Listing 6-12.

```
let sensor = new SMBus({address: 0x48});

let configuration = sensor.readWord(CONFIGURATION_REG, true);
sensor.writeWord(CONFIGURATION_REG, configuration | EM_MASK,
                true);

let value = sensor.readWord(TEMPERATURE_REG, true) >> 3;
if (value & 0x1000) {
    value -= 1;
```

```
    value = ~value & Ox1FFF;
    value = -value;
}

value /= 16;
trace(`Celsius temperature: ${value}\n`);
```

Setting the Conversion Rate

The conversion rate is the number of times a second the TMP102 completes a temperature measurement and updates the value in the temperature register. The TMP102 takes about 26 milliseconds to complete a temperature measurement. By default, the conversion rate is four times per second. During the 224 milliseconds between when a reading has been taken and the next reading is begun, the TMP102 enters a low power mode, reducing energy consumption by about 94%, from 40 µA to 2.2 µA.

Knowing the conversion rate is important to your application. If you read the temperature from the sensor more frequently than it's updated, you receive the same value, using limited CPU cycles unnecessarily. On the other hand, if the sensor is performing temperature readings more frequently than your application requires, it's using more energy than needed, as it generates readings that go unused.

The conversion rate is controlled by 2 bits in the configuration register, so it has four possible values, as shown here (and in Table 8 of the datasheet):

- **00** – once every 4 seconds (0.25 Hz)

- **01** – once per second (1 Hz)

- **10** – four times per second (4 Hz, the default)

- **11** – eight times per second (8 Hz)

The code in Listing 6-13 sets the conversion rate to eight times per second.

Listing 6-13.

```
const CONVERSION_RATE_SHIFT = 6;
const CONVERSION_RATE_MASK = 0b0000_0000_1100_0000;

let configuration = sensor.readWord(CONFIGURATION_REG, true);
configuration &= ~CONVERSION_RATE_MASK;
sensor.writeWord(CONFIGURATION_REG,
        configuration | (0b11 << CONVERSION_RATE_SHIFT), true);
```

Saving Energy with Shutdown Mode

Reducing the frequency of temperature conversions saves energy.
However, the lowest frequency is still one conversion every 4 seconds,
which may be more often than your IoT product requires. The TMP102
provides *shutdown mode,* which completely disables the temperature
conversion hardware, reducing energy consumption to 0.5 µA. Your
application can enter shutdown mode in the interval between readings
and then reenable the conversion.

The code in Listing 6-14 enters shutdown mode by setting the
shutdown mode bit in the configuration register.

Listing 6-14.

```
const SHUTDOWN_MODE_MASK = 0b0000_0001_0000_0000;

let configuration = sensor.readWord(CONFIGURATION_REG, true);
sensor.writeWord(CONFIGURATION_REG,
                configuration | SHUTDOWN_MODE_MASK, true);
```

Exiting shutdown mode is similar to entering but clears the shutdown
mode bit instead of setting it:

```
let configuration = sensor.readWord(CONFIGURATION_REG, true);
sensor.writeWord(CONFIGURATION_REG,
                configuration & ~SHUTDOWN_MODE_MASK, true);
```

One important detail to keep in mind when exiting shutdown mode is that because conversions take about 26 milliseconds, reading the temperature register immediately after exiting shutdown mode returns a stale value. To wait for a fresh temperature reading to be completed without blocking execution, use a timer, as shown in Listing 6-15.

Listing 6-15.

```
Timer.set(() => {
    let value = sensor.readWord(TEMPERATURE_REG);
    // Perform conversion to Celsius as before
    ...
}, 27);
```

Taking One-Shot Temperature Readings

Up to this point, you've configured the TMP102 sensor to continuously take temperature readings at a regular interval. The TMP102 also supports *one-shot mode,* for taking just one reading (see Listing 6-16). The one-shot feature is available only when the device is in shutdown mode, and once the reading is complete the TMP102 returns to the shutdown state. This makes it the most energy-efficient way to take infrequent readings—for example, if your product takes readings once an hour or only in response to a button press by the user.

Listing 6-16.

```
const ONESHOT_MODE_MASK = 0b1000_0000_0000_0000;

let configuration = sensor.readWord(CONFIGURATION_REG, true);
sensor.writeWord(CONFIGURATION_REG,
                 configuration | ONESHOT_MODE_MASK, true);
```

After enabling one-shot mode, you need to wait for a reading to be ready—about 26 milliseconds. Rather than wait a fixed interval, however, you can use a special feature of one-shot mode that lets you know when a reading is ready. This is important because the actual time needed to take a reading varies depending on the current temperature. After you set the one-shot bit to 1 in the configuration register, you poll that same bit to know when a new reading is ready; the TMP102 returns 0 while the temperature reading is taking place and 1 when the reading is available. Listing 6-17 shows the code that waits for the reading to be ready.

Listing 6-17.

```
while (true) {
    let configuration = sensor.readWord(CONFIGURATION_REG, true);
    if (configuration & ONESHOT_MODE_MASK)
        break;
}
// new temperature reading now available
```

The preceding code blocks execution while waiting for the temperature reading. This is acceptable for some products but not for others. To perform non-blocking polling, use a timer (Listing 6-18).

Listing 6-18.

```
Timer.repeat(id => {
    let configuration = sensor.readWord(CONFIGURATION_REG, true);
    if (!(configuration & ONESHOT_MODE_MASK))
        return;
    Timer.clear(id);
    // new temperature reading now available
}, 1);
```

One-shot mode has another interesting use. Since reading a temperature takes about 26 milliseconds, in theory about 38 readings may be taken per second. However, recall that the maximum conversion rate supported by the configuration register is eight times per second. Using continuous, back-to-back one-shot readings enables temperature readings to be taken as quickly as the hardware supports, which is valuable for situations where you want to precisely capture how the temperature changes over time.

Conclusion

Now that you understand the basics of some hardware protocols and know how to interact with some sensors and actuators, there's a lot you can do to make the simple examples provided more interesting. For example, you could make actuators respond to the input from sensors, or take what you learned in Chapter 3 about communicating with cloud services and use it to stream data from your sensors to the cloud. In Chapters 8, 9, and 10, you'll learn how to work with a touch screen, which is great for displaying sensor data and building user interfaces that work with hardware.

Countless other sensors and actuators are available online and in electronics stores. This chapter used some from SparkFun and Adafruit, both of which are excellent resources for beginners to electronics. In addition to offering many sensors and actuators and their datasheets, they also provide tutorials for many of their products, which are helpful starting points for writing your own JavaScript modules to interact with them.

CHAPTER 7

Audio

Sound is a great way to communicate information to the user of a device. You can use sound to provide feedback for user actions like tapping a button, to alert the user when a background task such as a timer or a download has finished, and much more.

Both the ESP32 and the ESP8266 support audio playback. Some development boards, including the M5Stack FIRE, come with a speaker built in. If your board doesn't include a speaker, you can attach one yourself. In this chapter, you'll learn how to play sounds using an inexpensive speaker that's easy to attach directly to an ESP32 or ESP8266. You'll also learn how you can achieve higher-quality audio playback using an external I²S audio driver, and how to choose the optimal audio format, balancing quality and storage space, for your project.

Speaker Options

If you're not using a development board with a built-in speaker, you'll need to wire a speaker to your device before running the examples.

Figure 7-1 shows a mini metal speaker available from Adafruit (product ID 1890) that works with the ESP32 and ESP8266. It's a simple analog speaker with 8 Ohm impedance that uses 0.5W of power. You can find many others like it with different impedance and power use. An 8 Ohm, 0.5W speaker is a great place to start because it can be used with the same power source as the ESP32 and ESP8266, whereas a larger speaker requires an external power supply.

© Peter Hoddie and Lizzie Prader 2020
P. Hoddie and L. Prader, *IoT Development for ESP32 and ESP8266 with JavaScript*,
https://doi.org/10.1007/978-1-4842-5070-9_7

Figure 7-1. *Mini metal speaker from Adafruit*

The mini metal speaker can be wired directly to your device, and it's an easy way to get started quickly. However, you can get better sound quality by adding an I²S chip. Figure 7-2 shows an I²S chip available from Adafruit (product ID 3006). This chip also amplifies the sound.

Figure 7-2. *I²S chip from Adafruit*

An I²S chip does not play sound itself; you still have to attach a speaker to it. The mini metal speaker does work with an I²S chip; however, the quality will be compromised by the inexpensive speaker. For higher-quality audio, use a higher-quality speaker such as the mono enclosed speaker available from Adafruit (product ID 3351) shown in Figure 7-3.

Figure 7-3. *Mono enclosed speaker from Adafruit*

An I²S chip adds additional cost, but it may be necessary if your product needs high-quality sound. In addition, using an I²S chip has lower CPU overhead on the ESP8266, which may also make it worth the cost. You can decide which option works best for you.

If you simply want to try out the audio playback capabilities of the Moddable SDK, the fastest way to start is with the analog speaker. If you later decide you want higher-quality audio, you can always switch to using the I²S chip and mono enclosed speaker. The JavaScript APIs to play audio are identical regardless of which setup you choose, so you will not have to change your application code. You do, however, have to configure audio settings differently for each option. The hosts for this chapter take care of the audio configuration in their manifest.json files. They assume you're using the speaker shown in Figure 7-1 or the I²S chip and speaker shown in Figures 7-2 and 7-3.

Adding the Analog Speaker

This section explains how to connect the analog speaker to your ESP32 or ESP8266.

ESP32 Wiring Instructions

Table 7-1 and Figure 7-4 show how to connect the speaker to the ESP32.

Table 7-1. *Wiring to connect the speaker to ESP32*

Speaker	ESP32
Wire 1	GPIO25 (D25)
Wire 2	GND

It doesn't matter which wire of the speaker goes to GPIO25 and which wire goes to GND on the ESP32.

Figure 7-4. *Wiring diagram for connecting the speaker to ESP32*

ESP8266 Wiring Instructions

Table 7-2 and Figure 7-5 show how to connect the speaker to the ESP8266.

Table 7-2. *Wiring to connect the speaker to ESP8266*

Speaker	ESP8266
Wire 1	GPIO3 (RX)
Wire 2	GND

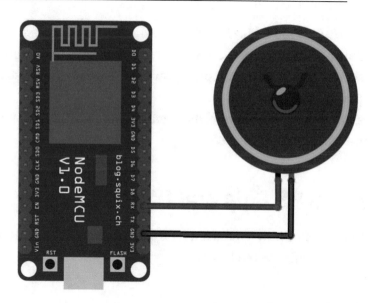

Figure 7-5. *Wiring diagram for connecting the speaker to ESP8266*

Note that GPIO3 on the ESP8266 is used for serial communication with your computer, for both installing and debugging. This means that you cannot use xsbug to debug audio examples and that installing audio examples requires a few extra steps:

1. Disconnect the speaker from GPIO3.

2. Install an example as usual.

3. Reconnect the speaker to GPIO3.

4. Reset the ESP8266 to run the example.

If you're using Moddable One, GPIO3 is on the small connector where you attach the programming adaptor. After installing an audio example, disconnect the programming adaptor, connect the speaker, and use a USB cable to power Moddable One.

It doesn't matter which wire of the speaker goes to GPIO3 and which wire goes to GND on the ESP8266.

Adding an I²S Chip and Digital Speaker

This section explains how to attach the I²S chip to your ESP32 or ESP8266 and the digital speaker to the I²S chip.

ESP32 Wiring Instructions

Table 7-3 shows how to connect the I²S chip to the ESP32.

Table 7-3. *Wiring to connect the I²S chip to ESP32*

I²S Chip	ESP32
LRC	GPIO12 (D12)
BCLK	GPIO13 (D13)
DIN	GPIO14 (D14)
GND	GND
Vin	3V3

Table 7-4 shows how to connect the speaker to the I²S chip.

Table 7-4. *Wiring to connect the speaker to the I²S chip*

Speaker	I²S Chip
Black wire	−
Red wire	+

Figure 7-6 shows a wiring diagram of the full setup.

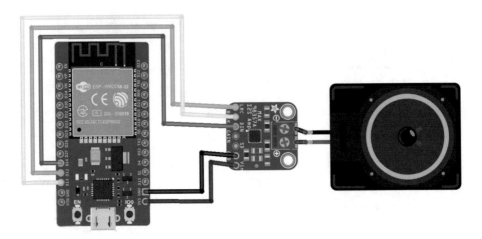

Figure 7-6. *Wiring diagram for speaker, I²S chip, and ESP32*

ESP8266 Wiring Instructions

Table 7-5 shows how to connect the I²S chip to the ESP8266. Note that GPIO2 and GPIO15 are not available on Moddable One, so you cannot use I²S on Moddable One.

Table 7-5. *Wiring to connect the I²S chip to ESP8266*

I²S Chip	ESP8266
LRC	GPIO2 (D4)
BCLK	GPIO15 (D8)
DIN	GPIO3 (RX)
GND	GND
Vin	3V3

Table 7-6 shows how to connect the speaker to the I²S chip.

Table 7-6. *Wiring to connect the speaker to the I²S chip*

Speaker	I²S Chip
Black wire	−
Red wire	+

Figure 7-7 shows a wiring diagram of the full setup.

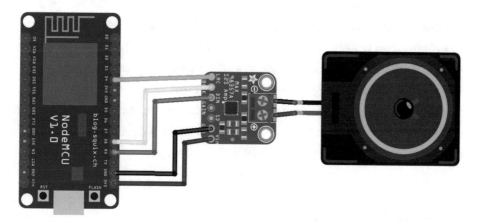

Figure 7-7. *Wiring diagram for speaker, I²S chip, and ESP8266*

Installing the Audio Host

The examples in this chapter are installed using the pattern described in Chapter 1: you install the host on your device using mcconfig, then install example applications using mcrun.

There are two host apps available in the $EXAMPLES/ch7-audio/host-pdm and $EXAMPLES/ch7-audio/host-i2s directories. The difference between the two is how they configure audio settings. Use host-i2s if you're using the I²S chip and speaker combination and host-pdm if you're using just the speaker. Navigate to the directory from the command line and install it with mcconfig.

The AudioOut Class

Sound is delivered to speakers using the AudioOut class:

```
import AudioOut from "pins/audioout";
```

The AudioOut class supports playback of uncompressed mono or stereo audio at 8 or 16 bits per sample and playback of mono audio compressed using the IMA ADPCM algorithm. The built-in mixer can combine up to four channels of audio for simultaneous playback. It can generate callbacks at specified points during audio playback—for example, to synchronize onscreen drawing with audio playback. AudioOut generates output in either 8-bit or 16-bit audio and sends it to a pseudo-analog output or a digital I²S digital-to-analog convertor.

With so many features, working with audio requires understanding the tradeoffs of the options available to help you make a decision about the best way to play audio in your product.

AudioOut Configuration

This section describes the audio hardware protocols, data formats, and other configuration options for the AudioOut class. For the examples in this chapter, the settings are configured in the manifest of the host.

Audio Hardware Protocols

The AudioOut class supports two different hardware protocols, PDM and I²S, as described in this section.

Pulse-Density Modulation (PDM)

Pulse-density modulation, or *PDM,* is a variation of PWM that rapidly toggles a digital output pin to create energy levels that correspond to the desired output signal. This way of playing audio is sometimes called an analog audio output because the PDM conversion synthesizes a signal that, when averaged over time, matches the energy levels output by an analog signal.

The advantage of PDM is that it works with only the built-in digital output hardware of your microcontroller. One disadvantage of PDM is that the audio is of lower quality; for this reason, PDM audio is primarily useful for sound effects in a user interface or game, not for music or spoken word.

The ESP32 has built-in hardware to convert audio data to PDM, so there's no CPU overhead when using this protocol. The ESP8266, however, has no PDM conversion hardware; the conversion occurs in software, thereby using some CPU cycles.

The `defines` section of the manifest configures the PDM output. For the ESP32, it looks like Listing 7-1.

Listing 7-1.

```
"defines": {
    "audioOut": {
        "i2s": {
            "DAC": 1
        }
    }
}
```

When set to 1, the `DAC` property tells the `AudioOut` implementation to use PDM output. No output pin is specified because only digital pin 25 on the ESP32 supports PDM output.

For the ESP8266, the manifest section is a bit different (Listing 7-2).

Listing 7-2.

```
"defines": {
    "audioOut": {
        "i2s": {
            "pdm": 32
        }
    }
}
```

The pdm property with a nonzero value indicates to use PDM output. The value must be 32, 64, or 128. The value 32 specifies that no oversampling should be performed in the conversion; this requires less time and memory but results in lower-quality output. The greater values provide better quality.

I²S

The other hardware protocol supported by the AudioOut class is *I²S*, a protocol designed to connect digital audio devices. I²S transmits unmodified audio samples over a digital connection from the microcontroller to a dedicated audio output component that performs the digital-to-analog conversion using specialized algorithms and hardware to generate a high-quality result. Both the ESP32 and the ESP8266 have built-in hardware support for transmitting audio data using I²S, so there's very little CPU overhead on the microcontroller for playing audio.

Using I²S requires an external component, which is an additional cost, and uses at least two, and often three, digital pins, whereas PDM output uses just a single digital pin. On the other hand, I²S audio hardware generates a very high-quality audio output, so the limiting factor for quality becomes the speaker used for output, not the way digital samples are converted to an analog signal.

I²S parts vary widely. Some have no configuration options, while others include an I²C connection to configure the part and do not operate correctly until they've been configured. This section assumes you're using an I²S part that either requires no configuration or has already been configured.

The defines section of the manifest configures the I²S output. For an ESP32, this looks like Listing 7-3.

Listing 7-3.

```
"defines": {
    "audioOut": {
        "i2s": {
            "bck_pin": 13,
            "lr_pin": 12,
            "dataout_pin": 14,
            "bitsPerSample": 16
        }
    }
}
```

The bck_pin, lr_pin, and dataout_pin properties correspond to the three pins of the I²S hardware protocol. The default values are 26, 25, and 22, respectively. The bitsPerSample property indicates the size of the sample in bits to transmit over the I²S connection. For many I²S components, this is 16, the default value, but for others 32 bits is required.

For the ESP8266, the manifest section is much simpler, as shown in Listing 7-4, because the I²S pins are defined in the hardware and cannot be changed. Setting the pdm property to 0 disables PDM output and uses the I²S hardware protocol instead. The I²S pins are 15 (bck_pin), 2 (lr_pin), and 3 (dataout_pin).

Listing 7-4.

```
"defines": {
    "audioOut": {
        "i2s": {
            "pdm": 0
        }
    }
}
```

The ESP8266 implementation supports 16-bit sample output only, so there's no bitsPerSample property.

Audio Data Formats

The audio data your application plays must be stored in a format compatible with the AudioOut class and the audio output hardware connected to the microcontroller. For maximum efficiency and simplicity, AudioOut uses a custom data format to store digital audio; this format is called MAUD, short for Moddable Audio. It consists of a simple header followed by the audio samples. The tools you use to build your application know how to convert standard WAVE audio files (files with a .wav file extension) containing uncompressed audio into MAUD resources, eliminating the need for you to create MAUD files yourself. The conversion tool is called wav2maud and is automatically invoked by mcconfig and mcrun. If your audio is stored in another format—for example, MP3—you must first convert it to a WAVE file; the free Audacity application is a good tool for this task.

For simplicity, the AudioOut class requires that all audio samples played have the same bits per sample, number of channels, and sample rate as the audio output. This eliminates the need to perform format conversion in software on the microcontroller. These AudioOut properties are configured in the manifest as shown in Listing 7-5.

Listing 7-5.

```
"defines": {
    "audioOut": {
        "bitsPerSample": 16,
        "numChannels": 1,
        "sampleRate": 11025
    }
}
```

The `bitsPerSample` property may be either 8 or 16, although 16 is more common. Similarly, the `numChannels` property may be 1 (mono) or 2 (stereo); however, it's rare to play stereo sounds for user interface interactions on a microcontroller, so the value is usually 1.

To include audio data in your application, you add them as resources to the manifest, as shown in Listing 7-6.

Listing 7-6.

```
"resources": {
    "*": [
        "./bflatmajor"
    ]
},
```

When `mcconfig` and `mcrun` process the manifest, they invoke `wav2maud` to convert the file `bflatmajor.wav` to a resource in the MAUD format. The audio is converted so that the bits per sample, number of channels, and sample rate of the audio in the MAUD resource match those defined in the `audioOut` section of the manifest. Based on the preceding example, the audio samples are 16-bit mono at 11,025 Hz sample rate.

Audio Compression

Audio data can take up a great deal of storage space. Ten seconds of 16-bit mono audio at 8 KHz uses 160,000 bytes of storage, or about 15% of the 1 MB flash address space of an ESP8266, and is still only about the quality of an analog telephone call. Audio compression is commonly used to reduce the size of audio stored on digital devices and transmitted over the internet. The algorithms used there, including MP3, AAC, and Ogg, just barely run on most microcontrollers, so they aren't practical here. A simpler audio compression format, IMA ADPCM (adaptive differential pulse-code modulation), provides 4:1 compression of 16-bit audio samples and is significantly less complex than MP3, AAC, or Ogg, making it suitable for real-time use on the ESP32 and ESP8266.

To use IMA ADPCM, add the `format` property to the `audioOut` section of your `manifest.json` file:

```
"audioOut": {
    ... // other audioOut configuration
    "format": "ima"
}
```

Your audio is automatically compressed during the build. The 10 seconds of 16-bit mono 8 KHz audio mentioned previously shrinks from 160,000 to 40,000 bytes. There's some reduction in quality, but for many purposes—for example, user interface sound effects—the difference may be unnoticeable.

Setting the Audio Queue Length

The length of the audio queue is fixed at build time, to improve the runtime efficiency of audio playback by eliminating the need for memory allocations when the queue is modified. The default queue length is eight entries, which is enough for most purposes, including all the examples in this chapter. If you need more queue entries, you can change the queue length by defining the queueLength property in the audioOut section of the manifest.

```
"audioOut": {
    ... // other audioOut configuration
    "queueLength": 20
}
```

Each queue entry uses some memory (24 bytes as of this writing), so you should not allocate more than you need. If your project makes simple use of audio, you can reduce the default to recover that memory.

Playing Audio with AudioOut

The AudioOut class provides a variety of different audio playback capabilities to help you incorporate audio feedback into your project's user experience. The playback engine is able to seamlessly play back sequences of samples. It provides a callback mechanism to synchronize audio with other parts of the user experience. It even supports real-time mixing together of multiple channels of audio, a capability that's quite unusual on microcontrollers. This section introduces these capabilities and many others.

Instantiating AudioOut

The AudioOut constructor accepts a dictionary to configure the audio output. The $EXAMPLES/ch7-audio/sound example configures the AudioOut instance as follows:

```
let speaker = new AudioOut({streams: 1});
```

The number of streams indicates the number of sounds that may be played simultaneously, up to a maximum of four. Since each stream uses some additional memory, it's best to configure the AudioOut instance for only as many as needed. The basic sound example plays a single sound, so it needs only one stream.

The sample rate, number of bits per sample, and number of channels are defined in the manifest, so they're not passed as properties in the dictionary to configure the AudioOut instance. The audio resources are stored in that same format, because mcconfig, mcrun, and wav2maud perform any needed format conversion.

Playing a Single Sound

To play a sound, you first use the enqueue method to enqueue an audio sample on a stream of the AudioOut instance. The $EXAMPLES/ch7-audio/ sound example enqueues the audio resource bflatmajor.maud on stream 0 as follows:

```
speaker.enqueue(0, AudioOut.Samples,
                new Resource("bflatmajor.maud"));
```

To begin playing the enqueued audio samples, call the start method:

```
speaker.start();
```

To stop all audio playback on the AudioOut instance, call the stop method:

```
speaker.stop();
```

Repeating a Sound

If you want to play a sound more than once, you can pass in an optional repeat parameter to the enqueue method. Here's how to play a sound four times:

```
speaker.enqueue(0, AudioOut.Samples,
                new Resource("bflatmajor.maud"), 4);
```

To repeat the sound indefinitely, pass Infinity for the repeat value:

```
speaker.enqueue(0, AudioOut.Samples,
                new Resource("bflatmajor.maud"), Infinity);
```

Using Callbacks to Synchronize Audio

The enqueue method can be used to enqueue more than just sounds; you can, for example, enqueue callbacks to be invoked at a particular point in a stream's playback. Enqueuing callbacks is useful for triggering other events in response to the completion of a sound, as in onscreen animations. In Listing 7-7, the callback simply traces to the debug console and blinks the on-board LED once when the sound finishes playing.

Listing 7-7.

```
speaker.enqueue(0, AudioOut.Samples,
                new Resource("bflatmajor.maud"));
speaker.callback = function() {
    trace("Sound finished\n");
    Digital.write(2, 1);
    Timer.delay(500);
    Digital.write(2, 0);
};
speaker.enqueue(0, AudioOut.Callback, 0);
```

Using Commands to Change Volume

You can also enqueue a command to adjust the volume of individual sounds. The command changes the volume of samples enqueued after it; it does not change the volume of samples already enqueued. The code in Listing 7-8 plays the sound three times in a row: once at the lowest volume (1), once at medium volume (128), and once at full volume (256).

Listing 7-8.

```
let bFlatMajor = new Resource("bflatmajor.maud");
speaker.enqueue(0, AudioOut.Volume, 1);
speaker.enqueue(0, AudioOut.Samples, bFlatMajor);
speaker.enqueue(0, AudioOut.Volume, 128);
speaker.enqueue(0, AudioOut.Samples, bFlatMajor);
speaker.enqueue(0, AudioOut.Volume, 256);
speaker.enqueue(0, AudioOut.Samples, bFlatMajor);
```

Playing a Sequence of Sounds

The $EXAMPLES/ch7-audio/sound-sequence example plays a sequence of sounds. Because it plays only a single sound at a time, it needs only one stream and so is configured with the same settings as the AudioOut instance in the basic sound example.

```
let speaker = new AudioOut({streams: 1});
```

Each sound is then enqueued using the AudioOut instance's enqueue method. As shown in Listing 7-9, all sounds in the sound-sequence example are enqueued on the same stream, causing them to play sequentially in the order in which they're enqueued.

Listing 7-9.

```
speaker.callback = function() {
    speaker.enqueue(0, AudioOut.Samples,
                    new Resource("ding.maud"));
    speaker.enqueue(0, AudioOut.Samples,
                    new Resource("tick-tock.maud"));
    speaker.enqueue(0, AudioOut.Samples,
                    new Resource("tada.maud"));
    speaker.enqueue(0, AudioOut.Callback, 0);
}
speaker.callback();
speaker.start();
```

A callback is enqueued after the samples; once all the samples have played, the callback is invoked and enqueues the samples again, causing the sequence to play repeatedly.

Playing Sounds Simultaneously

The $EXAMPLES/ch7-audio/sound-simultaneous example plays two sounds at the same time, so the AudioOut instance needs two streams.

```
let speaker = new AudioOut({streams: 2});
```

The AudioOut instance's enqueue method is called once to enqueue a ticking sound on stream 0. This sound repeats indefinitely.

```
speaker.enqueue(0, AudioOut.Samples,
                new Resource("tick.maud"), Infinity);
speaker.start();
```

Then the example sets a repeating timer whose callback enqueues a dinging sound on stream 1. Because the sound is enqueued on a different stream than the ticking sound, both sounds play at the same time.

```
Timer.repeat(() => {
    speaker.enqueue(1, AudioOut.Samples,
                    new Resource("ding.maud"));
}, 5000);
```

Playing Part of a Sound

The $EXAMPLES/ch7-audio/sound-clip example demonstrates how to play parts of a sound. The AudioOut instance is configured with the same settings as in the basic sound example.

```
let speaker = new AudioOut({streams: 1});
```

The tick-tock audio file is a recording of a clock. The full sound is played first.

```
let tickTock = new Resource("tick-tock.maud");
speaker.enqueue(0, AudioOut.Samples, tickTock);
```

Then the first half-second is played twice. To play portions of sounds, you specify the optional repeat, offset, and count arguments of the enqueue method. In the following line, repeat is 2, so the sound plays twice; offset is 0, so it starts at the beginning of the sound; and count is 11,025/2, so half a second plays:

```
speaker.enqueue(0, AudioOut.Samples, tickTock, 2, 0, 11025 / 2);
```

Flushing the Audio Queue

In some situations, you want to stop playing audio on one channel while continuing playback on others. The way to do this is to flush the audio queue of the stream you want to stop.

```
speaker.enqueue(0, AudioOut.Flush);
```

One situation where this is useful is when you have one channel playing a background sound effect on infinite repeat using channel 0 while using channel 1 for interactive audio sound effects. You can stop the background sound effects by flushing channel 0, which allows channel 1 to continue playing without interruption. This is in contrast to calling stop on the AudioOut instance, which immediately ends playback on all channels.

Conclusion

Now that you understand how to configure audio settings and use the many features of the AudioOut class to play audio, you're ready to get started adding sounds to your projects. The information in this chapter is most useful when combined with information from other chapters:

- In Chapter 5, you learned how to interface with sensors and actuators. Now you can trigger sound effects in response to sensor readings or to indicate when an actuator is performing an action.

- In the next few chapters, you'll learn how to work with a touch screen. You can provide audio feedback for user actions onscreen or add alert sounds to draw the user's attention back to the display. Pairing audio feedback and visual feedback delivers a more complete user experience.

CHAPTER 8

Graphics Fundamentals

This chapter and the two that follow show you how straightforward it is to create modern user interfaces using only a low-cost microcontroller and a small, inexpensive touch screen. This chapter first addresses how adding a display to your IoT product can deliver a better user experience and be much more cost-effective and practical now than in the past. The sections after that cover the fundamentals of graphics on microcontrollers, including important background on optimizations and constraints, information about how to add graphics assets to projects, and an introduction to various drawing methods. More detailed information is provided in the next two chapters, which describe the following in the Moddable SDK:

- *Poco,* a rendering engine for embedded systems that you can use to draw to displays

- *Piu,* an object-oriented user interface framework that uses Poco for drawing and simplifies the process of creating complex user interactions

With this knowledge, you'll be ready to begin building IoT products with built-in displays—and to explain to your friends and colleagues that this goal is in reach for your products.

P. Hoddie and L. Prader, *IoT Development for ESP32 and ESP8266 with JavaScript,*
https://doi.org/10.1007/978-1-4842-5070-9_8

Why Add a Display?

Displays with beautifully rendered user interfaces are taken for granted today on computers and mobile phones; however, they remain rare on IoT products. You're probably familiar with how difficult it is to set up and use IoT products that have extremely limited user interfaces, such as devices with just one button and a few blinking lights. It seems obvious that adding a display to many of these products would deliver a better user experience and make the product more valuable to the customer. Here are just some of the benefits to consider:

- Far more information is conveyed by a display than by a few pulsing status lights or alert sounds. A display shows the user what the product is doing in detail, and if there's a problem it tells the user what went wrong.

- A display makes it possible to include complete configuration options for all the capabilities of the product. This level of precision for configuration is generally not possible with a few buttons and knobs.

- A display enables the user to perform sophisticated interactions directly, with no other device required. Compare this to the user's downloading and installing a mobile app to interact with the product and pairing the app to the product before being able to begin configuring it.

- The graphical richness of a display lets you combine images with animations to bring style and character to the product, making it more enjoyable for the user and reinforcing the brand image of the manufacturer.

With so many benefits to incorporating a display, why don't more IoT products include one? The main reason is cost. The IoT products that do include displays tend to be high-end models, often so-called "hero" products that are intended to showcase the brand but not expected to sell many units. But is it really prohibitively expensive to add a screen to a product? At one time, the answer was yes. Here are some of the common reasons manufacturers cite for not adding displays to their products:

- The display itself is expensive. A small touch screen can easily cost $20 before adding the microcontroller and communication components.

- The software to interact with the display requires adding more RAM, and the graphics assets (images and fonts) for building a user interface require adding more storage.

- A special microprocessor with hardware graphics acceleration—that is, a GPU—is needed to achieve acceptable frame rates for animations.

- Graphics programming for microcontrollers requires highly specialized skills, making it more difficult to find qualified engineers and more expensive to hire them.

- The licensing costs for graphics and user interface SDKs for microcontrollers are too high.

- Preparing graphics assets for embedded systems is time-consuming and error-prone.

These were all valid reasons in the past, but today the situation is quite different. Unfortunately, most product planners, designers, and engineers working on IoT products are not aware that it's possible to get a touch screen, microcontroller, RAM, and ROM to deliver a beautifully rendered modern user interface for under $10, even for products in very low volume (comfortably under 10,000 units). Further, that same microcontroller can also provide Wi-Fi and Bluetooth support. The software and asset concerns are addressed by Poco and Piu.

Overcoming Hardware Limitations

The hardware in today's computers and mobile phones is designed to perform extremely complex graphical operations with amazing efficiency. This remarkable performance is achieved through a combination of sophisticated hardware and software. It should be no surprise that a typical microcontroller does not have that same graphics hardware and lacks the speed and memory to run the same complex graphics algorithms.

The natural consequence of these differences is that when IoT products powered by microcontrollers do include a display, the user interfaces they provide often appear quite primitive, like those of computers and video games from the dawn of the personal computer era in the 1980s and early 1990s. In some ways, that makes sense, because, like early personal computers and video games, these microcontrollers are considerably less powerful than modern computers. But an ESP32 today runs six times faster than the microprocessor in the top-of-the-line 1992 Macintosh IIfx, so there's enough performance in a modern microcontroller to match or exceed the results of this early hardware.

The Moddable SDK achieves great graphics results on a microcontroller by applying techniques used on early hardware, before modern high-speed display buses, plentiful memory, and GPUs. The implementations are inspired by classic techniques that have successfully been used for computer animation, video games, fonts, and more. Modern microcontrollers are still memory-constrained, but they're faster, so more calculations are possible. This makes some techniques possible that were not on older hardware.

The details of how these techniques work are beyond the scope of this book. All of the code that implements them is available to you in the Moddable SDK if you're interested in learning more. This book focuses on how to use these capabilities to build a great user interface for your product.

Pixel Rate Impacts Frame Rate

In modern mobile apps and web pages, the frame rate is the fundamental measure of graphics performance. Higher frame rates provide smoother animation. The GPU in computers and mobile phones is so powerful that it's able to update every pixel of the display on every frame. For a variety of reasons, a microcontroller just can't do the same; however, it's possible to achieve animations at 30 or even 60 frames per second (fps).

Because a microcontroller cannot render a high frame rate when updating the entire display, the solution is to update only a subset of the display. You can design your user interface so that only relatively small parts of the display are updated at any one time. This significantly reduces the work required of the microcontroller, so the user sees a smooth, high frame rate animation just as on a mobile app or web page.

To achieve a high frame rate using a microcontroller, it's helpful to think in terms of pixel rate—the number of pixels updated per second. The ESP32 and ESP8266 use a SPI bus to communicate with the display, and this connection runs at 40 MHz, providing a pixel rate of about 1,000,000 pixels per second, about 15 fps. Achieving the full theoretical pixel rate is generally not possible because of other factors; still, if your application updates only about 40% of the pixels in each frame—a pixel rate of about 30,000 pixels per frame—it can achieve a reliable frame rate of 30 fps. On the QVGA (320 x 240) displays used in this book, 30,000 pixels is about 40% of the total display area, which is more than enough motion to create a smooth, compelling user interface. Updating only 10,000 pixels per frame achieves 60 fps.

You might expect that the area of the screen updated on each frame must be a single rectangle. That would limit the design possibilities by limiting motion to one area of the display. Fortunately, though, this isn't the case. As you'll soon learn, you can have several different areas updating simultaneously, which can give the user the impression of motion on the full screen even though only a fraction of the actual pixels are changing.

Drawing Frames

Most graphics libraries used for microcontrollers are *immediate mode* APIs, meaning that the renderer performs the requested drawing operation when you call the drawing function. Poco, on the other hand, is a *retained mode* renderer, which works like this:

1. You tell Poco when you're starting to draw.

2. When you call drawing functions, they don't draw immediately but rather are added to a list of drawing commands.

3. When you tell Poco you're done drawing, it executes all the drawing commands.

Obviously retained mode rendering is more complex, and maintaining a list of drawing commands requires additional memory. Usually on microcontrollers, you try to keep software simple and memory use as small as possible, but the following benefits of retained mode justify its costs:

- Retained mode rendering eliminates flicker. For example, when you draw the background of the screen in an immediate mode renderer, all the pixels of the screen are drawn in the background color; when you then draw the controls, text, and pictures that make up the user interface, the user may first see the background screen without these user interface elements, causing a distracting momentary flicker. Because retained mode rendering executes all drawing commands before sending the result to the screen, it combines the background erase with the drawing of the user interface elements on the microcontroller before transmitting them to the display, thus eliminating the flicker.

- Retained mode improves performance by reducing the number of pixels transmitted from the microcontroller to the display. Consider that in every user interface there are some overlapping pixels—for example, the background of a button and its text label. In an immediate mode renderer, the overlapping pixels are sent to the display twice, whereas in a retained mode renderer each pixel is sent only once per frame. Because it's much faster to render a pixel than to transmit it to the display, this increases the overall pixel rate.

- Retained mode improves rendering quality by enabling efficient pixel blending. Modern computer graphics make heavy use of blending to smooth the edges of objects—for example, to anti-alias fonts to eliminate sharp edges ("jaggies"). This is one reason that text on today's computers and mobile phones looks so much crisper than screen text did in the 1980s. Blending is computationally more complex, and there's enough performance to do it because the microcontrollers are so much faster; however, blending also requires access to the pixel *behind* the pixel you're currently drawing. In typical microcontroller hardware, the previous pixel is stored in the display's memory, not the microcontroller's memory, making it either entirely unavailable or impractically slow to access.

The retained mode renderer, because it only transmits pixels to the display when they're fully rendered, always has the current value of the pixel available in memory and so is able to perform blends efficiently.

There are other advantages of retained mode renderers, but these three should be enough to convince you that the memory and complexity costs justify using a retained mode renderer like Poco instead of the more common immediate mode renderer. The quality of the user interface rendering is so much higher that users have the impression they're using a higher-quality product—one that belongs alongside their computer and phone rather than in a computer history museum.

Scanline Rendering

A QVGA display has 76,800 pixels, which means that a display with 16-bit pixels requires 153,600 bytes of memory to store one full frame. The ESP8266 has about 80 KB of total memory—only enough for a half frame, if your IoT product doesn't use any other memory! The ESP32 has much more, but still, holding an entire frame in memory uses 50% or more of the total free memory at startup. The displays used in this book include memory for a single frame, so the microcontroller doesn't have to store the entire frame, but it does need memory in which to render the frame. To minimize the memory required, the Poco renderer implements *scanline rendering*, a technique that divides the frame into horizontal strips as small as a single row of pixels; after each strip is rendered, it's immediately transmitted to the display. This approach is more complex than rendering the entire frame at once, but it reduces the rendering memory requirements for a single 16-bit QVGA display from 153,600 bytes to 480 bytes—one 240-pixel scanline at two bytes per pixel—a memory savings of 99.68%!

There's some performance overhead for each strip rendered, so there's a benefit to reducing the number of strips by increasing their size—but of course this also increases the memory needed. The performance benefit decreases somewhat with each line added to a strip, so increasing beyond about eight scanlines isn't usually worthwhile. If your project has some free memory or requires the highest performance rendering, you may want to have Poco render a few scanlines at a time; the upcoming chapters explain how to configure this.

Many modern microcontrollers, including the ESP32 and ESP8266, are able to use SPI asynchronously to transmit data to the display, which means that the microcontroller can do other work while that data is being transmitted. Poco uses asynchronous SPI transmission to render the next section of the display while the previous section is being transmitted to the display, and this simple parallel processing allows for a significant performance boost. To use this technique, Poco must have enough memory to hold at least two scanlines in memory: the previously rendered scanline that's now being transmitted and the current scanline that's now being rendered. Because this technique provides such a significant performance increase, Poco allocates two scanlines by default.

Restricting the Drawing Area

As you've seen in the sections "Pixel Rate Impacts Frame Rate" and "Scanline Rendering," a key technique used with graphics on microcontrollers is to update the display in parts rather than all at once. Note the following aspects of this technique in Poco and Piu:

- **In Poco** – The feature of the Poco rendering engine that enables restricting drawing to subsections of the display is called *clipping*. Poco uses a single rectangle to describe the *clipping area*; the portion of each drawing operation that intersects this clipping rectangle is drawn, whereas any portion of the operation that falls outside the clipping rectangle is not drawn. This feature is used by Poco to implement scanline rendering (and by Piu to implement partial frame updates). It's also available for use in your applications—for example, to draw a subset of an image.

- **In Piu** – Updating the smallest possible area of the display increases rendering performance on microcontrollers; however, determining the smallest possible area to update is quite difficult in the general case. Poco can't determine the optimal drawing areas for you because, being a rendering engine, it has no knowledge of what your code is drawing. Piu, on the other hand, is a user interface framework with complete knowledge of the different objects that make up your onscreen display. As a result, Piu is able to calculate the smallest possible update areas for you automatically, behind the scenes.

To understand the challenges of calculating the smallest possible update area, let's look at an example of a bouncing ball. In each frame, the ball moves some number of pixels. In Figure 8-1, the ball moves a few pixels down and to the right. The smallest rectangle that encloses the previous and current position of the ball is a good first estimate of the smallest possible area of the screen to update.

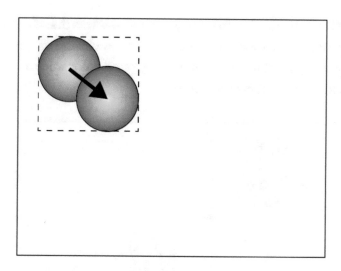

Figure 8-1. *Ball moving slightly, one update rectangle*

Now consider the case in which the ball moves a much longer distance (Figure 8-2): the smallest rectangle that encloses the previous and current positions includes many pixels that didn't actually change, but they're redrawn because they're included in the area to be updated.

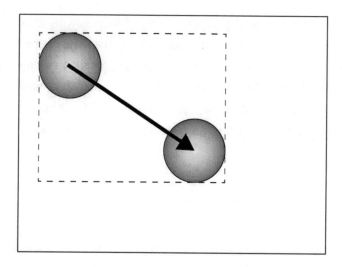

Figure 8-2. *Ball moving farther, one update rectangle*

As shown in Figure 8-3, in this case Piu recognizes that it's more efficient to update two separate areas: the area enclosing the previous location of the ball, which fills to the background color, and the area enclosing the current location of the ball.

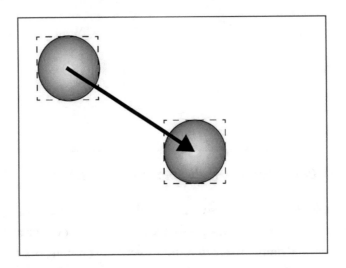

Figure 8-3. *Ball moving farther, two update rectangles*

Piu actually goes one step further. In the first example, where the ball moves only a small distance—a distance that causes the current position to overlap with the previous position—Piu recognizes that a single enclosing rectangle isn't the smallest possible update area; consequently (as shown in Figure 8-4), it updates *three* separate rectangles in this case, which avoids unnecessarily updating many background pixels that haven't changed.

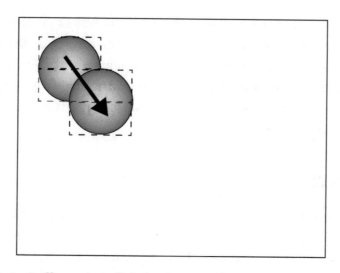

Figure 8-4. *Ball moving slightly, three update rectangles*

The calculations involved in optimizing the drawing area for a single bouncing ball are already surprisingly complex, and they would be even more complicated in an application with several bouncing balls that sometimes overlap. Piu automatically calculates the minimal set of rectangles for you; this does require time and memory, but the performance boost it gives makes it worthwhile. That's because rendering performance is largely limited by the pixel rate of your application and Piu is automatically minimizing the pixel rate of your code.

Pixels

Every display contains pixels, but not all displays have the same kind of pixels. Pixels come in different sizes and colors. This has always been the case but is easy to forget, because nearly all modern computers and mobile devices support the same 24-bit color pixel format. Like many areas of embedded development, the variety of pixel formats is partly a consequence of trying to keep hardware costs low. A display that's able to display colors tends to cost more, but there are factors other than cost that influence the pixel format used. For example, an ePaper display (often referred to by the name of the company that pioneered it, E Ink) that uses a technology only capable of displaying a handful of colors—typically black, white, and a few shades of gray—has no need for a pixel format that holds more than a few colors.

Pixel Formats

Most displays support a single type of pixel. The QVGA color displays used in most of the examples in this book use a color 16-bit pixel that has 5 bits for red, 6 bits for green, and 5 bits for blue. Your mobile phone probably has 24-bit color pixels, with 8 bits each for red, green, and blue. While both kinds of pixels are adequate for displaying full-color user experiences, the 24-bit color pixels are able to show 256 times more colors (16,777,216 vs. 65,536). That difference means that images on an embedded device may have a less refined appearance, especially in areas filled with similar colors, such as a sunset. This can be a problem for photos, but it's generally not an issue for user interfaces driven by microcontrollers if the design of the interface takes this limitation into consideration.

In addition to 16-bit color, a few displays support only 8-bit color. This is much more limited, allowing only 256 colors. Each pixel contains 3 bits for red, 3 bits for green, and 2 bits for blue. It's possible to build a reasonable user interface with a display that uses this type of pixel, but it takes some work to carefully select colors that look good within the limits. In some cases, it can be beneficial to use 8-bit color pixels on a display that supports 16-bit pixels. This clearly doesn't improve quality, but it does reduce the storage space required by assets and the time needed to render images. If you find your project is struggling to fit into available storage space or if rendering performance isn't quite what you need, using 8-bit color pixels on a 16-bit display may be a viable solution.

There are also 4-bit color pixels, but it's so difficult to achieve a professional result with these that they aren't addressed here. However, 4-bit gray pixels—which can display 14 levels of gray plus black and white—are very useful. An ePaper display that's unable to display color needs only gray pixels; since most ePaper displays are capable of showing only a few levels of gray, a 4-bit gray pixel is sufficient. Grayscale rendering is even faster than color rendering. You can use 4-bit gray pixels with a 16-bit color display to save even more storage space. There are also 8-bit gray pixels, which can display 254 levels of gray plus black and white; these provide excellent quality, but for many practical purposes 4-bit gray rendering is almost indistinguishable in quality from 8-bit gray pixels.

Some displays are just black and white. These displays tend to be small and low quality and to be used more for industrial IoT products than for consumer IoT products. A 1-bit pixel is sufficient for these displays; however, rendering well at 1 bit per pixel is very difficult. The Poco renderer does not support 1-bit pixel displays directly. Instead, the display driver receives 4-bit gray pixels and then reduces the image to 1-bit when transmitting it to the display.

Configuring a Host for a Pixel Format

In Chapter 1, you learned how to build a host using the `mcconfig` command line tool. On the command line, you use the `-p` option to pass the name of the hardware platform you're targeting—for example, `-p esp32` to build for an ESP32. For device targets that include a display, such as development boards from Moddable and M5Stack, the default pixel format is automatically configured for you. For example, when you build for Moddable One, Moddable Two, or M5Stack FIRE, the pixel format is set to `rgb565le`, for 16-bit color pixels; for Moddable Three, which has an ePaper display, it's set to `gray16`, for 4-bit gray pixels.

The most common display driver for 16-bit pixels is the ILI9341 driver, which implements the MIPI display standard used by the display controllers in both the Moddable and M5Stack development boards. The hardware uses 16-bit pixels, but the driver supports other pixel formats as well. You can experiment with different pixel formats by specifying the format on the command line using the -f option. For example, to use 4-bit gray pixels:

```
> mcconfig -d -m -p esp32/moddable_two -f gray16
```

When you configure the host this way, the ILI9341 driver converts the 4-bit gray pixels rendered by Poco to 16-bit color pixels when transmitting them to the display. But there are more changes going on than that:

- When you change the pixel format, the Poco renderer itself is recompiled. In this example, all the support for rendering to 16-bit pixels is removed and replaced with support for rendering to 4-bit gray pixels. This is one technique Poco uses to keep its code size small while still supporting many different pixel formats.

- Poco requires that certain graphics assets be stored in the same pixel format as the display, which normally would require you to recreate your graphics in a compatible format. But because that's tedious, time-consuming, and error-prone, mcconfig automatically invokes other tools in the Moddable SDK to convert your assets to a compatible format. This means you can switch pixel formats simply by specifying a different format, making it as easy as rebuilding your project to try different formats and see tradeoffs.

The ILI9341 driver also supports 8-bit color and 8-bit gray pixels. You can use those with mcconfig by specifying rgb332 and gray256, respectively, in the -f command line option.

If you find that the pixel format that works best for your product is different from the default, you can specify your preferred format in your project's manifest. That way you don't need to remember to include it on the command line each time you build. To do this, define a `format` property in the `config` section of your manifest:

```
"config": {
    "format": "gray256"
},
```

Freedom to Choose a Display

While the large variety of pixel formats available can seem confusing, it gives you options when creating a product. You can choose the display that best meets your requirements for quality, cost, and size. Poco is able to render pixels that work with your display, so you don't have to choose a display based on your software stack's limitations. In the next section, you'll learn how to automatically transform the graphics assets in your project to match the display you're using.

Graphics Assets

User interfaces built using Poco and Piu are composed of three different elements: rectangles, bitmap images, and text. That's everything; there are no graphics operations to draw lines, circles, round rectangles, arcs, splines, or gradients. At first, this may seem a little too simple, and you might conclude that it's impossible to build a modern user interface with such a small number of drawing operations. In the coming chapters, you'll see how to combine these elements to create a rich user experience that runs well on inexpensive microcontrollers. This section focuses on graphics assets—the images and fonts you use to build your user interface.

Masks

The most common type of asset used to build user interfaces with Poco and Piu is a mask. A mask is a grayscale image; you can think of it almost as a shape. Because the mask contains gray pixels, and not just black and white pixels, it can have smooth edges. Figure 8-5 shows two versions of a circle, the first as a grayscale mask and the second as a simple 1-bit mask, with their edges magnified to show the difference; note the gray edges in the magnification of the grayscale mask.

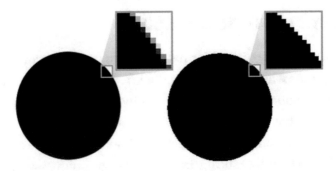

Figure 8-5. *Grayscale mask (left) and 1-bit mask (right)*

When Poco renders a grayscale mask, it doesn't draw it as an image. If it did, the white pixels would hide the background, as illustrated in Figure 8-6.

Figure 8-6. *Grayscale mask if drawn as image*

Instead, Poco renders masks by treating black pixels as solid (fully opaque), white pixels as transparent (fully invisible), and the grayscale levels between as different levels of blending. The result corresponding to Figure 8-6 is shown in Figure 8-7, where the black circle is superimposed on the background (which is visible through the transparent white pixels) and the gray edges of the circle blend with the background, eliminating any jagged edges.

Figure 8-7. *Grayscale mask drawn as mask*

You probably want to include color in your user interface, in which case gray images don't seem like an obvious solution. However, Poco lets you draw grayscale masks in any color. The black pixels are replaced by the color you choose, and the gray pixels blend that color with the background. Figure 8-8 shows the same circle mask drawn in blue (which appears gray in printed versions of this book).

Figure 8-8. *Grayscale mask drawn as mask in color*

The ability to draw a single grayscale mask in a variety of colors is very powerful, as it enables a single graphics asset to be displayed in different colors. This reduces the number of assets needed, saving storage space in your project.

Figure 8-9 shows some examples of grayscale masks used as user interface elements.

Figure 8-9. *Grayscale masks used as user interface elements*

As you know from the "Pixel Formats" section, Poco defines two different kinds of grayscale pixels: 4-bit and 8-bit. All Poco masks are 4-bit grayscale, which allows for the smallest storage size and fastest rendering without sacrificing much quality.

Adding Masks to Your Project

You add masks to your project as PNG files, the same kind of image file used by desktop applications, mobile apps, and web pages for user interface elements. Being able to use PNG files in your project is convenient; however, the ESP32 and ESP8266 aren't able to work efficiently with PNG images because of the memory requirements and CPU overhead needed to decode PNG images. Instead, the build tools convert your PNG files to formats that can be handled efficiently on these microcontrollers. Because of this automatic conversion, it's not necessary for you to understand the details of these nonstandard image formats (although the details are available in the Moddable SDK).

To include a PNG mask image in your project, add it to your project's manifest file in the resources section as shown in Listing 8-1.

Listing 8-1.

```
"resources": {
    "*-mask": [
        "./assets/arrow",
        "./assets/thermometer"
    ]
}
```

Keep in mind that resources specified in the manifest do not include a file extension. In the example in Listing 8-1, the file names of the image files are arrow.png and thermometer.png.

Mask Compression

Grayscale masks are small enough to use in products targeting microcontrollers. The thermometer image shown earlier in Figure 8-9 is 2,458 bytes when stored as a 4-bit grayscale mask. Still, it would be nice if it were smaller. Poco has a solution: it includes a compression algorithm specifically for 4-bit grayscale images. The algorithm is optimized for use on microcontrollers and therefore doesn't require much CPU time or additional memory.

For the thermometer image, the compression algorithm reduces the data size to 813 bytes, 67% smaller than the original uncompressed version. Compression ratios vary depending on the image. The Poco mask compression ratio improves for images that contain larger continuous white and black areas.

Uncompressed Masks

When drawing the masks for the user interface, it's often convenient to group several related elements together in a single graphics file. Many graphic designers prefer to work this way since it makes modifying the masks faster and easier. Because Poco supports clipped rendering, it's able to use only part of a mask when drawing, so you have the option to organize your graphics files this way. The masks in Figure 8-10, showing several different states of a Wi-Fi connection, are combined in a single graphics file.

Figure 8-10. *Multiple masks combined in single graphics file*

You can compress these combined mask images as described previously. However, there's a performance penalty for using compression with a mask containing multiple images. That's because to render a part of the compressed image, the decompressor must skip over the parts of the image above and to the left of the target area, which takes additional time. For some projects, the storage size reduction benefit of compression is more important than the performance reduction. You can keep the mask uncompressed by adding it to your manifest in a *-alpha section rather than the *-mask section (see Listing 8-2). Of course, your manifest may include both *-mask and *-alpha, to compress some masks while leaving others uncompressed.

Listing 8-2.

```
"resources": {
    "*-alpha": [
        "./assets/wifi-states"
    ]
}
```

Fonts

Fonts are a unique challenge in embedded development. Your computer and mobile phone have dozens, if not hundreds, of fonts built in. One or more of those fonts include nearly all the characters defined in the Unicode standard, meaning that there's no text character your devices can't display. On a microcontroller, there are no built-in fonts; the only fonts available to your project are the fonts you include in your project.

There are many fonts available for your computer, and it would be convenient to be able to use those same fonts in your IoT products. Most, if not all, of the fonts on your computer are stored in a format based on the TrueType scalable font technology created by Apple (the OpenType font format is a derivative of TrueType). Rendering these fonts on a microcontroller is possible but challenging, and the amount of code, memory, and CPU resources needed for rendering makes it impractical for many projects. The examples in this book use a simpler font format, a high-quality bitmap font. A TrueType-compatible renderer is available on the ESP32 and is introduced in this section.

Converting TrueType Fonts to Bitmap Fonts

Even though it's probably impractical to use TrueType fonts in all of your projects, you can still use the fonts on your computer, by using your computer to convert the TrueType fonts to a format that can be easily handled by a microcontroller. The TrueType font is rendered in a specific point size to a bitmap, with all the characters being stored in a single bitmap. The bitmap uses 4-bit gray pixels, rather than black and white, to maintain the anti-aliasing of the original font. In addition, a .fnt file is generated that maps between Unicode character codes and rectangles in the font bitmap. This font format that combines a bitmap image with a map file is called *BMFont*, for "bitmap font." There are several variations of BMFont; the Moddable SDK uses the binary BMFont format. Figure 8-11 shows an example of what the Open Sans font at 16-point size looks like in the BMFont format.

Figure 8-11. *Character images of font in BMFont format*

Notice that the characters are not arranged in the same order as in the Unicode or ASCII standard. For example, the letters A, B, and C do not appear in sequence. Instead, characters are arranged by height, to make the bitmap image as small as possible by minimizing the amount of unused white space.

The tools that may be used to create these bitmap files are not part of the Moddable SDK. Glyph Designer from 71 Squared works well. The Moddable SDK includes a suite of pre-built fonts in the BMFont format, so you can get started developing without any additional investment in tools.

The BMFont format has two files for each font: an image file, usually in the PNG format, and a font map file with a .fnt file extension. These two files should have the same name with different file name extensions, as in OpenSans-Regular-16.png and OpenSans-Regular-16.fnt. To add these to your project, include the name in your project manifest as shown in Listing 8-3.

Listing 8-3.

```
"resources": {
    "*-mask": [
        "./assets/OpenSans-Regular-16"
    ]
}
```

Notice that the *-mask section is the same one used for compressed grayscale masks. Fonts included in this way are compressed too; however, rather than the entire image being compressed, each character is compressed individually. This enables each character to be decompressed directly, avoiding the overhead that would otherwise be required to skip over the pixels above and to the left of each glyph.

The compressed glyphs are merged with the data from the .fnt file into a single resource. This results in compact font files that still retain excellent quality and can be rendered efficiently. The preceding Open Sans 16-point font example uses just 6,228 bytes of storage in total for both the compressed characters and the font metric information needed for layout and rendering. Additionally, because fonts are stored using the same compression format as grayscale masks, they may also be rendered in any color.

The BMFont format does not require fonts to be grayscale. This format is popular with game designers because it enables them to include creative, colorful fonts in their games. Full-color fonts are supported by Poco and Piu. They're not commonly used on microcontrollers because they require significantly more storage. In case you want to try them out, the Moddable SDK contains examples to get you started.

Using Scalable Fonts

The BMFont format is convenient and efficient, but it eliminates one of the key benefits of TrueType fonts: the ability to scale the fonts to any size. If your project uses the same font at three different sizes, you need to include three different versions of it, one for each point size. It's possible to use scalable fonts directly on some more powerful microcontrollers, including the ESP32. A high-quality implementation of scalable TrueType fonts that's optimized for microcontrollers is available as a commercial product from Monotype Imaging, a leading provider of fonts and font technology. The Monotype Spark scalable font renderer has been integrated with the Moddable SDK and so can be used with both Poco and Piu. For more information, contact Moddable or Monotype.

Font Copyright

For commercial products, you need to make sure you have the rights to use any font you include in your products. Just like books and computer software, fonts can be copyrighted by their creators. Fortunately, there are many excellent fonts available in the public domain or under a FOSS (free and open source software) license. The Open Sans font created by Google for Android is one such font that works well in the user interfaces of IoT products.

Color Images

While grayscale masks are a powerful tool for building user interfaces, there are times when you need full-color images. Poco uses uncompressed bitmaps to support color images. These bitmaps provide excellent quality and performance; however, they can be quite large and so are typically used sparingly in interfaces for microcontrollers.

You can use standard JPEG and PNG files for color images. As with grayscale masks, mcconfig converts them at build time to the optimal format for your build target. To include color images in your project, add them to a *-color section in the resources section of your manifest (see Listing 8-4). Note that the .jpg or .png file extension is omitted.

Listing 8-4.

```
"resources": {
    "*-color": [
        "./quack"
    ]
}
```

Full-color images are fully opaque; they have no blended or transparent areas. Figure 8-12 shows the quack JPEG image from the preceding manifest fragment rendered in a simple user interface.

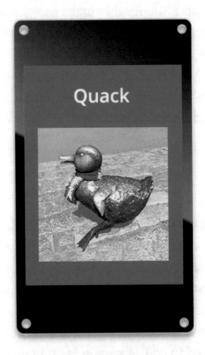

Figure 8-12. *Rendering of full-color image*

The shape is a rectangle because all of the pixels in the image are drawn. Images stored in a PNG file may contain an optional *alpha channel.* An alpha channel is like a grayscale mask: it indicates which pixels from the image should be drawn, which should be skipped, and which should be blended with the background. Alpha channels are usually created when you edit the image in tools like Adobe Photoshop. Poco supports rendering alpha channels; you indicate that you want to preserve the alpha channel by putting the image into the *-alpha section of the resources section of your manifest (see Listing 8-5).

Listing 8-5.

```
"resources": {
    "*-alpha": [
        "./quack-with-alpha"
    ]
}
```

Figure 8-13 shows the result. The duck image is the same one used in Figure 8-12; however, an alpha channel has been added to mask the background. Consequently, only the duck is drawn when the image is rendered.

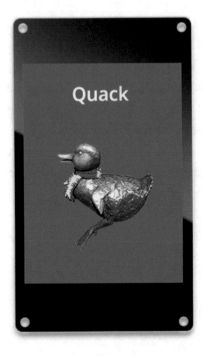

Figure 8-13. *Rendering of full-color image with alpha channel*

When you include images with an alpha channel in your project, the build tools create two separate images: the full-color image as if you'd put the image into the *-color section and the uncompressed alpha channel as a 4-bit grayscale mask. The color resource is named quack-color.bmp and the compressed mask resource is named quack-alpha.bm4. Figure 8-14 shows the alpha channel used to mask the drawing of the duck image.

Figure 8-14. *Alpha channel used in Figure 8-13*

When Poco and Piu render the image, they use both the color image and the mask. You'll learn how to do this in the next two chapters.

Display Rotation

Each display has a native orientation, meaning there's one edge that is the "top." This orientation is defined by the position of the first pixel that the hardware draws and the direction in which drawing proceeds from there. The native orientation is determined by the hardware and cannot be changed. Still, it's often desirable to treat a different edge of the screen as the top, to effectively rotate the image on the display. This is common on mobile devices that automatically rotate the image on the display to match the orientation in which the user is holding the device. This ability is also present in most LCD televisions, so that the user can mount the display however is most convenient and then manually adjust the orientation to display the image "right side up."

While many IoT products don't allow the user to change the orientation, either by configuration or by rotating the device, these products may still need to rotate the display—for example, when the product's design requires a landscape orientation but the display's native orientation is portrait mode, or when the display is mounted upside down in the product to save space (which may seem unusual, but it really does happen). Also, sometimes the hardware designer mistakenly mounted the display upside down, and to save time the software team is asked to compensate. For these reason and more, the ability to render the user interface at orientations of 0, 90, 180, and 270 degrees is necessary for many IoT products.

As described in the following sections, there are two different techniques for rotating the display: a software approach that works with all displays and a hardware approach that works with some displays.

Rotating in Software

The most common technique for rotating the user interface is to draw the full interface into an offscreen memory buffer as if the display was at the rotated orientation. Then, when the pixels are transmitted to the display, they're transformed to match the hardware orientation. This approach isn't feasible on low-cost microcontrollers because there's not enough memory available to store a full frame in an offscreen buffer.

Poco takes a very different approach: it rotates all image assets to the desired orientation during the build so that they don't need to be rotated at runtime. This rotation is performed at the same time as any needed pixel format conversions. Then, when the application on the embedded device makes drawing calls, Poco only needs to rotate the drawing coordinates to the target orientation. With those two steps done, Poco renders as usual and the result appears rotated on the display. This approach has almost no measurable runtime overhead—no additional memory is used, and only a trivial amount of additional code is run to perform the coordinate transformation—so it's almost a no-cost feature. Because software rotation is implemented entirely in the Poco renderer, it works with all displays.

When using software rotation, you can change orientation with the -r command line option to mcconfig. The supported rotation values are 0, 90, 180, and 270.

```
> mcconfig -d -m -p esp/moddable_one -r 90
```

As with the pixel format configuration, you may also specify the software rotation in your project manifest:

```
"config": {
    "rotation": 90
}
```

There's one notable limitation to software rotation: the rotation is fixed at build time and therefore can't be changed at runtime. Consequently, this technique is useful for situations where the IoT product user interface needs to be at a different orientation than the native orientation of the display but not when it needs to respond to a user action, such as turning the screen. Hardware rotation, when available, overcomes this limitation.

Rotating in Hardware

Hardware rotation uses features of the display controller to rotate the image as the display receives the pixels from the microcontroller. Using hardware rotation requires both the display controller and the display driver to support the capability. Hardware rotation is fully supported by the ILI9341 driver for MIPI-compatible display controllers.

Hardware rotation is performed entirely at runtime, so there's nothing to define in your build command line or project manifest. In fact, it's important that you do not use both hardware and software rotation in your project; they're not designed to work together, so the results can be unpredictable.

When using hardware rotation, you set the rotation at runtime instead of configuring it at build time. You use the screen global variable to communicate with the display driver. For displays that support hardware rotation, the screen global has a rotation property; you can check whether hardware rotation is supported by seeing whether this property is defined.

```
if (screen.rotation === undefined)
    trace("no hardware rotation\n");
else
    trace("hardware rotation!\n");
```

To change the rotation, set the `rotation` property:

```
screen.rotation = 270;
```

Your code can read `screen.rotation` to retrieve the current rotation:

```
trace(`Rotation is now ${screen.rotation}\n`);
```

When the hardware rotation is changed, the display does not change. The full content of the display must be redrawn before the user sees the changed orientation. If you update only part of the screen after changing the rotation, the user will see part of the display drawn in the original orientation and other parts with the new orientation.

The host for the M5Stack target includes support to automatically rotate the user interface of projects using Piu, to match the hardware orientation. This results in the same behavior as a mobile phone with a display that adjusts to how the user is holding the device. This feature is possible because the M5Stack includes a built-in accelerometer sensor, which provides the current device orientation. For M5Stack projects that don't want to use this feature, you can disable it in your project manifest.

```
"config": {
    "autorotate": false
}
```

Poco or Piu?

Throughout this chapter, you've learned about the Poco rendering engine for graphics and the Piu user interface framework, both of which can be used to build the user interface of IoT products running on inexpensive microcontrollers (including the ESP32 and ESP8266). Poco and Piu have similar graphics capabilities, because Piu uses Poco for rendering. When you start creating your own projects, you must decide whether to use the Poco API, the Piu API, or perhaps both. This section explains some of the differences, to help you make your choice.

Poco and Piu are inherently different APIs:

- Poco is a graphics API. You make function calls that eventually cause parts of the screen to be drawn.

- Piu is an object-oriented API for building user experiences. You create user interface objects with Piu such as text labels, buttons, and images. Adding these objects to the application causes parts of the screen to be drawn; you do not make drawing function calls yourself.

Piu takes care of many details for you, so you'll likely write less code; for example, it calls Poco to render your user interface objects when necessary. Because you tell Piu about all the active user interface objects on the current screen, Piu is able to minimize the amount of drawing necessary when you move, change, show, or hide an element. For example, with Piu you change the color of a user interface element using a mask with just a single line of code; Piu determines what pixels on the screen must be updated and automatically draws the changed element along with any objects that intersect it. By contrast, Poco has no knowledge about the user interface of your application, so you must write the code to refresh the screen and minimize the update areas. The code to do that often starts simple but becomes increasingly difficult to maintain as the user interface grows more complex.

Piu uses memory to keep track of the active user interface objects and consequently uses more memory than Poco alone. Of course, if you don't use Piu your code must keep track of the active user interface objects itself, which also requires memory.

Piu has built-in support for responding to touch events. In fact, Piu automatically supports multi-touch. (The displays on Moddable One and Moddable Two both support two touch points.) Being a graphics engine, Poco is focused on drawing and has no support for touch input, so your application must interact with the touch input driver directly; while this isn't too difficult to do, it's more code for you to write and maintain.

Perhaps the biggest advantage of using Piu is that, as a framework, it provides the basic structure of your project. The following predefined objects give your project a well-defined, well-designed organization that's backed by the very efficient implementation of Piu itself:

- The `Application` object maintains global state and exists for the entire application lifetime.

- The `Texture` and `Skin` objects organize your graphics assets.

- The `Style` objects manage font face, size, and style using cascading style sheets like CSS on the web.

- The `Container` and `Content` objects define the elements of your user interface.

- The `Behavior` objects group together event handlers for a specific purpose, such as providing a touch button behavior.

- The `Transitions` objects each implement a unique transition, either of the entire display or parts of it.

When you use Poco, you have to design and implement the application structure yourself. If your project user interface looks somewhat similar to a mobile app, desktop application, or web page, it's probably a good idea to use Piu, because it's designed and optimized for that. If you enjoy writing user interface frameworks or if your user experience is quite different—for example, a game—then using Poco directly is probably the right choice.

Some projects have a standard user interface style but need to provide a specialized rendering of part of the screen. One example of this is an IoT product showing a real-time graph of sensor data; the buttons and labels on the screen are a good fit for Piu, but the graph would be most efficiently rendered with Poco. The solution for a project like this is to use Piu for the screen and, to draw the graph, embed a Piu `Port` object, which lets you issue drawing commands similar to Poco within a Piu layout.

Conclusion

The next chapter further discusses Poco and its graphics framework, Commodetto, and the chapter following that one discusses Piu. As you read through these two chapters, consider the needs of your own project and whether the high-level Piu user interface API or the low-level Poco graphics rendering API is a better fit. Poco and Piu are quite different to work with, so it would be worthwhile to experiment with both of them to understand which is best for your needs.

CHAPTER 9

Drawing Graphics with Poco

The Poco renderer is at the core of all graphics and user interface code in this book. As you learned in Chapter 8, the design and implementation of Poco are optimized for delivering high-quality, high-performance graphics on the inexpensive microcontrollers used in many IoT products. This chapter introduces all the major capabilities of the Poco API through a series of examples. The name Poco is a term from classical music meaning "a little," reflecting the compact size and scope of the rendering engine.

Poco is part of *Commodetto,* a graphics library that provides bitmaps, instantiation of graphics assets from resources, offscreen graphics buffers, display drivers, and more. Some of the examples in this chapter use these Commodetto features. The name Commodetto, also a term from classical music, means "leisurely," reflecting the ease of working with the graphics library.

Installing the Poco Host

You can run all of this chapter's examples by following the pattern described in Chapter 1: install the host on your device using `mcconfig`, then install example applications using `mcrun`.

© Peter Hoddie and Lizzie Prader 2020
P. Hoddie and L. Prader, *IoT Development for ESP32 and ESP8266 with JavaScript,*
https://doi.org/10.1007/978-1-4842-5070-9_9

All the Poco examples require the use of a screen, making it essential for your `mcconfig` command line to specify a platform with a screen driver for your development board. The examples are intended to run on screens with 240 x 320 resolution. The following command lines are for Moddable One, Moddable Two, and M5Stack FIRE:

```
> mcconfig -d -m -p esp/moddable_one
> mcconfig -d -m -p esp32/moddable_two
> mcconfig -d -m -p esp32/m5stack_fire
```

If you're wiring the screen to your development board using a breadboard and jumper wires, follow the instructions in Chapter 1. The wiring provided there for the ESP32 works with the `esp32/moddable_zero` target; likewise for the ESP8266 and the `esp/moddable_zero` target.

If your device doesn't have a screen, you can run this chapter's examples on the desktop simulator provided by the Moddable SDK. The following command lines are for macOS, Windows, and Linux:

```
> mcconfig -d -m -p mac
> mcconfig -d -m -p win
> mcconfig -d -m -p lin
```

The host for this chapter is in the `$EXAMPLES/ch9-poco/host` directory. Navigate to this directory from the command line and install it with `mcconfig`.

If you're using the desktop simulator, make sure you change the dimensions of the screen to 240 x 320 before you install examples. You do this by selecting **240 x 320** from the **Size** menu in the application's toolbar.

Preparing to Draw

To use the Poco renderer, you need to import the Poco class from the `commodetto/Poco` module:

```
import Poco from "commodetto/Poco";
```

Poco is a general-purpose renderer. The pixels it renders can be sent to a screen, a memory buffer, a file, or the network. Poco doesn't know how to send pixels to any of these destinations; instead, it outputs pixels to an instance of the PixelsOut class, and each subclass of PixelsOut knows how to send pixels to a particular destination. For example, the display driver is a subclass of PixelsOut that knows how to send pixels to the screen. BufferOut, another subclass of PixelsOut, sends pixels to a memory buffer (as you'll see in the "Efficiently Rendering Gradients" section of this chapter).

When you instantiate Poco, you provide an instance of a PixelsOut class for Poco to call with rendered pixels. The host for this chapter automatically creates an instance of PixelsOut for the display driver of your development board and stores it in the screen global variable. To work with the screen, you simply pass screen to the Poco constructor.

```
let poco = new Poco(screen);
```

The pixel format and display dimensions of the display driver are configured in the host's manifest. The screen instance has width and height properties, but these do not include the effects of software rotation. Instead, when working with Poco, use the width and height properties of the Poco instance to get the bounds of the display with any rotation adjustments (hardware or software) applied.

```
trace(`Display width is ${poco.width} pixels.`);
trace(`Display height is ${poco.height} pixels.`);
```

As noted in Chapter 8, Poco is a retained mode renderer, meaning that instead of executing drawing commands immediately, it builds up a list of drawing operations to render all at once. This display list requires memory. The default display list is 1,024 bytes. If your drawing overflows the display list allocation, you need to increase it. If your project doesn't use all of the default display list allocation, you can decrease it to free memory for other uses. The following example adjusts the display list to 4 KB:

```
let poco = new Poco(screen, {displayListLength: 4096});
```

You can monitor how much of the display list your project is using by watching the "Poco display list used" row of the Instrumentation panel in xsbug (see Figure 9-1).

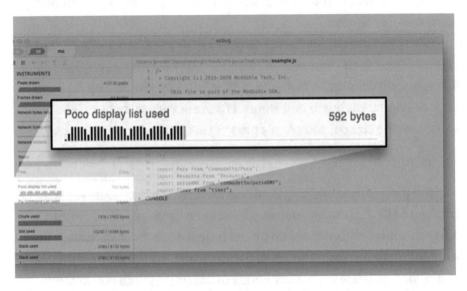

Figure 9-1. *Monitoring display list use in* xsbug *Instrumentation panel*

Poco also allocates memory for rendering. The default rendering buffer is two hardware scanlines. The width of one hardware scanline is available from screen.width. If memory is very tight in your product, you can reduce this to a single scanline, though no smaller.

```
let poco = new Poco(screen, {pixels: screen.width});
```

Poco is able to render faster when it renders several scanlines at once. The following code increases the rendering buffer to eight full scanlines, while setting the display list to 2 KB.

```
let poco = new Poco(screen,
          {displayListLength: 2048, pixels: screen.width * 8});
```

As an optimization, Poco shares the memory allocated for the display list and the rendering buffer. If the display list for the frame being rendered isn't entirely full, Poco includes those unused bytes in the rendering buffer, often enabling it to render a little faster.

The three fundamental drawing operations Poco provides are those for drawing rectangles, bitmaps, and text. As mentioned in Chapter 8, this may not sound like much, but you can combine these elements to create a rich user experience. The next sections cover them in detail.

Drawing Rectangles

Drawing rectangles is the simplest of the three fundamental drawing operations that Poco provides. In introducing this first drawing operation, this section also presents some fundamentals about drawing with Poco.

Filling the Screen

The $EXAMPLES/ch9-poco/rectangle example simply fills the entire screen with a solid color. The code is shown in Listing 9-1.

Listing 9-1.

```
let poco = new Poco(screen);
let white = poco.makeColor(255, 255, 255);
poco.begin();
    poco.fillRectangle(white, 0, 0, poco.width, poco.height);
poco.end();
```

The first line invokes the Poco constructor to create an instance of Poco. The instance delivers rendered pixels to screen. This step is common for all examples in this chapter and so will be omitted from the remaining examples shown here.

Let's look in turn at each of the methods called in this example:

1. The three arguments to poco.makeColor receive the red, green, and blue color components, each with a range from 0 (none) to 255 (full). Here the color specified is white, so the red, green, and blue components are each 255. The makeColor method combines these three values to a single value that's optimal for rendering to the destination (screen in this example). Poco uses different algorithms to create the color value from the color components, depending on the destination. Therefore, you should only pass the value returned by makeColor to the same Poco instance that created it.

2. The call to poco.begin tells Poco that you're beginning to render a new frame. All drawing operations that occur after this are added to the display list for the frame.

3. The poco.fillRectangle call adds a command to draw a full-screen white rectangle to the display list. The color is the first argument, followed by the x and y coordinates, and then the width and height. The coordinate plane puts (0, 0) at the top-left corner of the screen with the height and width progressing down and right.

4. The call to poco.end tells Poco that you've completed issuing the drawing operations for this frame. Poco then renders the pixels and sends them to screen; this may take some time, depending on the size of the display, the speed of the microcontroller, and the difficulty of rendering the frame. On a Moddable One or Moddable Two, it finishes quickly.

Important   Poco doesn't automatically fill the background with a color, because that would reduce rendering performance. This means your code must draw to every pixel in the frame. If you don't specify a color for a pixel, Poco outputs an undefined color. Make sure your code fills the background with a color, as this example shows, or ensure that the combination of drawing calls you make covers every pixel.

Updating Part of the Screen

When you call the begin method, you have the option to specify the area of the screen to update. You may recall that updating smaller parts of the screen is one technique for achieving higher frame rates.

The following example fills a square of 20 x 20 pixels with red; the other pixels on the display are unchanged. If you append this code to the earlier rectangle example, the screen will be white except for a small red square in the top-left corner.

```
let red = poco.makeColor(255, 0, 0);
poco.begin(0, 0, 20, 20);
    poco.fillRectangle(red, 0, 0, 20, 20);
poco.end();
```

Here the call to begin defines the area in which to draw—called the *update area*—to be only the 20 x 20 square in the top-left corner of the display. Only the pixels in the update area are drawn, so the white pixels outside the update area remain unchanged. When you call begin with no arguments, as in the rectangle example, the update area is the entire screen. In this example, the call to fillRectangle uses the same coordinates and dimensions as the call to begin, filling the entire update area with red pixels.

As noted previously, the code between begin and end must make drawing calls that cover every pixel to generate a correct result—but what happens if that code draws outside the area specified in the call to begin? Consider the following example, which calls fillRectangle with parameters specifying the full screen:

```
let red = poco.makeColor(255, 0, 0);
poco.begin(0, 0, 20, 20);
    poco.fillRectangle(red, 0, 0, poco.width, poco.height);
poco.end();
```

This example produces exactly the same result as the preceding example. Instead of responding to the request by fillRectangle to draw to the full screen, Poco limits the output of fillRectangle to the update area specified in the call to begin. This approach is convenient for many rendering situations—especially for animations—as it enables you to limit the area to update without changing your code to restrict its drawing to the update area.

Drawing Random Rectangles

A classic computer graphics demonstration is to continuously render randomly colored rectangles of random sizes and at random locations. The $EXAMPLES/ch9-poco/random-rectangles example does exactly that, by specifying coordinates in the call to Poco's begin method to limit the drawing to the current rectangle being drawn. If you run the example, you'll see an animated version of the screen shown in Figure 9-2.

Figure 9-2. *Rendering from* `random-rectangles` *animation*

The first step is to instantiate Poco and clear the screen:

```
let black = poco.makeColor(0, 0, 0);
poco.begin();
    poco.fillRectangle(black, 0, 0, poco.width, poco.height);
poco.end();
```

Next, a repeating timer (Listing 9-2) is scheduled to run at about 60 frames a second. When the timer fires, random coordinates and dimensions of a rectangle are generated along with a random color. The `begin` method limits the drawing to the area of the rectangle.

Listing 9-2.

```
Timer.repeat(function() {
    let x = Math.random() * poco.width;
    let y = Math.random() * poco.height;
    let width = (Math.random() * 50) + 5;
    let height = (Math.random() * 50) + 5;
    let color = poco.makeColor(255 * Math.random(),
                    255 * Math.random(), 255 * Math.random());
    poco.begin(x, y, width, height);
        poco.fillRectangle(color, 0, 0, poco.width,
                            poco.height);
    poco.end();
}, 16);
```

The random values are all floating-point because the call to Math.random returns a number from 0 to 1. All Poco functions expect integer values for coordinates, so makeColor and begin automatically round the floating-point numbers provided to the nearest integer. In Chapter 11, you'll learn how to add your own random integer function to increase performance by eliminating these floating-point operations.

Drawing Blended Rectangles

The rectangles drawn up to this point have all been solid: the pixels are entirely opaque and completely obscure the pixels behind them. A blended rectangle combines a single color with the pixels behind it, which creates an effect like looking through a pair of tinted glasses. Blended rectangles are used in user interfaces to provide a layered effect and to draw shadows.

To draw a blended rectangle, use the blendRectangle method. The parameters are similar to those of fillRectangle, with the addition of the blend level as the second parameter. The blend level is a number from 0 to 255, where 0 means fully transparent (entirely invisible) and 255 means fully opaque. The following line blends over the entire screen with red at a blend level of 128 (50%). Like all other drawing operations, this must occur between calls to begin and end.

```
poco.blendRectangle(red, 128, 0, 0, poco.width, poco.height);
```

If you pass blendRectangle a blend level of 0, it ignores the drawing operation entirely, not even adding an entry to the display list. If you pass a blend level of 255, blendRectangle behaves exactly like fillRectangle.

To explore what blended rectangles look like and their rendering performance, the $EXAMPLES/ch9-poco/blended-rectangle example animates a blended rectangle. Figure 9-3 shows images of the blended rectangle in several positions on the screen.

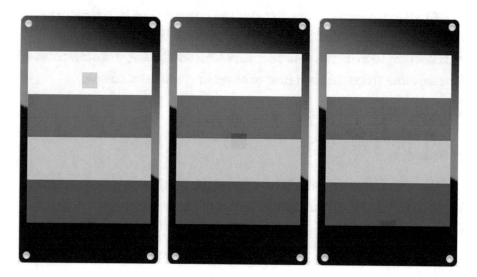

Figure 9-3. *Renderings from blended-rectangle animation*

The background of the animation consists of four colored bars—white, red, green, and blue. The bars are drawn by the drawBars helper function, shown in Listing 9-3.

Listing 9-3.

```
function drawBars(poco) {
    let w = poco.width;
    let h = poco.height / 4;
    poco.fillRectangle(poco.makeColor(255, 255, 255),
                       0, 0, w, h);
    poco.fillRectangle(poco.makeColor(255, 0, 0),
                       0, h, w, h);
    poco.fillRectangle(poco.makeColor(0, 255, 0),
                       0, h * 2, w, h);
    poco.fillRectangle(poco.makeColor(0, 0, 255),
                       0, h * 3, w, h);
}
```

When the example starts, it covers the entire screen by drawing the colored bars. Notice that drawBars doesn't begin with a single call to fillRectangle to fill the entire screen with a solid color, but rather draws four separate strips that combine to cover the entire screen area.

```
poco.begin();
    drawBars(poco);
poco.end();
```

Next, variables are defined to control the animation of a blended black box that drops from the top center of the screen to the bottom (see Listing 9-4).

Listing 9-4.

```
let boxSize = 30;
let boxBlend = 64;
let boxStep = 2;
let boxColor = poco.makeColor(0, 0, 0);
let x = (poco.width - boxSize) / 2, y = 0;
```

The size of the box in pixels is defined by boxSize. The blend level is 64 (25%). On each frame of the animation, the box steps two pixels, as defined by boxStep. The boxColor variable defines the box to be drawn in black. Finally, the initial coordinates of the box's top-left corner are set in the x and y variables.

The motion of the box is animated with a repeating timer, shown in Listing 9-5. The call to begin specifies a drawing area that includes both the current and the previous positions of the box, ensuring that the previous position is fully erased and the new position is fully drawn in one operation. The call to drawBars specifies coordinates that fill the screen, but those are limited to the update area passed to begin. At the end of the timer callback function, the y coordinate is incremented by boxStep. Once the box slides off the bottom of the screen, the y coordinate is reset to 0 to continue animating from the top of the screen.

Listing 9-5.

```
Timer.repeat(function() {
    poco.begin(x, y - boxStep, boxSize, boxSize + boxStep * 2);
        drawBars(poco);
        poco.blendRectangle(boxColor, boxBlend, x, y, boxSize,
                            boxSize);
    poco.end();

    y += boxStep;
    if (y >= poco.height)
        y = 0;
}, 16);
```

This animation runs at a smooth 60 frames per second on both the ESP32 and the ESP8266. That's because the code optimizes the drawing area so that the microcontroller sends only about 60,000 pixels per second to the display, or less than one full frame. The rendering and transmission to the screen of those pixels is spread across 60 frames. This reduces the number of pixels rendered and transmitted by 98.6% compared with rendering full frames. Experiment by changing the variables that control the animation to see the effects of changing the size of the box, the blend level, and the box color.

When running the example, you may notice a small artifact of the box at the bottom of the screen when the box returns to the top. It's possible to modify the code to eliminate the artifact, but doing so makes the code more complex. This is one of the details automatically taken care of by Piu, as you'll see in Chapter 10.

Drawing Bitmaps

Drawing bitmaps is the second fundamental drawing operation provided by Poco. It's used for both mask bitmaps and image bitmaps. Because there are so many different kinds of bitmaps and so many uses for bitmaps in building a user interface, there are several different functions for drawing bitmaps. This section introduces you to some of the most commonly used functions.

Drawing Masks

As you learned in Chapter 8, masks are the most common type of bitmap used in building user interfaces with microcontrollers. There are many reasons for that: they provide excellent quality because they support anti-aliasing, they can be rendered in different colors, they render quickly, and they can be compressed to minimize storage requirements.

Masks are stored in resources. You choose the mask images to use in your project by including them in your project's manifest as shown in Listing 9-6 (and as you learned in the section "Adding Masks to Your Project" in Chapter 8).

Listing 9-6.

```
"resources": {
    "*-mask": [
        "./assets/mask"
    ]
}
```

To use a mask bitmap, you must first access the resource it's stored in. The resource is just data; a Poco bitmap object is needed to render the mask using the Poco API. Commodetto provides functions to create Poco objects from the resource's data.

To instantiate a bitmap object from a compressed mask, use Commodetto's parseRLE function. ("RLE" stands for "run-length encoding," the algorithm used to compress the mask.) The following code retrieves a resource and uses parseRLE to create the bitmap object:

```
import parseRLE from "commodetto/parseRLE";

let mask = parseRLE(new Resource("mask-alpha.bm4"));
```

There are some important details to understand in this small example:

- As you saw in Chapter 5, the Resource constructor references the resource data in flash memory rather than loading it into RAM. The parseRLE function also references the data in place rather than copying the data from flash memory to RAM; however, parseRLE does allocate a small amount of RAM for the Poco bitmap object that references that data.

- Notice that the path the resource is loaded from is mask-alpha.bm4, not mask.png. Remember that tools that are run at build time convert PNG files to an optimized format for the microcontroller, and these tools put the optimized image data into a file of type bm4. Because the image is used as an alpha channel, -alpha is appended to the name. The code running on the microcontroller therefore needs to load the data with a different name than the original. (Piu automatically uses the correct name and extension for you.)

Once you have the bitmap object for the mask, you draw the mask by calling the drawGray method:

```
poco.drawGray(mask, red, 10, 20);
```

The first argument is the mask, the second is the color to apply, and the final two arguments are the x and y coordinates. Note that you do not specify the dimensions; Poco always renders bitmaps at their original size, without applying any scaling. This is done because high-quality scaling would use more CPU time and increase the amount of rendering code in Poco.

The mask bitmap object returned by parseRLE has width and height properties that give the dimensions of the bitmap in pixels. These can be useful in your drawing by enabling it to adapt automatically when you change the dimensions of graphics assets. For example, the following code draws a blue rectangle in the area behind the mask, so any pixels that the mask doesn't draw are blue and any pixels in the mask with transparency blend against the blue background. The size of the blue background rectangle always precisely matches the size of the mask.

```
poco.fillRectangle(blue, 10, 20, mask.width, mask.height);
poco.drawGray(mask, red, 10, 20);
```

Using an Uncompressed Mask

As you know from Chapter 8, drawing only a subset of a compressed mask has some inefficiency because the decompressor must skip over the parts of the image above and to the left of what you want to draw. You can use an uncompressed mask instead. To do that, put the mask image in the *-alpha section (rather than the *-mask section) of your manifest's resources to have it stored in uncompressed form. Then, instead of using parseRLE to load it, use parseBMP with a resource extension of .bmp.

```
import parseBMP from "commodetto/parseBMP";

let mask = parseBMP(new Resource("mask-alpha.bmp"));
```

When switching between compressed and uncompressed masks, remember to do the following:

- Put the resource in the correct section: *-alpha for uncompressed and *-mask for compressed.

- Use the correct loading function to instantiate the bitmap: parseBMP for uncompressed and parseRLE for compressed.

- Use the correct extension in the resource name: .bmp for uncompressed and .bm4 for compressed.

Once you have the bitmap, you use drawGray to render masks whether they're compressed or uncompressed.

Drawing Part of a Mask

The image in Figure 9-4 (which you first saw in Chapter 8) is a single uncompressed mask image that contains icons depicting several different Wi-Fi states.

Figure 9-4. *Wi-Fi icon strip*

An obvious use for this image is to draw an icon that reflects the current Wi-Fi status. Your application will want to draw only one of the icons at a time, reflecting the current status. As discussed in the preceding section, for reasons of efficiency the image combining the different states should not be compressed.

To draw only part of a bitmap, you specify a *source rectangle*, the area of the bitmap to use. In the $EXAMPLES/ch9-poco/wifi-icons example, the source rectangle's *x* and *y* coordinates, width, and height are passed to drawGray as optional arguments following the drawing coordinates. Each individual status icon is 27 pixels square. The following code from the wifi-icons example draws four status icons as shown in Figure 9-5:

```
poco.drawGray(mask, black, 10, 20, 0, 0, 27, 27);     // top left
poco.drawGray(mask, black, 37, 20, 0, 27, 27, 27);    // bottom left
poco.drawGray(mask, black, 10, 47, 112, 0, 27, 27);   // top right
poco.drawGray(mask, black, 37, 47, 112, 27, 27, 27);  // bottom right
```

Figure 9-5. *Icons created from Wi-Fi icon strip*

Fading a Mask In and Out

Fading an image in or out is a common transition in a user interface. The drawGray method has an option to blend the mask with the background pixels. This is the same idea as blended rectangles, but using a mask enables you to blend any shape. The $EXAMPLES/ch9-poco/fade-mask example fades a volume icon in and out, as shown in Figure 9-6.

Figure 9-6. *Renderings from fade-mask animation*

The blend level is specified in the optional ninth argument to drawGray. As in blendRectangle, the blend level is a number from 0 to 255, where 0 means fully transparent and 255 means fully opaque.

Listing 9-7 shows the code from the fade-mask example that fades the mask resource from transparent to opaque. The same drawBars function as in the blended-rectangle example (Listing 9-3) draws the mask over a background.

Listing 9-7.

```
let mask = parseRLE(new Resource("mask-alpha.bm4"));
let maskBlend = 0;
let blendStep = 4;
let maskColor = poco.makeColor(0, 0, 255);
```

```
Timer.repeat(function() {
    let y = (poco.height / 4) - (mask.height / 2);
    poco.begin(30, y, mask.width, mask.height);
        drawBars(poco);
        poco.drawGray(mask, maskColor, 30, y,
                        0, 0, mask.width, mask.height, maskBlend);
    poco.end();

    maskBlend += blendStep;
    if (maskBlend > 255)
        maskBlend = 0;
}, 16);
```

Notice that to use the blend level, you must also provide the source rectangle, even when drawing the entire mask. The dimensions of the bitmap rectangle—mask.width and mask.height in this example—are used for the source rectangle; this ensures that the code doesn't need to change when the dimensions of the asset are changed.

Drawing Color Images

You add color images to your project using JPEG and PNG files. The build tools convert these to uncompressed bitmaps for rendering on the device, because it's generally impractical to use the JPEG and PNG compression formats on a microcontroller to build a high-performance user interface. The bitmap is stored in a BMP file (with a .bmp extension) and can be quite large because it's not compressed. For example, an image 40 pixels square for a display using 16-bit pixels takes up 3,200 bytes of storage.

You create a Poco bitmap for a BMP image using the parseBMP function, as you saw earlier, and you draw it using the drawBitmap method, passing as arguments the x and y coordinates of where to draw the image.

```
let image = parseBMP(new Resource("quack-color.bmp"));
poco.drawBitmap(image, 30, 40);
```

As with drawGray, you can optionally draw only part of the image by specifying the source rectangle. The following example draws only the top-left quadrant of the image:

```
poco.drawBitmap(image, 30, 40, 0, 0,
                image.width / 2, image.height / 2);
```

Drawing JPEG Images

Because of their memory and CPU requirements, compressed JPEG images aren't a good general-purpose way to store images on microcontrollers; however, they're useful when you need to store a large number of images in a relatively small space—for example, a slide show or a collection of images to use in a user interface. Commodetto includes a JPEG decompressor that you can use together with Poco to draw JPEG images in your projects. This section explains two different ways to do that.

Storing JPEG Data in Resources

As you know, the build tools automatically convert images in your manifest to BMP files. If you want to keep a JPEG file in its original compressed format, put the JPEG image in the data section of the manifest instead of the resources section (see Listing 9-8). The contents of the data section are always copied without any transformation.

Listing 9-8.

```
"data": {
    "*": [
        "./piano"
    ]
}
```

The approaches to drawing a JPEG image that are introduced in the following section are incompatible with software display rotation. That's because software rotation depends on rotating the image at build time, and here the manifest tells the build tools not to transform the images. These techniques for drawing JPEG images work only when you're using hardware rotation or when software rotation is 0 degrees.

Drawing a JPEG Image from Memory

On computers and phones, JPEG images are usually decompressed once to an offscreen bitmap; then, when the JPEG image is needed, that bitmap is drawn. This approach gives excellent rendering performance, because the complex operation of decompressing the JPEG image happens only once. However, storing the decompressed JPEG image uses a great deal of memory. Consequently, this approach is typically appropriate on microcontrollers for only relatively small images.

The following example uses the loadJPEG function to decompress a resource containing JPEG data to a Poco bitmap. Once the image is in a bitmap, you use drawBitmap to render it as described previously.

```
import loadJPEG from "commodetto/loadJPEG";

let piano = loadJPEG(new Resource("piano.jpg"));
poco.drawBitmap(piano, 0, 0);
```

The call to loadJPEG takes some time to complete, because decompressing JPEG images is a relatively difficult operation for a microcontroller. The time varies based on the size of the image, compression level, and microcontroller performance.

Drawing a JPEG Image During Decompression

If you don't have enough memory to hold the full decompressed JPEG image in memory, you can still display the image, by displaying it in blocks as it's decompressed. The $EXAMPLES/ch9-poco/draw-jpeg example demonstrates how to decompress a full-screen (240 x 320) JPEG image directly to the screen. When you run the example, you'll see the screen shown in Figure 9-7.

Figure 9-7. *JPEG image from* draw-jpeg *example*

First you use the JPEG class to create a Poco bitmap for the JPEG image:

```
import JPEG from "commodetto/readJPEG";

let jpeg = new JPEG(new Resource("harvard.jpg"));
```

The JPEG decompressor always decodes one block at a time. The size of the block varies depending on how the JPEG image is compressed, and is between 8 x 8 and 16 x 16 pixels. As the blocks are decompressed, your code can draw them directly to the screen.

Listing 9-9 shows the code from the draw-jpeg example that decompresses the JPEG image to the screen. The read method decompresses one block of the image and returns it as a Poco bitmap. The bitmap object includes x and y properties that provide the coordinates of the block in the JPEG image and width and height properties that provide the block's dimensions. The ready property of the JPEG class returns true while there are more blocks to display and false after all blocks have been decoded.

Listing 9-9.

```
while (jpeg.ready) {
    let block = jpeg.read();
    poco.begin(block.x, block.y, block.width, block.height);
        poco.drawBitmap(block, block.x, block.y);
    poco.end();
}
```

Filling with Color Images

Filling an area of the screen with a texture can create a more interesting user interface than a solid color. The $EXAMPLES/ch9-poco/pattern-fill example demonstrates how to tile an image of earth to cover part of the screen, as shown in Figure 9-8.

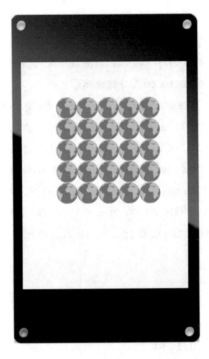

Figure 9-8. *Repeated earth texture from* `pattern-fill` *example*

Using a large image of a textured pattern takes more storage than it needs to. A good alternative is to use a small pattern that can be tiled. Your code can simply draw the small image multiple times; however, it takes time to issue all those calls to `drawBitmap`, and doing so may overflow Poco's display list. A better option is to use Poco's `fillPattern` method, which tiles a rectangular area with a Poco bitmap. For example, here's how to fill the entire screen with a bitmap stored in a variable named `tile`:

```
poco.fillPattern(tile, 0, 0, poco.width, poco.height);
```

The arguments after the bitmap are the *x* and *y* coordinates, width, and height of the rectangle to fill. The `fillPattern` method also supports an optional source rectangle, which enables you to use only a section of the bitmap for the tile. For example (as shown in Figure 9-9), the image from the pattern-fill example combines 11 different versions of the same texture, each in a different step of an animation.

Figure 9-9. *Image from pattern-fill example*

The pattern-fill example uses the source rectangle to fill an area of the screen with an animated pattern. Listing 9-10 shows the code that creates the animation. A timer is used to move sequentially through the eight different images in the combined image. The phase variable keeps track of which of the eight steps of the animated pattern to draw.

Listing 9-10.

```
let tile = parseBMP(new Resource("tiles-color.bmp"));
let size = 30;
let x = 40, y = 50;
let phase = 0;
Timer.repeat(function() {
    poco.begin(x, y, size * 5, size * 5);
        poco.fillPattern(tile, x, y, size * 5, size * 5,
                            phase * size, 0, size, size);
    poco.end();

    phase = (phase + 1) % 8;
}, 66);
```

Drawing Masked Color Images

Drawing a color image through a mask (an alpha channel) is a common technique in mobile apps and web pages. As you saw in Chapter 8, it enables you to draw a full-color image of any shape, not just rectangles.

Using the drawMasked method of Poco, you can draw an uncompressed color image through an uncompressed grayscale mask.

The drawMasked call takes many arguments, all but one of which is required. These are the parameters, in order:

- image – The color bitmap image.

- x, y – The coordinates at which to draw.

- sx, sy, sw, sh – The source rectangle to use from the color bitmap.

- mask – The mask bitmap (uncompressed 4-bit grayscale; compressed masks are not supported).

- mask_sx, mask_sy – The coordinates of the top left of the source rectangle to use from the mask bitmap. (The width and height are the same as those of the color bitmap source rectangle.)

- blend – *(Optional)* The blend level, from 0 to 255; defaults to 255 (fully opaque).

To try drawing a color image through a mask, you'll need an image and a mask. The $EXAMPLES/ch9-poco/masked-image example uses the circle mask in Figure 9-10 to create a spotlight effect with the train image in Figure 9-11.

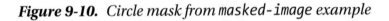

Figure 9-10. *Circle mask from masked-image example*

Figure 9-11. *Train image from masked-image example*

The mask and color image are loaded with parseBMP because they're both uncompressed:

```
let image = parseBMP(new Resource("train-color.bmp"));
let mask = parseBMP(new Resource("mask_circle.bmp"));
```

As shown in the following code, the drawing location is set to the coordinates (30, 30) in the x and y variables. The variable sx is the left side of the source rectangle; it's initialized to the right side of the image so that the train rendering begins at the front of the train. The step variable is set to 2 to advance the train two pixels on each frame.

```
let x = 30, y = 30;
let sx = image.width - mask.width;
let step = 2;
```

Listing 9-11 shows the code that does the animation. A timer is used to move the train at regular intervals. The location of the drawing is always the same, with the train moving through the mask. The train moves by adjusting sx, the left edge of the image's source rectangle.

Listing 9-11.

```
Timer.repeat(function() {
    poco.begin(x, y, mask.width, mask.height);
        poco.fillRectangle(gray, x, y, mask.width, mask.height);
        poco.drawMasked(image, x, y,
                    sx, 0, mask.width, mask.height, mask, 0, 0);
    poco.end();

    sx -= step;
    if (sx <= 0)
        sx = image.width - mask.width;
}, 16);
```

Figure 9-12 shows the result of drawing part of the train through the mask. Notice that the edges of the mask blend with the gray background.

Figure 9-12. *Masked train with default blend level (255)*

The optional blend argument to drawMasked changes the relative opacity of each pixel. Figure 9-13 shows the same train image rendered with a blend level of 128 (about 50%). Notice now that all the pixels, not only the edges, blend with the background.

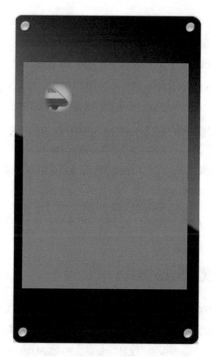

Figure 9-13. *Masked train with blend level of 128*

Drawing Text

The third and last of the fundamental drawing operations supported by Poco is drawing text. To draw text, you first need a font. Fonts are stored as bitmaps and are usually compressed.

In your applications, fonts are loaded from a resource using the parseBMF function. For compressed fonts, the extension is .bf4. This chapter identifies a font resource with a name consisting of hyphen-separated parts according to the convention that's typically used in applications built with Piu (as described further in Chapter 10).

```
import parseBMF from "commodetto/parseBMF";

let regular16 = parseBMF(new Resource("OpenSans-Regular-16.bf4"));
let bold28 = parseBMF(new Resource("OpenSans-Semibold-28.bf4"));
```

Poco doesn't impose a limit on the number of fonts your project may contain. Of course, the available flash storage space on your target microcontroller limits the number and size of fonts in your project.

The characters in a font are grayscale masks, so they can be drawn in any color. The drawText method requires as arguments a text string, font, color, and drawing coordinates. The coordinates specify the location of top-left corner of the first character drawn. The following line draws the string Hello in 16-point, regular-weight Open Sans in black starting at the top-left corner of the screen:

```
poco.drawText("Hello", regular16, black, 0, 0);
```

Drawing a Text Shadow

You can achieve a drop shadow effect by drawing the text twice, each time with different coordinates—first as a shadow and then as the primary text. The $EXAMPLES/ch9-poco/text-shadow example begins by drawing the text in the shadow color down and to the right of where the primary text will go and then overlays that with the same string in the primary color drawn at the primary coordinates. This results in the text shown in Figure 9-14.

```
let text = "Drop Shadow";
poco.drawText(text, bold28, lightGray, 0 + 2, 100 + 2);
poco.drawText(text, bold28, blue, 0, 100);
```

Figure 9-14. *Text drawn by* text-shadow *example*

Measuring Text

The height of the text drawn is the same as the height of the font, which is contained in the height property of the font object. The width of the text drawn is determined by using the getTextWidth method. The following code fills the area behind the text with green before drawing the text:

```
let text = "Hello";
let width = poco.getTextWidth(text, regular16);
poco.fillRectangle(green, 0, 0, width, regular16.height);
poco.drawText(text, regular16, black, 0, 0);
```

Note   The font is passed to getTextWidth because it contains the measurements for each character. Take care not to measure with one font and draw with another; their measurements are likely different, so you could get unexpected results.

Truncating Text

In situations where the text you want to draw is wider than the space available for it, a common solution is to draw an ellipsis (...) at the point where the text is cut off. The drawText method does this for you automatically when you tell it the width that's available for drawing.

The following example draws a sentence on a single line, truncating it to the width of the screen. The result is shown in Figure 9-15.

```
let text = "JavaScript is one of the world's most widely used
            programming languages.";
poco.drawText(text, regular16, black, 0, 0, poco.width);
poco.drawText(text, bold28, black, 0, 40, poco.width);
```

Figure 9-15. *Truncated text in two different fonts*

Wrapping Text

In some situations, you may want to draw text across multiple lines of the display. In the general case of supporting written languages from around the world, such word wrapping is challenging. The $EXAMPLES/ch9-poco/ text-wrap example presents a basic approach that's sufficient for common situations when you're working with languages written with Roman characters.

The example uses the split method of String objects to create an array containing the words of the string:

```
let text = "JavaScript is one of the world's most widely used
            programming languages.";
text = text.split(" ");
```

It then loops through all the words, one at a time, as shown in Listing 9-12. If there's enough room on the line to fit the current word or if the word is wider than the full line, the text is drawn; otherwise, width is reset to the full line width and y is increased by the font's height so that drawing resumes on the next line down.

Listing 9-12.

```
let width = poco.width;
let y = 0;
let font = regular16;
let spaceWidth = poco.getTextWidth(" ", font);
while (text.length) {
    let wordWidth = poco.getTextWidth(text[0], font);
    if ((wordWidth < width) || (width === poco.width)) {
        poco.drawText(text[0], font, black, poco.width - width, y);
        text.shift();
    }
    width -= wordWidth + spaceWidth;
    if (width <= 0) {
        width = poco.width;
        y += font.height;
    }
}
```

Figure 9-16 shows the result of running this example with the font set to regular16 and bold28, respectively.

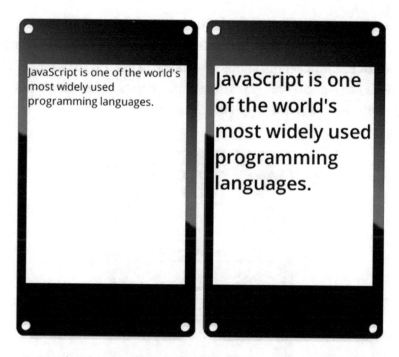

Figure 9-16. `text-wrap` *example with font size 16 (left) and 28 (right)*

Additional Drawing Techniques

Poco and Commodetto provide many tools to simplify and optimize drawing for specific needs. The following sections introduce three of them: using clipping to restrict text to a box, using the origin to easily reuse drawing code, and drawing offscreen to efficiently render gradients.

Restricting Text to a Box

As you know, Poco does not draw outside the update area defined when you call Poco's begin method; it clips to that area, by setting the initial clipping area to be the same as the update area. Your code can also adjust the clipping area during drawing. The clipping area is always limited by the update area defined by begin; you can shrink the clipping area, but you can ever expand it beyond the initial drawing area.

One place where clipping is useful is a ticker—a scrolling text message that fits into a section of the screen. The text must never be drawn outside the bounds of the ticker but should be drawn all the way to its edges. The $EXAMPLES/ch9-poco/text-ticker example demonstrates how to do this; Figure 9-17 shows a rendering of the example.

Figure 9-17.   Ticker tape drawn by text-ticker *example*

Listing 9-13 shows some of the variables used throughout the drawing code. There's a black frame around the outside, with its size in pixels stored in the frame variable. There's a small margin inside the frame, where the text cannot be drawn; its size in pixels is stored in the margin variable. The width of the area reserved for the ticker text is stored in tickerWidth. The overall width and height are calculated from these values.

Listing 9-13.

```
let frame = 3;
let margin = 2;
let x = 10, y = 60;
let tickerWidth = 200;
let width = tickerWidth + frame * 2 + margin * 2;
let height = regular16.height + frame * 2 + margin * 2;
```

The text is measured once, before drawing starts, to avoid redundant calculations during rendering. The result is stored in textWidth.

```
let text = "JavaScript is one of the world's most widely used
            programming languages.";
let textWidth = poco.getTextWidth(text, regular16);
```

The variable dx stores the current horizontal offset of the text from the left edge of the ticker text area. The text starts just off the right edge and scrolls in from there.

```
let dx = tickerWidth;
```

The ticker is drawn in two parts. First, the black frame and yellow ticker background are drawn:

```
poco.fillRectangle(black, x, y, width, height);
poco.fillRectangle(yellow, x + frame, y + frame,
                   tickerWidth + margin * 2,
                   regular16.height + margin * 2);
```

Next, the text is drawn (Listing 9-14). The example first uses the clip method to change the clipping area. It calls clip with the *x* and *y* coordinates, width, and height of the clipping rectangle. This pushes the current clipping area onto a stack and then intersects it with the requested clip. Calling clip with no arguments pops the clip stack and restores the previous clip. This approach makes it easy to nest clipping area changes.

Listing 9-14.

```
poco.clip(x + frame + margin, y + frame + margin, tickerWidth,
          regular16.height);
poco.drawText(text, regular16, black, x + frame + margin + dx,
              y + frame);
poco.clip();
```

Finally, the horizontal offset of the ticker is advanced, to prepare for the next animation frame. When the text completely scrolls off the left edge, it resets to again scroll in from the right edge.

```
dx -= 2;
if (dx < -textWidth)
    dx = tickerWidth;
```

Easily Reusing Drawing Code

The origin for drawing, (0, 0), is the top-left corner of the screen after you call Poco's begin method, and the origin has remained there in all the examples so far. You can use the origin method to offset the origin. This simplifies writing a function to draw a user interface element at different locations on the screen. The $EXAMPLES/ch9-poco/origin example uses the origin method to draw identical yellow rectangles with black frames in different locations, as shown in Figure 9-18.

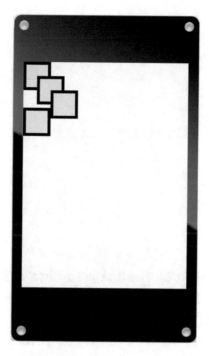

Figure 9-18. *Rectangles drawn by the* origin *example*

The following function from the origin example draws a yellow rectangle with a black frame:

```
function drawFrame() {
    poco.fillRectangle(black, 0, 0, 20, 20);
    poco.fillRectangle(yellow, 2, 2, 16, 16);
}
```

In this function, drawing is done at the origin. Moving the origin before calling drawFrame causes the drawing to appear at a different location on the screen. Listing 9-15 shows the code from the origin example that calls the origin method to offset the origin before each call to drawFrame. The result is the four rectangles you saw in Figure 9-19.

Listing 9-15.

```
drawFrame();
poco.origin(20, 20);
drawFrame();
poco.origin(20, 20);
drawFrame();
poco.origin();
poco.origin();
poco.origin(0, 65);
drawFrame();
poco.origin();
```

The origin starts at (0, 0). The first call to poco.origin(20, 20) moves the origin to (20, 20). Because the values are relative, the second call to poco.origin(20, 20) moves the origin to (40, 40).

The origin method stores the current origin on a stack. Calling origin with no arguments pops the origin stack and restores the previous origin. As with the clip method, this approach makes nested origin changes easy. In this example, the call to poco.origin(0, 65) occurs after all items on the stack are removed, so the origin is back at (0, 0). After the call, the origin is at (0, 65).

While the final call to origin may appear unnecessary, since no further drawing is performed, Poco considers it an error if you fail to fully clear the origin or clip stack before calling the end method. If this unbalanced situation occurs, the end method reports an error.

Efficiently Rendering Gradients

Your projects aren't limited to bitmaps created at build time; you can also create bitmaps while your project is running. You've already seen one example of this: the loadJPEG function creates a bitmap in memory from compressed JPEG data. Because these bitmaps must be stored in RAM, they're limited by the amount of available memory. You can create a bitmap at runtime using the BufferOut class, which also creates a virtual screen for the bitmap. This enables you to draw to the offscreen bitmap using Poco in the same way you draw to a physical screen.

```
import BufferOut from "commodetto/BufferOut";
```

The $EXAMPLES/ch9-poco/offscreen example creates an offscreen bitmap, draws a simple gradient to the bitmap, and then animates the bitmap on the screen. When creating the offscreen bitmap, you specify its width and height and the pixel format for the new bitmap. Here the pixel format is set to poco.pixelsOut.pixelFormat so that the offscreen bitmap and the screen have the same pixel format.

```
let offscreen = new BufferOut({width: 64, height: 64,
                    pixelFormat: poco.pixelsOut.pixelFormat});
```

This offscreen bitmap is a 64 x 64 pixels square. To draw to it, you create another instance of Poco bound to offscreen, instead of to screen like the first instance.

```
let pocoOff = new Poco(offscreen);
```

The example then uses pocoOff to draw to the bitmap exactly as if it were drawing to the screen. Listing 9-16 shows the code it uses to draw the gray gradient shown in Figure 9-19.

Listing 9-16.

```
pocoOff.begin();
    for (let i = 64; i >= 1; i--) {
        let gray = (i * 4) - 1;
        let color = pocoOff.makeColor(gray, gray, gray);
        pocoOff.fillRectangle(color, 0, 0, i, i);
    }
pocoOff.end();
```

Figure 9-19. *Gray gradient drawn by* offscreen *example*

The bitmap attached to offscreen is available from its bitmap property. The following line draws the offscreen bitmap to the screen:

```
poco.drawBitmap(offscreen.bitmap, 0, 0);
```

Rendering the content of this offscreen bitmap requires drawing 64 different rectangles, each of a slightly different size and color. Drawing those rectangles over and over in an animation would be too much calculation for a microcontroller. Fortunately, drawing the offscreen bitmap is much easier.

The offscreen example goes on to animate 19 copies of an offscreen bitmap by sliding them left and right at different speeds. Listing 9-17 shows the animation code, and Figure 9-20 shows a rendering of the animation.

Listing 9-17.

```
let step = 1;
let direction = +1;
Timer.repeat(function() {
    poco.begin(0, 0, 240, 240);
        poco.fillRectangle(white, 0, 0, poco.width, poco.height);
        for (let i = 0; i < 19; i += 1)
            poco.drawBitmap(offscreen.bitmap, i * step, i * 10);
```

```
        step += direction;
        if (step > 40) {
            step = 40;
            direction = -1;
        }
        else if (step < 1) {
            step = 0;
            direction = +1;
        }
    poco.end();
}, 33);
```

Figure 9-20. *Rendering of offscreen animation*

Touch Input

If you're using Poco to draw your product's user interface and you want to incorporate touch capabilities, you need to implement support for touch input by reading directly from the touch input driver. When you use Piu, touch input is automatically taken care of for you. Fortunately, reading the touch input is not very difficult.

Accessing the Touch Driver

The most common capacitive touch input is the FocalTech FT6206. This part is used in Moddable One and Moddable Two boards. You import the touch driver in your project and create an instance as follows:

```
import FT6206 from "ft6206";

let touch = new FT6206;
```

Older resistive touch screens commonly use the XPT2046 touch controller.

```
import XPT2046 from "xpt2046";

let touch = new XPT2046;
```

Both touch drivers implement the same API, so once you've instantiated the driver your code to read from them is the same for both.

Reading Touch Input

To retrieve touch points from the touch driver, you call the read method. You pass an array of touch points to the read call, and the driver updates the points. Usually you allocate the touch points once, after instantiating the touch driver to minimize the work done by the memory manager and garbage collector. The following line allocates an array with a single touch point. The array is assigned to the points property of the touch input driver instance.

```
touch.points = [{}];
```

To retrieve the current touch points, call read with the array of points:

```
touch.read(touch.points);
```

The driver sets the state property for each touch point. The values of the state property are as follows:

- **0** – no touch
- **1** – touch input begin (finger down)
- **2** – touch input continue (finger still down)
- **3** – touch input end (finger lifted)

For all state values except 0, the x and y properties of the touch point indicate the current touch location. The code in Listing 9-18, which is excerpted from $EXAMPLES/ch9-poco/touch, samples the touch driver 30 times a second, outputting the current state to the debug console.

Listing 9-18.

```
Timer.repeat(function() {
    let points = touch.points;
    let point = points[0];
    touch.read(points);
    switch (point.state) {
        case 0:
            trace("no touch\n");
            break;
        case 1:
            trace(`touch begin @ ${point.x}, ${point.y}\n`);
            break;
```

```
        case 2:
            trace(`touch continue @ ${point.x}, ${point.y}\n`);
            break;
        case 3:
            trace(`touch end @ ${point.x}, ${point.y}\n`);
            break;
    }
}, 33);
```

Some versions of the FT6206 do not reliably generate the touch end state. When you run the example, you can see the behavior of your component. If the touch end state is not generated, you can determine that a touch sequence has ended when the touch point enters state 0 (no touch).

Using Multi-touch

The reason that the read method takes an array of points rather than a single point is so that it can support multi-touch. The FT6206 capacitive touch sensors support two simultaneous touch points, as long as they're not too close together. To use multi-touch, you just need to pass an array with two points.

```
touch.points = [{}, {}];
touch.read(touch.points);
```

Applying Rotation

The touch driver always provides points that have neither hardware nor software rotation applied. If you're using rotation, you need to apply it to the touch points. As you might expect, Piu takes care of rotating the touch points for you.

You can use code from Listing 9-19 to transform coordinates for rotations of 90, 180, and 270 degrees.

Listing 9-19.

```
if (90 === rotation) {
    const x = point.x;
    point.x = point.y;
    point.y = screen.height - x;
}
else if (180 === rotation) {
    point.x = screen.width - point.x;
    point.y = screen.height - point.y;
}
else if (270 === rotation) {
    const x = point.x;
    point.x = screen.width - point.y;
    point.y = x;
}
```

Conclusion

The Poco renderer provides all the basic tools you need to build the user interface of an IoT product. You can draw rectangles, bitmaps, and text with many different options. The rendering capabilities include anti-aliased text, grayscale masks drawn in any color, and rendering of color images through alpha channel masks. You can optimize rendering performance using clipping to restrict the area of the screen that you update.

Poco gives you a great deal of control—but that power brings with it some inconveniences. You must load resources and invoke the appropriate functions to parse them, you must calculate the area of the screen to update, and you must take care of some details of rotation. The next chapter introduces the Piu user interface framework, which takes care of many of these details for you.

CHAPTER 10

Building User Interfaces with Piu

Piu is an object-oriented user interface framework that simplifies the process of creating sophisticated user interfaces. It uses the Poco renderer to draw. This chapter provides an overview of how Piu works and introduces some of its major capabilities through a series of examples. The name Piu means "more" in classical music and reflects the remarkably rich set of capabilities that Piu builds on Poco.

Keep in mind that learning a new user interface framework can be challenging. Every framework has its own way of addressing the problem of building a user interface and its own suite of APIs to solve the problem. It takes more than following the examples in this chapter to fully understand the intricacies of Piu. The goal of the chapter is to teach you the most important and commonly used features of Piu, show simple examples of where they're used, and explain them enough that you can use them in your own user interfaces for your own products.

Some parts of Piu will look familiar to you if you already know *Cascading Style Sheets*, or *CSS*, a language for defining styles—for example, of text—that's most commonly used in designing web pages written in HTML. The similarities between Piu and CSS are no accident; Piu incorporates many CSS conventions to provide consistency for developers working on both web and IoT products.

© Peter Hoddie and Lizzie Prader 2020
P. Hoddie and L. Prader, *IoT Development for ESP32 and ESP8266 with JavaScript*,
https://doi.org/10.1007/978-1-4842-5070-9_10

Key Concepts

It's important to understand a few of the key concepts behind Piu before diving into code. If you're new to working with object-oriented user interface frameworks, the information in this section is particularly important because it gets you in the right mindset to work with Piu. If you're already comfortable working with object-oriented frameworks, this section is still important because it introduces information specific to Piu.

Everything Is an Object

The most important concept to grasp is that every element of the user interface in a Piu application has a corresponding JavaScript object. The JavaScript objects are instances of the classes Piu provides. Piu is unlike the other Moddable SDK features introduced in this book in that you don't have to import most Piu classes. Instead, Piu stores the constructors for commonly used classes in global variables, making it easy for you to use them from any module in your application.

Every Piu application begins with the same object: an instance of the Piu Application class. The host for this chapter creates the instance, so none of the examples in this chapter need to create it. Listing 10-1 shows how the host instantiates the Application instance by calling the Application constructor.

Listing 10-1.

```
new Application(null, {
    displayListLength: 8192,
    commandListLength: 4096,
    skin: new Skin({fill: "white"}),
    Behavior: AppBehavior
});
```

Don't worry about the details of the various properties for now. Do notice that the `displayListLength` property from Poco is used here, since Piu uses Poco for drawing.

As part of the `Application` constructor, Piu stores the instance in the application global variable. The examples access the `Application` instance through the `application` global.

The `application` object is the root of a Piu application. Think of it as a container that holds all the graphical elements that appear on the screen. Graphical elements added to the container are called *content objects*. To display a content object on the screen, you create an instance of it and add it to the `application` object. To display a line of text, for example, you create an instance of Piu's `Label` class, a kind of content object, and add that to the `application` object.

Note   This chapter refers to classes by their capitalized names, as in "the `Label` class," and to instances of classes by the uncapitalized class name, as in "a `label` object" (or simply "a label").

You can create Piu content objects without adding them to the `application` object, but they're not drawn until they're added. When you use Piu, you don't call drawing functions yourself. The content objects know how to draw themselves; they call the drawing functions for you as needed to update the screen.

Of course, you can also remove content objects from the screen. As you may have guessed, you do this by removing them from the `application` object.

Every User Interface Element Is a Content Object

As you now know, every element of the user interface in a Piu application is associated with a content object. More specifically, every user interface element is associated with an instance of a class that inherits from the Content class. There are many such classes, including the Label class mentioned previously. You'll learn about various types of content objects throughout this chapter.

Note   In this chapter, "content object" refers to an instance of the Content class, whereas the generic term *content object* refers to an instance of any class that inherits from the Content class.

When you create a content object, you specify its properties in a JavaScript dictionary. In the case of a label object, properties include the label's string and text style. The dictionary is passed to the constructor of the class.

```
let sampleLabel = new Label(null, {
    style: textStyle,
    string: "Hello"
});
```

The properties of a content object can be changed at any time. You change a property by setting its value in the instance, usually using the same property name you used to initialize the property when you called the constructor.

```
sampleLabel.style = OpenSansBold12;
sampleLabel.string = "Goodbye";
```

When you change the properties of a content object that you added to the application object, the screen is updated automatically. Piu causes an update by invalidating the appropriate parts of the display, and the content object calls the needed drawing functions to update the screen.

Not All Piu Objects Are Content Objects

In addition to content objects, Piu has several other kinds of objects, the most common of which are introduced in this section. They're all used to modify content objects in some way—their appearance, how they behave, or how they animate. None of these objects inherit from the Content class. The classes that define them are introduced here and described in greater detail later in this chapter.

Defining Appearance

The Skin, Texture, and Style classes modify the appearance of content objects: skin and texture objects are used by content objects to fill an area with color and images, while style objects define the appearance of text, including its font and color. In the preceding section, for example, sampleLabel was instantiated with a dictionary containing a style property set to a style object named textStyle. The style object is not associated with a single content object; rather, it may be applied to one or more label objects and other content objects.

Similarly, skin objects are associated with content objects through the skin property of the content objects, and, like style objects, they may be shared by many content objects. The Texture class, on the other hand, is not used directly by content objects; texture objects are associated with skin objects, through the texture property of the skin objects, and they may be shared by many skin objects.

As with content objects, you specify the properties of skin, texture, and style objects with a dictionary passed to their constructor. Unlike with content objects, the properties of skin, texture, and style objects cannot be changed. This means, for example, that to change the font used by a label, you change the style property of the label object, not the font property of the style object.

Controlling Behavior

Behaviors perform actions in response to *events*, such as taps on the screen, changes in sensor values, or the expiration of a timer. The behavior of content objects is defined by subclasses of the Behavior class. Behaviors are part of how Piu enables an event-driven programming style. If you're new to event-driven programming, don't worry; this chapter thoroughly explains how behavior objects and events work in Piu.

A content object must have a behavior assigned to it to be able to respond to events. A content object need not have an assigned behavior, but it won't respond to events without one. Usually a content object has its own instance of a Behavior subclass, though it's possible for multiple content objects to share one behavior instance.

Animating

To animate content objects, you use the Timeline and Transition classes. You can animate content objects by changing their properties to make them move, change color, fade in or out, and more, and you can swap one content object for another—for example, to move between screens.

Content objects do not have timeline or transition properties; instead, timeline and transition objects refer to the content objects they animate.

Installing the Piu Host

You can run all of this chapter's examples by following the pattern described in Chapter 1: install the host on your device using mcconfig, then install example applications using mcrun.

All the Piu examples require the use of a screen, making it essential for your mcconfig command line to specify a platform with a screen driver for your development board. The examples are intended to run on screens with 320 x 240 resolution. The following command lines are for the Moddable One, Moddable Two, and M5Stack FIRE:

```
> mcconfig -d -m -p esp/moddable_one
> mcconfig -d -m -p esp32/moddable_two
> mcconfig -d -m -p esp32/m5stack_fire
```

If you're wiring the screen to your development board using a breadboard and jumper wires, follow the instructions in Chapter 1. The wiring provided there for the ESP32 works with the esp32/moddable_zero target; likewise for the ESP8266 and the esp/moddable_zero target.

The screen driver for the Moddable Zero, Moddable One, Moddable Two, and M5Stack FIRE supports the use of hardware rotation. The host configures the screen rotation so that it renders pixels in landscape (320 x 240) orientation rather than the default portrait (240 x 320) orientation.

If your device doesn't have a screen, you can run this chapter's examples on the desktop simulator provided by the Moddable SDK. The following command lines are for macOS, Windows, and Linux:

```
> mcconfig -d -m -p mac
> mcconfig -d -m -p win
> mcconfig -d -m -p lin
```

The host for this chapter is in the $EXAMPLES/ch10-piu/host directory. Navigate to this directory from the command line and install it with mcconfig.

If you're using the desktop simulator, make sure you change the dimensions of the screen to 320 x 240 before you install examples. You do this by selecting **320 x 240** from the **Size** menu in the application's toolbar.

"Hello, World" with Piu

When you run the $EXAMPLES/ch10-piu/helloworld example, you see the screen shown in Figure 10-1.

Figure 10-1. *helloworld example*

This isn't the most exciting user interface, but it's a good starting point to demonstrate the basics of creating Piu objects to build a simple screen. The text displayed is defined in a label object, and the first line of code in the example creates a *style*—an instance of the Style class—to define the appearance of the text.

```
const textStyle = new Style({
    font: "24px Open Sans"
});
```

The details of the font property are covered in the next section. For now, just notice that the properties of the style object are defined in a dictionary passed to the constructor of the Style class. As you learned earlier, this is the convention for both Piu content objects and the objects that define their appearance. Each Piu object requires certain properties to be specified, while other properties are optional. For example, the Style constructor requires a font property, but the properties associated with the color, horizontal and vertical alignment, and line height are optional.

The helloworld example then creates a content object: a label object named sampleLabel (see Listing 10-2). A label object renders text on a single line with a single style.

Listing 10-2.

```
const sampleLabel = new Label(null, {
    style: textStyle,
    string: "Hello, World",
    top: 0, bottom: 0, left: 0, right: 0
});
```

The string property specifies the text that the label displays, and the style property defines the style of the text (textStyle, as created earlier). The top, bottom, left, and right properties define the position of the label by specifying the margins between the label object and its container, the application object; setting these all to 0 makes the label object fill the entire screen. Text is centered horizontally and vertically by default, so the text is drawn in the center of the screen.

Note   Keep in mind that top, bottom, left, and right are not absolute coordinates but rather specify margins from the corresponding edge of the parent container.

As you learned earlier, simply creating a content object doesn't make it appear on the screen. You have to add content objects to the application object in order for Piu to draw them. This is done by calling application.add.

```
application.add(sampleLabel);
```

In this example, textStyle is attached to just one content object, but recall that one style object can be attached to more than one content object. You could add a second label that uses the same style but with different text displayed at a different location. For example, adding the code in Listing 10-3 to the example would display the text Second string in the bottom-right corner of the screen.

Listing 10-3.

```
application.add(new Label(null, {
    style: textStyle,
    string: "Second string",
    bottom: 0, right: 0
}));
```

Note that top and left properties are not specified for this label. If you specify a bottom property of a label but no top, or vice versa, the height of the label is the height of the text in the style specified by its style property. Similarly, if you specify only one of left and right, the width of a label is the width of the text in its style.

Fonts

The font property of a style object indicates the font to use to draw text when the style is applied to content objects. Fonts are typically compressed bitmaps stored in a resource, as explained in Chapter 8. Piu doesn't include any built-in fonts; instead, the host and the application may include fonts in their manifests. The host for this chapter provides two fonts, which are used by all the examples that draw text. Listing 10-4 shows the fragment of the manifest that includes the fonts.

Listing 10-4.

```
"resources": {
    "*-alpha": [
        "./OpenSans-Regular-24",
        "./OpenSans-Semibold-16"
    ]
},
```

Font Names

Piu uses the font property of a style to locate the font resource to use. This section introduces the naming convention for fonts, and the next section explains how those names are mapped to a font resource.

In the helloworld example, the font name is specified by the string "24px Open Sans". This Piu format for the font name is a subset of the CSS font name format. There are five parts to a Piu font name, in this order:

1. **Style** - *(Optional)* The font style, specified as italic or omitted if normal.

2. **Weight** - *(Optional)* The thinness or thickness of the font. You can use the same keywords and numerical values as in CSS (for example, light, bold, or 800). Each keyword has an equivalent numeric value; for example, the weight light is equivalent to 300 and bold is 700. Table 10-1 lists the weight keywords and their equivalent numeric values. The default value of normal (400) is used if this part of the font name is omitted.

3. **Stretch** – *(Optional)* The spacing between characters, specified as condensed or omitted if normal.

4. **Size** – The height of the font in pixels. The height extends from the bottom of the descender to the top of a typical uppercase letter, as shown in Figure 10-2. You can use the absolute-size keywords from CSS (for example, x-small or medium) or specify the size in pixels (as in 24px). Note that the actual height varies depending on the font family. Table 10-2 lists the size keywords and their corresponding pixel sizes.

5. **Family** – The name of the font family (for example, Times New Roman or Open Sans).

Figure 10-2.   *Font size*

Table 10-1. *Weight keywords*

Keyword	Equivalent Number
ultralight	100
thin	200
light	300
normal	400
medium	500
semibold	600
bold	700
heavy	800
black	900

Table 10-2. *Size keywords*

Keyword	Equivalent Size
xx-small	9px
x-small	10px
small	13px
medium	16px
large	18px
x-large	24px
xx-large	32px

Table 10-3 lists and explains examples of font names that might be specified in a text style's font property.

Table 10-3. *Example font names*

Piu Font Name	Explanation
24px Open Sans	The font family is Open Sans and the size is 24px. No stretch, weight, or style is specified, so they're all normal.
bold 16px Fira Sans	The font family is Fira Sans, the size is 16px, and the weight is bold (equivalent to 700). No stretch or style is specified, so they're both normal.
italic bold medium Open Sans	The font family is Open Sans and the size is medium, or 16px. The weight is bold (equivalent to 700) and the style is italic. No stretch is specified, so it's normal.
italic bold condensed small Open Sans	The font family is Open Sans and the size is small, or 13px. The stretch is condensed, the weight is bold (equivalent to 700), and the style is italic.

Font Resources

The font name 24px Open Sans refers to a font stored in a resource named OpenSans-Regular-24.fnt. Although the font name and resource name are clearly similar, they're not identical. Piu gets from the font name to the font's resource data by applying a set of rules to create a resource name from the font name. You need to understand these rules to match the font names you specify in your code with the font resources you include in your project's manifest.

The following list shows, in order, the parts of the resource name (excluding the .fnt extension) and explains how Piu generates them from the font name.

Note   The keywords here (such as Light and Regular) are case-sensitive, so their capitalization is significant.

---

1. **Family** – The name of the font family, with any spaces removed. For example, Open Sans becomes OpenSans.

2. **Hyphen (-)** – A hyphen separating the font family name from what follows.

3. **Stretch** – Omitted if the stretch of the font is normal; otherwise, Condensed.

4. **Weight** – Omitted if the font weight is normal; otherwise, the font weight—for example, Light, Bold, or a numeric value such as 200.

5. **Style** – Omitted if the font style is normal; otherwise, Italic.

6. Regular – If the stretch, weight, and style are normal, the resource name includes the keyword Regular in place of all three.

7. **Hyphen (-)** – A hyphen separating the stretch, weight, and style (or Regular) from the size that follows.

8. **Size** – The height in pixels, as a number—for example, 16 or 24.

Table 10-4 gives examples of Piu font names and the resource names that they map to.

Table 10-4. *Example font names mapped to resource names*

Piu Font Name	Resource Name	Notes
24px Open Sans	OpenSans-Regular-24.fnt	Spaces are removed from the font family name. Because the stretch, weight, and style are all normal, Regular is used in place of those three parts in the resource name.
bold 16px Fira Sans	FiraSans-Bold-16.fnt	The font size is moved to the end and the style, bold, is capitalized in the resource name.
italic bold 16px Open Sans	OpenSans-BoldItalic-16.fnt	Although the font name places italic before bold, the resource name specifies BoldItalic because the weight always precedes the style. Also note that there's no space or hyphen between Bold and Italic.

When creating your own bitmap font files, name the files in accordance with Piu's resource naming conventions. Doing so ensures that when your code specifies a font name, Piu will find the corresponding font data in your resources.

Additional Notes on Fonts

The font naming conventions Piu takes from CSS are designed to be convenient for developers while expressive enough for building sophisticated user interfaces. They also provide consistency for web developers. However, although CSS is powerful, some developers find it more confusing than helpful. If you prefer, you can simply use the name of the font resource as the font name. For example, `textStyle` in the `helloworld` example can be defined as follows:

```
const textStyle = new Style({
    font: "OpenSans-Regular-24"
});
```

Remember that the only fonts available to your project are those that you include in your manifest or are provided by the host. In many cases, that's just a few fonts. If you specify a font that's not installed, Piu cannot render it. This is different from desktop and web development environments, where there's always a fallback font.

Because each font resource corresponds to only one family, stretch, weight, style, and size, you need a separate resource for each variation. If you create a text style whose font property is 24px Open Sans, you must have a font resource named `OpenSans-Regular-24.fnt`. Even if you have a related font resource available, such as `OpenSans-Regular-12.fnt`, Piu cannot resize it to match the 24px size specified in your text style. This too is different from desktop and web development environments, where resizable fonts are common.

Adding Color

The `$EXAMPLES/ch10-piu/helloworld-color` example adds color to the `helloworld` example to make it a little more interesting. It has just a few changes from `helloworld`.

First, the `style` object in `helloworld-color` specifies a `color` property that causes the label to draw the string in yellow:

```
const textStyle = new Style({
    font: "24px Open Sans",
    color: "yellow"
});
```

The example also creates a `skin` object, named `labelBackground`. *Skins* control the drawing of the background of content objects. The `skin` object here specifies the `fill` property in hexadecimal notation, as the color #1932ab, a shade of blue.

```
const labelBackground = new Skin({
    fill: "#1932ab"
});
```

The `sampleLabel` object (Listing 10-5) adds a `skin` property to set its background, causing the label to fill its background with the shade of blue specified in `labelBackground`.

Listing 10-5.

```
const sampleLabel = new Label(null, {
    left: 0, right: 0, top: 0, bottom: 0,
    style: textStyle,
    string: "Hello, World",
    skin: labelBackground
});
```

When you run the `helloworld-color` example on your device, you see the same text and layout as for `helloworld` but with yellow text on a blue background instead of black text on a white background.

When no `skin` property is specified, as in the `helloworld` example, the label doesn't draw anything for its background, causing the text to appear in front of whatever is behind it. The background is white because, in the absence of a skin, the text appears in front of the `application` object itself (created by the host as shown in the section "Everything Is an Object"); since the host sets the application's `skin` property to white, that's the background color for the entire screen.

Specifying Color

The color property in the helloworld-color example's style object is set to a color name, while the fill property in the skin object denotes a color in hexadecimal notation. You can specify the color for these two properties in either way, as discussed in this section.

The color property in the example's style object is set to the string "yellow". Piu supports 18 color names: black, silver, gray, white, maroon, red, purple, fuchsia, green, lime, olive, yellow, navy, blue, teal, aqua, orange, and transparent. The colors and their RGB values are taken from the CSS Level 2 specification.

The fill property in the example's skin object is "#1932ab", a shade of blue specified in hexadecimal notation. As shown in Listing 10-6, Piu supports specifying colors as strings in any of four hexadecimal notations: "#RGB", "#RGBA", "#RRGGBB", and "#RRGGBBAA". In these notations, A stands for "alpha channel" and represents the level of transparency of the color: an alpha value of 0xFF means fully opaque, 0 means entirely transparent, and values in between perform blending. (The alpha value is the same as the blend level used in some Poco rendering functions, such as blendRectangle and drawGray.)

Listing 10-6.

```
const redSkin = new Skin({
    fill: "#f00"
});
const blendedRedSkin = new Skin({
    fill: "#f008"
});
const greenSkin = new Skin({
    fill: "#00ff00"
});
```

```
const blendedGreenSkin = new Skin({
    fill: "#00ff0080"
});
```

All these forms of hexadecimal color notation are also used in CSS.

Changing Color Based on State

Earlier in this chapter, you learned that the properties of skin and style objects cannot be changed. So, for example, you can't change the color of a content object by changing the color property of its skin and style objects; instead, you create a different skin or style object to change the color. However, there's another approach to changing color that's more common and convenient.

Often the reason you want to change the color of a user interface element is to indicate its current state. A button, for example, might have three states: disabled, enabled but not being tapped, and enabled and being tapped. Or a label displaying a sensor reading might have states for when it's within 5% of a target value, within 15% of a target value, and more than 15% off a target value. To support these situations, every content object has a state property, a number that indicates its current state. Piu uses the state property together with properties of style objects to change the appearance of the user interface element.

The state property is just a number; the state that the number corresponds to is up to you as the developer. It's also up to you to determine how the user interface changes when a content object changes state. For example, you might choose to make a button light gray when disabled, green when enabled but not being tapped, and darker green when enabled and being tapped.

An easy way to change the color of content objects is to use their state property as an index to properties in skin and style objects. You do this by setting the fill or color properties of skin or style objects to an array of two, three, or four colors, rather than a string representing a single color. For example:

```
const blackAndWhiteStyle = new Style({
    color: ["black", "white"]
});
```

Following from this example, Listing 10-7 creates a label with black text because the state is 0 and the color at index 0 is "black".

Listing 10-7.

```
const sampleLabel = new Label(null, {
    top: 0, bottom: 0, left: 0, right: 0,
    style: blackAndWhiteStyle,
    state: 0,
    string: "Hello, World"
});
```

When you change the state property, the user interface element is redrawn with the corresponding color from its style. Changing the state to 1 here causes the label to be redrawn with white text.

```
sampleLabel.state = 1;
```

You can also use non-integer values for the state, causing colors from surrounding states to be blended. For example, you can make the text gray in this example as follows:

```
sampleLabel.state = 0.5;
```

The ability to specify fractional values for the state may seem odd conceptually; what does it mean, for instance, for a button to be halfway between the disabled and enabled states? However, there are some interesting uses, such as when you're animating between two states: you can create a style with two colors and slowly fade a label from the first color to the second by changing its state from 0 to 1 in small increments.

Responding to Events with Behaviors

Once you have some content objects on the screen, the next step is to enable them to perform actions in response to events. You do this with behavior objects.

A behavior object is a collection of methods. You attach a behavior object to a content object by setting its behavior property. When the content object receives an event, it looks in its behavior object for a method corresponding to that event; if it finds a method with the same name as the event, it calls that method to handle the event.

Piu defines a set of events that it triggers as needed. For example, it triggers the onTouchBegan event when a finger is placed on a content object and the onTouchEnded event when the finger is removed. The TraceBehavior class in Listing 10-8 contains methods that respond to Piu's onTouchBegan and onTouchEnded events by tracing to the debug console.

Listing 10-8.

```
class TraceBehavior extends Behavior {
    onTouchBegan(label) {
        trace("touch began\n");
    }
    onTouchEnded(label) {
        trace("touch ended\n");
    }
}
```

Events defined and triggered by Piu are called *low-level events*. You can also define your own events, using any you name like; these are called *high-level events*. For example, you might create an onSensorValueChanged event that your application triggers when the value of a sensor changes. The rest of this section introduces some commonly used low-level events; later in this chapter, you'll learn how to define and trigger your own high-level events.

"Hello, World" with a Behavior

The $EXAMPLES/ch10-piu/helloworld-behavior example adds a behavior to the helloworld example to make the string "Hello, World" appear one character at a time as you tap the screen. This simple behavior shows how Piu delivers events to content objects.

The sampleLabel object in the helloworld-behavior example (Listing 10-9) is similar to the one from helloworld. However, there are three important differences:

- The string property of sampleLabel starts out as the empty string so that it may be filled in one character at a time in response to taps.

- The active property is set to true. This property specifies whether the content object should respond to touch events. If it's set to true, Piu triggers touch-related events such as onTouchBegan. The default value is false, so you have to explicitly set active to true to make contents tappable.

- A Behavior property is specified in the dictionary passed to the constructor. This sets the behavior of sampleLabel as the LabelBehavior class.

Listing 10-9.

```
const sampleLabel = new Label(null, {
    top: 0, bottom: 0, left: 0, right: 0,
    style: textStyle,
    string: "",
    active: true,
    Behavior: LabelBehavior
});
sampleLabel.message = "Hello, World";
```

LabelBehavior is a class that extends the built-in Behavior class:

```
class LabelBehavior extends Behavior {
    ...
}
```

When sampleLabel is created, Piu also creates an instance of LabelBehavior and assigns it to the behavior property of sampleLabel. Notice that the Behavior property is capitalized in the dictionary passed to the Label constructor, whereas the behavior property of a created instance is lowercase; that's because property names follow the same capitalization convention as the values they take: the class is passed to the constructor in the Behavior property (and class names in JavaScript are uppercase by convention), whereas the behavior property of sampleLabel contains an instance of the class (and instance names in JavaScript are lowercase by convention).

LabelBehavior has just one method, onTouchBegan, shown in Listing 10-10. The argument to this method is the label object itself. The first argument to all event handler methods invoked in a behavior is the content object they're attached to. When called, this method adds the next character from the string "Hello, World" to the label object until all characters have been added. Then it sets the label object's active property to false to stop it from receiving further touch events.

Listing 10-10.

```
onTouchBegan(label) {
    const message = label.message;
    label.string = message.substring(0, label.string.length + 1);
    if (label.string === message)
        label.active = false;
}
```

That's all it takes to implement a basic touch behavior. When you run the example and tap the label object (which covers the entire screen), Piu triggers the object's onTouchBegan event. The label object then checks its behavior to see if it has an onTouchBegan method; it does, so it calls that method, passing a reference to itself as the first argument.

Many low-level events have additional arguments that may be useful in your projects. For example, the onTouchBegan event also passes these four arguments:

- id – The identifier of the touch point used to support multi-touch. This example supports only one touch point, so id is always 0. The id value is a number that comes from the touch controller, enabling you to distinguish between different touch points on the screen.

- x and y – The global coordinates of the event—that is, of the point touched—in pixels.

- ticks – The global time of the event in milliseconds. This value is not the time of day and is unrelated to UTC; it's used only to determine the time elapsed between two events.

When you're working with an event for the first time, a good way to understand it well is to add a method to the behavior to trace the arguments it receives to the debug console. For example, to observe details of how and when onTouchBegan is invoked, change the helloworld-behavior example to the function shown in Listing 10-11.

Listing 10-11.

```
onTouchBegan(label, id, x, y, ticks) {
    trace(`id: ${id}\n`);
    trace(`{x, y}: {${x}, ${y}}\n`);
    trace(`ticks: ${ticks}\n`);
}
```

The onTimeChanged and onDisplaying Events

This section introduces these commonly used low-level events:

- The onTimeChanged event gives you access to the clock built into every Piu content object.

- The onDisplaying event gives your behavior a chance to configure itself before the content object appears on the screen.

These events are introduced through the $EXAMPLES/ch10-piu/ helloworld-ticking example, which is similar to the helloworld-behavior example in that it adds one character of "Hello, World" to the screen at a time; however, instead of adding characters when the screen is tapped, it adds them at a regular interval. Note the following about this example:

- The sampleLabel object is identical to the one in helloworld-behavior except that its active property is not set to true, because it doesn't respond to touch events.

- The LabelBehavior class includes onDisplaying
  and onTimeChanged methods (Listing 10-12) instead
  of an onTouchBegan method. Their first argument is
  a reference to the label object associated with the
  behavior, as with all events defined by Piu.

Listing 10-12.

```
class LabelBehavior extends Behavior {
    onDisplaying(label) {
        ...
    }
    onTimeChanged(label) {
        ...
    }
}
```

The onDisplaying event is triggered after the content object is
added to the application object but before it's visible to the user. This
is useful for initializing the state of the object, especially content objects
that may be hidden and later shown several times. One common use
of the onDisplaying event is to start a timer that's used to animate the
appearance of the content object.

Because animation is such a pervasive part of modern user interfaces,
Piu gives every content object a built-in clock. The clock "ticks" at the
interval specified by the content object's interval property. Both the
interval property and the clock express the time in milliseconds. Each
time the clock ticks, it generates an onTimeChanged event. The clock is not
always running and is initially stopped; you use a content object's start
and stop methods to control when its clock is running.

In this example, the behavior's onDisplaying method (Listing 10-13) begins by resetting the index property, which stores the number of characters of the string that are in the label object at any given time. The code sets the interval property to 250 milliseconds to request that the onTimeChanged event be generated every quarter of a second. Finally, the method starts the label's clock ticking by calling its start method.

Listing 10-13.

```
onDisplaying(label) {
    this.index = 0;
    label.interval = 250;
    label.start();
}
```

The behavior's onTimeChanged method (Listing 10-14) adds one new character to the label object's string property at each interval. It uses the substring method, which returns part of a string. The arguments to substring specify the indexes of the first character to include and the first character to exclude, respectively. When the complete string has been displayed, onTimeChanged calls the label's stop method to prevent the clock from ticking so that onTimeChanged is no longer triggered.

Listing 10-14.

```
onTimeChanged(label) {
    const message = label.message;
    this.index += 1;
    if (this.index > message.length)
        label.stop();
    else
        label.string = message.substring(0, this.index);
}
```

Later examples show how to use a content object's clock to drive animations.

Adding Images

Images are a fundamental part of building a user interface. Just as Piu uses skin objects to fill an area of the screen with a solid color, it also uses them to fill an area of the screen with an image, enabling any content object to draw images. A *texture* in a skin object specifies the image to use.

To show how to render an image, the $EXAMPLES/ch10-piu/js-icon example draws the JavaScript logo. The example draws the screen shown in Figure 10-3.

Figure 10-3. js-icon *example*

A skin object is used to create the icon. The first step is to create a reference to the image file to use, by instantiating a texture object. The path property of the dictionary passed to the Texture constructor is the name of the resource that contains the image.

```
const jsLogoTexture = new Texture({
    path: "js.png"
});
```

Notice that the resource name has a .png extension, instead of .bmp as you saw for Poco in Chapter 9. While the PNG image is still converted to another format for rendering on the microcontroller, Piu is aware of the conversion and automatically changes the .png extension to the correct extension for the device.

In the helloworld-color example, you used a skin object with a fill property to create a solid-colored background. In this example, instead of fill you use a texture property, together with height and width properties, to create a skin, jsLogoSkin, that fills content objects using jsLogoTexture. The height and width properties are set to match the dimensions of the js.png image file, 100 x 100 pixels.

```
const jsLogoSkin = new Skin({
    texture: jsLogoTexture,
    height: 100, width: 100
});
```

The final step is to create a content object that references jsLogoSkin:

```
const jsLogo = new Content(null, {
    skin: jsLogoSkin
});
```

Because the skin is defined to be 100 x 100 pixels, the jsLogo content object has those same dimensions by default.

Drawing Part of an Image

You may have wondered why you had to specify height and width properties in the Skin constructor earlier. Why didn't the skin just use the entire image by default? The reason is a feature of the skin object that enables you to draw only part of the texture. To specify the area of the texture to draw, you use the x, y, height, and width properties to define the source rectangle in pixels. The x and y properties default to 0, but the height and width properties are required.

The code in Listing 10-15 is an alternative to jsLogoSkin in the js-icon example. Here the skin is defined to draw a square of 70 x 70 pixels from the bottom right of the image. The result is shown in Figure 10-4.

Listing 10-15.

```
const jsLogoSkin = new Skin({
    texture: jsLogoTexture,
    x: 24, y: 30,
    height: 70, width: 70
});
```

Figure 10-4. *js-icon example with cropped jsLogoSkin*

Drawing a portion of a single icon is rare. After all, if you only want to draw the bottom-right corner, you might as well crop the image file and save some storage space. However, it's often convenient to store several icons in a single image, in which case being able to draw a portion of an image is very useful. The next section walks through an example.

Drawing Multiple Icons from One Image

Recall the icons in Figure 10-5, which you first saw in Chapter 8. These icons show several different states of a Wi-Fi connection and are combined into a single image.

Figure 10-5. *Wi-Fi icons*

The icons are organized into a uniform grid, in which the columns and rows are as follows:

- Each column is a different state of the Wi-Fi icon, representing signal strength levels from weak to strong.

- Each row is a different variant of the Wi-Fi icon. The top row is the open Wi-Fi access point variant and the bottom row is the secure Wi-Fi access point variant.

Just as Piu uses a content object's state property to determine which color to draw from a style, it can use a content object's state and variant properties to determine which icon to draw from a texture containing a grid of icons. To do this, the skin containing the texture here must specify the width of each column and the height of each row, using the states and variants properties, respectively, in the dictionary used to create the skin (see Listing 10-16).

Listing 10-16.

```
const wifiTexture = new Texture({
    path: "wifi-strip.png"
});
```

```
const wifiSkin = new Skin({
    texture: wifiTexture,
    width: 28, height: 28,
    states: 28,
    variants: 28
});
```

The image in this example contains icons that are 28 pixels square, so the states and variants properties are both 28. In addition, the height and width properties are both set to 28 so that the size of the skin is exactly the size of one icon.

The $EXAMPLES/ch10-piu/wifi-status example draws one icon from this image at a time, changing the icon once a second. It starts with the top-left icon (state and variant both 0), as shown in Listing 10-17.

Listing 10-17.

```
const wifiIcon = new Content(null, {
    skin: wifiSkin,
    state: 0,
    variant: 0,
    Behavior: WifiIconBehavior
});
```

The state and variant properties of a content object can be updated at any time. This example changes them to move through the icon strip one icon at a time, from left to right, first across the top row and then across the bottom row; then it goes back to the top row and repeats this indefinitely. As shown in Listing 10-18, the onDisplaying and onTimeChanged event handlers in the behavior of wifiIcon use the content object's built-in clock to drive the animation (as you saw in the helloworld-ticking example): the behavior changes the variant property on each tick, moving across a row of icons; when the last icon in a row is reached, it changes the state property to switch to the other row.

Listing 10-18.

```
class WifiIconBehavior extends Behavior {
    onDisplaying(content) {
        content.interval = 1000;
        content.start();
    }
    onTimeChanged(content) {
        let variant = content.variant + 1;
        if (variant > 4) {
            variant = 0;
            content.state = content.state ? 0 : 1;
        }
        content.variant = variant;
    }
}
```

Using Masks

Compressed grayscale masks are more efficient for storing grayscale images than full-color bitmap images are, and (as you learned in Chapter 8) masks may be drawn in any color. Many icons drawn in user interfaces are only a single color and consequently can be stored as a mask. A texture object may refer to a mask image resource as well as a color bitmap resource, enabling your user interface to include both.

Adding a mask image to your application is very similar to adding a full-color bitmap. The $EXAMPLES/ch10-piu/mask-icon example displays an icon stored as a mask. When you tap the icon, it changes color.

The example's texture and skin properties (Listing 10-19) should look familiar. The key difference is that maskSettingsSkin specifies a color property with two colors, "orange" for when the content object's state property has a value of 0 and "yellow" for when it's 1. (Note that there are two different ways to specify the color of a skin: when you use a skin to draw a mask texture, you specify the color property; to create a solid-colored background, you specify the fill property.)

Listing 10-19.

```
const maskSettingsTexture = new Texture({
    path: "settings-mask.png"
});

const maskSettingsSkin = new Skin({
    texture: maskSettingsTexture,
    width: 80, height: 80,
    color: ["orange", "yellow"]
});
```

As usual, you have to create a content object that references the skin. Listing 10-20 shows the one created in this example: a content object that also has a behavior and an active property (set to true so that the object can receive touch events).

Listing 10-20.

```
const maskSettingsIcon = new Content(null, {
    skin: maskSettingsSkin,
    state: 0,
    active: true,
    Behavior: SettingsIconBehavior
});
```

When the icon is first drawn, the mask is drawn in orange, because the state value of 0 means it uses the color at index 0 of the array in the color property.

As shown in Listing 10-21, this example provides touch feedback using the onTouchBegan and onTouchEnded events triggered at the beginning and end of a tap:

- When maskSettingsIcon receives an onTouchBegan event, its behavior sets its state to 1, causing it to redraw with the color at index 1 of its color property—in this case, yellow.

- When maskSettingsIcon receives an onTouchEnded event, its behavior changes its state to 0, making the icon orange again.

Listing 10-21.

```
class SettingsIconBehavior extends Behavior {
    onTouchBegan(content) {
        content.state = 1;
    }
    onTouchEnded(content) {
        content.state = 0;
    }
}
```

Tiling Images

You can draw repeating patterns by tiling the texture of a skin. This is another way to reduce storage space, because you can use image files that are a single tile of a background rather than the full size of the screen.

Tiling a Single Image

The $EXAMPLES/ch10-piu/tiled-background example uses the image in Figure 10-6 to create the tiled background shown in Figure 10-7.

Figure 10-6. *Image from* `tiled-background` *example*

Figure 10-7. `tiled-background` *example*

Like the skin of an icon, a tiled skin uses a texture object and defines height and width properties to specify the area of the texture to draw (in this case all of it). As shown in Listing 10-22, you also include a tiles property—an object with left, right, top, and bottom properties indicating different parts of the texture to tile; here they're all 0 because this example uses the entire image as a repeating tile. (The following section, on drawing 9-patch images, explains how to use these four properties with other values.)

Listing 10-22.

```
const tileTexture = new Texture({
    path: "tile.png"
});
```

```
const tileSkin = new Skin({
    texture: tileTexture,
    height: 50, width: 50,
    tiles: {
        left: 0, right: 0, top: 0, bottom: 0
    }
});
```

When you attach tileSkin to a full-screen content object, it draws as shown in Figure 10-7:

```
const background = new Content(null, {
    left: 0, right: 0, top: 0, bottom: 0,
    skin: tileSkin
});
```

Drawing 9-Patch Images with Tiles

A 9-patch image is used to efficiently draw rectangular shapes, such as a rounded rectangle, at different sizes. The term "9-patch" comes from the Android mobile OS, although the concept is widely used elsewhere; it refers to the way the image asset is divided into nine parts, as you'll see in a moment. Many interesting effects can be created with 9-patch images. Piu incorporates this concept through the use of a tiled skin.

Recall from earlier that the properties of a tiles object indicate different sections of the texture to tile. More specifically, these properties define the parts of a 9-patch image by specifying a number of pixels in from the edges of the image, as shown in Figure 10-8 for a tiles object whose properties all specify 14. The light gray lines in the figure delineate the nine parts and assign a number to each one. The whole image is 56 pixels square.

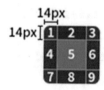

Figure 10-8. *Rounded rectangle with nine parts delineated*

A tiled skin for this image would be defined as in Listing 10-23.

Listing 10-23.

```
const tileSkin = new Skin({
    texture: tileTexture,
    height: 56, width: 56,
    tiles: {
        left: 14, right: 14, top: 14, bottom: 14
    }
});
```

When this skin is applied to a content object, Piu draws the nine parts of the image using the following rules:

- Zones 1, 3, 7, and 9 are each drawn once at the corresponding corner of the content object.

- Zones 2 and 8 repeat horizontally across the top and bottom of the content object, respectively.

- Zones 4 and 6 repeat vertically along the left and right sides of the content object, respectively.

- Zone 5 repeats vertically and horizontally to fill space in the middle of the content object not covered by other tiles.

Figure 10-9 shows how this tiled skin is rendered by content objects with the following dimensions (from left to right): 28 x 28, 56 x 56, 110 x 100, and 70 x 165. Note that the nine parts of the image are only repeated and never resized.

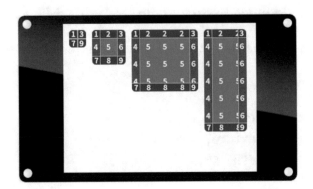

Figure 10-9. *tileSkin rendered in different sizes*

The $EXAMPLES/ch10-piu/rounded-buttons example uses a simple, solid-colored rounded rectangle to create buttons of different sizes (Figure 10-10).

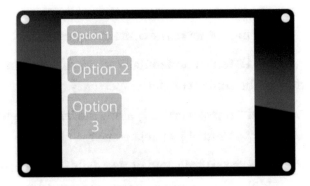

Figure 10-10. *rounded-buttons example*

The skin in this example is defined as shown in Listing 10-24. It looks similar to the preceding skin example, but the image asset is smaller and the left, right, top, and bottom properties of the tiles object are all set to 5. It also specifies a color property; tiled skins can use masks.

Listing 10-24.

```
const roundedTexture = new Texture({
    path: "button.png"
});

const roundedSkin = new Skin({
    texture: roundedTexture,
    width: 30, height: 30,
    color: ["#ff9900", "#ffd699"],
    tiles: {
        top: 5, bottom: 5, left: 5, right: 5
    }
});
```

The three buttons in this example are label and text objects (Listing 10-25). They have different heights and widths, but roundedSkin tiles its texture as described previously to fit all the different sizes.

Listing 10-25.

```
const button1 = new Label(null, {
    top: 10, left: 10,
    skin: roundedSkin,
    style: smallTextStyle,
    string: "Option 1",
    active: true,
    Behavior: ButtonBehavior
});
```

```
const button2 = new Label(null, {
    top: 60, left: 10,
    skin: roundedSkin,
    style: textStyle,
    string: "Option 2",
    active: true,
    Behavior: ButtonBehavior
});

const button3 = new Text(null, {
    top: 120, left: 10, width: 90,
    skin: roundedSkin,
    style: textStyle,
    string: "Option 3",
    active: true,
    Behavior: ButtonBehavior
});
```

Recall that a label object renders text on a single line; this example uses a text object for the third button to illustrate that text objects, unlike label objects, can render text on multiple lines.

The behavior ButtonBehavior in this example is identical to SettingsIconBehavior in the mask-icon example, with onTouchBegan and onTouchEnded methods providing feedback when the buttons are tapped.

Building Compound User Interface Elements

The user interfaces of real products are composed of more complex elements than just a string of text or single icon in the middle of the screen. The initial examples in this chapter use a simple structure to introduce fundamental Piu concepts; you're now ready to put those elements together to build more sophisticated interfaces.

Adding content objects to the `application` object creates a tree data structure called a *containment hierarchy*. The simple examples so far have created a two-level containment hierarchy, with the `application` object at the root and content objects as leaves, but there can be many levels in the hierarchy.

The containment hierarchy organizes the content objects in your user interface by placing them into groups called *containers*. Containers are implemented by the `Container` class, a key built-in Piu class. The `application` object itself is a container, which is how it's able to hold other content objects. The containment hierarchy does more than group content objects together; it also affects how the objects are drawn and how they receive events.

The idea of a containment hierarchy should be familiar to you if you've ever built a user interface with HTML or with other object-oriented user interface frameworks. If not, the example in the next section will get you started by taking you through the steps of building a containment hierarchy.

Creating a Header

Like previous examples in this chapter, the `$EXAMPLES/ch10-piu/header` example adds text and an icon to the screen. But rather than treating them as standalone elements as in those examples, it groups them together into one compound user interface element, the header shown in Figure 10-11.

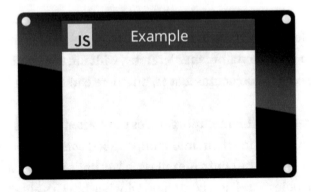

Figure 10-11. *header example*

The jsLogo and headerText objects in the header example (Listing 10-26) are similar to the content and label objects in the previous examples.

Listing 10-26.

```
const jsLogo = new Content(null, {
    left: 10,
    skin: jsLogoSkin
});

const headerText = new Label(null, {
    style: textStyle,
    string: "Example"
});
```

The header object (Listing 10-27) is an instance of the Container class. The Container class inherits from the Content class and extends it with the ability to hold other content objects.

Listing 10-27.

```
const header = new Container(null, {
    top: 0, height: 50, left: 0, right: 0,
    skin: headerSkin,
```

```
contents: [
    jsLogo,
    headerText
  ]
});
```

The header object contains the jsLogo and headerText objects, which are placed in the contents property array. The skin property gives the header object a blue background (because headerSkin has a fill property of "#1932ab").

Because the jsLogo and headerText objects are contained by the header object, when the header object is added to the application object all the elements—the blue background, icon, and text—appear on the screen:

```
application.add(header);
```

Similarly, removing the header object makes all the elements disappear, and moving the header object around the screen moves all the elements it contains simultaneously.

When a content object is added to a container, the content object is said to be a *child object*, or simply *child*, of the container; correspondingly, the container is said to be the content object's *parent object*, or simply *parent*. In this example, the header is the parent container, and the text and icon are child objects of the header.

You can use the container property of an object to access its parent container object and the length property to determine the number of child objects in a container. If an object has no parent container, its container property is null. If there are no child objects, the length property is 0. Several different methods of accessing the objects in a container are described in the section "Accessing Content Objects in a Container" later in this chapter.

Relative and Absolute Coordinates

As you've learned, the left, right, top, and bottom properties passed to a content object's constructor define the position of the content object by specifying the margins between the object and its container. Since these properties express the location of points relative to the parent container, they're called *relative coordinates*. For example, when you pass left with a value of 10, it doesn't necessarily mean the content object will be 10 pixels from the left side of the screen when it's drawn; it means the content will be 10 pixels from the left side of whatever container it's placed in.

The coordinates of a content object once it's drawn on the screen are called *absolute coordinates*, which express the location of points as the distance from the edges of the screen. When the container is the entire screen, which is usually the case for the application object, the relative and absolute coordinates of the container's child objects are the same.

When a container moves, Piu adjusts the absolute coordinates of all of the container's child content objects. This makes it much easier to animate compound user interface elements, like the header in the header example, since your code needs to move only the container of the compound element rather than each individual content element.

Adding and Removing Container Contents

The contents of a container are not fixed. Just as you can add and remove objects from the application object, you can add and remove objects from a container object at any time. The Container class and all classes that inherit from it have add and remove methods that you use to modify their contents array. The Application class is one common class that inherits from the Container class.

You can call a container's add method at any time, whether or not the container is part of the containment hierarchy. For example, instead of passing a contents array to the constructor when you create the header object (as in Listing 10-27 earlier), you can add each content object to the header after instantiating all the objects but before adding the header to the application object (see Listing 10-28).

Listing 10-28.

```
const header = new Container(null, {
    top: 0, height: 50, left: 0, right: 0,
    skin: headerSkin
});

header.add(jsLogo);
header.add(headerText);
application.add(header);
```

Either way, the result is the same: jsLogo and headerText are contained by header, and header is contained by the application object. This creates a three-level containment hierarchy, with the application object at the root, header as a branch, and jsLogo and headerText as leaves.

Here's how you could use the remove method to take jsLogo out of the header's child list:

```
header.remove(jsLogo);
```

The empty method removes all child elements from a container. This is useful when you need to rebuild the content of a compound node, such as when moving to another screen (as you'll see later, in the section "The Application Logic").

```
header.empty();
```

One Container for Each Content Object

A content object can be a child of only one container at any time. You can add and remove an object from its container as many times as you want, and you can move an object into a new container by removing it from its current container and adding it to a new one; however, you can't add the same content object to multiple containers at the same time. If you attempt to add a content object already in one container to another container, Piu throws an error.

This may seem strange. You might think that adding the same object to multiple containers would just create identical objects that go into different containers, but that's not the case. Every graphical element that shows up on the screen is associated with a single content object.

If this still seems strange, a metaphor to the real world may help you understand it. Imagine you have two boxes and one physical object—a pen, for example. You can put the pen in either box but not in both boxes at the same time. The same rule applies to content objects and containers in Piu.

Of course, you can always create identical contents and put them in different containers. Later in this chapter, you'll learn about an easy way to create similar or identical contents, using templates.

Building Responsive Layouts

The screen shown in Figure 10-12 displays a navigation bar consisting of three buttons, each with an icon and text in it that identify its purpose. If asked to describe the position of these buttons, most people would say something like, "There's a row of evenly spaced buttons in the middle of the screen." Few would say, "There's one button that's 20 pixels from the left and 74 pixels from the top of the screen, one that's 120 from the left and 74 from the top, and another that's 220 from the left and 74 from the top." To put this another way, people would most likely describe the layout rule rather than the coordinates of each button.

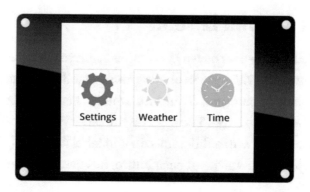

Figure 10-12. *Row of buttons in centered navigation bar*

A layout rule is a concise way of describing how to arrange the content objects in a container. The layout rule may be independent of the current container size, adjusting to whatever the current size happens to be. For example, the layout shown here can evenly space the buttons whether the width of the container (the screen) is 320 or 480 pixels. A layout rule that adjusts intelligently to changes to the size of its parent container is called a *responsive layout*.

If you have a background in web design or in writing mobile apps, you're likely familiar with the concept of responsive layout. Good web pages are designed to render well regardless of the size of the browser window or screen; in other words, they respond to differences in size. Many mobile apps rotate based on the orientation of the screen; that is, they respond to changes in orientation.

Piu has features that enable you to create responsive layouts as well. These features are often useful, as demonstrated in the next few examples, even if the size of the screen in all the models of your product is the same.

Row and Column Layouts

The $EXAMPLES/ch10-piu/nav-bar example displays the navigation bar shown in Figure 10-12. A column object groups together the icon and label for each of the three compound button elements. Listing 10-29 shows the code for the leftmost button. The code for the other two buttons follows the same pattern but with a different skin and label for each. (To keep the example simple, the behavior of each button has been omitted.)

Listing 10-29.

```
const settingsButton = new Column(null, {
    skin: outlineSkin, width: 80,
    contents: [
        Content(null, {
            top: 5,
            skin: settingsSkin
        }),
        Label(null, {
            top: 0,
            style: textStyle,
            string: "Settings"
        })
    ]
});
```

The Column class extends the Container class with a layout rule to arrange its contents in a vertical column. In this example, the content object has a top margin of 5 and the label object has a top margin of 0. If you placed them in a container, they would overlap; however, because they're in a column object, the content object's top margin is relative to the column object, and the label object's top margin is relative to the bottom of the content object. If you add another object, its top margin will be relative to the bottom of the label object, and so on.

The `column` objects for all three buttons are placed in a `row` object, as shown in Listing 10-30. The Row class is another subclass of the `Container` class.

Listing 10-30.

```
const navBar = new Row(null, {
    left: 0, right: 0,
    contents: [
        Content(null, {left: 0, right: 0}),
        settingsButton,
        Content(null, {left: 0, right: 0}),
        weatherButton,
        Content(null, {left: 0, right: 0}),
        timeButton,
        Content(null, {left: 0, right: 0})
    ]
});
```

A `row` object arranges its contents horizontally and, like a `column` object, relative to each other. The left margin of the first item in a `row` object's `contents` array is relative to the left of the row, the left margin of the second item is relative to the first item, and so on.

You're likely wondering why there are `content` objects in Listing 10-30. Here are a few important things to note about them:

- They have no skin and therefore are transparent. They represent the blank space around the buttons in the row.

- No width is specified for them; instead, the `row` object calculates the amount of blank space to put around the buttons.

- Their `left` and `right` margins (like those of the three buttons) are 0; otherwise, the margins would enter into the calculations that the `row` object does, which isn't normally what you'd want.

To understand this further, let's first look at what the result would be if the `content` objects were removed from the row, leaving only the three buttons. Because the buttons all have a defined width of 80 but no left or right margins, placing them in the `navBar` row on their own causes them to be pushed together into 240 pixels on the left side of the screen, as shown in Figure 10-13.

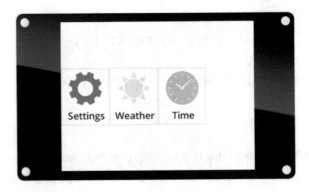

Figure 10-13. *navBar without* content *objects*

If you then give each button a left margin of 20, you get the desired layout on a 320 x 240 screen, as shown earlier in Figure 10-12. But now imagine a different-sized screen is used—say, a 480 x 320; Figure 10-14 shows the result in that case.

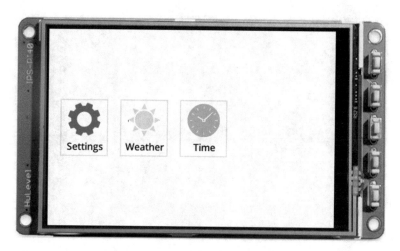

Figure 10-14. *navBar without* content *objects but with margins,*
larger screen

The content objects are what make the layout responsive to different
screen sizes. Since the content objects have no width, the row object
figures out how wide to make them in order to achieve the desired layout:
it calculates the width taken up by the three buttons on their own—240 in
this case—and the rest of the pixels available in the row are distributed
evenly among the remaining contents (resulting in the same amount of
space before the first button, between the buttons, and after the last one).
On the 320 x 240 screen in Figure 10-12, this comes to (320 – 240) / 4, or 20
pixels per content object; on a 480 x 320 screen (Figure 10-15), it comes to
60 pixels each.

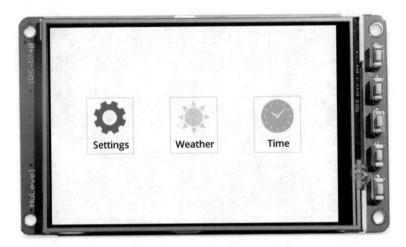

Figure 10-15. *navBar on larger screen, properly centered*

If you wanted the buttons in this example to be exactly 20 pixels apart but still centered on the screen, you could specify a width of 20 for the two middle content objects. The row object would then calculate only the amount of space to put before the first button and after the last one.

If you're sure the size of the screen won't change or rotate, adding transparent content objects isn't necessary; you can just define left and right margins to space items as desired. Still, it's a useful trick to know if you're designing for multiple screen sizes.

Scrolling Content

When you have more content than you can fit on the screen at once, one common solution is to use scrolling to move through the content. The $EXAMPLES/ch10-piu/scrolling-text example uses scrolling to display content that's too large to fit on a 320 x 240 screen. Figure 10-16 shows the screen as it initially appears.

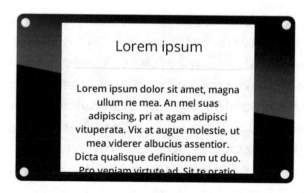

Figure 10-16. *scrolling-text example*

This example scrolls a header, a gray bar, and sample text, defined by label, content, and text objects, respectively. These objects are in a column container, laying them out vertically. The column is the first item in a scroller object's contents array, as shown in Listing 10-31.

Listing 10-31.

```
const sampleVerticalScroller = new Scroller(null, {
    left: 0, right: 0, top: 0, bottom: 0,
    contents: [
        Column(null, {
            left: 0, right: 0, top: 0,
            contents: [
                sampleHeader,
                grayBar,
                sampleText
            ]
        })
    ],
    active: true,
    Behavior: VerticalScrollerBehavior
});
```

The Scroller class extends the Container class with a layout rule that scrolls the first item in its contents array while leaving the other contents (none, in this example) to follow the default container layout behavior. The Scroller class can scroll horizontally, vertically, or both; this example scrolls vertically. The way a scroller object scrolls is determined by its behavior.

The behavior VerticalScrollerBehavior in this example (Listing 10-32) uses touch input to control the scrolling. When you touch the screen and drag up or down, the scroller moves the content up or down. The onTouchMoved event is a low-level event that's triggered when a finger is moved on the screen. A content object may receive many onTouchMoved events after an onTouchBegan event (and before the onTouchEnded event, if any).

Listing 10-32.

```
class VerticalScrollerBehavior extends Behavior {
    onTouchBegan(scroller, id, x, y, ticks) {
        this.initialScrollY = scroller.scroll.y;
        this.initialY = y;
        scroller.captureTouch(id, x, y, ticks);
    }
    onTouchMoved(scroller, id, x, y, ticks) {
        const dy = y - this.initialY;
        scroller.scrollTo(0, this.initialScrollY - dy);
    }
}
```

Note the following about this code:

- The onTouchBegan method calls the scroller object's captureTouch method, which prevents other content objects from triggering touch events related to the touch. This isn't necessary here, because there are no other active content objects to receive touch events, but it's included because it makes the behavior more reusable.

- The onTouchMoved method calls the scrollTo method of the scroller object to scroll the content vertically based on finger movements. It's best to use scrollTo rather than changing the coordinates of the content; scrollTo prevents the content from moving off screen, so you don't have to write additional code to avoid doing so.

- There's no onTouchEnded method because no feedback is provided at the end of the touch.

Templates for Content Objects

User interfaces often use the same element, sometimes with small variations, in many places. For example, each screen of an application may use a header with the same icon in it but different text, or each button in a navigation bar may have a different icon and text in it, as in the nav-bar example. To create each of its three buttons, the nav-bar example used essentially the same code. Piu *templates* are a more concise and efficient way to achieve the same result. A template is a class that you create using a content object's template method. The ability to create classes at runtime like this is a powerful feature of JavaScript that Piu builds on.

Creating a Button Template Class

Recall that the nav-bar example creates the row of buttons using three column objects, each containing a content object (for the icon) and a label object. These column objects differ only in the skin property of the content object and the string property of the label object. The buttons are placed in a row object along with invisible content objects to make the layout responsive to multiple screen sizes.

463

Writing nearly identical code to create each of three buttons may not seem unreasonable, but imagine you want to create ten buttons: you'd have over a hundred lines of code that look similar. And if you then decided to make each of those buttons a few pixels wider, it would be tedious and error-prone to change each width property individually.

The $EXAMPLES/ch10-piu/nav-bar-template example creates a Button class for the nav-bar buttons. It does this by calling the static template method of the Column class, as shown in Listing 10-33.

Listing 10-33.

```
const Button = Column.template($ => ({
    skin: outlineSkin,
    width: 80,
    contents: [
        Content(null, {
            top: 5,
            skin: $.skin
        }),
        Label(null, {
            top: 0,
            style: textStyle,
            string: $.string
        })
    ]
}));
```

The template method called here creates and returns a constructor for the Button class. This new class extends Column because the template method is part of the Column class. All Piu content objects have a static template method.

Even though the Button class isn't created using the class keyword, you still create instances using the new keyword, as in new Button. Before getting into how to use the Button class, let's look at the implementation of the class.

The sole argument to `Column.template` is a function that returns an object. The syntax is a little unusual, in that the arrow function body is a value rather than a series of statements; that value becomes the return value of the function. To illustrate this with a simple example, the following code defines an arrow function named `test`:

```
let test = () => ({one: 1});
test();    // returns {one: 1}
```

When the arrow function is called, it returns the object. Now consider this example, which defines a version of `test` that takes a single argument:

```
let test = $ => ({one: $});
test(1);    // returns {one: 1}
```

The argument to the arrow function is assigned to a variable named $. Although $ is an unusual variable name, it's valid JavaScript, and the $ variable behaves like any other. (Note this is unrelated to $ used in template literals for string substitution, as described in Chapter 2.)

Similarly, in the `Button` class implementation shown in Listing 10-33, the argument to `Column.template` is an anonymous arrow function that returns an object for which some property values are taken from the $ variable passed in. When you invoke the `Button` constructor, as shown for `settingsButton` in the following code, you pass a dictionary that contains properties to substitute in the template where the $ variable is used, here substituting for `$.skin` and `$.string`; the constructor calls the arrow function specified in its implementation, passing the dictionary shown here as the $ argument:

```
const settingsButton = new Button({
    skin: settingsSkin,
    string: "Settings"
});
```

Using the Button template, each additional button is created with a concise invocation of the Button constructor, as shown in Listing 10-34. (The rest of the code that creates the navigation bar is the same as in the nav-bar example.)

Listing 10-34.

```
const weatherButton = new Button({
    skin: sunSkin,
    string: "Weather"
});

const timeButton = new Button({
    skin: clockSkin,
    string: "Time"
});
```

As you can see, defining a template class has these advantages:

- It significantly improves the code's readability by eliminating redundant code to define each button (which also saves flash memory).

- It makes your code easier to maintain. To change a common property, like the width of each column, all you have to do is change that property of the template.

Content Constructor Arguments

You probably noticed that the Button constructor invocations in the nav-bar-template example look different from the content object constructors in the earlier examples: the calls to the Button constructor pass a dictionary as the first argument rather than null, and they omit the second argument (which, when present, is the dictionary that configures the object). In looking more closely at these two arguments, which every Piu content constructor takes, this section explains these differences.

The Instantiating Data Argument

The first argument a content constructor takes is called the *instantiating data*. This concept is most relevant when working with templates. For example, the Button template class created earlier uses the data passed as the first argument to create the dictionary from which to instantiate the class (in other words, the dictionary normally passed as the second argument).

The instantiating data can be any JavaScript value or object. The class you instantiate determines what data is valid. For example, the Button class template as defined in Listing 10-33 expects the instantiating data to be an object with skin and string properties. An alternative implementation of the Button class is shown in Listing 10-35.

Listing 10-35.

```
const Button = Column.template($ => ({
    skin: outlineSkin,
    width: 80,
    contents: [
        Label(null, {
            top: 0,
            style: textStyle,
            string: $
        })
    ]
}));
```

This `Button` class has no icon and expects a string to be passed as the `$` argument, as in these examples:

```
const weatherButton = new Button("Weather");
const timeButton = new Button("Time");
```

The instantiating data has another interesting property: it's passed to the `onCreate` method of the created instance's behavior. For example, Listing 10-36 shows another way to implement the `Button` class from Listing 10-35.

Listing 10-36.

```
const Button = Column.template($ => ({
    skin: outlineSkin,
    width: 80,
    contents: [
        Label(null, {
            top: 0,
            style: textStyle
        })
    ],
    Behavior: class extends Behavior {
        onCreate(column, $) {
            column.first.string = $;
        }
    }
}));
```

The functionality of the instantiating data is not limited to templates; any content object constructors can use it. For example, Listing 10-37 creates a label with the string `"Hello, World"`.

Listing 10-37.

```
const sampleLabel = new Label("Hello, World", {
    top: 0, bottom: 0, left: 0, right: 0,
    style: textStyle,
    Behavior: class extends Behavior {
        onCreate(label, data) {
            label.string = data;
        }
    }
});
```

Later in this chapter, you'll learn an advanced use of the instantiating data argument: defining content anchors.

The Content Dictionary Argument

The second argument to a content constructor is a dictionary that defines properties of the created instance. The properties you include in this content dictionary are associated with built-in properties of the content class you're instantiating—for example, the instance's skin or width. Except for the Button template examples shown earlier, all the examples in this chapter define the content dictionary argument; however, it's optional and is undefined by default.

Listing 10-37 demonstrated the use of both the instantiating data argument and the content dictionary argument to create a label object. The $EXAMPLES/ch10-piu/colored-squares example demonstrates how to use both these arguments when calling a template constructor to create the colored squares shown in Figure 10-17.

Figure 10-17. *colored-squares example*

Listing 10-38 shows the code for creating the template and constructing the squares.

Listing 10-38.

```
const Square = Content.template($ => ({
    width: 80, height: 80,
    skin: new Skin({fill: $})
}));

const redSquare = new Square("red", {left: 20, top: 20});
const yellowSquare = new Square("yellow");
const blueSquare = new Square("blue", {right: 20, bottom: 20});
```

In this example, the instantiating data is a string that defines the fill color of the square. The position of the red and blue squares is defined by the second dictionary argument, while the yellow square omits the second argument and therefore defaults to being centered in its parent container.

Accessing Content Objects in a Container

In the examples you've seen so far, you've accessed content objects through local variables, but you haven't seen how to access content objects when you don't have a reference to them in a local variable. There are many situations where you may need to access objects directly from the containment hierarchy, such as when working with compound objects you created using a template.

You've already learned that a container object contains a list of child objects, the number of which is available from the container's length property. The following sections introduce several methods for accessing content objects within the containment hierarchy.

Using first, last, next, and previous

You can use the first property of a container to retrieve its first child, and the last property to retrieve its last child. If a container has no child objects, first and last are null.

Every content object has a next property that you can use to access the following content object in its container, or null if there is none. Likewise, a previous property returns the preceding content object (or null).

Using these properties is a simple way to access contents in a container. They work well for some situations but not all. For example, the code to access the fourth child of a container named myContainer using first and next is difficult to read and tedious to write.

```
let button = myContainer.first.next.next.next;
```

The next section introduces a better solution for these situations.

Accessing Children by Index and Name

The content method provides access to a container's child objects by index. The index values begin at 0, so you can access the third child in a container named myContainer as follows:

```
myContainer.content(2);
```

Like the first, last, next, and previous properties, this method of accessing child objects is simple, but it requires you to modify your code when the order of contents in the container changes. Alternatively, you can use the content method to access child objects by their name. You define a name property for a content object in the dictionary passed into the constructor.

```
let myContent = new Content(null, {
    name: "foo"
});
```

If myContent is a child of myContainer, you can access it as follows:

```
let foo = myContainer.content("foo");
```

This method works well for many containment hierarchies, but note that the content object has to be a direct child of the container for it to work. You can't use the content method to access grandchildren, great-grandchildren, and so on, of a container.

Accessing Content with Anchors

An *anchor* is a reference to a content object saved as a property in the instantiating data of the content object. Anchors are the best method of accessing contents in complex interfaces with many levels in their containment hierarchy; however, they're the most difficult to understand. Trying to explain anchors conceptually is often more confusing than helpful, so let's go right into looking at them through an example.

The $EXAMPLES/ch10-piu/anchors example demonstrates a basic use of anchors to create an animated user interface. When you tap the **Start** button, the background and a colored square flash between two different colors. Figure 10-18 shows the two states the screen toggles between when the **Start** button is tapped.

Figure 10-18. *anchors example*

This interface consists of three content objects:

- The **Start** button (an instance of the StartButton class)
- A colored square (an instance of the AnimatedSquare class)
- A background object (an instance of the MainContainer class) that fills the background with color and, as shown in Listing 10-39, contains the **Start** button and colored square

Listing 10-39.

```
const MainContainer = Container.template($ => ({
    ...
    contents: [
        new StartButton($),
        new AnimatedSquare($)
    ],
    ...
}));
```

Note that all three objects are passed the same instantiating data, through the $ variable. In this example, the instantiating data starts out as an empty dictionary.

```
let instantiatingData = {};
application.add(new MainContainer(instantiatingData));
```

The colored square and background objects have behaviors that change their fill color twice a second when their internal clock is running—that is, when each object's start method is called and the object begins receiving onTimeChanged events. The **Start** button is responsible for calling the start method of these objects when tapped; the colored square and the background object create anchors so that the **Start** button can reference them to do this.

To create an anchor for a content object, you specify an anchor property in the dictionary passed to its constructor. The MainContainer template sets the anchor property to the string "BACKGROUND", as shown in Listing 10-40.

Listing 10-40.

```
const MainContainer = Container.template($ => ({
    ...
    anchor: "BACKGROUND",
    ...
}));
```

Likewise, the AnimatedSquare template sets the anchor property to the string "SQUARE" (Listing 10-41).

Listing 10-41.

```
const AnimatedSquare = Content.template($ => ({
    ...
    anchor: "SQUARE",
    ...
}));
```

When a content object with an anchor property is instantiated, Piu assigns the instance to a property with the anchor's name in the instantiating data. Recall that instantiatingData started out as an empty dictionary; if you are using anchors, the instantiating data must be a dictionary so anchors can be added to it. After the colored square and background objects are instantiated, instantiatingData looks like this:

```
{
    BACKGROUND: <reference to the background object>,
    SQUARE: <reference to the colored square object>
}
```

The BACKGROUND and SQUARE properties of instantiatingData are anchors to the background and colored square objects. Anything with access to instantiatingData can use these anchors to reference these objects. In this example, the **Start** button uses the anchors to trigger the start of the background and square's animations. The code that uses the anchors and triggers the animations is all contained within StartButton template's behavior.

As you know, the instantiating data passed to the constructor of a content object is passed to the onCreate method of the created content's behavior. StartButtonBehavior saves a reference to the instantiating data in a data property so that it can be used in other methods.

```
class StartButtonBehavior extends Behavior {
    onCreate(label, data) {
        this.data = data;
    }
}
```

StartButtonBehavior then uses its data property in its onTouchEnded
method (Listing 10-42) to access the anchors to the background and
colored square so that it can call their start methods, which in turn causes
the animation to start.

Listing 10-42.

```
onTouchEnded(label) {
    ...
    this.data.SQUARE.start();
    this.data.BACKGROUND.start();
}
```

Note that the level of content objects in the containment hierarchy
does not matter when you use anchors. In this example, the **Start** button
and colored square are both children of the background object, but you
could rearrange the containment hierarchy—for example, you could make
the colored square a child of the application object—without having
to change the implementation of StartButtonBehavior to trigger the
animations. This flexibility makes anchors very useful when you create
containment hierarchies that may change.

Defining and Triggering Your Own Events

You've seen several examples with behavior objects that respond to the
low-level events defined and triggered by Piu. Your applications may need
other events, high-level events not defined by Piu; for example, a product
with a sensor attached can trigger an onSensorValueChanged event when

a sensor detects a change, so that the application can update the display or report the change to a network service. To handle high-level events, you add methods to your behavior just as you do for low-level events.

Often several content objects need to respond to a single event. For example, when a sensor value changes, multiple elements in the user interface may require an update. Your event handler for one object can propagate events—the event it received or others it creates—to other objects throughout the containment hierarchy. Piu provides the delegate, distribute, and bubble methods for propagating events.

This section shows how to define and trigger your own events. It also introduces methods to propagate events to one or more content objects in the containment hierarchy.

Triggering Events on a Content Object

The $EXAMPLES/ch10-piu/counter example stores a counter in a label object and enables another object, in this case a button, to increment the counter using a high-level increment event. Figure 10-19 shows the steps in the example, with the counter starting at 0, the user touching the button, and finally the counter being incremented to 1 when the touch ends.

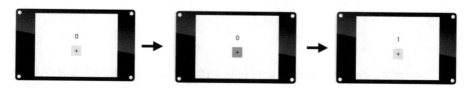

Figure 10-19. *counter example*

As shown in Listing 10-43, the counter is a label object with a behavior named CounterBehavior.

Listing 10-43.

```
const counter = new Label(null, {
    top: 70, height: 30, left: 0, right: 0,
    style: textStyle,
    string: "0",
    Behavior: CounterBehavior
});
```

The counter is stored in the count property of the label's behavior (Listing 10-44) and is initialized to 0 by the onDisplaying event handler of CounterBehavior. The behavior also implements an increment event handler, which increments the label object's counter and updates its string property with the new value.

Listing 10-44.

```
class CounterBehavior extends Behavior {
    onDisplaying(label) {
        this.count = 0;
    }
    increment(label) {
        label.string = ++this.count;
    }
}
```

The incrementButton object (Listing 10-45) is also a label object, with a behavior named IncrementButtonBehavior.

Listing 10-45.

```
const incrementButton = new Label(null, {
    top: 120, height: 40, left: 140, width: 40,
    style: textStyle,
```

```
    string: "+",
    skin: buttonSkin,
    active: true,
    Behavior: IncrementButtonBehavior
});
```

When the button is tapped, IncrementButtonBehavior (Listing 10-46) provides feedback by changing the button's state property in the onTouchBegan and onTouchEnded methods. The onTouchEnded method also *delegates* the increment event to the counter object. The delegate method of a content object immediately triggers the event named in the method's first argument. Here the increment event is triggered on the counter object.

Listing 10-46.

```
class IncrementButtonBehavior extends Behavior {
    onTouchBegan(label) {
        label.state = 1;
    }
    onTouchEnded(label) {
        label.state = 0;
        counter.delegate("increment");
    }
}
```

You can pass additional arguments to the event handler by passing them to the delegate method after the event name; for example, an onSensorValueChanged event could receive the new sensor reading as part of the event. To change the counter example to increment by any number, you could change the increment method in Listing 10-44 to accept an additional argument specifying the amount to increment by, as shown in Listing 10-47.

Listing 10-47.

```
class CounterBehavior extends Behavior {
    ...
    increment(label, delta) {
        this.count += delta;
        label.string = this.count;
    }
}
```

You'd then pass a number to the delegate method in the onTouchEnded method. For example:

```
counter.delegate("increment", 1); // increments by 1
counter.delegate("increment", 5); // increments by 5
```

Distributing Events Inside a Container

The $EXAMPLES/ch10-piu/color-scheme example provides buttons to change the appearance of the application between light and dark modes. When the user taps the **Light** or **Dark** button, the button triggers an event to all objects inside the application container. The objects respond by updating their colors to the requested mode. Figure 10-20 shows the interface starting in light mode, the **Dark** button while being tapped, and the interface in dark mode. Text displayed above the buttons indicates the current mode.

Figure 10-20. *color-scheme example*

The **Light** and **Dark** buttons trigger an event named onModeChanged. Each button is an instance of ModeButton, a template based on Label as shown in Listing 10-48.

Listing 10-48.

```
const ModeButton = Label.template($ => ({
    top: 110, height: 40, width: 120,
    skin: buttonSkin,
    active: true,
    Behavior: ModeButtonBehavior
}));
```

ModeButtonBehavior (Listing 10-49) provides feedback when the button is tapped, by changing the state property of the button in the onTouchBegan and onTouchEnded methods. The onTouchEnded method also *distributes* the onModeChanged event throughout the application container, by calling the distribute method of the application object. The distribute method triggers the event on each content object in the container. In its call to application.distribute, ModeButtonBehavior passes the name of the button, either "Light" or "Dark" in this example, as an argument to indicate the mode to change to.

Listing 10-49.

```
class ModeButtonBehavior extends Behavior {
    onTouchBegan(label) {
        label.state = 1;
    }
    onTouchEnded(label) {
        label.state = 0;
        application.distribute("onModeChanged", label.string);
    }
}
```

All container objects have a `distribute` method, which triggers a specified event on the container and all content objects downward in the containment hierarchy. Distribution of the event ends when the event is delivered to all objects in the container or when one of the event handlers returns `true` to indicate that the event has been fully handled. You can think of the `distribute` method as a way to broadcast an event to the contents of a container. In this example, it would be easy to directly call `delegate` on the few content objects with an `onModeChanged` handler in their behavior; however, as your application becomes more complex, it's easier to use the `distribute` method to traverse everything in a container automatically.

Now that you know how `distribute` triggers events on the contents of containers, let's look at how content objects respond to those events. The `state` property plays a key role. The `LightDarkScreen` container, which holds the buttons and the string of text, has a skin that's white when its `state` property is 0 and black when its `state` property is 1.

```
const backgroundSkin = new Skin({
    fill: ["white", "black"]
});
```

The string of text is a `label` object that has a style that will do the reverse, causing the text to be black when its `state` property is 0 and white when its `state` property is 1. (See Listing 10-50.)

Listing 10-50.

```
const textStyle = new Style({
    font: "24px Open Sans",
    color: ["black", "white"],
    top: 10, bottom: 10, left: 10, right: 10
});
```

The code for LightDarkScreen is shown in Listing 10-51.

Listing 10-51.

```
const LightDarkScreen = new Container(null, {
    top: 0, bottom: 0, left: 0, right: 0,
    skin: backgroundSkin,
    style: textStyle,
    contents: [
        Label(null, {
            top: 50, height: 30, left: 0, right: 0,
            string: "Light",
            Behavior: TextBehavior
        }),
        ModeButton(null, {
            left: 30,
            string: "Dark"
        }),
        ModeButton(null, {
            right: 30,
            string: "Light"
        })
    ],
    Behavior: LightDarkScreenBehavior
});
```

Both LightDarkScreen and the label object it contains have behaviors that change their state property when they receive an onModeChanged event. The label changes its string property to reflect which button was tapped. Listing 10-52 shows these behaviors.

Listing 10-52.

```
class LightDarkScreenBehavior extends Behavior {
    onModeChanged(container, mode) {
        container.state = (mode === "Dark")? 1 : 0;
    }
}

class TextBehavior extends Behavior {
    onModeChanged(label, mode) {
        label.state = (mode === "Dark")? 1 : 0;
        label.string = mode;
    }
}
```

Bubbling Events Up the Containment Hierarchy

The $EXAMPLES/ch10-piu/background-color example provides buttons
to change the background color of the screen. When the user taps the
buttons, they trigger an event upward in the containment hierarchy. The
buttons' parent container spans the whole screen and updates its skin
property in response to the event. Figure 10-21 shows the background in
its initial white state, the **Yellow** button while being tapped, and then the
background after it has changed to be yellow.

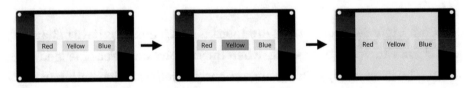

Figure 10-21. *background-color example*

As shown in Listing 10-53, the buttons are created with a template that
creates a label object with a behavior named ColorButtonBehavior.

Listing 10-53.

```
const ColorButton = Label.template($ => ({
    height: 40, left: 10, right: 10,
    skin: buttonSkin,
    active: true,
    Behavior: ColorButtonBehavior
}));
```

ColorButtonBehavior (Listing 10-54) provides feedback when the button is tapped, by changing the state property of the button in the onTouchBegan and onTouchEnded methods. The onTouchEnded method also *bubbles* the onColorSelected event up the containment hierarchy, by calling the bubble method and passing it the string property of the button—"Yellow", "Red", or "Blue"—as an argument to the event handler.

Listing 10-54.

```
class ColorButtonBehavior extends Behavior {
    onTouchBegan(label) {
        label.state = 1;
    }
    onTouchEnded(label) {
        label.state = 0;
        label.bubble("onColorSelected", label.string);
    }
}
```

All content objects have a bubble method, which causes them, their parent container, and all container objects upward in the containment hierarchy to trigger a specified event. Propagation of the event ends when the event has been delivered to all objects up to the application object or when one of the event handlers returns true to indicate that the event has been fully handled. As with the delegate and distribute methods, the event is specified by name and passed as the first argument to the bubble method.

Now that you know how to use the bubble method to trigger events, let's look at how the containment hierarchy of the example is organized before exploring the details of how the onColorSelected event propagates through this particular containment hierarchy.

The buttons are contained in a row object. This row is part of a container object, named colorScreen, which is added to the application object. As shown in Listing 10-55, the row doesn't have a behavior associated with it, but colorScreen references a behavior named ColorScreenBehavior.

Listing 10-55.

```
const colorScreen = new Container(null, {
    top: 0, bottom: 0, left: 0, right: 0,
    skin: whiteSkin,
    style: textStyle,
    contents: [
        Row(null, {
            height: 50, width: 320,
            contents: [
                new ColorButton(null, {string: "Red"}),
                new ColorButton(null, {string: "Yellow"}),
                new ColorButton(null, {string: "Blue"})
            ]
        })
    ],
    Behavior: ColorScreenBehavior
});

application.add(colorScreen);
```

ColorScreenBehavior changes the background color when it receives the onColorSelected event; as shown in Listing 10-56, the new color is passed as an argument. The first letter of each button string is uppercase ("Red"), but CSS colors are all lowercase, so the event handler uses toLowerCase to convert the string to all lowercase letters.

Listing 10-56.

```
class ColorScreenBehavior extends Behavior {
    onColorSelected(container, color) {
        container.skin = new Skin({
            fill: color.toLowerCase()
        });
    }
}
```

Here's what happens when one of the buttons is tapped:

1. The onColorSelected event is first triggered on the button itself. The button's behavior has no corresponding onColorSelected method, so the event bubbles up to its parent container.

2. The parent container of the button is the row object. This object has no behavior and therefore no onColorSelected method, so the event moves on to the row's parent container.

3. The parent container of the row is the colorScreen container. The behavior of this container has an onColorSelected method, so the method is called when the behavior triggers the onColorSelected event. Then the event moves on to this container's parent container.

4.   The parent container of the `colorScreen` container
is the `application` object. This object has no
`onColorSelected` method and is the root of the
containment hierarchy, so the traversal is complete.

As with the other examples of propagating events, it would be easy to
simply delegate the event to all of the contents that have a corresponding
`onColorSelected` method in their behavior. But applications with many
levels in their containment hierarchy can use the `bubble` method of
content objects to simplify the code that propagates an event and to
minimize the code changes needed when the containment hierarchy
changes.

Animation

Incorporating animations into user interfaces can significantly improve the
user experience. Animations are used for meaningful, functional purposes,
such as to provide feedback when a user taps a button. They're also used
for aesthetic purposes, to give the product a particular feel—for example,
to create an animated transition when moving between screens.

Easing Equations

Animations that linearly modify the properties of content objects often
appear unnatural. Easing equations are a common tool for implementing
animations that feel more natural, or to add a visual style.

Piu extends the JavaScript `Math` object with Robert Penner's well-
known easing equations. The names of these functions in Piu are self-
explanatory—for example, `bounceEaseInOut` creates a bouncing effect at
the start and end of the animation. Details on the Penner equations are
available at `robertpenner.com/easing/`.

The Piu implementations of these easing equations all take a single argument, a number in the range [0, 1], and return a number in the range [0, 1] with the easing function applied. The equations are used extensively in all types of animations. The input value is the fraction of the animation that has completed; the easing function adjusts the fraction to another value which is then used to calculate the state of values in the animation. You'll see examples of this in the sections that follow.

Some of the easing equations create a subtle effect to make the animations feel more natural. For example, the quad easing functions—`Math.quadEaseIn`, `Math.quadEaseOut`, and `Math.quadEaseInOut`—vary the speed slightly throughout the duration of the animation to make the beginning and/or end of the animation less abrupt. Others create a bold effect. For example, the bounce easing functions—`Math.bounceEaseIn`, `Math.bounceEaseOut`, and `Math.bounceEaseInOut`—make objects bounce at the start and/or end of the animation.

Of course, you're not limited to the easing functions that are included by default; you can easily add your own easing equations to suit your product's needs. The details of creating your own easing equations are outside the scope of this book, but there's plenty of information online should you decide it's necessary for your product.

Animating Content Objects

The `helloworld-ticking` example showed how to use the built-in clock of a content object to create a simple animation. Creating more complex animations, particularly those that independently move several interface elements simultaneously, is difficult.

The `$EXAMPLES/ch10-piu/timeline` example demonstrates how to create an animation sequence involving multiple objects on the screen. The animation in this example is simple, but understanding the code will give you a foundation to create much more sophisticated animations of your own. Figure 10-22 shows the user interface at a few points during the animation.

Figure 10-22. `timeline example`

The interface in the example consists of a `container` object named `animatedContainer` (Listing 10-57), which contains a `label` object and a `content` object.

Listing 10-57.

```
const animatedContainer = new Container(null, {
    top: 0, bottom: 0, left: 0, right: 0,
    skin: whiteSkin,
    contents: [
        new Label(null, {
            style: textStyle,
            top: 80, left: 0, right: 0,
            string: "Hello, World"
        }),
        new Content(null, {
            top: 115, height: 3, left: 0, width: 320,
            skin: colorfulSkin
        })
    ],
    Behavior: TimelineBehavior
});
```

The animation is driven by `TimelineBehavior`, the behavior of `animatedContainer`. `TimelineBehavior` instantiates a `timeline` object in its `onDisplaying` event handler. Piu provides the `Timeline` class to simplify and structure the code for implementing animations. This class can be used both for animating elements within a single screen and for animating transitions between screens. Using the Timeline class is generally the best way to organize and implement animations of multiple content objects; for example, it easily handles the situation where the time that each content object begins animating is staggered. The API for the Piu Timeline class is based on the API for TimelineLite by GreenSock, a popular JavaScript library used to animate web pages.

The onDisplaying event handler also initializes the reverse property, which is used to enable the timeline animation to run both forward and backward. Listing 10-58 shows the relevant code.

Listing 10-58.

```
class TimelineBehavior extends Behavior {
    onDisplaying(container) {
        let timeline = this.timeline = new Timeline();
        this.reverse = false;
        ...
```

A timeline object consists of a set of *tweens*, each of which describes how one or more properties of one content object change from an initial value and an ending value. Tweens are added to the timeline by its from and to methods, which define the tween based on the following arguments:

1.   target – the content object to animate

2.   properties – a dictionary whose keys are properties of the target object to animate

3.   duration – the duration of the tween, in milliseconds

4.   easing – *(optional)* an easing function to use for the tween

5.   delay – *(optional)* the number of milliseconds that this tween should start after the previous tween in the timeline completes; defaults to 0

A tween added by a timeline's from method—called a *from-tween*—eases the properties of the target object from the values specified in the properties object to the original values of the target object over duration milliseconds. The onDisplaying method in Listing 10-58 continues by adding the following from-tween. In this example, the label object moves from a y position off the top of the screen to its original position of 80 pixels from the top of the screen. At the same time, its state animates from state 1 to state 0, causing it to fade from white to black. Note that the label here is accessed as container.first because it's the first content object added to the container. The tween has a duration of 750 milliseconds and uses the quadEaseOut easing function.

```
timeline.from(container.first, {
        y: -container.first.height,
        state: 1
    }, 750, Math.quadEaseOut, 0);
```

As shown in the following code, a second call to the timeline's from method then adds a tween to move the color bar from an x position off the left edge of the screen to its original position of 0 pixels from the left edge. Each call to from extends the timeline by the duration of its animation and, unless the delay argument is used, the tween added by the next call to from begins at the end of the timeline. To make the two tweens run at the same time, this example sets the delay property to –750 milliseconds, which causes it to start at the same time as the first tween. This tween doesn't change the timeline's duration, because it ends at the same time as the first tween.

```
timeline.from(container.last, {
        x: -320
    }, 750, Math.linearEase, -750);
```

A tween added by a timeline's to method—called a *to-tween*—eases the properties of the target object from its current values to the target values specified in the properties object over duration milliseconds.

The onDisplaying method continues by adding the to-tween shown as follows. In this example, the color bar goes from its current state of 0 to a state of 1. The delay property here isn't specified, so it defaults to 0, which causes this tween to begin immediately after the previous one completes.

```
timeline.to(container.last, {
        state: 1
    }, 750, Math.linearEase, 0);
```

After all the tweens are added, the timeline is ready to use, as shown in the following code in the remaining calls in the onDisplaying method. The timeline has a current time, between 0 and the timeline's duration, that indicates the progress in the animation and can be set using its seekTo method. Like the duration property (and a content object's clock), seekTo expresses time in milliseconds. This example rewinds the timeline to the beginning by using seekTo to set the timeline's current time to 0. It then uses the content object's clock—in this case the container's clock—to drive the animation: after setting the container's duration to match the duration of the timeline, it rewinds the container's clock and starts it ticking.

```
timeline.seekTo(0);
container.duration = timeline.duration;
container.time = 0;
container.start();
```

TimelineBehavior includes two additional event handlers, onTimeChanged and onFinished (Listing 10-59):

- With the clock ticking, onTimeChanged is invoked at regular intervals. Because the duration of the timeline is equal to the duration of the container's clock, onTimeChanged uses seekTo to synchronize the timeline with the time property of the container's clock.

- When the container's clock reaches its duration, the onFinished event is triggered. This also means that the animation sequence is complete. In this example, the timeline moves in reverse after it reaches the end, and loops back and forth indefinitely.

Listing 10-59.

```
onTimeChanged(container) {
    let time = container.time;
    if (this.reverse)
        time = container.duration - time;
    this.timeline.seekTo(time);
}
onFinished(container) {
    this.reverse = !this.reverse;
    this.timeline.seekTo(0);
    container.time = 0;
    container.start();
}
```

Animating Transitions

The Piu Transition class provides another method of implementing animations. It's most often used to swap one content object for another in the containment hierarchy—for example, to move between screens. This section focuses on the built-in wipe and comb transitions, which are subclasses of the Transition class. Unlike timeline animations, which modify the properties of content objects, the wipe and comb transitions are purely graphical operations that operate on the pixels of the display. Because they're optimized to minimize the number of pixels drawn in each frame, these transitions achieve high frame rates, even on an ESP8266 microcontroller. You can also create your own transitions, by subclassing the Transition class, but that's outside the scope of this book.

You import the wipe and comb transitions classes from modules:

```
import WipeTransition from "piu/WipeTransition";
import CombTransition from "piu/CombTransition";
```

The wipe transition reveals the new screen starting from either an edge or a corner of the screen. The constructor for this transition has the following arguments to control the wipe:

1. A duration in milliseconds

2. An easing equation

3. A horizontal direction, as "center", "left", or "right"

4. A vertical direction, as "middle", "top", or "bottom"

The horizontal and vertical directions determine where the transition starts. For example, if they're center and top, the transition begins from the top edge; if they're right and bottom, the transition begins from the bottom-right corner.

```
const wipeFromCenter = new WipeTransition(250,
                         Math.quadEaseOut, "center", "top");
const wipeFromTopRight = new WipeTransition(250,
                         Math.quadEaseOut, "right", "bottom");
```

The comb transition reveals the new screen through a series of interleaved bars that emerge from either the top and bottom edges of the screen or the left and right edges of the screen. The constructor for the comb transition has the following arguments:

1. A duration in milliseconds

2. An easing equation

3. A direction, as either "horizontal" or "vertical"

4. The number of bars

If the direction is set to horizontal, the bars emerge from the left and right edges; if it's set to vertical, the bars emerge from the top and bottom edges.

```
const horizontalComb = new CombTransition(250,
                          Math.quadEaseOut, "horizontal", 4);
const verticalComb = new CombTransition(250,
                          Math.quadEaseOut, "vertical", 8);
```

Once you have an instance of a transition, you call the run method of the parent container of the object to transition from, passing as arguments the transition, the content object to transition from, and the content object to transition to. The transition runs asynchronously and therefore doesn't block execution of your code. When the transition completes, the content object to transition from is replaced in the containment hierarchy by the content object to transition to. For example, the code in Listing 10-60 runs the wipeFromTopRightTransition transition to replace firstScreen with nextScreen.

Listing 10-60.

```
const firstScreen = new Content(...);
const nextScreen = new Content(...);
const sampleContainer = new Container(null, {
    ...
    contents: [
        firstScreen
    ]
});

sampleContainer.run(wipeFromTopRightTransition, firstScreen,
                nextScreen);
```

The $EXAMPLES/ch10-piu/transitions example shows several variations of the wipe and comb transitions. It transitions between two screens at a regular interval.

Drawing a Graph in Real Time

Sometimes there are elements of your user interface that are more convenient or efficient to render using drawing functions like those provided by Poco instead of creating and updating objects as Piu does. For example, imagine you want to create a bar graph like the one shown in Figure 10-23, which updates in real time based on readings from a sensor.

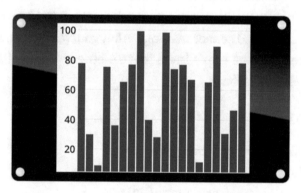

Figure 10-23. *Bar graph that updates in real time*

You could use Piu content objects, but that's not the most efficient implementation. You'd have many content objects to keep track of and update—at least one content object for every bar in the graph and the background of the graph, plus one or more label objects for the labels on the *y* axis. Every object takes up some RAM, so your RAM usage would quickly add up.

Fortunately, you don't have to choose between the approaches of Piu and Poco; you can combine them by using Piu's Port class. A port is a content object that lets you issue drawing commands similar to Poco within a Piu layout, making it great for user interface elements like graphs that would otherwise require many content objects.

The $EXAMPLES/ch10-piu/graph example uses a single port object to efficiently render the real-time bar graph shown in Figure 10-23:

```
const graph = new Port(null, {
    top: 0, bottom: 0, left: 0, right: 0,
    Behavior: GraphBehavior
});
```

This port's behavior, GraphBehavior (Listing 10-61), maintains a list of sample values to graph in an array stored in the values property. Every 100 milliseconds, the onTimeChanged event handler removes the first value in the list and replaces it with a random number from 0 to 100. These random numbers are simulated sensor readings. After generating a new value, onTimeChanged calls the port's invalidate method, which tells Piu that the port needs to be redrawn.

Listing 10-61.

```
class GraphBehavior extends Behavior {
    onDisplaying(port) {
        this.values = new Array(20);
        this.values.fill(0);
        port.interval = 100;
        port.start();
    }
    onTimeChanged(port) {
        this.values.shift();
        this.values.push(Math.random() * 100);
        port.invalidate();
    }
```

The call to invalidate causes the port object to trigger an onDraw event on itself. Note that onDraw is invoked not from inside the call to the invalidate method but a short time after. As shown in Listing 10-62, in this case the onDraw event handler fills the background with white, draws the y-axis labels and corresponding gray lines, and then draws a blue bar for each randomly generated value.

Listing 10-62.

```
onDraw(port, x, y, width, height) {
    port.fillColor(WHITE, x, y, width, height);

    for (let i = 100, yOffset = 0; yOffset < height;
            yOffset += height / 5, i -= 20) {
        port.drawString(i, textStyle, "black",
                        30 - textStyle.measure(i).width,
                        yOffset);
        port.fillColor(GRAY, 35, yOffset + 10, width, 1);
    }

    let xOffset = 35;
    const values = this.values;
    for (let i = 0; i < values.length; i++) {
        let value = values[i];
        let barHeight = (value / 100) * (height - 10);
        port.fillColor(BLUE, xOffset, height - barHeight,
                       12, barHeight);
        xOffset += 14;
    }
}
```

This example uses two of the drawing methods provided by the `port` content object:

- It calls `drawString` to draw a line of text the way a `label` object would, with the style and color specified. The `measure` method of the `textStyle` object is called to calculate the width of the label strings so that they'll be positioned precisely.

- It calls `fillColor` to draw a rectangle in the color specified.

The `port` object has several other drawing methods, including `drawTexture` to draw the image specified by a texture and `drawSkin` to draw a rectangle with a skin, just as any content object would. For details on all the drawing commands available to `port` objects, see the Piu documentation in the Moddable SDK.

Adding an Onscreen Keyboard

In many IoT products, there are situations that require the user to enter text—for example, to enter a Wi-Fi password when setting up the product. Today this operation is usually done in a companion app on a mobile phone, requiring the user to install a new mobile app and follow a complex, error-prone process to configure Wi-Fi. On IoT products that incorporate a touch screen, the user can configure Wi-Fi, and enter text for other purposes, directly on the product. To enable that, you just need an onscreen keyboard.

The challenge is that accurate typing is easier when the keyboard is bigger, but bigger touch screens are more expensive. To solve this problem, the Moddable SDK includes a module that provides an expanding onscreen keyboard, making it possible to enter text accurately on small touch screens. Typing a character on this keyboard is a two-step process:

first you tap in the vicinity of the character you want to type (either on or near that character); the keyboard expands around where you tapped, and you then tap the character you want. You tap **OK** when you're done entering the text.

You can try this out by running the $EXAMPLES/ch10-piu/keyboard example. When the example is launched, you see the keyboard in its unexpanded state (Figure 10-24) with a blinking cursor in the text field above the keyboard.

Figure 10-24. *Unexpanded keyboard*

In Figure 10-25, the left image shows how the keyboard expands after you tap on or near the letter *a*, and the right image shows how it expands after you tap on or near the letter *g*.

Figure 10-25. *Keyboard expanded around letter* a *(left) and* g *(right)*

You then tap the character you want, which appears before the blinking cursor in the text field, and the keyboard returns to the unexpanded state. (Notice that in the expanded state, the **OK** button changes to display a keyboard icon; you'd tap it if you didn't want to type a character after all but instead wanted to return to the unexpanded keyboard and the **OK** button.)

Two variants of the expanding keyboard are available: VerticalExpandingKeyboard for screens that are 240 pixels wide and HorizontalExpandingKeyboard for screens 320 pixels wide. The keyboard example uses the horizontal variant, so it imports HorizontalExpandingKeyboard and KeyboardField objects from the keyboard modules.

```
import {HorizontalExpandingKeyboard} from "keyboard";
import {KeyboardField} from "common/keyboard";
```

These modules are part of the Moddable SDK, so you can see the source code and full documentation for them. Everything in the modules will look familiar now that you've read this chapter; all elements of the keyboard are built with Piu classes you've learned about, including Port, Timeline, and Behavior. This section doesn't describe the implementation of the keyboard modules but only focuses on how to use the modules to incorporate a keyboard in your projects.

The KeyboardContainer template (Listing 10-63) is a good place to begin exploring this example. The first item in its contents is an instance of KeyboardField, a content object class imported from the common/keyboard module. This field is where the text you type will go. The KeyboardField class has a behavior that responds to text input and blinks the cursor. The second item is a container to hold the keyboard, although it starts as an empty container. Note that both of these content objects have an anchor property, so anchors to them are created in the instantiating data.

Listing 10-63.

```
const KeyboardContainer = Column.template($ => ({
    left: 0, right: 0, top: 0, bottom: 0,
    contents: [
        KeyboardField($, {
            anchor: "FIELD",
            left: 32, right: 0, top: 0, bottom: 0,
            style: fieldStyle
        }),
        Container($, {
            anchor: "KEYBOARD",
            left: 0, right: 0, bottom: 0, height: 164
        })
    ],
    active: true,
    Behavior: KeyboardContainerBehavior
}));
```

In KeyboardContainerBehavior (Listing 10-64), the methods
associated with onDisplaying and onTouchEnded events (which you're
already familiar with) both do the same thing: they call the addKeyboard
method.

Listing 10-64.

```
class KeyboardContainerBehavior extends Behavior {
    ...
    onDisplaying(column) {
        this.addKeyboard();
    }
```

503

```
onTouchEnded(column) {
    this.addKeyboard();
}
 ...
}
```

The addKeyboard method (Listing 10-65) checks whether the container object referenced by data.KEYBOARD already contains a keyboard. If it doesn't, the method adds an instance of HorizontalExpandingKeyboard to the empty container object, based on three arguments passed in:

- The style is the style of the characters on the keys of the keyboard.

- The target is the object that should receive events when a key is tapped, which in this case is the KeyboardField object referenced by data.FIELD.

- The doTransition parameter specifies whether the keyboard should transition in. If true, the keyboard transitions in, one row at a time; if false, it appears all at once.

Listing 10-65.

```
addKeyboard() {
    if (1 !== this.data.KEYBOARD.length) {
        this.data.KEYBOARD.add(HorizontalExpandingKeyboard(
            this.data, {
                style: keyboardStyle,
                target: this.data.FIELD,
```

```
            doTransition: true
        }
    ));
    }
}
```

When the user taps the **OK** button, the keyboard distributes the onKeyboardOK event to the application container with the text string the user entered. In this example, KeyboardContainerBehavior responds to the event by tracing the string entered and hiding the field that displays the string and the cursor.

```
onKeyboardOK(application, string) {
    trace(`User entered: ${string}\n`);
    this.data.FIELD.visible = false;
}
```

The keyboard appears with a slide-in transition and slides out to disappear when the user taps **OK**. When either of these transitions completes, the keyboard bubbles an onKeyboardTransitionFinished event with a parameter indicating whether the transition is for appearance or disappearance of the keyboard. Your code can use these events to take actions such as showing user interface elements hidden while the keyboard is in use.

In this example, the onKeyboardTransitionFinished method (Listing 10-66) responds to the disappearance of the keyboard by removing it from the containment hierarchy, and the method responds to the appearance of the keyboard by making the text field above the keyboard visible.

Listing 10-66.

```
onKeyboardTransitionFinished(application, out) {
    if (out) {
        let keyboard = this.data.KEYBOARD;
        keyboard.remove(keyboard.first);
    }
```

```
    else
        this.data.FIELD.visible = true;
}
```

Note that the keyboard doesn't have to be removed from the containment hierarchy after being transitioned out; you could keep transitioning the same instance in and out of view. In many applications, however, tapping **OK** triggers a transition to another screen, so it's better to remove the keyboard from the containment hierarchy so that it can be garbage-collected.

Organizing User Interface Code Using Modules

Every example in this chapter has been contained in one module, and consequently one source code file. As your applications become more complex—with multiple screens, interactions with cloud services and other devices, and more—you'll likely want to divide your code among multiple modules. Separating code into modules has these benefits:

- Reusing code is easier because code that's not specific to one product can be stored in separate source code files. The keyboard modules are an example of this.

- Editing and maintaining code is easier when it's organized in logical modules.

- It's easier to distribute work across a team.

The $EXAMPLES/ch10-piu/multiple-screens example discussed in this section shows a common way to organize your user interface. It's a simple application with two screens: a splash screen and a home screen, as pictured in Figure 10-26. The application first displays an animated splash screen and then transitions to a home screen that has a restart button and label on it. Tapping the restart button returns to the splash screen. Along the way, the example demonstrates useful techniques for building maintainable, memory-efficient applications with multiple modules and screens.

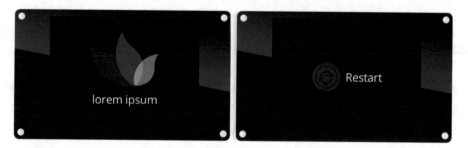

Figure 10-26. *Splash screen (left) and home screen (right) from* `multiple-screens` *example*

The Modules

The `multiple-screens` example consists of three modules:

- `example.js` – the application logic for navigating between screens

- `assets.js` – `texture`, `skin`, and `style` objects used throughout the application

- `screens.js` – templates for the two screens of the application

In this example, the `assets` and `screens` modules aren't especially long, and therefore it might seem strange to separate them, since the `assets` module exports objects that only the `screens` module uses. However, this is often a useful separation in larger applications, because you need to modify only one file to change the colors and assets used across all screens. It's also useful when you're building a line of products with similar branding; you can give all your products a consistent look and feel by creating a shared `assets` file that defines the common textures, skins, and styles used by your screens.

You've already seen many examples of texture, skin, and style objects in this chapter, so the assets module isn't described in detail here. The next sections focus on the example and screens modules and how they interact.

The Application Logic

The example module contains all the application-specific logic, which in this application is the simple logic to move between screens. At startup, the example instantiates the MainContainer template (Listing 10-67) and adds it to the application object. This container is what the example uses to hold the screens.

Listing 10-67.

```
const MainContainer = Container.template($ => ({
    top: 0, bottom: 0, left: 0, right: 0,
    Behavior: MainContainerBehavior
}));

application.add(new MainContainer({}));
```

The instance of MainContainer is initially empty. Its behavior adds and removes the screens that are defined in the screens module. As shown in Listing 10-68, the behavior adds the first screen in the onDisplaying event handler by calling its switchScreen method with the name of the screen, "SPLASH".

Listing 10-68.

```
class MainContainerBehavior extends Behavior {
    onCreate(container, data) {
        this.data = data;
    }
```

```
onDisplaying(container) {
    this.switchScreen(container, "SPLASH");
}
...
}
```

The next event handler in the behavior is switchScreen, which
the application calls each time it needs to switch to a new screen. The
switchScreen method triggers the doSwitchScreen event in order to
move to the new screen; however, rather than triggering the event with the
delegate method, which would trigger it immediately, it uses the defer
method, which *defers* delivery of the event until the next iteration of the
event loop. The only difference between defer and delegate is the timing
of when the event is delivered.

```
switchScreen(container, nextScreenName) {
    container.defer("doSwitchScreen", nextScreenName);
}
```

One reason you'd want to defer delivery of the event is to avoid a
stack overflow. The stack on the microcontroller is small, and the code
to create a screen often takes up quite a bit of stack space. If you switch
screens immediately, some of the stack has already been used by the calls
that invoke your behavior's event handler. By deferring the delivery of the
event, your event handler runs on a nearly empty stack, thereby reducing
the peak stack usage.

Another reason to defer delivery of the event is to reduce peak memory
use when switching screens. Because of the way garbage collection works,
if you deliver the doSwitchScreen event immediately, the garbage collector
keeps both the previous and the next screens in memory for a brief period

of time. Using defer makes it possible to first release the previous screen before instantiating the next screen. That's what the doSwitchScreen method (Listing 10-69) of MainContainer does, as follows:

1. It uses the empty method to empty the current screen. Because this is done from a deferred event, the objects associated with that screen become eligible for garbage collection.

2. It calls application.purge, which frees caches that Piu created and runs the garbage collector, freeing up the memory used by the objects from the old screen.

3. It instantiates and adds the next screen.

Listing 10-69.

```
doSwitchScreen(container, nextScreenName) {
    container.empty();
    application.purge();
    switch (nextScreenName) {
        case "SPLASH":
            container.add(new SCREENS.SplashScreen(this.data));
            break;
        case "HOME":
            container.add(new SCREENS.HomeScreen(this.data));
            break;
    }
}
```

This process is a good way to manage an application's RAM usage, because it helps ensure that there are never two screens' worth of objects in RAM at the same time. Putting the logic for switching screens in the behavior of the MainContainer is also useful because it prevents you from having to repeat it in the behavior of every screen template; instead, each screen can simply delegate the switchScreen event when it's time to go to a new screen.

The Splash Screen

Like many mobile and web apps, this example displays a simple splash screen when the application is launched. As shown in Listing 10-70, the logo on this screen is created by layering three content objects, which enables each piece to be animated individually with a timeline object. The title on the screen is a simple label object.

Listing 10-70.

```
const SplashScreen = Container.template($ => ({
    top: 0, bottom: 0, left: 0, right: 0,
    skin: ASSETS.backgroundSkin,
    contents: [
        Content($, {
            anchor: "LOGO1",
            top: 30,
            skin: ASSETS.logoSkin1
        }),
        Content($, {
            anchor: "LOGO2",
            top: 30,
            skin: ASSETS.logoSkin2
        }),
        Content($, {
            anchor: "LOGO3",
            top: 30,
            skin: ASSETS.logoSkin3
        }),
```

```
        Label($, {
            anchor: "TITLE",
            top: 155,
            style: ASSETS.bigTextStyle,
            string: "lorem ipsum"
        })
    ],
    Behavior: SplashScreenBehavior
}));
```

As usual, the timeline is defined in the behavior (Listing 10-71) and is driven by the container object's internal clock.

Listing 10-71.

```
class SplashScreenBehavior extends Behavior {
    ...
    onDisplaying(container) {
        let data = this.data;
        let timeline = this.timeline = new Timeline;
        ...
    }
    onTimeChanged(container) {
        this.timeline.seekTo(container.time);
    }
}
```

When the animation completes, the behavior's onFinished method (Listing 10-72) does the following:

- It deletes the anchors for all the content objects on the screen. Note that this doesn't delete the content objects themselves but only deletes the references to them in the data object. It's important to delete these references because the data object is shared by the MainContainer object and passed to all the screens it creates; if the references aren't deleted, the garbage collector won't be able to free up the RAM associated with the content objects when application.purge is called in the doSwitchScreen method.

- It then bubbles the switchScreen event, which eventually reaches the MainContainer object. It passes the string "HOME" as the second argument, so the MainContainer loads the home screen next.

Listing 10-72.

```
onFinished(container) {
    let data = this.data;
    // Delete anchors
    delete data.LOGO1;
    delete data.LOGO2;
    delete data.LOGO3;
    delete data.TITLE;
    // Transition to next screen
    container.bubble("switchScreen", "HOME");
}
```

The Home Screen

The home screen (Listing 10-73) is a row that centers a restart button and a label. The restart button and the home screen have behaviors named RestartButtonBehavior and HomeScreenBehavior, respectively.

Listing 10-73.

```
const HomeScreen = Row.template($ => ({
    top: 0, bottom: 0, left: 0, right: 0,
    skin: ASSETS.backgroundSkin,
    contents: [
        Content($, {
            left: 0, right: 0
        }),
        Container($, {
            anchor: "BUTTON",
            skin: ASSETS.buttonBackgroundSkin,
            contents: [
                Content($, {
                    skin: ASSETS.restartArrowSkin
                })
            ],
            active: true,
            Behavior: RestartButtonBehavior
        }),
        Label($, {
            anchor: "TEXT",
            left: 10,
            style: ASSETS.bigTextStyle,
            string: "Restart",
            left: 0, right: 0
        })
    ],
    Behavior: HomeScreenBehavior
}));
```

The HomeScreenBehavior class's onDisplaying event handler animates the restart button and the label, as shown in Listing 10-74.

Listing 10-74.

```
class HomeScreenBehavior extends Behavior {
    onCreate(container, data) {
        this.data = data;
    }
    onDisplaying(container) {
        let data = this.data;
        let timeline = this.timeline = new Timeline();
        ...
        container.start();
    }
    ...
}
```

Unlike the splash screen, the home screen doesn't automatically switch screens after it animates in. Instead, it waits to receive an animateOut event; its behavior's animateOut method (Listing 10-75) creates a timeline object and sets the transitioningOut property to true.

Listing 10-75.

```
animateOut(container) {
    let data = this.data;
    this.transitioningOut = true;
    let timeline = this.timeline = new Timeline();
    ...
    container.start();
}
```

When the onFinished event is triggered at the end of the animation, the corresponding event handler (Listing 10-76) checks the transitioningOut property to determine which action to take:

- If transitioningOut is true, the anchors to the button and the label are deleted, and the switchScreen event is bubbled to the MainContainer object.

- If transitioningOut is false, the timeline property is deleted, making the timeline object eligible for garbage collection. Since the garbage collector runs only when it needs to free up RAM, and no other objects are instantiated between the transitions in and out, the garbage collector won't run, so deleting the timeline property is unnecessary here. Still, it's good to get in the habit of deleting references to objects that are no longer in use.

Listing 10-76.

```
onFinished(container) {
    if (this.transitioningOut) {
        let data = this.data;
        // Delete anchors
        delete data.BUTTON;
        delete data.TEXT;
        // Transition to next screen
        container.bubble("switchScreen", "SPLASH");
    }
    else
        delete this.timeline;
}
```

The restart button's behavior (Listing 10-77) responds to just one event: onTouchEnded. The behavior's onTouchEnded method simply delegates the onAnimateOut event to the button's container, which is an instance of the HomeScreen template. As you just saw, this triggers the animation out and eventually leads to the transition back to the splash screen.

Listing 10-77.

```
class RestartButtonBehavior extends Behavior {
    onTouchEnded(content) {
        content.container.delegate("animateOut");
    }
}
```

Adding More Screens

Now that you know how to switch between two screens, it's straightforward to add more screens. These are the steps:

1. Define a template for a new screen.

2. Add it to the default export of the screens module.

3. In the example module, add a case to the switch statement in the doSwitchScreen method of MainContainerBehavior to instantiate the screen template and add it to MainContainer.

4. Trigger the switchScreen event as needed in your code, passing in the name you used for the new screen in the switch statement.

Conclusion

In this chapter, you learned the fundamentals of building user interfaces with Piu, including how to add graphics and text, give them event-driven behaviors, and create animations. You learned several techniques to save RAM, such as reusing textures and skins and removing references to unused objects. You also learned techniques to save ROM, including using templates. With the information from this chapter, you can build beautiful, modern user interfaces using inexpensive hardware.

This chapter introduced the key features of Piu that are used to build user interfaces for embedded products. Piu has many other features that you may find useful in your products—for example, support for efficiently localizing the text strings for products that must support multiple languages. For extensive documentation of all of Piu's features and links to examples that use them, see the Piu documentation in the Moddable SDK.

CHAPTER 11

Adding Native Code

There are times when JavaScript isn't the best language to use to implement parts of your IoT product. Fortunately, you don't need to choose either JavaScript or C (or C++) to build your product: you can choose both. *XS in C* is a low-level C API provided by the XS JavaScript engine so that you can integrate C code into your JavaScript projects (or JavaScript code into your C projects!).

Here are three common reasons for using use native code in your project:

- **Performance** – High-level languages, including JavaScript, can't outperform optimized native code at high-performance tasks. You can add your own optimized native functions and invoke them from your JavaScript code.

- **Accessing hardware features** – As a general-purpose programming language, JavaScript doesn't have built-in support for the unique features of your host hardware. You can implement your own functions and classes to configure and use these.

- **Reusing existing native code** – You may have a large body of existing native code that works well for your products, and you'd prefer not to have to rewrite it in JavaScript. You can use that code in your JavaScript projects by using XS in C to bridge between it and your JavaScript code.

© Peter Hoddie and Lizzie Prader 2020
P. Hoddie and L. Prader, *IoT Development for ESP32 and ESP8266 with JavaScript*,
https://doi.org/10.1007/978-1-4842-5070-9_11

XS in C lets you work with JavaScript features from C. As you know, JavaScript has capabilities that C doesn't directly support, such as dynamic types and objects. Working with these features using XS in C can be awkward, but it becomes straightforward as you get some practice and learn some common patterns. This chapter introduces XS in C through a series of examples that demonstrate different techniques to build a bridge between JavaScript and C code.

Note that many engines that implement a high-level programming language provide an API to bridge between that language and native code. The Java language defines the Java Native Interface (JNI) for this purpose, and the V8 JavaScript engine provides a C++ API.

Important   The information introduced in this chapter is an advanced topic. It assumes you're comfortable programming in C and have a solid understanding of the basic JavaScript concepts discussed in this book.

Installing the Host

There's no host to install for this chapter, because all native code must be part of the host itself; therefore, you build each example in this chapter as a standalone host. Rather than using mcrun to install the examples, you use mcconfig. The following command lines are for ESP32 and ESP8266 targets, respectively:

```
> mcconfig -d -m -p esp32
> mcconfig -d -m -p esp
```

These command lines don't specify a development board (for example, esp32/moddable_two) because the examples use only common features of the microcontroller and don't depend on board-specific features.

When you build the examples with mcconfig, both the JavaScript and the C code are built. If an error occurs building either, it's reported to the command line.

Generating Random Integers

The first example of native code integration generates random integers. You saw in Chapter 9 that the random-rectangles example uses random numbers generated by the JavaScript built-in function Math.random. That example is less efficient than it could be because Math.random returns a floating-point value, forcing Poco to convert several floating-point values to integers for each rectangle. Floating-point operations are generally slow on microcontrollers, and here they have no benefit. The C standard library's rand function generates random integers, and the $EXAMPLES/ ch11-native/random-integer example begins by using rand to generate random integers for JavaScript code.

Creating a Native Function

The first step is to create a JavaScript function that JavaScript code can call to invoke your C function. The random-integer example declares a randomInt function in the main.js source code file.

```
function randomInt() @ "xs_randomInt";
```

This syntax creates a JavaScript function named randomInt which, when called, invokes the native function xs_randomInt, essentially building a bridge from JavaScript to C. The use of @ here is not standard JavaScript syntax but a language extension provided by XS to simplify adding native code to your projects. Consequently, this code is unlikely to compile or work the same with other JavaScript engines.

After creating the function, you can call it like any other JavaScript function. The main.js module calls it 100 times, tracing the result to the debug console.

```
for (let i = 0; i < 100; i++)
    trace(randomInt(), "\n");
```

Implementing a Native Function

The implementation of xs_randomInt is contained in main.c. When you build a file with a .js extension, mcconfig also builds a file with a .c extension that has the same name. Listing 11-1 shows the entire contents of main.c.

Listing 11-1.

```
#include "xsmc.h"

void xs_randomInt(xsMachine *the)
{
    xsmcSetInteger(xsResult, rand());
}
```

The include preprocessor command brings in the header file for XS in C. (The file name, xsmc, stands for "XS Microcontroller.") There's also an xs.h header file that's used by some code. The two headers provide equivalent functionality, but the functions in the xsmc.h header file are more efficient and therefore preferred for use on microcontrollers.

The native function prototype of xs_randomInt is used for all functions that implement native methods using XS in C. The JavaScript arguments are not passed as arguments to the C function. You'll see later in this chapter how to access the arguments.

This example needs to return a value—the result of calling rand. The result of rand is an integer, so this example uses xsmcSetInteger, a function that assigns a native 32-bit integer value to a JavaScript value. Here the JavaScript value is xsResult, which refers to the return value of the function on the JavaScript stack.

Using the Hardware Random Number Generator

You've seen how simple it is to declare, call, and implement a simple native function. When you run the random-integer example, you see 100 random numbers from 0 to 2,147,483,647 traced to the debug console. But when you restart the microcontroller and run the example a second time, you see the exact same list of numbers. That's not very random. Why does it happen?

The rand function is a pseudo-random number generator. It's an algorithm to generate numbers that appear random; however, when you restart the microcontroller you also restart the pseudo-random number generator algorithm, causing it to generate the same sequence of numbers. You can use the srand function to have the algorithm start a different sequence, but you must provide srand with a different starting point on each restart. The most common way to initialize the sequence is to use the current time. Unfortunately, many microcontrollers, including the ESP32 and ESP8266, don't know the time at startup, so this technique can't be applied.

Fortunately, many microcontrollers, including the ESP32 and ESP8266, have hardware to generate random numbers, and these values are more random than those generated by rand. The $EXAMPLES/ch11-native/ random-integer-esp example shows how to use the hardware random number generator.

Important   Not all random numbers are guaranteed to be sufficiently unpredictable to be safely used in security solutions, such as the TLS protocol that protects network connections. (Random numbers that have this guarantee are called cryptographically secure.) You should always verify that the source of random numbers you use meets the security requirements of your project. This isn't easy to do, but it's important, as a weak random number generator is a vulnerability in your project's overall security.

On the ESP32, accessing the hardware random number generator requires just substituting the call to rand with a call to the ESP-IDF function esp_random. The degree of randomness that esp_random provides depends on a number of factors, including whether the radio (Wi-Fi or Bluetooth) is enabled.

```
xsmcSetInteger(xsResult, esp_random());
```

On the ESP8266, there's an undocumented hardware random number generator that appears to work well. It should be used with care, as its precise characteristics are not known. To access the random number generator, you read its hardware register directly.

```
uint32_t random = *(volatile uint32_t *)0x3FF20E44;
```

Listing 11-2 shows the revised native implementation using the native random number generators. Because the generator is accessed differently on the ESP32 and the ESP8266, the C code uses conditional compilation to select the correct version and to generate an error when the code is compiled for an unsupported target.

Listing 11-2.

```
void xs_randomInt(xsMachine *the)
{
#if ESP32
    xsmcSetInteger(xsResult, esp_random());
#elif defined(__ets__)
    xsmcSetInteger(xsResult, (*(volatile unt32_t *)0x3FF20E44));
#else
    #error Unsupported platform
#endif
}
```

There are two problems with using this randomInt function:

- Both the ESP32 and ESP8266 hardware random number generators return 32-bit unsigned values. The xsmcSetInteger function requires a 32-bit signed value. Consequently, using the hardware random number technique changes the result of the JavaScript randomInt function to return a range of values from –2,147,483,648 to 2,147,483,647. Recall that when you use rand, all values are positive. You could use xsmcSetNumber instead to return the unsigned 32-bit value as a floating-point number; however, that runs counter to the goal of returning a random number as an integer value.

- Usually you want a random number within a certain range, and generating a value within a range requires a division or modulo operation. The division operation typically requires a floating-point operation, since the result may have a fractional part. The modulo operation can use an integer divide if both operands are integers.

However, instead of requiring the caller of `randomInt` to efficiently restrict the return value to the desired range, you can modify the native function to do that.

The next section addresses these issues.

Restricting Random Numbers to a Range

The `$EXAMPLES/ch11-native/random-integer-esp-range` example restricts random numbers to a range. The first step is to declare a function that accepts a range for the random values. The `randomIntRange` function accepts a single argument indicating the range of random values, starting at 0 and ending at `max`.

```
function randomIntRange(max) @ "xs_randomIntRange";
```

The calling code in `main.js` is updated to pass in the range, which is 1,000 in this example.

```
for (let i = 0; i < 100; i++)
    trace(randomIntRange(1000), "\n");
```

The native function must first retrieve the range passed as the first argument. The arguments are accessed by index using `xsArg`. Arguments are numbered starting at 0, so the first argument is accessed as `xsArg(0)`. If the caller didn't pass any arguments, `xsArg(0)` throws an exception; therefore, it's not usually necessary for your native code to check the number of arguments passed. (If your function needs to know the number of arguments, use the `xsmcArgc` integer value.) The exceptions thrown by XS in C are ordinary JavaScript exceptions, which may be caught with a familiar `try` and `catch` blocks in the JavaScript code.

The C code can't make any assumption about the type of the argument, because JavaScript doesn't enforce any rules about the types of arguments passed to a function. XS in C provides functions to convert a JavaScript value to a specific native type. In the xs_randomIntRange function (Listing 11-3), the call to xsmcToInteger asks XS to convert the JavaScript property to a signed 32-bit integer. If XS is able to perform the conversion, it returns the result; otherwise, it throws a JavaScript exception. For example, passing a string value of "100" or a number value of 100.1 succeeds because JavaScript knows how to convert them to an integer; however, passing an empty object {} fails.

Listing 11-3.

```
void xs_randomIntRange(xsMachine *the)
{
    int range = xsmcToInteger(xsArg(0));
    if (range < 2)
        xsRangeError("invalid range");

    ...
}
```

The native function implementation next validates the requested range. A range smaller than two values makes no sense for integer random numbers. If the range is invalid, the function calls xsRangeError to throw the JavaScript error RangeError. The preceding C code is equivalent to these lines of JavaScript:

```
if (range < 2)
    throw new RangeError("invalid range");
```

It's important to include error checking in the native code that bridges between your JavaScript and C code. JavaScript programmers expect the language to be safe—there should be no way to crash or corrupt the device—and the JavaScript engine and runtime do their best to achieve this goal. Your native code must do the same. For example, should the JavaScript code pass 0 for the range, the result is undefined by the C language. The modulo operation with a 0 on the right side on ESP32 generates an IntegerDivideByZero exception and on ESP8266 an Illegal Instruction exception, both of which reset the microcontroller.

The remaining implementation of xs_randomIntRange (Listing 11-4) is straightforward. Instead of returning the 32-bit unsigned integer value directly, the modulo operator (%) restricts the random value to the specified range.

Listing 11-4.

```
#if ESP32
    xsmcSetInteger(xsResult, esp_random() % range);
#elif defined(__ets__)
    xsmcSetInteger(xsResult,
                    (*(volatile uint32_t *)0x3FF20E44) % range);
#else
    #error Unsupported platform
#endif
```

Comparing Random Number Approaches

The native randomIntRange function is just a few lines of native code, but those few lines have many advantages for IoT development compared to the built-in Math.random function:

- The returned values are integers, not floating-point, allowing for more efficient execution on microcontrollers.

- The returned values are efficiently limited to a requested range.

- The numbers are more random because they use a hardware random number generator.

Of course, there are also disadvantages:

- The native code isn't portable. It builds successfully for only two microcontrollers.

- You must build your native code as part of a host.

- Native code is more complex to implement and debug and requires additional specialized knowledge.

When you have the option of adding native functionality to your project, you should base your decision on a balance of the advantages and the disadvantages.

The BitArray Class

JavaScript typed arrays, such as Uint8Array and Uint32Array, enable you to work with arrays of 8-, 16-, and 32-bit integer values using a minimum of memory. The BitArray class implements a 1-bit array—that is, an array that stores only the values 0 and 1. This is useful for efficiently storing a large number of samples received from a digital input.

This section introduces two variations of BitArray, each with the same JavaScript API. The first one uses a JavaScript ArrayBuffer to store the bits, while the second uses native memory allocated with the C calloc function.

The BitArray class constructor takes a single argument: the number of bits the array needs to store. The class provides get and set methods to access the values in the array. Listing 11-5 shows test code that uses the BitArray class.

Listing 11-5.

```
import BitArray from "bitarray";

let bits = new BitArray(128);
bits.set(2, 1);
bits.set(3, bits.get(3) ? 0 : 1);
```

The first argument to both get and set is the index of the bit in the array to get or set. The index of the first array element is 0. The final line of the example toggles the value of the bit at index 3.

Using Memory Allocated by ArrayBuffer

The implementation of BitArray in the $EXAMPLES/ch11-native/ bitarray-arraybuffer example is shown in Listing 11-6. It begins by declaring the class in JavaScript. As in the earlier random-integer examples, the special XS @ syntax is used to connect the JavaScript function to a native C function. Notice that the constructor is implemented in JavaScript while the get and set methods are implemented in C. There's no requirement that the class be implemented entirely in JavaScript or C; you can choose the language that works best for each method.

Listing 11-6.

```
class BitArray {
    constructor(count) {
        this.buffer = new ArrayBuffer(Math.ceil(count / 8));
    }
    get(index) @ "xs_bitarray_get";
    set(index, value) @ "xs_bitarray_set";
}

export default BitArray;
```

The constructor allocates an `ArrayBuffer` to hold the bit values. Because the memory of a new `ArrayBuffer` is always initialized to 0, no further initialization is needed. The number of bits to store is divided by 8 to determine the number of bytes needed and then rounded up using `Math.ceil` to ensure that there are enough bytes allocated when the number of bits isn't evenly divisible by 8. The `ArrayBuffer` is assigned to the `buffer` property of the `BitArray` instance. The native implementations of get and set access the memory using the `buffer` property.

The get Function

The native implementation of the get function, `xs_bitarray_get`, begins by retrieving the index of the bit, the first argument to the function. It uses the `index` argument to calculate `byteIndex`, the index of the byte that contains the bit, and `bitIndex`, the index of the bit within that byte.

```
int index = xsmcToInteger(xsArg(0));
int byteIndex = index >> 3;
int bitIndex = index & 0x07;
```

Next, `xs_bitarray_get` gets a pointer to the memory allocated by the `ArrayBuffer` stored in the `buffer` property. To do this, it first allocates one temporary JavaScript variable on the JavaScript stack, by calling `xsmcVars` with the argument 1 specifying the number of temporary variables.

```
xsmcVars(1);
```

Variables allocated using `xsmcVars` are accessed with `xsVar`, which is similar to `xsArg` but accesses local temporary variables instead of arguments to the function. The variables are automatically released when the native function that allocated them—in this case, `xs_bitarray_get`—returns. You should call `xsmcVars` only one time in a function, allocating all needed temporary variables at once.

The implementation of xs_bitarray_get retrieves a reference to its instance's buffer property by calling xsmcGet. The value of the buffer property is placed in xsVar(0).

```
xsmcGet(xsVar(0), xsThis, xsID_buffer);
```

The second argument, xsThis here, tells xsmcGet which object you want to retrieve the property from. The third argument, xsID_buffer here, specifies that the name of the property you want to retrieve is buffer.

The preceding steps use many unfamiliar calls from XS in C. What they do is quite simple in JavaScript, and much more verbose to express in C. The JavaScript equivalent to the calls to xsmcVars and xsmcGet is as follows:

```
let var0;
var0 = this.buffer;
```

The buffer property is not a pointer to the memory buffer used by the ArrayBuffer instance; it's a reference to the instance. Just as you use xsmcToInteger to convert a JavaScript value to an integer, you use xsmcToArrayBuffer to convert a JavaScript value to a native pointer. If the JavaScript value is not an ArrayBuffer instance, the call to xsmcToArrayBuffer throws an exception.

```
uint8_t *buffer = xsmcToArrayBuffer(xsVar(0));
```

Now that xs_bitarray_get has the buffer pointer, it uses the byteIndex and bitIndex values calculated earlier to read the bit and set the return value of the JavaScript function call to 0 or 1.

```
if (buffer[byteIndex] & (1 << bitIndex))
    xsmcSetInteger(xsResult, 1);
else
    xsmcSetInteger(xsResult, 0);
```

The set Function

The implementation of the set function (Listing 11-7) in xs_bitarray_set is very similar to the implementation of get. The values of byteIndex, bitIndex, and buffer are determined in the same way. The sole difference is that the value of the second argument, accessed with xsArg(1), is used to determine whether to set or clear the specified bit.

Listing 11-7.

```
int value = xsmcToInteger(xsArg(1));
if (value)
    buffer[byteIndex] |= 1 << bitIndex;
else
    buffer[byteIndex] &= ~(1 << bitIndex);
```

Security Vulnerability

This implementation of BitArray, using memory allocated by ArrayBuffer, works well, but it has a critical flaw that makes it unsuitable for safe use in real products. The get and set functions don't verify that the index argument is inside the bounds of the memory allocated. This enables code using this implementation of BitArray to read and write arbitrary memory on embedded devices, which can cause a crash or be used as the basis of a privacy attack. There are multiple ways to solve this problem; the next section discusses one of them.

Using Memory Allocated by calloc

The implementation of BitArray in the $EXAMPLES/ch11-native/bitarray-calloc example solves the security problem presented by the bitarray-arraybuffer example as just discussed. It stores the number of bits allocated by the constructor and then validates the index passed to the get and set calls against that stored value.

The BitArray implementation in the bitarray-calloc example uses calloc instead of ArrayBuffer to allocate memory. The memory allocated by these two approaches comes from two different pools of memory: memory allocated by calloc is taken from the native system memory heap, whereas memory allocated by ArrayBuffer is inside the memory heap managed by XS. Some hosts are configured with more free space in one of these pools than the other, which may influence your decision about where to allocate memory from. A little bit less code is required to work with the memory allocated by calloc, though that difference may not be significant.

The bitarray-calloc example illustrates some important techniques for integrating native code into your project. In addition to a native constructor, this BitArray class also has a native destructor to perform cleanup when an instance of the class is garbage-collected. In XS, an object with a native destructor is called a *host object*.

The Class Declaration

Listing 11-8 shows the class declaration. This implementation of BitArray uses primarily native methods, unlike the implementation from the bitarray-arraybuffer example. Notice that the name of the native C function that implements the destructor, xs_bitarray_destructor, follows the declaration of the class name.

Listing 11-8.

```
class BitArray @ "xs_bitarray_destructor" {
    constructor(count) @ "xs_bitarray_constructor";
    close() @ "xs_bitarray_close";

    get(index) @ "xs_bitarray_get";
    set(index, value) @ "xs_bitarray_set";
```

```
    get length() @ "xs_bitarray_get_length";
    set length(value) {
        throw new Error("read-only");
    }
}
```

The declarations of the get and set methods are the same as in the previous example, though the implementations are somewhat different.

The native constructor, destructor, and close functions are closely related. The next sections look at each in turn.

The Constructor

The native constructor in Listing 11-9 begins much like the JavaScript implementation, by calculating the number of bytes needed to store the requested number of bits and then allocating those bytes. The constructor allocates additional space, the size of an integer, to hold the bit count. If the allocation fails, the constructor calls xsUnknownError to throw an exception. The use of Unknown in the name xsUnknownError means that this a general-purpose error, which uses the JavaScript Error class, rather than a specific error such as RangeError.

Listing 11-9.

```
void xs_bitarray_constructor(xsMachine *the)
{
    int bitCount = xsmcToInteger(xsArg(0));
    int byteCount = (bitCount + 7) / 8;
    uint8_t *bytes = calloc(byteCount + sizeof(int), 1);
    if (!bytes)
        xsUnknownError("no memory");

    *(int *)bytes = bitCount;
    xsmcSetHostData(xsThis, bytes);
}
```

Once the memory is allocated, the number of bits requested is stored at the start of the block. Because the memory is allocated using `calloc`, all bits are initialized to 0.

The call to `xsmcSetHostData` stores a reference to the memory allocated with this host object. This pointer is then available to all native methods of the object, through a call to `xsmcGetHostData`. You might be tempted to simply store the `bytes` pointer in a global variable; however, that approach fails when there's more than one instance of the object, since the two objects can't share a single C global variable. Using `xsmcSetHostData` to store the data pointer means that the implementation of `BitArray` supports an arbitrary number of simultaneous instances.

The Destructor

This is the first time in this book that you've seen a destructor. They're common in C++ in working with objects, but they're not a visible part of the JavaScript language. Instead, JavaScript automatically frees the memory used by objects when they're garbage-collected. The JavaScript engine doesn't know how to free the resources your host object allocated, such as the memory allocated with `calloc`. Therefore, you must implement a destructor.

For `BitArray`, the destructor (Listing 11-10) simply calls `free` to release the memory allocated by `calloc`.

Listing 11-10.

```
void xs_bitarray_destructor(void *data)
{
    if (data)
        free(data);
}
```

Here are some details to be aware of when implementing a destructor:

- The function prototype of a destructor is different from regular native method calls. Instead of being passed a reference to the XS virtual machine as the, it has an argument that's a data pointer, the same value you passed to xsmcSetHostData.

- Because there's no reference to the XS virtual machine (no the argument), you can't make calls to XS in C. For example, you can't call xsmcGetHostData, which is why the data pointer is always passed to the destructor function. That also means your destructor can't create new objects, change the values of properties, or make function calls to the object. These limitations are necessary because the destructor is called from inside the garbage collector when such operations are unsafe.

- The value of data may be NULL. This happens, for example, when the memory allocation in the constructor fails. As you'll see in the next section, it also happens after the close method is called. Therefore, a good practice is to always check that the data argument isn't NULL in your destructor before using it, as this example does.

The close Function

Chapters 3 and 5 contain examples of JavaScript objects that have a close method. This method releases any native resources—memory, file handles, network sockets, and so on—that the object owns. If the object isn't explicitly closed, those resources are eventually released when the garbage collector determines that the object is no longer in use. However, there's no way to know when the garbage collector will make that determination, which means it may be a very long time until the resources are freed. The close call solves this problem by giving code a way to explicitly free those resources.

Many host objects have an implementation of close like the one for BitArray (Listing 11-11).

Listing 11-11.

```
void xs_bitarray_close(xsMachine *the)
{
    uint8_t *buffer = xsmcGetHostData(xsThis);
    xs_bitarray_destructor(buffer);
    xsmcSetHostData(xsThis, NULL);
}
```

Here's what these lines of code do:

1. The call to xsmcGetHostData retrieves the data pointer that was allocated in the constructor and associated with this object by the call to xsmcSetHostData.

2. The data pointer is passed to the destructor, which does the work of releasing the resources.

3. The call to xsmcSetHostData sets the saved data pointer to NULL. This ensures that, should close be called twice, the data pointer is freed only once.

The get and set Functions

This implementation of xs_bitarray_get calculates the bit and byte index values in the same way as in the ArrayBuffer version of get:

```
int index = xsmcToInteger(xsArg(0));
int byteIndex = index >> 3;
int bitIndex = index & 0x07;
```

As shown in Listing 11-12, xs_bitarray_get uses xsmcGetHostData to retrieve the data buffer. If the buffer is NULL, that indicates that the instance has already been closed, and get throws an error. The count of the number of bits allocated is stored in the first integer of the buffer; it's extracted to the local variable bitCount, and then the buffer pointer is advanced to point to the bit array values.

Listing 11-12.

```
uint8_t *buffer = xsmcGetHostData(xsThis);
int bitCount;

if (NULL == buffer)
    xsUnknownError("closed");

bitCount = *(int *)buffer;
buffer += sizeof(int);
```

Before accessing the requested bit, the implementation first checks to see whether the value is in range. Because the index is a signed integer, it checks that it's not greater than the number of bits allocated and that the index is not negative.

```
if ((index >= bitCount) || (index < 0))
    xsRangeError("invalid bit index");
```

With that check complete, reading the requested bit and setting the return value is identical to the previous version:

```
if (buffer[byteIndex] & (1 << bitIndex))
    xsmcSetInteger(xsResult, 1);
else
    xsmcSetInteger(xsResult, 0);
```

The implementation of set applies the same changes described for get in this section and so is not repeated here.

The `length` Property

The typed array classes include a `length` property in their instances which, as in instances of `Array`, indicates the number of elements in the array. This value is useful when you're iterating over the array. Because this implementation of `BitArray` stores the number of bits allocated, it can also provide a `length` property.

The `length` property is implemented with a getter and a setter, two special kinds of JavaScript functions that are called when code accesses a property. Using the getter and setter for `length` enables you to write code like the following to initialize all bits to 1:

```
let bits = new BitArray(55);
for (let i = 0; i < bits.length; i++)
    bits.set(i, 1);
```

The first step in implementing the `length` property is to add the getter and setter to the `BitArray` class. Here the getter is the `xs_bitarray_get_length` native function. The `length` property is read-only, so instead of native code the setter implementation is a JavaScript function that always throws an exception. Notice that a host object may have JavaScript methods.

```
get length() @ "xs_bitarray_get_length";
set length(value) {
    throw new Error("read-only");
}
```

The implementation of `xs_bitarray_get_length`, shown in Listing 11-13, is straightforward. It uses `xsmcGetHostData` to retrieve the data pointer created in the constructor. If the instance has been closed—that is, if `buffer` is `NULL`—it throws an exception; otherwise, it sets the return value to the bit count extracted from the start of the data pointer.

Listing 11-13.

```
void xs_bitarray_get_length(xsMachine *the)
{
    uint8_t *buffer = xsmcGetHostData(xsThis);
    if (NULL == buffer)
        xsUnknownError("closed");

    int bitCount = *(int *)buffer;
    xsmcSetInteger(xsResult, bitCount);
}
```

Advantages to This Approach

This second implementation of BitArray, using memory allocated by calloc, has many advantages over the first version:

- It validates the input values, eliminating the ability of sloppy code to cause a crash and of malicious code to breach privacy.

- It provides a length property, making it more convenient to work with.

- It uses system memory to store the bit data, reducing the memory used in the memory heap managed by the JavaScript engine.

- It uses the host data feature of XS in C to keep track of the memory buffer, requiring less code and running faster than using a JavaScript property.

Wi-Fi Signal Notifications

You've learned how to implement a class to manage native resources as a host object. This next example shows how to make calls from C code back to JavaScript and how to configure a host object using a dictionary. Both these techniques are used by many of the host objects in the Moddable SDK.

The $EXAMPLES/ch11-native/wifi-rssi-notify example implements the WiFiRSSINotify class, which lets you register callbacks to invoke when the Wi-Fi signal strength crosses above and below a specified threshold. You might use this in your product to give the user an indication of when Wi-Fi is likely to perform well or to throttle the amount of network traffic you generate when the signal is weak. The class could be implemented entirely in JavaScript using Timer together with the net module introduced in the "Getting Network Information" section of Chapter 3. This implementation using native code is a bit more efficient and provides a convenient starting point to show how to configure your host object from a dictionary and how to invoke callback functions.

When you run this example, you must specify a Wi-Fi access point for the microcontroller to connect to. That's because RSSI measures the strength of the signal between your microcontroller and the access point it's connected to; if there's no connection, there's nothing to measure. Here's a typical command line to build and run this example:

```
> mcconfig -d -m -p esp32 ssid="My Wi-Fi" password="secret"
```

The Test Code

The WiFiRSSINotify class follows the common pattern of having a constructor that accepts a dictionary object of configuration options. Listing 11-14 shows test code in main.js that constructs an instance of this class. You need to specify the RSSI threshold below which the signal is considered weak and at which the signal is considered strong. An optional poll property configures how often the signal strength is checked; it's set to 1,000 milliseconds in this example. The default polling frequency is 5,000 milliseconds.

Listing 11-14.

```
import WiFiRSSINotify from "wifirssinotify";

let notify = new WiFiRSSINotify({
    threshold: -66,
    poll: 1000
});
```

Once the notification instance is created, you can install an onWeakSignal and/or onStrongSignal callback, as shown in Listing 11-15. The onWeakSignal callback is invoked when the RSSI reaches or falls below the specified threshold, and onStrongSignal is invoked when the RSSI exceeds the threshold. The functions are called when the threshold is crossed, not each time the RSSI is polled. The current RSSI value is passed to the callback functions.

Listing 11-15.

```
notify.onWeakSignal = function(rssi) {
    trace(`Weak Wi-Fi signal. RSSI ${rssi}.\n`);
}
notify.onStrongSignal = function(rssi) {
    trace(`Strong Wi-Fi signal. RSSI ${rssi}.\n`);
}
```

The `WiFiRSSINotify` Class

The JavaScript class for `WiFiRSSINotify` is just a host object with a destructor, constructor, and `close` function all implemented in native code:

```
class WiFiRSSINotify @ "xs_wifirssinotify_destructor" {
    constructor(options) @ "xs_wifirssinotify_constructor";
    close() @ "xs_wifirssinotify_close";
}
```

Default functions for the `onWeakSignal` and `onStrongSignal` callbacks are not part of the class. Before invoking a callback, `WiFiRSSINotify` confirms that the instance has a property with the callback's name.

The Native `RSSINotifyRecord` Structure

The `WiFiRSSINotify` class needs to maintain state to perform its work. That state is stored in a C language structure named `RSSINotifyRecord`, shown in Listing 11-16. You can think of this data structure as the C equivalent of the properties in a JavaScript instance.

Listing 11-16.

```
struct RSSINotifyRecord {
    int         threshold;
    int         state;
    modTimer    timer;
    xsMachine   *the;
    xsSlot      obj;
};
```

Before looking at the code that uses this data structure, it's helpful to review how each field is used:

- threshold – The RSSI threshold below which the signal is considered weak and at which the signal is considered strong.

- state – The WiFiRSSINotify instance is always in one of three states: kRSSIUnknown when it's created and then either kRSSIWeak or kRSSIStrong. This state is used to eliminate redundant callbacks when the state has not changed.

- timer – A native timer used to implement polling.

- the – A reference to the XS virtual machine that contains the WiFiRSSINotify instance. It's used to invoke callbacks from the timer.

- obj – A reference to the WiFiRSSINotify object that's used to invoke callbacks from the timer. The type of this field, xsSlot, is used by XS to hold any JavaScript value. The xsArg, xsVar, and xsGet functions that you already know return values of type xsSlot.

Additional details about how these fields are used are provided in the following sections.

The implementation also defines RSSINotify as a pointer to RSSINotifyRecord for convenience:

```
typedef struct RSSINotifyRecord *RSSINotify;
```

The Constructor

The WiFiRSSINotify constructor begins by allocating storage for the RSSINotifyRecord structure. Once this structure is fully initialized, it's attached to the object using xsmcSetHostData. As a rule, the data structure is not attached to the object before being initialized, to avoid having a partially initialized structure in case an error occurs during execution of the constructor.

```
RSSINotify rn = calloc(sizeof(RSSINotifyRecord), 1);
if (!rn)
    xsUnknownError("no memory");
```

Next, the constructor initializes the state, the, and obj fields:

```
rn->state = kRSSIUnknown;
rn->obj = xsThis;
rn->the = the;
```

The constructor performs several operations that may fail. When they fail, they throw an error that can be caught by the calling JavaScript code. Because the first operation the constructor performs is allocating memory, it needs to free that memory if an exception occurs. If it doesn't do so, the memory is orphaned, causing a memory leak that could eventually lead to a system failure. To guard against this, the constructor surrounds those operations with xsTry, catching any exceptions with xsCatch. After catching the exception, the constructor frees the memory stored in rn and then uses xsThrow to throw the error again. In C, that use of xsTry and xsCatch has the structure shown in Listing 11-17.

Listing 11-17.

```
xsTry {
    ...
}
xsCatch {
    free(rn);
    xsThrow(xsException);
}
```

Recall that XS in C provides ways to access and implement basic JavaScript capabilities in your C code. The C code for xsTry-xsCatch is similar to the JavaScript version of the code, shown in Listing 11-18.

Listing 11-18.

```
try {
    ...
}
catch(e) {
    ...
    throw e;
}
```

The xsTry block begins by declaring a local variable, poll, to hold the requested polling interval from the dictionary argument and using xsmcVars to reserve space for a temporary value on the JavaScript stack:

```
int poll;

xsmcVars(1);
```

As shown in Listing 11-19, the constructor then calls xsmcHas to see if the dictionary argument contains the poll property. If it does, the property is retrieved, converted to an integer, and assigned to the local variable poll; otherwise, a default value of 5,000 is used.

Listing 11-19.

```
if (xsmcHas(xsArg(0), xsID_poll)) {
    xsmcGet(xsVar(0), xsArg(0), xsID_poll);
    poll = xsmcToInteger(xsVar(0));
}
else
    poll = 5000;
```

The xsmcHas function is similar to the in operator used in JavaScript. The preceding code is about the same as the JavaScript code in Listing 11-20.

Listing 11-20.

```
let poll;
if ("poll" in options)
    poll = options.poll;
else
    poll = 5000;
```

The constructor next calls xsmcHas again, this time to confirm that the required threshold property is present. If not, it throws an error; otherwise, the JavaScript threshold property is retrieved, converted to an integer, and assigned to the threshold field of rn.

```
if (!xsmcHas(xsArg(0), xsID_threshold))
    xsUnknownError("threshold required");
xsmcGet(xsVar(0), xsArg(0), xsID_threshold);
rn->threshold = xsmcToInteger(xsVar(0));
```

Finally, the xsTry block allocates a native timer using modTimerAdd from the Moddable SDK. You may use another timer mechanism here, one specific to your microcontroller. This code uses modTimerAdd for convenience, as it's available for both ESP32 and ESP8266 devices. If the timer can't be allocated—for example, because there's insufficient memory available—the constructor throws an exception.

```
rn->timer = modTimerAdd(1, poll, checkRSSI, &rn, sizeof(rn));
if (!rn->timer)
    xsUnknownError("no timer");
```

The call to modTimerAdd creates a timer that first fires after 1 millisecond and then fires at the interval specified by poll. When the timer fires, it calls the checkRSSI native function, passing it the value of rn. A later section shows how the native callback retrieves this value and invokes the JavaScript callbacks.

That's the end of the xsTry block. Even in this relatively simple object, there are two exceptions that the constructor itself generates. In addition, the calls to xsmcToInteger throw exceptions when passed a value that can't be converted to an integer. These many potentials for exceptions make it important for the constructor to ensure that no memory or other resources are orphaned if an exception is thrown. Using xsTry with xsCatch often helps with this.

There are two more steps remaining in the constructor. The first is to store the rn data pointer with the object:

```
xsmcSetHostData(xsThis, rn);
```

The second is to ensure that the object is garbage-collected only after the JavaScript code calls close on the object. This behavior is common for JavaScript host objects that support callbacks. To do this, the constructor calls the xsRemember function with the object stored in the RSSINotifyRecord.

```
xsRemember(rn->obj);
```

You can only pass xsRemember a value in storage that your code allocated. If you call xsRemember with values such as xsThis, xsArg(0), xsVar(1), or other XS-provided values, it silently fails. As you might expect, there's a corresponding xsForget call that needs to be called in close. The memory where the object is stored, rn->obj here, must persist until xsForget is called and therefore must not be a local variable in the constructor.

The Destructor

The destructor for WiFiRSSINotify (Listing 11-21) is similar to the other destructors in this chapter, with the addition of code to free the timer allocated in the constructor. To access the timer in the RSSINotifyRecord structure, the data pointer argument is cast to an RSSINotify pointer. The constructor implementation guarantees that the timer field is never NULL in the destructor when rn is non-NULL. Therefore, there's no need to check that rn->timer is non-NULL before calling modTimerRemove.

Listing 11-21.

```
void xs_wifirssinotify_destructor(void *data)
{
    RSSINotify rn = data;
    if (rn) {
        modTimerRemove(rn->timer);
        free(rn);
    }
}
```

The close Function

The close method of WiFiRSSINotify (Listing 11-22) also follows a familiar pattern. However, in addition it must call xsForget to make the object eligible for garbage collection, counteracting the call to xsRemember in the constructor. Because the call to xsForget accesses the obj field of rn, the close implementation must guard against being called more than once by checking that xsmcGetHostData returns a non-NULL value.

Listing 11-22.

```
void xs_wifirssinotify_close(xsMachine *the)
{
    RSSINotify rn = xsmcGetHostData(xsThis);
    if (rn) {
        xsForget(rn->obj);
        xs_wifirssinotify_destructor(rn);
        xsmcSetHostData(xsThis, NULL);
    }
}
```

The call to xsForget can't be made in the destructor because the destructor can't use XS in C, as explained previously.

The Callback

The checkRSSI function, shown in Listing 11-23, is at the heart of the WiFiRSSINotify class. It's invoked at the polling interval to detect when the RSSI value crosses the specified threshold value. The function begins by recovering the value of rn, the pointer to the RSSINotifyRecord structure allocated in the constructor. Because the checkRSSI callback isn't called directly by XS, but by modTimer, the pointer can't be retrieved using xsmcGetHostData as usual, but is instead retrieved by dereferencing the refcon argument.

Listing 11-23.

```
void checkRSSI(modTimer timer, void *refcon, int refconSize)
{
    RSSINotify rn = *(RSSINotify *)refcon;
    ...
}
```

The next step is to get the current RSSI value, which is done differently on the ESP32 and the ESP8266. Listing 11-24 has conditional cases for each, and an error for other targets.

Listing 11-24.

```
int rssi = 0;

#if ESP32
    wifi_ap_record_t config;

    if (ESP_OK == esp_wifi_sta_get_ap_info(&config))
        rssi = config.rssi;
#elif defined(__ets__)
    rssi = wifi_station_get_rssi();
#else
    #error Unsupported target
#endif
```

As shown in Listing 11-25, the polling function uses the current RSSI value to decide if it's necessary to invoke either the onStrongSignal or the onWeakSignal JavaScript callback function. It checks to see if the current value is above or below the specified threshold stored in rn->threshold. If the RSSI value is on the same side of the threshold as the previous check, checkRSSI returns immediately; otherwise, it updates rn->state to the new state and assigns the ID of the callback to invoke, either xsID_onStrongSignal or xsID_onWeakSignal, to the local variable callbackID.

Listing 11-25.

```
if (rssi > rn->threshold) {
    if (kRSSIStrong == rn->state)
        return;
    rn->state = kRSSIStrong;
```

```
        callbackID = xsID_onStrongSignal;
}
else {
    if (kRSSIWeak == rn->state)
        return;
    rn->state = kRSSIWeak;
    callbackID = xsID_onWeakSignal;
}
```

Invoking a JavaScript function from native code requires a valid JavaScript stack frame. When a native method is called from JavaScript, XS has already created that stack frame. The checkRSSI function isn't called by XS, but by modTimer, and therefore must set up the stack frame itself. It does this by calling xsBeginHost before the callback. It calls xsEndHost afterward to remove the stack frame that xsBeginHost creates. Both functions take the, a reference to the JavaScript virtual machine, as their sole argument. Between xsBeginHost and xsEndHost, you can make calls to XS in C as usual.

The code in Listing 11-26 creates a temporary JavaScript variable using xsmcVars(1) and assigns it an integer value of rssi using xsmcSetInteger. It then calls xsmcHas to confirm that the object has the callback function. If it does, it uses xsCall to invoke the callback function, passing the RSSI value stored in xsVar(0).

Listing 11-26.

```
xsBeginHost(rn->the);
    xsmcVars(1);
    xsmcSetInteger(xsVar(0), rssi);
    if (xsmcHas(rn->obj, callbackID))
        xsCall1(rn->obj, callbackID, xsVar(0));
xsEndHost(rn->the);
```

You use xsCall1 to call functions with one argument (and xsCall0 to call functions with no arguments, xsCall2 for functions with two arguments, and so on, up to xsCall9).

Additional Techniques

You now know how to invoke native code from JavaScript code and JavaScript code from native code, giving you the power to integrate native code and scripts in whatever way makes the most sense for your project. This section briefly introduces several important topics that you may find useful when integrating native code into your own JavaScript-powered products. Along with discussing a variety of techniques to help you build the bridge between your native and JavaScript code, it includes warnings about some common mistakes.

Debugging Native Code

As you develop increasingly complex native code, you may need to debug that code. Although you may not have a native debugger available, your code can interact with xsbug.

A common debugging technique is to send diagnostic output to the debug console. In embedded JavaScript, you use trace to do this. Using XS in C, you can do the same with xsTrace.

```
xsTrace("about to get RSSI\n");
```

The argument to xsTrace is a string, making it convenient to output the progress of a function. If you need to output more detailed information, use xsLog, which provides printf-style functionality.

```
xsLog("RSSI is %d.\n", rssi);
```

Both xsTrace and xsLog require a valid XS stack frame; therefore, they must be called either from a method invoked directly by XS or between an xsBeginHost-xsEndHost pair. For example, to output the current RSSI level to the debug console from the checkRSSI callback, you use this code:

```
xsBeginHost(rn->the);
    xsLog("RSSI is %d.\n", rssi);
xsEndHost(rn->the);
```

It can be useful to trigger a breakpoint in xsbug from your native code to see the stack frames leading up to your native function being called and the arguments passed to it. Although you can't set a breakpoint in native code using xsbug, you can trigger a breakpoint by calling xsDebugger in your C code.

```
xsDebugger();
```

Accessing Global Variables

Your code can get and set the value of global variables directly. All global variables are part of the global object, which is accessed in JavaScript using globalThis. In XS in C, the global object is available to your native code as xsGlobal. You can use xsGlobal in your native code like any other object. For example, you use the xsmcSet* functions to assign values to a global variable, and the following lines set the global variable status to 0x8012:

```
xsmcSetInteger(xsVar(0), 0x8012);
xsmcSet(xsGlobal, xsID_status, xsVar(0));
```

You get the value of a global using xsmcGet:

```
xsmcGet(xsVar(0), xsGlobal, xsID_status);
int status = xsmcToInteger(xsVar(0));
```

The following code checks to see if there's a global variable named onRestart. If there is, it calls the function stored in the onRestart global.

```
if (xsmcHas(xsGlobal, xsID_onRestart))
    xsCall0(xsGlobal, xsID_onRestart);
```

Getting a Function's Return Value

When you use the family of xsCall* functions to invoke a JavaScript function from C, you can access the return value by assigning the result to a JavaScript value. For example, the following code calls the function on the callback property of this and traces the result to the console:

```
xsmcVars(1);
xsVar(0) = xsCall0(xsThis, xsID_callback);
xsTrace(xsVar(0));
```

Getting Values

The examples in this chapter use xsmcToInteger to get an integer value from a JavaScript value. There are similar functions for getting a boolean, floating-point number, string, and ArrayBuffer from a JavaScript value, as shown in Listing 11-27.

Listing 11-27.

```
uint8_t boolean = xsmcToBoolean(xsArg(0));
double number = xsmcToNumber(xsArg(1));
const char *str = xsmcToString(xsArg(2));
uint8_t *buffer = xsmcToArrayBuffer(xsArg(3));
int bufferLength = xsmcGetArrayBufferLength(xsArg(3));
```

All of these functions fail if the JavaScript value can't be converted to the requested type. For example, xsmcToArrayBuffer fails if the value is a string.

Special care is required when working with the pointers to strings and with ArrayBuffer pointers. See the section "Ensuring Your Buffer Pointers Are Valid" for details.

Setting Values

You've already seen how to use xsmcSetInteger to set a JavaScript property to an integer value. In addition, there are xsmcSet* functions for setting other basic JavaScript values, as shown in Listing 11-28.

Listing 11-28.

```
xsmcSetNull(xsResult);
xsmcSetUndefined(xsVar(0));

xsmcSetBoolean(xsVar(2), value);
xsmcSetTrue(xsVar(3));
xsmcSetFalse(xsResult);

xsmcSetNumber(xsResult, 1.2);

xsmcSetString(xsResult, "off");

const char *string = "a dog!";
xsmcSetStringBuffer(xsResult, string + 2, 3); // "dog"
```

You can also create objects using XS in C. The following code creates an ArrayBuffer object of 16 bytes and sets the first byte to 1:

```
xsmcSetArrayBuffer(xsResult, NULL, 16);
uint8_t *buffer = xsmcToArrayBuffer(xsResult);
buffer[0] = 1;
```

Listing 11-29 creates an object and adds several properties to it. Using this approach, your code can return objects just as the next method of the File class does.

Listing 11-29.

```
xsmcSetNewObject(xsResult);

xsmcSetString(xsVar(0), "test.txt");
xsmcSet(xsResult, xsID_name, xsVar(0));

xsmcSetInteger(xsVar(0), 1024);
xsmcSet(xsResult, xsID_length, xsVar(0));
```

The JavaScript equivalent of that code is as follows:

```
return {name: "test.txt", length: 1024};
```

Listing 11-30 creates an array with eight elements and uses xsmcSet to set each array element to the square of its index. You've already seen xsmcSet used to set the value of a property of an object; here it's used to set the value of an array element by passing the element's index instead of an xsID_*-style symbol identifier.

Listing 11-30.

```
xsmcSetNewArray(xsResult, 8);

for (i = 0; i < 8; i++) {
    xsmcSetInteger(xsVar(0), i * i);
    xsmcSet(xsResult, i, xsVar(0));
}
```

Determining a Value's Type

Your native code sometimes needs to know the type of a JavaScript value. For example, some functions change their behavior depending on whether an argument is an object or a number. You use xsmcTypeOf to determine the basic type of a value.

```
int typeOf = xsmcTypeOf(xsArg(1));
if (xsStringType == typeOf)
    ...;
```

The types returned by xsmcTypeOf are xsUndefinedType, xsNullType, xsBooleanType, xsIntegerType, xsNumberType, xsStringType, and xsReferenceType. Most of these correspond directly to JavaScript types you're already familiar with. Notice, however, that there are types for both integers and numbers (floating-point values). While JavaScript itself uses the Number type for both, XS stores them as distinct types, as an optimization. If your native code checks whether a JavaScript value is of type Number, it needs to check for both xsIntegerType and xsNumberType.

The type xsReferenceType corresponds to a JavaScript object. This single type constant is used for all JavaScript objects. You use the xsmcIsInstanceOf function to determine whether the object is an instance of a particular class. The type xsmcIsInstanceOf is similar to JavaScript's instanceof operator. XS defines values for built-in objects—for example, xsArrayPrototype. The following code sets the variable isArray to 1 if the first argument to the native method is an array or 0 if it's not:

```
int typeOf = xsmcTypeOf(xsArg(0));
int isArray = (xsReferenceType == typeOf) &&
              xsmcIsInstanceOf(xsArg(0), xsArrayPrototype);
```

The xsmcIsInstanceOf function returns true if the object is a subclass of the specified type. For example, the section "Accessing Values of a Data View" in Chapter 2 defines the Header class as a subclass of DataView. Passing an instance of Header to the following call returns true:

```
if (xsmcIsInstanceOf(xsArg(0), xsDataViewPrototype))
    ...;    // is a data view
```

Other useful prototypes defined by XS that may be used with xsmcIsInstanceOf include xsFunctionPrototype, xsDatePrototype, xsErrorPrototype, and xsTypedArrayPrototype. For a complete list, see the xs.h header file in the Moddable SDK.

Working with Strings

Strings are commonly used in JavaScript. Because XS stores them in UTF-8 encoding, strings are convenient to work with in C. Here are a few details to keep in mind:

- You're guaranteed that strings you receive from XS are valid UTF-8. You must ensure that any strings you pass to XS are also valid UTF-8.

- XS treats a null character (ASCII 0) as the end of the string, so don't include any null characters in your strings. (Since the C language also uses the null character to terminate a string, this should be familiar.) Your code probably doesn't intentionally create invalid UTF-8 strings or include null characters in a string, but they can sneak in when you import strings from a file or a network connection; it's a good practice to validate these strings before passing them to XS.

- In JavaScript, strings are read-only. No functions are provided to change the content of a string. You could choose to break this rule in your native code—but don't! Doing so would break a fundamental assumption that JavaScript programmers rely on. Furthermore, it could cause a crash, as some strings are stored in read-only flash memory and attempting to write to them causes the microcontroller to reset.

- The string pointer returned from `xsmcToString` can be invalidated when you make other calls using XS in C. The next section explains the details.

Ensuring Your Buffer Pointers Are Valid

When you call `xsmcToString` or `xsmcToArrayBuffer`, they don't return a copy of the data; they return a pointer into an XS data structure. This behavior is important on microcontrollers, where the extra time and memory required to make a copy are unacceptable. The pointer may become invalid when you make a call to XS in C that causes the garbage collector to run. The garbage collector cannot free the `ArrayBuffer` or string, because they're in use. However, the garbage collector may move the data structure when it compacts the memory heap to make more space by combining areas of free space.

With some care, as in the following approaches, you can avoid any problems when the garbage collector compacts the heap:

- Never use a pointer returned by XS in C after making another call to XS in C. This may seem challenging, but all the examples so far in this chapter have done exactly that.

- Make a copy of the data. While this approach is not optimal, it's occasionally necessary.

Two functions can help when you're working with pointers to strings and `ArrayBuffer` pointers. The `xsmcToStringBuffer` function is similar to xsmcToString, but instead of returning a string pointer it copies the string to a buffer. If the buffer is too small to hold the string, it throws a RangeError error.

```
char str[40];
xsmcToStringBuffer(xsArg(0), str, sizeof(str));
```

The xsmcGetArrayBufferData function copies all or part of an ArrayBuffer into another buffer. The second argument is the ArrayBuffer offset (in bytes) from which to begin copying the data, the third argument is the destination buffer, and the final argument is the size of the destination buffer in bytes. This example copies five bytes starting at offset 10 from an ArrayBuffer to the local variable buffer.

```
uint8_t buffer[5];
xsmcGetArrayBufferData(xsResult, 10, buffer, sizeof(buffer));
```

Integrating with C++

XS in C enables you to bridge not only between C and JavaScript code but also between C++ and JavaScript code. Although both JavaScript and C++ support objects, the details of how they implement objects and their features are quite different. Therefore, it's usually unrealistic to try to create a direct mapping between your C++ classes and your JavaScript classes. Instead, design your JavaScript classes to make sense to JavaScript programmers and your C++ classes to make sense to C++ programmers. The bridge code you write using XS in C can translate between the two.

Using Threads

JavaScript is a single-threaded language; for this reason, the XS JavaScript engine is also single-threaded. This means that all calls to a single JavaScript virtual machine, as represented to native code by the, should be made from the same thread or task. You shouldn't call XS in C from an interrupt or a thread other than the one that created the virtual machine.

Techniques that provide multitasking execution of JavaScript code, such as the Web Workers class, are built outside the JavaScript language. The Moddable SDK supports a subset of the Web Workers class on the ESP32, which enables several JavaScript virtual machines to coexist, each in their own thread. Each virtual machine is single-threaded, but several machines may run in parallel. The implementation of Web Workers for ESP32 respects the requirement that each individual JavaScript virtual machine is single-threaded.

Conclusion

The ability to bridge between JavaScript and native code using the XS in C API opens the door to many new possibilities for your projects. It enables you to optimize memory use, improve performance, reuse existing C and C++ code libraries, and access unique hardware capabilities. However, using XS in C is considerably more difficult than working in JavaScript, and consequently more error-prone. As a rule, using as little native code as practical tends to minimize the risks.

To help you learn more about working with XS in C, these two excellent resources are available:

- The XS in C documentation is a complete reference to the API. It's part of the Moddable SDK.

- All the classes in the Moddable SDK that access native capabilities are implemented using XS in C. If you're curious about how they work, the source code is there for you to read and learn from.

Glossary

absolute coordinates (in Piu)

The coordinates of a content object on the screen, expressed as distance from the edges of the screen. See also **relative coordinates**.

access point

In this book, the point of connection between your Wi-Fi network and the internet; also called a *base station* (or *router*). The access point creates a local network that allows devices connected to it to communicate directly, without using the internet.

alpha channel

An indication of the degree of transparency (or opacity) of a solid color or pixels in a color image: which pixels should be drawn, which should be skipped, and which should be blended with the background.

anchor (in Piu)

A reference to a content object saved as a property in the instantiating data of the content object.

ArrayBuffer

In JavaScript, a block of memory of a fixed number of bytes, with no type associated with the data in it. The memory is initialized to 0. To access the data, you wrap the `ArrayBuffer` in a view; see also **data view** and **typed array**.

P. Hoddie and L. Prader, *IoT Development for ESP32 and ESP8266 with JavaScript*, https://doi.org/10.1007/978-1-4842-5070-9

arrow function

In modern JavaScript, a compact syntax for declaring functions (using => syntax) that, when called, has a this value that's the same as the this value of the function in which the arrow function is defined; formally known as a *lambda function.*

asynchronous networking

See **non-blocking networking**.

bare module specifier

In JavaScript, a module specifier that's not a path. This book uses only bare module specifiers, which are more common for embedded JavaScript.

base station

See **access point**.

behavior (in Piu)

A collection of methods that define the actions to be taken by a content object in response to events; specifically, an instance of a subclass of the Behavior class that's assigned to the content object.

BLE (Bluetooth Low Energy)

A wireless communication protocol that features low power consumption and is widely used between two devices in close proximity to each other.

block (in flash memory)

An organizational unit for flash memory. The size of a block varies depending on the flash memory component used; a common value is 4,096 bytes.

blocking networking

Networking in which the device will be unresponsive to user input during the network operation unless a more complex and memory-intensive technique, such as threads, is also used.

BMFont

A font format that combines a bitmap image with a map file. There are several variations of BMFont; the Moddable SDK uses the binary BMFont format.

bubble an event (in Piu)

To trigger a specified event on a content object, its parent container, and all container objects upward in the containment hierarchy, using the object's `bubble` method.

Central (in GAP)

One of the two main roles defined by GAP. A Central scans for devices acting as Peripherals and initiates requests to establish a new connection with a Peripheral.

characteristic (in GATT)

In the GATT hierarchy that defines the format of data, a value of a GATT service. See also **profile** and **service**.

child object, child (in Piu)

In a containment hierarchy, a content object that has been added to a container, which is said to be its parent object. The full term is often shortened to *child*.

chunked transfer encoding

A feature of the HTTP protocol that's often used to deliver large responses. The HTTP Request class decodes the chunks before invoking the callback function, so your callback function doesn't need to parse the chunk headers.

claiming (in mDNS)

The process whereby a device checks to see whether the mDNS name you chose for it is already in use because mDNS requires each device to have a unique name.

Client (in GATT)

See **GATT Client**.

clipping

Restricting drawing to subsections of the display. It's used by Poco to implement scanline rendering and by Piu to implement partial frame updates, and is also available for use in your applications—for example, to draw a subset of an image. See also **clipping area**.

clipping area

The area that restricts where drawing will occur in the update area; a single rectangle in Poco, but possibly multiple rectangles in Piu. Only the portion of each drawing operation that intersects the clipping area is drawn.

closure

In JavaScript, the binding of a function with a group of variables outside the function. The references to outside variables persist for the lifetime of the closure.

Commodetto

A graphics library that includes Poco and adds features such as offscreen graphics buffers, bitmaps, and instantiation of graphics assets from resources.

constructor

A special kind of function that, when invoked with new, creates an instance of the type specified by the constructor. The constructor function is executed to initialize the instance.

container (in Piu)

The organizing element of a containment hierarchy—a group into which content objects are placed within the hierarchy; specifically, an instance of any class that inherits from the Container class, which inherits from the Content class and extends it with the ability to hold other content objects.

containment hierarchy (in Piu)

The tree of content objects, with the application object at the root, that make up the user interface of a Piu application.

content object (in Piu)

A JavaScript object that's associated with a graphical element of the user interface; specifically, an instance of any class that inherits from the Content class.

CSS (Cascading Style Sheets)

A language for defining styles (for example, of text), most commonly used in web pages. Piu incorporates many CSS conventions to provide consistency for developers working on both web and IoT products.

data view

A view in which you can wrap an `ArrayBuffer` to access the data in it. Unlike typed arrays, in which all the values are of the same type, data views are used to read and write different-sized integers and floating-point values in a buffer.

defer an event (in Piu)

To trigger a specified event on a content object at the next iteration of the event loop, using the object's `defer` method.

delegate an event (in Piu)

To immediately trigger a specified event on a content object, using the object's `delegate` method.

distribute an event (in Piu)

To trigger a specified event on a container and all content objects downward in the containment hierarchy, using the container's `distribute` method.

easing equations

Equations that implement common accelerations and decelerations for animated state changes; also known as *easing functions*. These are often used to give animations a more natural feel by making something move more slowly at the start or near the end.

event (in Piu)

An occurrence, such as a tap on the screen, a change in a sensor value, or the expiration of a timer, that may trigger one or more content objects to take an action defined by the object's behavior.

extended mode (for TMP102 sensor)

A mode that increases the resolution of the TMP102 from the default of 12 bits to 13 bits, enabling the measurement of temperatures up to 150°C.

from-tween (in Piu)

A tween, added to a timeline by the timeline's `from` method, that modifies the properties of the `target` object from the values specified in the `properties` object to the original values of the `target` object over `duration` milliseconds.

GAP (Generic Access Profile)

The BLE protocol layer that defines how devices advertise themselves, how they establish connections with each other, and their connection security.

GATT (Generic Attribute Profile)

The BLE protocol layer that defines the way BLE devices transfer data back and forth after a connection is established between them—a client-server relationship.

GATT Client

A BLE device that accesses data from a remote GATT Server by sending read/write requests.

GATT Server

A BLE device that stores data locally, receives read/write requests, and notifies the remote GATT Client of changes to the values of its characteristics.

high-level event (in Piu)

An event defined and triggered by your application, using any name you like—for example, an onSensorValueChanged event to be triggered when the value of a sensor changes. See also **low-level event**.

host

A collection of JavaScript modules, configuration variables, and other software available that make up the environment in which your code runs. Each chapter in the repository for this book on GitHub has its own host, which contains the software environment needed to run that chapter's examples.

host object

In XS, an object with a native destructor, which performs cleanup when an instance of the class is garbage-collected.

I²C

A serial protocol for connecting multiple devices to a single two-wire bus.

I²S

A protocol to connect digital audio devices; one of two hardware protocols supported by the AudioOut class. It transmits unmodified audio samples over a digital connection from the microcontroller to a dedicated audio output component that performs the digital-to-analog conversion. See also **PDM**.

immediate mode rendering

A rendering technique, used in most graphics libraries used for microcontrollers, that performs the requested drawing operation when you call the drawing function. See also **retained mode rendering**.

immutable

A characteristic of JavaScript objects and values meaning they're read-only—that is, you cannot modify them. JavaScript strings are immutable and so can't be modified in place.

instantiating data (in Piu)

In a call to a content object constructor, a JavaScript value or object passed as the first argument and used to instantiate the class. This data is also passed to the onCreate method of the created instance's behavior.

iterator protocol

A protocol defined by JavaScript and implemented by the file module's Iterator class, which provides a standard way to implement and use iterators. For example, it enables the use of for-of loops.

lambda function

See **arrow function**.

lexical this

A feature of arrow functions whereby the value of this inside the arrow function is taken from the enclosing function.

low-level event (in Piu)

An event defined and triggered by Piu—for example, the onTouchBegan event when a finger is placed on a content object and onTouchEnded when the finger is removed. See also **high-level event**.

mDNS (Multicast DNS)

A protocol derived from DNS (Domain Name System) to allow devices to easily connect to each other on a local network. Whereas DNS is a centralized design that depends on authoritative servers to map names to IP addresses, mDNS is decentralized, with each individual device answering requests to map its name to an IP address.

MQTT (Message Queuing Telemetry Transport)

A publish-and-subscribe networking protocol (designed for use by lightweight IoT client devices) that organizes message into topics.

non-blocking networking

A characteristic of networking APIs which means, for example, that when you request data from the network using the HTTP protocol, your code continues running while the request is made; also called *asynchronous networking*. This is the way networking works when you use JavaScript on the web.

one-shot mode (for TMP102 sensor)

A mode for taking just one temperature reading from a TMP102 sensor. The most energy-efficient way to take infrequent readings, it's available only when the device is in shutdown mode.

parent object, parent (in Piu)

In a containment hierarchy, a container into which a content object (said to be its child object) has been added. The full term is often shortened to *parent*.

partition (in flash memory)

An organizational unit for the flash memory available to your microcontroller. For example, one partition contains your project's code, another the preference data, and another the storage for the SPIFFS file system. Each partition is identified by a name.

PDM (pulse-density modulation)

The rapid toggling of a digital output pin to create energy levels that correspond to the desired output signal; one of two hardware protocols supported by the AudioOut class. See also **I²S**.

Peripheral (in GAP)

One of the two main roles defined by GAP. Peripherals advertise themselves to Centrals and accept requests from Centrals to establish a connection.

Piu

In the Moddable SDK, an object-oriented user interface framework that simplifies the process of creating complex user interactions and uses Poco for drawing.

Poco

In the Moddable SDK, a rendering engine for embedded systems that you can use to draw to displays. See also **Piu**.

port (in Piu)

A content object that lets you issue drawing commands similar to Poco within a Piu layout; an instance of the Port class.

private method

A method that can only be called from within a class's implementation.

profile (in GATT)

In GATT, the top level of the hierarchy that defines the format of data. A profile defines a specific use of BLE for communication between multiple devices, including the roles of the devices involved and their general behaviors. See also **characteristic** and **service**.

promise

A feature of modern JavaScript that provides an alternative to callbacks to simplify asynchronous programming. Callbacks can be turned into promises using small helper functions so that applications can use asynchronous functions.

property

A characteristic of a JavaScript object that's similar to a field in C or C++, except that you can add properties to an object at runtime (without having to declare them in advance).

PWM (pulse-width modulation)

A type of digital signal whereby the digital pin outputs a square wave with varied widths of high and low values. Taking the average of these high and low pulses over time creates a power level between the high and low values, proportional to the pulse widths.

relative coordinates (in Piu)

The coordinates of a content object relative to the object's parent container, expressed as margins from the edges of the container; the left, right, top, and bottom properties specify margins from the corresponding edge. See also **absolute coordinates**.

responsive layout (in Piu)

A layout rule that adjusts intelligently to changes to the size of its parent container.

rest parameters

A feature of modern JavaScript that provides similar functionality to the special `arguments` variable, combining several arguments into an array, but is always available and is more flexible.

retained mode rendering (in Poco)

A rendering technique that doesn't draw immediately but rather maintains a list of drawing commands that executes only when you tell Poco you're done drawing. See also **immediate mode rendering**.

router

See **access point**.

RSSI (received signal strength indication)

A measure of the strength of the signal received from the Wi-Fi access point.

scanline rendering (in Poco)

A rendering technique that divides a frame into horizontal strips as small as a single row of pixels and, after each strip is rendered, immediately transmits it to the display.

Server (in GATT)

See **GATT Server**.

service (in GATT)

In the GATT hierarchy that defines the format of data, a collection of characteristics that describe the behavior of part of a BLE device. See also **characteristic** and **profile**.

shutdown mode (for TMP102 sensor)

A mode that completely disables the temperature conversion hardware in a TMP102 sensor, reducing energy consumption to 0.5 µA. Your application can put the TMP102 in shutdown mode in the interval between readings.

skin (in Piu)

An object that controls the drawing of the background of one or more content objects, filling the area with color or images. An instance of the Skin class, it's specified in a content object's skin property. See also **texture**.

sloppy mode

A JavaScript mode primarily used for backward compatibility for websites. Sloppy mode includes features that may be error prone or reduce performance. See also **strict mode**.

SMBus (System Management Bus)

A subset of I²C for register-based devices.

SNTP (Simple Network Time Protocol)

A lightweight way for an IoT device to retrieve the current time from the network.

source rectangle (in Poco)

When drawing a bitmap, the area of the bitmap to use, enabling you to specify that only part of a mask or image should be drawn.

sparse array

A JavaScript array in which not all elements have an assigned value.

spread syntax

A feature of modern JavaScript that separates the elements of an array or properties of an object into individual arguments.

SSID (service set identifier)

The human-readable name of a Wi-Fi network provided by a Wi-Fi base station.

strict equality operator

The JavaScript operator ===, which can be used in place of == to avoid type conversion. This operator never performs type conversion; if its operands are of different types, they're always unequal.

strict inequality operator

The JavaScript operator !==, which can be used in place of != to avoid type conversion. This operator never performs type conversion; if its operands are of different types, they're always unequal.

strict mode

A mode introduced in JavaScript 5th Edition which eliminates a handful of confusing and inefficient features. This book uses strict mode exclusively. See also **sloppy mode**.

style (in Piu)

An object that controls the appearance of text, including the text's font and color, in one or more content objects. An instance of the `Style` class, it's specified in a content object's `style` property.

tag

A JavaScript feature that enables a function to modify the default behavior of template literals. For example, you can use this feature to convert the string representation of a UUID to binary data.

template (in Piu)

A class, created using a content object's `template` method, that enables you to eliminate redundancy when creating several similar objects.

template literal

A way of delineating JavaScript strings that uses the backtick character (`` ` ``). Strings defined in this way may span multiple lines and include string substitutions.

texture (in Piu)

An object that provides an image to be drawn (entirely or in part) by one or more skins. An instance of the `Texture` class, it's specified in a skin's `texture` property.

TLS (Transport Layer Security)

A low-level tool for securing communication that works with many different protocols, including HTTP; a more recent version of Secure Sockets Layer (SSL).

to-tween (in Piu)

A tween, added to a timeline by the timeline's to method, that modifies the properties of the target object from its current values to the target values specified in the properties object over duration milliseconds.

topic (in MQTT)

In the MQTT protocol, an organizational unit for messages. Messages to and from an MQTT server are organized into topics; a particular server may support many topics, but a client receives only the messages for the topics it subscribes to.

tween (in Piu)

A description of what happens to a specified content object in a timeline. Each tween describes how one or more properties of the object change from an initial value and an ending value. See also **from-tween** and **to-tween**.

typed array

A view in which you can wrap an ArrayBuffer to access the data in it; a collection of classes (subclasses of TypedArray for specific types) that let you work with arrays of integers and floating-point values stored in an ArrayBuffer. See also **data view**.

update area (in Poco)

The initial drawing area, defined by Poco's begin method. It can be restricted by clipping; see also **clipping area**.

WebSocket

A peer-to-peer protocol whereby two devices communicate over a persistent network connection enabling efficient communication of brief messages. Unlike HTTP, in which only the client can make a request and the server always responds, WebSocket enables both devices to send and receive messages.

XS

A JavaScript engine optimized for resource-constrained environments such as microcontrollers. XS implements the full JavaScript language and supports on-device debugging, unlike other engines for embedded use. Created by Kinoma, XS is maintained by Moddable as the core of the Moddable SDK.

XS in C

A low-level C API provided by the XS JavaScript engine so that you can integrate C code into your JavaScript projects (or JavaScript code into your C projects).

Index

A

Absolute coordinates, 452, 565,
 See also Relative coordinates
Access point, 128–136, 137–138, 163,
 178–179, 438, 542, 565
Actuators, 255
Adafruit, 262, 277, 281, 294–297
Advertising
 BLE, 203–204
 multicast DNS, 167–168
Alpha channel, 347–349, 372, 383,
 425, 565
Analog class, 281
Analog input, 277, 281
Anchor, Piu, 472–476, 565
Animation, 320–321, 323, 488–489
 easing equations, 488–489, 570
 transitions, 491, 494–497,
 505–506, 508–511
Application class, Piu, 354,
 408–409
ArrayBuffer, 106–107
Arrays, 96–106
 typed, *see* Typed arrays
Arrow functions, 88–89, 101,
 465, 566

async keyword, 182
Asynchronous
 functions, 181–183, 190,
 327, 576
Asynchronous networking, *see*
 Non-blocking networking
Audio, 295–317
AudioOut class, 304–317, 572, 575
Automatic semicolon
 insertion (ASI), 27
await keyword, 182–183

B

Bare module specifier, 91, 566
Base station, *see* Access point
Behavior class, Piu, 354, 412,
 429–435, 566
Binary data, 25, 106–118
 BLE, 199, 201
 data views, 114–118, 570
 in files, 226, 227, 230–231
 HTTP, 141, 142, 158, 162
 MQTT, 174, 176
 typed arrays, 25, 107–113, 114,
 242, 250, 529, 581

© Peter Hoddie and Lizzie Prader 2020
P. Hoddie and L. Prader, *IoT Development for ESP32 and ESP8266 with JavaScript,*
https://doi.org/10.1007/978-1-4842-5070-9